Ex Villa, Ex Zaslav viola by J. B. Guadagnini, Turin, 1781

For Nomi

"LUV LUV"
A wedding gift painted by David Jackier.

The Viola in My Life
An Alto Rhapsody

Bernard Zaslav

Science & Behavior Books, Inc.

Copyright © 2011 Bernard Zaslav

Published by Science & Behavior Books, Inc.
P.O. Box 60519
Palo Alto, CA 94306
www.sbbks.com

All rights reserved. No part of this book may be reproduced or used in any form or by any means – graphic, electronic, or mechanical – without written permission from the publisher.

Printed in the United States of America.

Library of Congress Card Number 2011926570

ISBN 978-0-8314-0096-5

Cover Design by Jim Marin, Marin Graphics
Interior Design by Nikki Brown, Nikki, Ink
The line drawings on pages 217, 381, and the back cover are by Kris Yenney.

*"Live as if you were to die tomorrow.
Learn as if you were to live forever."*

MAHATMA GANDHI

TABLE OF CONTENTS

PRELUDE: GREAT SCOTT, HUGHIE		7
⌢	A Cult Figure	15
OVERTURE		20
ENTRATA		27
I	BROOKLYN BEGINNINGS	31
II	SAMUEL J. TILDEN HIGH SCHOOL: *Instruzione Scolastica*	51
III	"MY" JUILLIARD: *Gradus ad Parnassum*	59
IV	THE CHAUTAUQUA SYMPHONY: Learning the Ropes	81
V	THE CLEVELAND ORCHESTRA: Szell's Magnificent Instrument	89
VI	PLUMBING THE DEPTHS: *Miserere*	109
VII	NU, PHOENIX, RISE ALREADY? *Ad Astra*	123
⌢	The Carnegie Tavern	145
VIII	MY LANCE IS FREE: *Scorrevole*	157
IX	THE KOHON STRING QUARTET	177
X	SET FOR TWO	200
⌢	New York: My Vienna	217
XI	THE COMPOSERS STRING QUARTET	223
XII	THE FINE ARTS STRING QUARTET (PART 1): *Guadeamus Igitur*	241
⌢	My Peak Viola Experience: Performing Beethoven's *Grosse Fuga*	279
XIII	THE FINE ARTS STRING QUARTET (PART II)	283
⌢	Stage	305
XIV	THE VERMEER STRING QUARTET: *Ne Plus Ultra*	307
⌢	"Mainely" Music	337
XV	THE STANFORD STRING QUARTET: Westward Ho!	347
⌢	Oh, Fiddlesticks!	367
XVI	THE ZASLAV DUO: Tea for Two	381
POSTLUDE		399
ACKNOWLEDGMENTS		409
DISCOGRAPHY		411
ABOUT THE CDS		417
INDEX		423

Bernard Zasalv is second from the right in the back row.

Prelude
Great Scott, Hughie

"Hey Zazzy, it's Hugh Brown. Lissen up willya, 'cause I gotta talk real fast!"

It sure sounds like Hughie's voice on the phone all right, but where's that laid-back mid-western drawl I'm used to? Right now he's yammering away like an oboe in heat. Only a week before, May 17, 1946, to be exact, we both received our violin diplomas from the Institute of Musical Art, as the Juilliard School of Music was then called, but they hadn't provided us with the manual for getting ahead in the music world.

"So Hughie, what's up?" I ask.

"Look, Zazz, I'm sitting here with Raymond Scott's band arranger, and your name just came up. Tell me, what are you doin' this summer?"

"Oh, I'm so glad you asked, Hughie. Even as we speak, I'm waiting for a call from Arturo Toscanini to play the Beethoven Violin Concerto with the NBC Symphony."

"Uh, huh. Well Zazz, while you're waitin', Mr. Scott's band is gonna start their run at the New York Paramount Theater next week, and they're using four violins. They've already hired Normie Carr, Eddie DiBiase, Pete Tramontana, and me as backup for their featured singer, some crooner by the name of Andy Russell—kind of a Sinatra type. But now the arranger tells me he's wanting to add a viola to the mix, to make the string section kind of mellow. So I'm callin' to see if you'd be interested in a really great-paying summer gig."

"Slow down Hughie," I say. "What's so great about this gig, and why would I have to be the palooka playing viola?"

"Okay. First off, this thing pays union scale, and I gotta tell you it's a ton of money . . . you do play viola, right Zazz?"

"Oh sure," I lied, not missing a beat. Well I actually had played the second viola part of a Brahms Quintet in a chamber music class at Juilliard, but what the heck was I getting myself into?

"So tell me Hughie," I asked. "Exactly what would I have to do for this marvelous gig?"

"Aw it's a piece a cake Zazz. We only do four shows a day with the band on stage, in between the movie and the newsreels. Besides backing up Andy we'll back up the band's two regular singers, Dorothy Collins and Snooky Lanson. But get this: they've got this amazing alto sax player who crawls downstage on his belly to play his solo licks. Can you just see it?"

"Oh yeah," he said. "And there's one more thing I should tell you: we'll be singing along with the band, doing standing choruses of 'Cement Mixer, Puttee, Puttee' and 'Get Your Kicks on Route 66.' But all the moolah they're payin' us for this gig should keep you happy."

Now that was something to chew on.

After my first semester at Juilliard my folks realized that I needed a better instrument. My father's wholesale plumbing supply business had been doing okay, so he took me to Lazare Rudie's violin shop on West 46th Street in Manhattan, a dealer recommended by my violin teacher, Mischa Mischakoff.

Mr. Rudie took a couple of fiddles out of his violin safe for me to try, and the one that really caught my ear was an Italian instrument made in 1748 by Josephus Gagliano of Naples. It had a sweet tone, and was a real beauty, covered in a dark rich varnish. After they negotiated a while, my father sat down and wrote out a check for $1,200 (in 1945 dollars), and I walked out of Rudie's violin shop with a smile on my face, and a beautiful violin in my case. Lucky me.

After paying for my years of study at Juilliard, and buying me that expensive violin, I had to wonder what my folks would think if my very first job was playing viola with a commercial jazz band on the stage of a Broadway movie house. Every aspiring violinist dreams about making that successful debut at Carnegie Hall. My earlier dreams included conducting symphonies by Beethoven, and even writing a few of my own. Wouldn't I be "prostituting my art" by playing pop music? Even though the Paramount movie house was only thirteen blocks south of Carnegie, it certainly was worlds apart, musically. Wasn't this a comedown? Maybe even a sellout?

And then I thought, "What's the a big deal?" After all we're only talking about a six week summer gig, and I could chalk it up as my first real-world experience. There were no other employment opportunities on the horizon for that summer (Toscanini hadn't called), and this would be my first step to becoming self-sufficient one day. While I hesitated, Hughie, as if reading my mind, told me exactly what union scale came to in American dollars. I said, "Count me in."

"Terrific!" said Hughie. "No more working our fingers to the bone in some sweaty Juilliard practice room. Just make sure you're at the stage door of the Paramount, 44th and Broadway, at ten sharp tomorrow morning." With the band arranger sitting nearby, I could hear Hughie covering the phone as his voice descended from the range of the oboe to the lower register of the bassoon, while muttering, "Oh yeah, and don't forget to bring your . . . viola!"

I had to dig up a viola in time for the next morning's

rehearsal, but my real job was to convince Raymond Scott that I knew how to play the darned thing. I thought of my friend Mike, a tall "drink of water" blessed with a droll New York sense of humor. Mike was the genuine article: an honest-to-god certified violist. And he even admitted to being one. He was tall and looked kind of droopy, and almost clownish. There was talk that Mike was enjoying the favors of (or as some might put it *boffing*) a drop-dead beauty who was starring in a current musical hit at the Shubert Theatre. Perhaps Mike's physical endowments overshadowed his other talents.

I phoned Mike to ask him if he might have an unused "ax" kicking around in the back of his closet (in the commercial world a musician might call his instrument his "ax," because it's what he used to "cut the part"). I guess I lucked out that night. It seemed that he did have an old student model he was willing to part with, so I grabbed the subway up to 193rd Street and Broadway for a look-see. Upon opening the case, I could see that it was no work of art, but when Mike said he could part with the whole deal, including the ratty old case and the bow, for forty bucks, it was definitely a steal. I didn't have that much cash on me, but when I informed him about my upcoming pot of gold, he was willing to wait until my first paycheck. What a doll! Aren't all violists dolls?

According to Woody Allen, eighty percent of success is showing up, so at 10:00 I appeared at the stage door of the Paramount building clutching my "new" viola case. Inside that case four threadbare strings were holding on for dear life, and the beat-up bow badly needed a re-hair, but what the heck, I'd brought my ax.

Right next door stood the old Astor Hotel (it was demolished in 1982). The lobby of that hotel was famous for its enormous four-faced clock, a Broadway landmark. It was a favored spot where you might chat up an attractive someone by asking, "Can we meet under the clock at the Astor?" That's just what Judy Garland tells Robert Walker in *The Clock*, a 1945 film directed by Vincente Minnelli. The big question, of course, was whether *she* would show up. You'll just have to see the film to find out.

After I passed through the stage door, they sent me right off to makeup, since lots of pancake was required to counter the effects of the Paramount's harsh stage lighting. Next, along with the others, I was required to don a yucky-looking mud-brown-colored velvet suit. These ghastly outfits would serve as our "costumes" for the run of the show and, as we soon learned, we would be wearing these ridiculously hot outfits all day long.

This was all happening during the proverbial "big band" era, which meant there were saxes who doubled on all the woodwinds, a big brass section of trumpets and trombones, and a rhythm section of piano, string bass, and drums: the *gonsa megillah* cranking out enough decibels to fry your brain. The five string players sat in a back row behind the saxophones. Raymond Scott's initials were emblazoned across the fronts of our cardboard music stands, and we played from hastily-scrawled string parts that were still wet from the copyist's pen.

Our new boss wielded an almost mile-long white baton. It was even longer than the one used by Paul Whiteman. Scott seemed to be eyeing his five newly hired recruits suspiciously, as we clung together like a bunch of wet mussels. Those devilishly hot stage lights caused our makeup to run while we sawed away manfully at our parts.

I was still struggling to decipher the alto clef, when I looked up to see Mr. Scott standing directly in front of me with a scowl on his face. His lips were moving, and though I couldn't make out the words amid the surrounding bedlam, it sounded something like, "Hey kid, how come I see you bowing different from the other guys?"

Uh-oh, there went my musical future up in smoke. Surely Scott must have been aware that those "other guys" were playing the violin, and that I was playing a different instrument. Many arrangers in the 1940s used only violins for their vocal backgrounds, so perhaps Scott wasn't aware that his arranger had cleverly inserted a viola part. Trying to set him straight in front of everyone might prove embarrassing, so I just played dumb and continued to scrape away, while mumbling something inane in his general direction.

After a heart-stopping interval, Scott simply gave up on me and shrugged, saying, "Well make it look good," and then went off to deal with concerns more pressing than a numbskull violist. That was when I learned the one maxim known to every single member of the orchestral world: you're better off faking than to try explaining things to a conductor.

Andy Russell wasn't a household name like Frank Sinatra, but he was still able to attract his own bunch of bobbysoxers. They haunted the Paramount's stage door day and night, hoping for a glimpse of their idol. Many of them were mere nymphets, desperate for an autograph, a shred of clothing, or anything remotely connected to their dreamboat. We heard that a couple of wily stagehands had dropped water-filled balloons out of a window located directly over the stage door, but even a soaking failed to disperse Andy's loyal fans. They were known to have torn the clothes off anyone who dared to walk out that door, so the Paramount became a cinematic gulag. We were being held virtual prisoners while the bobbysoxers' collective lust awaited its proper target.

We had about two hours off during the film showings, but to trying fight our way through that stage door for a bite of food or a breath of Broadway's polluted air was foolhardy. We could phone out to the Edison Deli over on West 46th Street to have them send over a corned-beef sandwich, and kill time by reading or kibitzing the stagehands' nonstop poker game. Taking a hand in the game wasn't in the cards: the stagehand's union scale far exceeded the kind of dough we were making.

Normie Carr was our resident show biz maven, and as such it was his duty to regale us with its vagaries. He freelanced even while he was studying at Juilliard, and eventually left New York to work in the film studios (read "Salt Mines') of Los Angeles. Normie told us about a musical revue he had played called "Ice Capades" at Madison Square Garden on Fiftieth Street and Eighth Avenue. This long-running traveling show featured some notable ice skaters of the time, and Normie, always the operator, struck up a few casual friendships among them. One night he happened to show up late for work (he neglected to tell us her name), and he found the stage door locked.

While he stood outside feeling really stupid, Normie could hear the band strike up the overture through the door. He raced madly around the perimeter of the Garden (quite a feat in itself) and knocked desperately on every door he came across. A few skaters who were already in costume and were awaiting their cues heard his knock and let him in. Seeing his plight, two of those skater pals lifted Normie up, fiddle and all, and carried him all the way across the Garden's huge ice rink. They delivered him to his place, as the band played on. The audience probably regarded the spectacle as part of the show, but Normie was in deep doo-doo with his boss.

My only show-biz perk happened when the Folies Bergère of Paris appeared at a Broadway Theatre in 1964. As a lowly pit-dweller, my sole fringe benefit was to ogle a parade of semi-nude topless dancers, as they wandered backstage between acts. Such pleasures were denied the inmates of our Paramount dungeon.

Without much recourse, I decided to put my otherwise-wasted hours between shows to good use. One morning before my first show at the Paramount I went through the stacks of viola music on the shelves of the Joseph Patelson Music House on West 56th Street (sadly, it's no longer in business). I picked up a book of viola scales and some books of etudes, and I found a fairly secluded spot backstage where I could practice during the breaks without bothering anyone.

As I began to practice this instrument seriously, I found that my left hand adapted very easily to the slightly longer finger-board, and that my vibrato speed (the slight finger oscillation used by a player to color the tone) was just right for the instrument. As for the all-important bow arm, the viola's requisite degree of bow speed and pressure seemed to be second nature to me, and I was soon pulling a halfway decent sound from this crummy 40-dollar box. Who could have imagined that this instrument would be such a natural fit for me? I was hooked; completely won over by its rich throatiness and deep sound quality. The viola's bottom C string, just five notes lower than the violin's G string, provided a dimension of dark sonic beauty that was simply too tempting to pass up. I wondered if it might be foolish to switch to viola at this stage of my life, and though I knew that embarking on such a less-travelled road would be a bit scary, I felt it was worth the gamble.

That Raymond Scott gig was one of those accidents of fate that you only read about (and you are reading about it here). I needed to find the right teacher in order to make a proper transition to my newly-chosen instrument, and then there was that not-so-small matter of the damned viola clef. Learning to read that odd-looking doo-hickey (𝄡) would be my first challenge.

Could you call this turning point in my life a "clef-hanger?" Well, that's how it looked to me in the fall of 1946.

A Cult Figure

The strange-looking thing you see, vaguely resembling an eyebrow overhanging a dot, is called a *fermata* in music notation. The *fermata* symbol is placed over a single note, or sometimes over a bar line when a composer wishes to slow down the tempo, or even come to a complete halt. This usually signifies a phrase ending, after which the natural momentum is to be restored. The *fermata* is simply a means of stretching the duration of that note, phrase, or rest, giving the listener a bit of time to savor what was last heard, before the next musical event.

Occasionally a composer may want to add a few expressions that ask the performer not to jam on the brakes, but to kind of feather them before the music stops. How long this pause lasts depends on the discretion (and the imagination) of the performer, and is often a measure of his or her musical taste. This little hiccup in time must sound persuasive, especially to those acquainted with the conventions of particular historical periods. The noses of some early music scholars are easily turned out of joint by the blatant misuse of these *fermate*, but a performer may wish to lavish them on music of a more romantic character *a piacere* (at your pleasure).

When I read *The Castle in the Forest*, Norman Mailer's final novel, I noted that he blithely inserted a many-paged hiatus between two of his chapters. After sailing along with his fictional *noir* history of Adolph Hitler's horrific childhood, Mailer simply put a halt to the proceedings and slammed on the brakes, so that he could insert a few pages of alternate history in his narrative. Not to worry, he says to the reader (in so many words). If you're finicky, just skip ahead, and miss the more ghoulish stuff; you'll be able to catch up at the stated page. This feisty, two-time Pulitzer Prize-winner has always been one of my favorite writers, and at his advanced stage of life, he felt entitled to write as he pleased.

I have borrowed Mailer's clever idea by inserting *fermate* between various sections of this memoir. It gives me some leeway to digress for a bit, or to muse on a random topic, as it pleases me (*a piacere*). I hope that the reader will permit me this small indulgence, considering my own advanced age.

I have had the pleasure, through the years, of teaching many talented violists and chamber music students. The other day my former student John Sherba, who plays second violin in the famed Kronos Quartet, brought his violinist-brother, Charles, Charles' violist-wife and my student Consuelo Scribner, and Hank Dutt, the Kronos Quartet's excellent violist, to my home on campus at Stanford University. We spent a pleasant afternoon chatting, and we all took turns at the sacred rite of trying some of the viola bows in my collection.

How John came to join the Kronos Quartet was yet another accident of fate. A cello student of George Sopkin's (the cellist of the Fine Arts Quartet) heard that the San Francisco-based Kronos Quartet was looking for a new cellist. This young cellist asked John to accompany him on the long drive from Milwaukee to San Francisco for the audition. Though the cellist wasn't offered the position, John, who had come along only as a lark, became the second violinist of the Quartet.

In 2003, *Musical America* selected the Kronos Quartet, which was then celebrating its 30th anniversary, as Musicians of the

Year. Mark Swed credited them with "boisterously breaking down nearly every conceivable genre barrier that ever existed for the string quartet," and changing "our perception of not just what a string quartet can be, but what music can be in the 21st-century global village." Since its first concert in 1973, the Kronos Quartet premiered more than 450 original works and custom (usually in-house) arrangements. Swed calculated that the Kronos "has, in effect, given the world a new string quartet every three weeks, steadily, for three decades."

I might compare the Kronos Quartet to the avant-garde Composers Quartet that I helped to found in New York during the 1960s. The Composers Quartet came together under the aegis of composer Gunther Schuller to perform many of the complex string quartets that were being written by American composers like Milton Babbitt, Roger Sessions and Elliott Carter.

When I mentioned to John that my very first professional gig was playing with Raymond Scott's band at the Paramount Theater, he was incredulous. My stock reached an all-time high. John asked me whether I realized that Raymond Scott had become a cult figure. I knew it took ten Jewish males to make a minion, but how many warm (or bloodless) bodies of any denomination are required to make a cult?

I soon learned that my first boss wasn't the musical lightweight I imagined him to be. Raymond Scott (né Harry Warnow) was a piano prodigy from the age of two, and was a brilliant engineering student. Surpassing the late guitarist-composer Les Paul in electronic inventiveness, Scott created such highly-advanced musical instruments as the Scott Clavivox and the Electronium. He was best known for his much-recorded Raymond Scott Quintette, which consisted (as a gag) of six members rather than the nominal five. The composer of such deathless favorites as "Dinner Music for a Pack of Hungry Cannibals," "Confusion Among a Fleet of Taxicabs Upon Meeting with a Fare," and "War Dance for Wooden Indians" was called the "Mad Professor of Cartoon Music" because these pieces were used as background music by Merrie Melodies and

Looney Tunes. I was obviously way off base in thinking that Scott might not have known what a viola was. More likely, he saw right away what kind of neophyte he had hired.

The high point of this visit was when John told me the Kronos Quartet had recently transcribed and recorded "Dinner Music for a Pack of Hungry Cannibals." He had even brought along the CD they made, and he played it for us that night. The Kronos arrangement involves a lot of knuckle rapping on the belly of the cello, and the mad rhythmical figures reminded me of the kick I used to get from those cartoons as a kid, but does that make Raymond Scott worthy of a cult?

Go figure!

Several months after this visit, Michael Leddy, the husband of Elaine Fine, my patient editor, told me about a film by Stan Warnow (the son of Harry Warnow) called *Deconstructing Dad: The Music, Machines, and Mysteries of Raymond Scott*. Serendipity abounds. Harry Warnow grew up in a Russian-Jewish family on 845 Sutter Avenue, near where my father had his plumbing supply business. Warnow went to Brooklyn Tech (the high school my son Mark attended), and studied at Juilliard, my alma mater. He found a new professional name in a telephone book (to avoid being accused of nepotism when he went to work for his brother Mark Warnow, who was the music director of CBS Radio).

In 1942 Raymond Scott took over his brother's job at CBS, and organized the first racially integrated radio band. In 1949, after his brother died, Scott took Lucky Strike's *Your Hit Parade* to NBC television, and remained the show's conductor until 1957. I didn't know it during our run at the Paramount, but the singer Dorothy Collins had been his student and his protege since the age of 14. She lived with his family, along with his wife and two children, and once she became an adult, Collins and Scott got married.

First and foremost, Scott was a composer and had an early interest in the ways that electronics could be applied to the composition of music. Taking a leaf from the Theremin, an eerie-sounding electronic instrument, he invented a Rube Goldberg-style sequencing device he called the Electronium, into which he could insert various recorded clips of musical sounds and events. It was somewhat akin to Robert Moog's analog synthesizer, and used elements of pitch, tonality, and rhythm to compose music. Scott's obsessive tinkering constituted a few baby steps towards artificial intelligence. In addition to musical innovations, he invented an electronic telephone ringtone-generating machine, and a Fax machine.

His career laid the groundwork for Frank Zappa, *Musique Concréte* and Pierre Boulez. It seems that the composer of "Sleepwalker," "Toy Trumpet," "Twilight in Turkey," and "Wackiki Wabbit" was more than a cult figure, he was almost an "occult" figure.

Overture

"I don't get no respect . . . no respect at all."
RODNEY DANGERFIELD, COMEDIAN

In 500 B.C. Aeschylus wrote, "It is a profitable thing, if one is wise, to seem foolish." Taking a cue from the Ancient Greeks, stand-up comedian Rodney Dangerfield's shtick was to play the sempiternal loser. He used his deer-in-the-headlights eyes and plastic puss to portray himself as the luckless *schlimazel*, a poor sap who gets burning hot chicken soup spilled on his lap by a *schlemiel* (a blundering fool). In old-time vaudeville, the lead comic (the top banana) would get a huge laugh (boffo) from the audience when he bopped his partner (the second banana) on the head with a bladder. Violists had long been relegated to that second-banana status, and I was taking a gamble by joining their ranks. Because of this traditional bias, violists had become the butt of racist-style jokes. A rather antiquated slur defines the prototypical cultured English gentleman as "one who actually *can* play the viola, but refrains from doing so in public." We respond to these philistines (*vile-inists,* as we call them) by saying, "It's not the viola that's bigger, it's the violinist's *head* that's bigger."

Like lots of other Jewish kids in the 1920s, I took violin lessons. I dreamt about conducting Toscanini's NBC orchestra in a symphony of my own creation, but I didn't expect music to become my livelihood and to shape my life. I was deeply inspired by the violin teachers I worked with at Juilliard; Sascha Jacobsen, with his luscious sound, and Mischa Mischakoff, with his wonderful solidity and presence, but after being lured by the unique sound of the viola, I began to have a deeper appreciation of the luscious contrapuntal voices that create music's tapestry. Playing the viola showed me what actually takes place beneath the surface of the music, and the importance of the rhythm that drives music forward.

My first professional stroke of luck came in 1947, when I was accepted as a member of the Cleveland Orchestra. After two seasons I returned to New York where, following a nine-year hiatus from professional music-making, I became a freelance musician. This was during the 1950s and 60s, a time when all sorts of interesting and highly controversial innovations were happening in new music. I cut my quartet teeth by playing in three different New York string quartets, and at the age of 42 I crossed the Hudson River and successively became a member of three more highly distinguished string quartets, while maintaining a viola and piano duo.

Being members of the alto family, violists have historically lacked the breadth of classical repertoire (and hence the glamour) of the violin, or even the cello. Acousticians tell us that it's because the strings of the viola are too short for optimal body length, so it can't soar above the orchestral texture as easily as the violin or the cello. Perhaps that's one reason that only a few composers from the 18th and 19th centuries provided us with solo concerti. Good contemporary composers have learned to use clever orchestration to overcome these obstacles.

I'm excited about the new crop of young viola players who are almost fanatical in their dedication to the instrument's repertoire. These violists have raised the level of artistry on our instrument to new heights. I communicate almost daily with colleagues and ex-students living everywhere from London to New Zealand through a viola list hosted by a website (viola.com) devoted to all things having to do with the viola. We exchange helpful tips about instruments and strings, discuss new works written for the viola, catch up with the latest viola gossip, share video and audio files, and have fun "dissing" our screechier violinist brethren.

When friends would come calling to play *hausmusik* with Herr Mozart, he (wisely) elected to play the viola part. A single viola part didn't cut the mustard for Wolfgang, so he gave us six glorious two-viola quintets, which are masterpieces of the chamber music literature. Beethoven also chose to play the viola part at such sessions (though he wrote only one spectacular two-viola quintet). Playing *middle fiddle*, as the English called it, was also the choice of other great composers like Antonín Dvořák, Ernest Bloch, Paul Hindemith, and Benjamin Britten. Even Felix Mendelssohn played the instrument. A list of orchestral conductors who played the viola would include Pierre Monteux, Frederick Stock, Charles Dutoit, Carlo Maria Giulini, Leonard Slatkin, Pinchas Zukerman, Arthur Fiedler, Leon Barzin, Jorge Mester, Ferde Grofé, Milton Katims, and the late Rudolph Barshai.

The British violist Lionel Tertis (1876–1975) was the first viola soloist to gain international repute. In his two memoirs, *Cinderella No More,* and *My Viola and I,* Tertis tells of his efforts to popularize the viola by performing and expanding its then-current repertoire. He made arrangements of works originally written for other instruments, including a viola transcription of Edward Elgar's Cello Concerto (with the composer's blessing). 20th-century viola virtuosi like William Primrose, and my teacher Lillian Fuchs, continued to further the instrument's recognition by playing and recording concertos and chamber music. I have tried to follow in these illustrious footsteps by making arrangements and commissioning new works for viola and piano, as well as for string quartet.

Sitting in a quartet, between the soprano voice of the violins and the bass of the cello, the viola constitutes the alto voice. There's a bit of grit in the sound, but it's a lovely grit. I would guess that the sound of 1,176 HP being delivered from under the Clear Engine Bonnet of a Lamborghini Gallardo would cast a similar spell on an auto enthusiast. Playing the solo viola repertoire is fun and challenging, but there's no better place to make your special voice heard to advantage than in a string quartet. We are right in the middle of the action, occupying the best seat in the house, tossing fly balls back and forth with our colleagues. Choosing programs from the string quartet's vast canon is like having "Breakfast at Tiffany's."

Whales, wombats, and walleroos all use sounds to communicate, but the human brain seems to be pre-wired for speech (and probably music) at birth. When an air column moves in a regular pattern, the brain can translate pitch, frequency, harmony, rhythm, and decibel level into something we recognize as music. The (once) avant-garde composer Edgard Varèse defined music as merely organized sound, but music has the power to raise us to emotional heights or dump us into the depths of despair (a speciality of Gustav Mahler). Sound organizers (composers) have something important to tell us, not with mere words, but with melody, harmony, texture, and rhythm. And I've been blessed with the ability and training to act as a membrane between a composer's blueprint and you, the listener.

Whenever I meet up with a stranger in this country (Europeans generally find such behavior impolite at a first meeting), I may ask him about his "dodge" (what he does for a living). Perhaps he'll say he's in sales, and when I tell him I'm a musician, nine times out of ten he'll tell me that he always wanted to be one. He might wistfully say that he played the clarinet years ago, or maybe that he still fools around with the old guitar in his closet, but he never got around to taking lessons.

If he has kids he may say that he wants them to have at least some knowledge of good music in their lives. Perhaps he'll say he's thinking of buying a piano, but because of space problems, not one of those real jobs. How about one of those electronic keyboards; what do I think of those? What I want to tell him honestly is that it's a desecration of musical sound, but when he says he has no option, I change the conversation.

But the musical conversation in my head never stops. There's always a musical fragment playing back there. My synapses are overstuffed with the hypnotic creations of other minds that have been passed along to me. It might be the insistent rhythmic figure I happened to hear yesterday in Stravinsky's *Rite of Spring*, or a Bach fragment from one of the Cello Suites that violists have now claimed as their territory. Maybe it's one of those simple—gloriously simple and magical—Impromptus from Schubert's Opus 90 that my pianist wife plays constantly, and loves deeply. Any one of the above patiently waits its turn to claim my attention.

String quartet rehearsals offer their members an unparalleled learning experience. The amount of time spent in analysis, discussion, and making the countless number of repetitions that are necessary for ensemble (playing together), would seem unthinkable to the layman. In a string quartet we have a situation where four obsessive people are reaching for the ultimate: how many angels they can fit on the head of a pin. Young quartets have the opportunity to learn from chamber music coaches in graduate programs, but the better part of my musical learning came about "on the job," through repetition and reflection.

When I talk of performing a work, that doesn't begin to tell you how much actual rehearsal time and effort goes into making a performance possible. Learning one's own part is the bare beginning. In fact, I always advise a student group to simply play through a work, bloopers and all, and then make joint decisions concerning a composer's intentions. A pianist has (usually) only two music staves to deal with, but the quartet player must learn all four parts simultaneously, through visual means (the score), and by listening to who's got the ball in that place, and who's accompanying whom. Taking a piece of chamber music on the road is the best way to solve its logistical problems and get closer to understanding its inner meaning, because every concert venue has different acoustics and every audience has "fresh ears."

Touring (schlepping) for over forty years by train, plane, and taxi with my precious Guadagnini viola in hand, carrying my suitcase loaded with "frock coat" as they call it in Europe (i.e., tails mit cummerbund), silly-looking black patent leather shoes (in every kind of weather) and four our five programs worth of music (15 to 20 quartets) was a career in itself, before we even played a note. But there were plenty of *Noten* to play. In one (overstuffed) year the Fine Arts Quartet played 150 concerts. In addition to foreign and domestic touring, our university obligations involved teaching and chamber music coaching, faculty concerts, lectures, and recitals, and interminable *(pace mio dio)* faculty meetings. I'd say we earned our keep and then some.

Small bottles of *Slivovitz* (plum brandy) kept us from death's door while we waited on train platforms in Frankfurt, and we were required to offer the obligatory gift of duty-free Scotch whisky to our first London manager before he would even rise from his chair to greet us. Fritz Dietrich, our German manager, would often parcel out our fees (in U.S. currency) in a dimly lit upstairs café at midnight, while our Italian manager once took over a year to come up with our money.

Sometimes our concert sponsors would invite us (some even required us) to down a fulsome post-concert repast at one of their homes, or at one of the top local restaurants. In some great gastronomic cities, like Munich, Strassburg, or Montreux, we dined at restaurants listed in the Michelin Guide. We chose our *forelle blau mit Zahn-meerrettich* from a fish pool at the door of a great Bavarian restaurant in St. Georgen, and we were also given entree to places and sights normally inaccessible to most tourists, like a 15th-century monk's brewery. I came down with a case of gastroenteritis by eating bad eggs at the Jerusalem Hilton, and got the runs after imbibing *crème fraiche* in Paris. A well-aimed ice-cream bar once struck the scroll of my viola at an outdoor concert in New York's Battery Park, and the story made the papers. My hair was set afire from candles provided by the Westbury Hotel during a brown-out in London (a reviewer had fun with that). I wore huge amber beads and a bright red Nehru jacket when I soloed in Berlioz's *Harold in Italy*, but since it happened shortly after the 1960s, when such things were in style, barely an eyebrow was raised.

I borrowed the title of this memoir from Morton Feldman (1926–1987), the composer who is famous for writing "The Viola in My Life" during the early 1970s. I regret never having the chance to perform Feldman's piece (for flute, violin, viola, cello, piano, and percussion), but Karen Phillips recorded it with some of the people I was closest to during my days in New York. The word "rhapsody" comes from the Greek word for "songs stitched together," and was first used to describe poetry. Its connection with emotional poetry came about during the middle 17th century, and it was first used to describe a relatively free-flowing piece of music (one not dominated by structure and form) during the middle of the 19th century.

I hope I haven't confused the reader by beginning my tale at age 20, the beginning of my life as a violist. I found the viola to be my true voice during that first backstage encounter with the instrument back in 1946, and was truly smitten by its sound. I knew I was taking a gamble by switching to an instrument less well regarded by some, but from that point on everything simply fell into place. The feedback I've garnered through the years confirms that I made the right decision, and it's been a helluva run for a kid from Brooklyn.

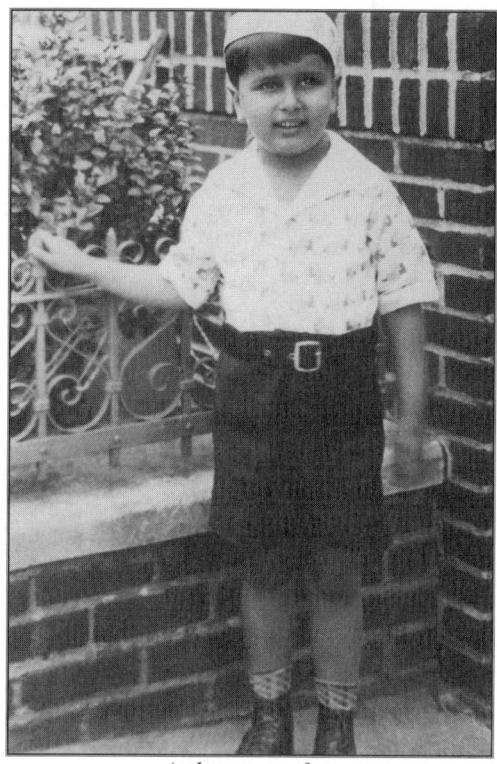
Author at age four

Entrata

So this psychiatrist visits an insane asylum, and he notices one of the inmates pushing a wheelbarrow back and forth, endlessly. That behavior seems odd enough, but the inmate also happens to have the wheelbarrow turned upside down. After observing this guy doing his thing for a while, our visitor decides to ask this character why he's doing this, and the reply comes back, "Whaddaya think, I'm crazy? Every time I turn the damned thing right-side up, someone fills it with dirt."

I suppose I should be having nightmares still because of one wheelbarrow in particular—dirt-filled, right-side-up, and only too real—that caused my mother to be so overprotective of me throughout my Brooklyn childhood, and for years to come.

It happened that this otherwise-innocent dirt-filled tool of the mason's trade was standing on the sidewalk in front of my mother's dependable kosher butcher shop on Church Avenue. While she was busy inside making her purchases and watching Mr. Schiffman wrap them (only the very best cut of flanken would do for Mrs. Zaslav), I joined some kids outside who were making mud pies near the wheelbarrow. My next memory was waking up in a strange hospital bed, and seeing my mother's face hovering anxiously over me.

I learned that the wheelbarrow had accidentally been tipped over on me, resulting in a skull fracture, and middle ear infections that necessitated two mastoidectomies. The infections resulting from this accident could easily have proved fatal during the 1930s, but with today's antibiotics the need for a mastoidectomy is rare.

My bad luck was followed by some very good luck. I developed pneumonia after the ear operations at Brooklyn Eye and Ear Hospital, and was moved to another hospital, where I was told that my temperature reached 107 degrees. I can still recall seeing the thermometer break in my bed, and seeing droplets of mercury hop merrily all over the sheets. If it happened to my granddaughter, she would call it "cool." I thought of it as "neat," another instance of the much-discussed generation gap.

During the 1930s it was taken for granted that all family doctors made house calls. In response to a frantic phone call from my mother, Dr. Isaac Salevitz would drive up to 440 East 96th Street, park his big black Buick sedan in front of our apartment house door, and mount the two flights of stairs for yet another examination of mother's little darling. He rediscovered all my ticklish spots with his ice-cold stethoscope, and tucked it back into his leather bag. He scowled briefly at his thermometer before shaking it down, and clasped my feverish head in both hands while delivering his prophecy: "Yes," he intoned, "I believe our Buddy will grow up to be a doctor."

Mary Zaslav and her son "Buddy" in 1932.
The automobile to their left is a 1927 Hupmobile.

CHAPTER I
Brooklyn Beginnings

My birth certificate clearly states that my official arrival on the planet took place at the Brooklyn Lutheran Hospital on April 7, 1926, which was roughly three years before the stock market crash of '29. It further affirms that person or persons unknown had conferred upon me the middle name of Manuel (there, my secret's out!), but this was hardly the best possible sobriquet for a kid of Jewish parentage in that milieu. I can only attribute this flight of fancy to my mother's innately romantic view of life, rosy to a fault, when it came to naming her children. In fact, I doubt that my father had even been consulted. At least I came off better in the name department than my kid brother, who was born seven years after me. He somehow wound up with the name of Blair. Lucky for him it was kept quiet. He wisely never answered to anything but Billy.

Nowadays people seem to be much more concerned with their family histories than they were when I was growing up. Both of my parents immigrated from Europe, but I can't recall anyone saying a word about their lives in the old country. I use Yiddish terms unabashedly, but my parents and other relatives rarely spoke Yiddish in my presence, except to keep me in the dark about something they thought wasn't my business.

By talking to my Aunt Loretta, I was able to tease out a few of our family stories, but I learned most of what I know from my late cousin Barry Siegel and his pastor-wife Martha, who traveled to Europe in order to learn about our family history.

During the first decade of the 20th century everyone was trying to reach the *Goldeneh Medina*, a fabled place where the sidewalks were paved with gold. My maternal grandfather Selig (Samuel) Knauer came to America to join his brothers. He had been a sawmill worker in the old country, and found employment as a pants cutter in a Lower East Side sweatshop. After his day's work was over, he would stroll the length of Canal Street with cheap wristwatches buckled under his sleeves and around both his arms, looking for buyers (greenhorns, who were even greener than he was) for his cheap merchandise.

My maternal grandmother Esther Knauer and her children, ten-year-old Malie (my mother changed her name to Mary), six-year-old Jetty (my Aunt Loretta), and four-year-old Baruch (my Uncle Ben), waited impatiently for their promised departure from the village of Stulpikany.*

---

* Stulpikany was near Gura Humora, in the district then known as Bukovina, in the Northern Carpathian mountains of Romania, which was part of Austria at the time.

With little news forthcoming from her faraway husband, Esther began to smell a rodent. Calling upon her Carpathian wiles, she wrote to him saying that a certain piece of land that he had coveted was coming up for sale. If he would rush her the required sum, she might just be able to grab it for him. Our entrepreneurial handler forked over the money, and Esther (who spoke no English) promptly bought passage in steerage class for the Knauer gang on the ship *Vaderland*. They sailed from Antwerp and landed at Ellis Island on June 21, 1909. Little Jetty came down with the measles during the voyage, so the whole family was quarantined on Ellis Island for several weeks until she recovered.

Mary Zaslav

My mother was really kind of classy for her time, a cut above some of my friend's mothers. She was close to her four sisters (three more sisters were born after they arrived in America) and her brother, who all lived nearby. She certainly was not a common gossip, like many of the *yentas* that Woody Allen depicts in his films. She dressed well, and was considered attractive, though she was somewhat unhappy about the shape of the nose she inherited from the Knauers. She kept a kosher middle-class home for her family, lit candles on Friday nights, said her prayers, and kept two sets of dishes. The cushions of our living room furniture had elaborately-embroidered slipcovers over the requisite heavy-zippered plastic covers, so prone to yellowing, that prevented possible destruction by the rear ends of guests, who rarely appeared. I wasn't allowed to escape her taste in dress either. Little protesting Buddy, even at eight years of age, was dragged to Abe Stark's fancy clothing emporium on Pitkin Avenue to be fitted for a pair of pants, a vest, and a jacket for the holidays. Every single one of Abe Stark's suits came with an extra pair of pants (you never can tell).

The maturity she developed as the eldest of six children, seemed to set her apart from her siblings. If she wasn't reading (in her spare time), she was seated at our upright piano playing kitschy waltzes by Johann Strauss, Joseph Lanner, Emile Waldteufel, and achingly sad love songs from Franz Lehar's operettas, which gave a quasi-Viennese flavor to our Brooklyn home. As my onset of puberty became manifest, I took note of the romantic images that adorned the covers of the sheet music on the piano rack. Those elegantly-swooning, lightly-draped nymphs, surrounded by courtly knights on horseback must have made a distinct impression on my psyche.

While the sounds of old Vienna floated rapturously from her right hand, I began to sense that her left hand was hitting a few clinkers: the harmony was definitely off. This leads me to speculate that I might have chosen to play the viola, which provides so much of a composition's harmony, in an unconscious (albeit noble) effort to correct those wrong notes. Was I riding (many years later) to my mother's harmonic rescue, like those pictured knights-in-shining-armor coming to save those diaphanously clad females? *Was glauben sie, Herr Doktor Freud?*

The classic Jewish mother's dream at the time was that at least one of her sons should become a doctor, so our own good doctor's prophecy that I would join his fold was understandable. But confident as he sounded, Dr. Salevitz would not win a cigar. In contrast to so many youngsters of Asian parentage who choose to play string instruments today, it was mostly kids of European parentage who could be seen schlepping their little violin cases, to the jeers of the other kids on the block, in the early decades of the 20th century.

My paternal genes reached Brooklyn by way of Odessa, the cradle city for many of the great Russian violinists, so perhaps it was *b'shert* that I would spend the greater part of my life with a fiddle tucked under my chin. As for becoming a doctor, I already knew that any medical question could be answered by consulting a big black volume sitting on our bookshelf. I used to show off to my friends by using some of the exotic Latin words I found in Dr. Morris Fishbein's *Modern Home Medical Adviser*, like "fallopian tubes" and "glans," and tossing them casually into conversations. The highly-detailed line drawings that showed how the human reproductive system actually looked really troubled me. But who would want to be a doctor anyway? They usually smelled of strong soap and seemed to frown a lot; but they sure as heck drove swell cars!

I was squatting on the ground for a game of marbles with my friends one day (I must have been around the age of 12), and I felt a sharp stabbing pain in my lower-right abdomen. Like Superman to the rescue, I took immediate control of the situation and ran (in some pain) to our bookshelf to consult with Dr. Fishbein. I didn't have to go beyond the letter A to reach my incontrovertible diagnosis: what we had here was a clear case of appendicitis.

You will understand my exultation when Dr. Salevitz, arriving this time in a new Buick, declared that it did indeed look like appendicitis to him. At the hospital, I was eager to display my medical erudition to the attending surgeon. While he gently prodded my tender abdomen, I suggested that, in this case, he might want to employ the classic right rectus incision. He suggested in turn that I might want to just shut up and mind my own business. But he did make the right rectus incision after all to remove my inflamed appendix, and I still bear the scar as a trophy of my astute diagnosis.

You might have noticed that Dr. Salevitz called me "Buddy." My teachers called me "Bernard," but everybody else called me "Buddy," even my mother. When she noticed a suspicious silence emanating from my room at practice time, she would call out, "Buddy, if you don't practice we'll have to stop the lessons—again." Some smart-alecks called me "Zazzy," inspired by Zasu Pitts a daffy character actress in the movies.

The nickname Buddy was not without its problems. Across the street from our apartment house there was a large vacant lot that was perfect for flying kites and model airplanes, and there was a small farm right next door. The farmer kept a few ratty-looking goats, and he called one of them "Buddy." Sharing a name with a goat was all the kids needed to razz me. It didn't help that I was a total klutz at stickball. I couldn't even hit the distance from one sewer cover to the next. I was quite nearsighted, but I couldn't wear regular eyeglasses because the temple piece wouldn't fit properly over my right ear (my mastoidectomies took a long time to heal). The optometrist solved the problem by outfitting me with a piece of old-fashioned eyewear known as a *pince-nez*, a silly-looking thing that clipped onto my nose, and was attached to a black silk ribbon that hung around my neck to keep it from falling to the ground. Presidents Teddy Roosevelt and Woodrow Wilson both wore a *pince-nez*, as did Margaret Hamilton when she played the Wicked Witch of the West in *The Wizard of Oz*. Sure, all those weird old fogies wore them, but a five year old? Enough said!

My tale of childhood woe should explain why I became known to one and all as a "sickly kid." I was somewhat pale and skinny, but I didn't feel sickly. I wanted to play with the other kids on the block, but my clearly-overwhelmed mother felt that I had to be kept in a kind of cocoon or else I would surely die. My mother's fears were further strengthened when I caught all of the childhood diseases going around. I wasn't allowed to ride a bike or roller skate ("Your cousin Nate broke his arm skating, and it never healed right!"). Of course there was the constant stricture about "running around" because "you could fall and kill yourself!" We used to rent a summer cottage at Salt Air Court, near Brooklyn's Brighton Beach, but because of my mastoid operations, I wasn't allowed to go into the ocean, and I never learned to swim.

Out of self defense, I did what any other red-blooded, one-hundred-percent American boy would have done in my situation: I read voraciously. I read everything I could find, until it felt like my eyes were coming out of my head. I can't ever remember a time when there wasn't a book in my hand. I even read under the covers with a flashlight when I was supposed to be asleep. I can still hear my mother's warning, You'll RUIN your EYES!

And there was such an enormous world of books out there. I read and reread Paul DeKrief's *Microbe Hunters*, lots of Sherlock Holmes, Madame Curie's discoveries of radium, mind-stretching sci-fi yarns, James Hilton's *Lost Horizons*, satire by Ambrose Bierce, and fun stuff by P.G. Wodehouse and S.J. Perelman. A big bookshelf in my Aunt Loretta's apartment, just across the hall, held the entire *Book of Knowledge*, which contained all the wonders of the known world, and *Anthony Adverse*, a novel by Hervey Allen that had 1,224 pages packed with unsheathed Spanish swords and heaving bosoms. We saved coupons from the *New York Post*, which was worth reading then, and bought complete editions of Charles Dickens and Mark Twain at a special low price. A tattered few of these well-thumbed volumes still inhabit my garage.

There were other exciting things to do besides reading all day and much of the night. I could blow up test tubes full of stuff (accidentally, of course) with my chemistry set, and seek exotic microscopic specimens in Brooklyn mud puddles. I could build model airplanes with balsa wood, airplane glue (we called it amberoid), and sheets of tissue paper, which was much more fun than assembling kits from the shelves of the toy stores. I designed throw gliders with the help of my cousin Byron, who was six years older than me and lived across the hall. We once built a large single-wing double-dihedral model plane with a 36-inch wingspan that was powered by a tiny Browning gasoline engine. If the wind was right, we could fly it in the lot across the street. Or we could go by car to Floyd Bennett Airport, where we would get the thrill of watching our creation lift ever so gracefully from the concrete tarmac, before it crashed.

So how did I come to play the violin? I often doodled around on our upright piano, but what I heard from the recordings of Mischa Elman and Jascha Heifetz that played on our wind-up Victrola was much more appealing. I wasn't pushed at all by my mother to learn the violin: I asked for the lessons. Although each of my violin teachers claimed that I was quite gifted musically, none of them tarred me with the dreaded word "prodigy," a cross many exceedingly talented individuals had to bear.

My father, Samuel Zaslavsky was born in Odessa in either 1894 or 1892 (we're not sure which). I would guess that any fiddle playing genes in my DNA chain would have come from his side of the family, since quite a few of Russia's best violinists, including Nathan Milstein, David Oistrakh, and Efrem Zimbalist, were either born in Odessa, or studied in Odessa. It remains a mystery why this particular spot on the shores of the Black Sea should have roiled the embryos of so many great fiddlers: perhaps it was something in the air. In his book, *Isaac Stern: My First 79 Years*, the American violinist (and possessor of a golden tongue) says that during the 1950s his manager, Sol Hurok, got close to the Soviet minister of culture in order to obtain permission for Soviet artists like Oistrakh to participate in an artist-exchange program between America and the USSR. When the actual invitation arrived in 1956 Stern remarked, "The Russians sent us their Jews from Odessa, and now we're sending them our Jews from Odessa." Nathan Milstein counters, "I know many Jews who are not good violinists" in *The Art of the Violin*. He continues by explaining that the climate was right in Russia/Odessa at the time for Jews to play the violin, and they did so with great fervor. It was a way to get ahead.

There have been several other Zaslavskys in the music world. From 1912 through 1918 a violinist named Alexander Saslavsky was the concertmaster of the New York Symphony Society under music director Walter Damrosch (which finally went through a series of changes to end up as the New York Philharmonic). The pianist Dora Zaslavsky taught for many years at the Manhattan School of Music, and violinist Isidor Saslav bears still another variant of the name. An attorney named Zaslavsky (who was herself born in Odessa) told me about a small section outside Odessa proper called Zaslavi that is still largely inhabited by Jews, anent the fictional shtetl of Anatevka in *Fiddler on the Roof*.

My father, who was not a fiddler, was sent off to work at the tender age of ten. When he passed through Ellis Island in 1906, his family name was duly shortened to Zaslav, one of the many differently truncated versions of Zaslavsky that I've seen. He was a bit short, slim, and proud of his physical strength. He enlisted to fight in World War I, apparently underage, with the U.S. Army. He was wounded and gassed in France, and was hospitalized for nearly a year as a result. He was honorably discharged in 1919, and he never spoke about his wartime service. I only learned about it from my mother, years later.

After working as a tinsmith, he joined his two older brothers, who had a wholesale plumbing and heating supply business in Brooklyn. I recall visiting their store when I was quite young and seeing my father at work behind the counter. When a customer requested a certain item, he would lift a trap door hidden behind the counter and then he would disappear bit by bit: first his torso, and then his head, as he descended an unseen flight of steps into the cellar. I always wondered what sort of world was hidden down there beneath the floor.

My Aunt Loretta, who we always called "Yetty," told me that my father worked his way up in the business, and that he was "persuaded" (more likely *inveigled*) by Grandma Esther to marry my mother. Yetty claimed that my dad had once lived the 1920's-style bachelor life of a "wild and crazy guy," and when he finally settled down to marriage, he had to part with his red Harley Davidson motorcycle, WITH sidecar.

Due to a few canny choices they made at the onset of the Great Depression, Zaslav Brothers Plumbing & Heating Supplies had become the largest-stocked plumbing and heating supply business in Brooklyn. Many of the manufacturers that provided society with the basic human necessities of life like toilets, sinks, bathtubs, faucets, furnaces, and the pipes and fittings they required, were failing. Noticing this trend, the three Zaslav brothers used their available cash to buy up the remaining inventory of the failing firms (which also helped to keep a few of them afloat) and rent a couple of extra warehouses. They sat out the difficult times, and their prescience paid off. When their competitor's shelves were bare, you "hadda' go" for what you needed to Zaslav Brothers.

The business was located on the corner of Sutter and Watkins Streets, in Brooklyn's crime-ridden Brownsville area, the home of the mob known as "Murder, Inc." One morning my father was delivered home by the police (my mother had been waiting up for him all night) after he had paid kidnappers the requisite shakedown money.

The store opened at 6:00 a.m., six days a week, so plumbers and contractors could pick up the materials that they required for the day's work, and then they would return for stuff they needed for the next day. I was already tucked in bed when my father got home, so I rarely saw him, except on Sundays. The plumbing business was his life, and he regarded it as his lot to work and provide financially for his family. Like many other fathers of the time, he basically didn't know how to be one, and he never learned.

Although it was not properly recognized at the time, my father suffered throughout his life from post-traumatic stress disorder as a result of his war experiences. Nobody spoke of "dysfunctional families" then. People argued, fought, broke up, and patched up their marriages, but divorce was rarely seen in our world. My Aunt Loretta was an exception to the rule, and it was thought scandalous when she divorced her husband, Sol, a house painter from New Orleans whom she had married at age sixteen.

Most fathers, as a breed, rarely took time off from their work to play ball with their children, so we kids figured out how to amuse ourselves by playing ball games in the street, or in nearby schoolyards. Sometimes, on a Sunday, I'd see somebody's father "toss a few" to his kid, and I'd try not to notice it too much. I never enjoyed that interaction with my own father; he was "busy at the store," and it just seemed normal to me.

Ebbett's Field, the home field of our beloved Brooklyn Dodgers, was on Bedford Avenue. There was also an automobile dealership (I think it was a Dodge dealership) on Bedford, and it had a big plate glass window that faced the back of the stadium. That window was often the victim of a long fly or (sigh) a homer by our hero Jackie Robinson (who joined the Dodgers after I returned to Brooklyn as an adult). I suspect the dealer thought the advertising he got on the sports pages was well worth the cost of replacing the window (which was often boarded up).

On Sundays we took the obligatory drive to Coney Island in our 1927 black Hupmobile sedan. Back then cars seemed to come only in black. Ours was huge, and it featured a unique innovation called "Free Wheeling." If you tugged at a dashboard-mounted lever with all your might, you could shift the gears without depressing the clutch pedal. When I was eleven I got to drive this monster around the block (not legally, of course) with my father sitting next to me. This model had eight cylinders with "double ignition," which meant that it had sixteen spark plugs.

For some reason, we would always follow the same predictably boring route down Ocean Parkway to Coney Island, but despite our requests, my father would never stop to park. I'll never figure out why. We missed all the fabled amusements that everyone else enjoyed, like walking along Surf Avenue and Stillman Street, eating one or two of Nathan's hot dogs with fries, or even better, the Feltman's Foot-Long Dog they sold next door to Nathan's, a nickel more and worth every penny (or so I'd been told). It was even more frustrating to miss all the great rides at Luna Park, like the Loop-the-Loops or "Steeplechase, the Funny Place." Once my cousin Barry (who was eight years younger than me) came along with us, and he couldn't believe that we weren't eveb allowed to get out of the car.

My Uncle Ben was once permitted to take me deep-sea fishing off Sheepshead Bay, but my mother warned her brother repeatedly that his nephew might get seasick on the boat. Instead of rods, we used hand lines with baited treble hooks that we dropped over the side. The ocean was a bit rough that day, but I kept hauling 'em in over the side, while my uncle Ben suffered from seasickness below decks. It was exciting, particularly when I got more than one fish on the line. We docked the boat at the pier, and schlepped home two muslin sacks of smelly dead fish on the Brooklyn Manhattan Transit. To the righteous disgust of the other riders, the sacks leaked all over the floor of the subway car, and after we got them home, nobody wanted to eat our catch. Weren't our fish kosher?

Sometimes on Saturdays my grandfather Selig, a great lover of children, would take me to the movies. We usually went to the old Bluebird Theater, located under the elevated track of the BMT at Saratoga and Livonia Avenues in Brownsville. For ten cents we got to see a double bill along with the Fox Movietone News, the Three Stooges, and two other serials (usually Flash Gordon and the Lone Ranger). I enjoyed one newsreel that showed Lucky Lindy barely lift off for his solo flight across the Atlantic. Whenever I heard the first strains of the Lone Ranger's theme, Rossini's "William Tell Overture," I'd hunker down in my seat and wait for the inevitable. Sure enough, when our hero was caught in a tight spot, trapped by the bad guys without Tonto, his trusty guide, at his side, my grandpa would jump to his feet in excitement and shout out in his old-country accent, *"Look ott, Lone Renjeh."* Lots of kids sitting around me snickered, but I did still get to the movies.

Public School 196 was just two blocks from our apartment house. I found school excruciatingly boring. You see, I already knew everything worth knowing from all my reading, so public school felt like a big fat waste of time. I could use that time better to read even more of my really good stuff.

When I got a bit older, we would spend our summers in the Catskill Mountains (known in some circles as the "Jewish Alps"). I was still skinny as a rail (my mother's words), and we went there in a vain effort to "fatten up little Buddy and bring some color to his cheeks" (my mother again). My sallow complexion didn't seem to bother little Jetta Becker, my official six-year-old summer girlfriend. Her father was the owner of the Becker House in Mountaindale, the hotel that my family favored. As a special perk, Jetta's father would pick us up from the train station in his magnificent silver Pierce-Arrow Town Brougham, an automobile unforgettable for its opulence. My appreciation of beauty, both female and automotive, stems from those heady days, though

I didn't rank them in that order.

Food-wise, the Borscht Belt more than lived up to its reputation. Every hotel in the Catskills catered to a particular clientele, and they all competed for the best Jewish chefs to be found. Tables sagged under the weight of blintzes and borscht, and you risked a case of snow-blindness from all the sour cream. My favorite borscht-belt food was a cold dish called Fruit Soup, a rich dark-purple concoction made from plums and sour cherries.

Everyone knew that the main reasons to go to the Catskills were to play pinochle by day, and to "carry on" by night at the hotel casino, where a movable cast of desperate and underpaid comics plied their trade. They were paid to keep you in stitches, so you wouldn't complain to the management about your crummy room; and they were strenuously encouraged to flirt outrageously with the ladies of all ages, married and otherwise. These aptly named tummlers* were hired to brighten up the otherwise drab lives of paying guests with hilariously vulgar material. I enjoyed them all. Luminaries like Danny Kaye, Red Buttons, and Jerry Lewis, rose from the salt mines of the Catskills to Hollywood stardom, but the supreme virtuoso of them all, and the one whom I most admired, was a classy, sober-looking gentleman by the name of Myron Cohen, a murderously funny storyteller, who might be described today as a minimalist. His humor was very different from the coarse jokes of all the others. By merely dropping one eyelid while telling his tales of the Yiddish absurd, he could make you laugh so hard that your belly hurt.

Once my father's business was doing well enough, we would take an annual two-week winter vacation in Miami Beach. During the years following the Depression it was affordable to stay at one of the small family-style hotels right on the ocean on Collins Avenue, and my parents had no problem getting their delicate genius excused from public school. We enjoyed the luxury of our own sleeping compartment aboard the Orange Blossom Special, an express train with Pullman sleeper cars that went non-stop from New York to Miami. When we alit from the train, we really

---

* In Yiddish *tumler* comes from *tumlen,* which means to make a racket.

did smell oranges, just as the advertisements had promised.

One special Florida event stands out in my memory. While strolling down Collins Avenue, one warm evening, we passed a house with a traditional white picket fence, and windows that were wide open, to let in the evening air. Through the windows, I could see (and hear) a small group of people playing a piece of classical music on string instruments. I had, of course, heard solo violin and orchestral works before, but this was my very first taste of live chamber music. It was different from anything I had ever experienced, and I was transported by the rich sound and the complexity of the music.

Our mail was postmarked "New York," but when you said "the city," you meant Manhattan; certainly not Brooklyn, the Bronx, Queens, or far-flung Staten Island. Due to the improved economy after the Depression, many people began to leave these increasingly-crowded boroughs to buy the affordable houses being built in the open spaces of Long Island. New townships, such as Levittown, were springing up all over the Island, and our part of Brooklyn was benefiting as well. The Ferrante Brothers builders put up some inexpensive single-family attached homes on East 49th Street and Avenue D in East Flatbush, and my father and his brother (my Uncle Louis) decided to purchase two adjoining units. Flatbush (as well as the Bushwick, Flatlands, Gravesend, and New Utrecht sections), felt more like "shirtsleeve" communities than the densely-populated sections of downtown Brooklyn.

The Zaslav brothers always seemed to do things in threes. When it came to trading in their cars, they would always buy the same model (I liked their Chrysler New Yorkers best). I imagine that, as in their business, they got a bargain by buying in quantity. They always placed their trust in the oldest brother, my Uncle William, and why not? He hadn't steered them wrong during the Depression!

Our new house at 811 East 49th Street cost exactly $3,990

in 1936 dollars. It had a two-car garage, a small front lawn, and a basement apartment, where I could read late at night to my heart's content. It had a large backyard where we planted radishes, carrots, beans, and two small fruit trees. I even raised a few rabbits back there, but they never multiplied.

One spring day, my grandfather, who lived within walking distance, came to visit us. With a mysterious twinkle in his eyes, and without explanation, he reached into the cabinet under the kitchen sink, and hauled out my mother's bag of potatoes. He cut a few of them into small pieces, making sure that each piece contained an "eye." I couldn't figure out what he was doing. We went into the garden, and he stuck the little pieces of potato into loosened soil. I had planted seeds before, but planting potatoes was new to me. After a week or so, I noticed green shoots coming up through the soil, and in about two months, we were digging up his potatoes. I guess memories of the old country still lived in my Grandpa's heart.

An Italian family lived on a large corner lot down the street from us, and the dignified old Italian gentleman who owned it took care of our garden. He was tall, erect, and formal in his bearing, and he sported a handsome white handlebar mustache. He usually wore overalls over the heavy underwear we called a "union suit." He walked solemnly past our house every morning holding an empty galvanized pail, and promptly returned, for some unfathomable reason, with his pail filled with beer from the bar around the corner. He went through the same routine in the early evening, though by that time he would be walking a little more deliberately.

His own huge garden was filled with peach trees, pear trees, and apple trees. My mother asked him if he might plant a fruit tree for us. He showed up next day with something that looked to me only like a leafy stick, which he planted in our back yard. After a few years we had small sweet peaches to enjoy in the summer. I've tried my amateur hand at gardening everywhere I lived. I planted three different shades of lilacs in Milwaukee, Eastern white pines and lupines around our shore cottage in Surry, Maine, and English hybrid roses in our back patio in Stanford, all this in memory of my wonderful grandfather, and that gentle Italian man who taught me to love the earth.

Since our new house was located about a mile away from our old house, I was now enrolled at P.S. 208, right on the next corner. There was a synagogue directly across the street, but for some mysterious reason, I was sent to another one a block up the street to prepare for my upcoming Bar Mitzvah. I had read many books on science and evolution, so I was skeptical of the religious studies that my folks tried to foist on me. I was already certain that religion was just a "crock," but a Jewish male child comes "of age" at thirteen, and my folks insisted on the ceremony.

I had to fold again on this one, and I dutifully sang out my *haftarah* in a high, strained soprano. The reception was held at a Lower East Side Manhattan restaurant-cum-night club known as the Little Rumanian. This was the club where Sophie Tucker, the "Red Hot Momma," sang her big hit song, "Some of These Days," and where I got my first close-up view of middle-age cleavage. The predictable avalanche of gifts from relatives and friends followed: Waterman fountain pens and small checks peeking out of colored envelopes were stuffed into my undeserving hands.

Our move to East 49th Street meant that I was cut off from my three cousins who lived across the hall in our old building. But I had two other cousins, Gary Zaslav and Nate, his 6-foot-plus brother, who lived in the adjoining house at 809 East 49th Street. P.S. 208 was just across the street, and it had a newly-instituted program for "gifted" children called IPC, (Individual Progress Classes), for which I signed a so-called contract promising to work on a subject of my choice. This was a terrific opportunity to delve deeply into my favorite subjects at my own pace, with the luxury of a teacher's individual attention.

Through the offices of our beloved Mayor Fiorello H. LaGuardia, the P.S. 208 orchestra was selected to play the 1939 New York World's Fair in Flushing Meadows, Queens. Billed as "The World of Tomorrow," it gave us a look into futuristic technologies, and offered hope to a world already threatened by the horrific events happening in Europe and in Asia. The Trylon and Perisphere, two architectural wonders, rose high over exhibits like the General Motors Futurama, the Lagoon of Nations, and a great number of international exhibits.

Spurred on by the memory of that evening of chamber music in Florida and my beloved records, I was eager to resume my off-again, on-again violin lessons. Signor Felice D'Alfino, my new violin teacher, came highly recommended. Signor D'Alfono was intimidatingly Italian, and luxuriously handlebar-mustachioed. He had four or five certificates hanging on the wall of his studio, all in Italian, that proved he was a professor of violin. He had a stern manner, and gestured with his hands as he spoke mellifluously, in a richly-accented voice.

Signor D'Alfino brooked absolutely no excuse for not practicing. My mother took me once a week on the Utica Avenue trolley to his dark little studio apartment on Eastern Parkway. Once there, Signor D'Alfino strove mightily to unearth any dormant violinistic genius hiding within. In addition, he took some of our lesson time to work through a fascinating Italian book called *The Art of Rhythmical Articulation* (his translation of the title). Using this book, which he translated, as well as he could into his flavorful English, we tackled the mysteries of musical and rhythmical notation like solfeggio, key signatures, time signatures, and the various beat patterns used when conducting. After two months of lessons with Signor D'Alfino, I was at last able to mount my imaginary podium in front of my unseen orchestra, and beat out, with some bare semblance of correctness, the rhythmic patterns of the music I played on my records.

It was a long trolley ride to Signor D'Alfino's apartment, so my mother found me a new and slightly-balding violin teacher named Hartley M. Shellans, who came to our house twice a week for my lessons. In contrast to the flowing white handlebar model that was affected by the Maestro, Mr. Shellans made do with a small black pencil mustache, which underscored his rather academic manner. He pronounced me highly talented, but improperly schooled, and made it clear that everything had to be changed, something not uncommon when one changes violin teachers, and something that is always painful for both parties.

We plugged away at my technical deficiencies, using scales, arpeggios, and études that I hadn't worked on previously. We worked very well together during lessons, and I was making significant progress. He kept telling me how talented I was, but Mr. Shellans seemed to exude an air of sadness, and I feared that it was because of me. I really liked Mr. Shellans, and thought he played very well, but I thought that music making ought to be more pleasurable. I was also confused about the violin, because I considered playing it only a small part of music. My innermost dream of conducting a symphony orchestra was still uppermost, and though I continued to play, my lessons with Mr. Shellans eventually petered out.

A huge Stromberg-Carlson radio occupied a corner of our living room, and like most Americans, I waited impatiently on Sundays to hear Fred Allen and Jack Benny, and their famous radio duel. I got a kick out of the sounds of stuff dropping out of Fibber McGee and Molly's famous overstuffed closet. We were treated to the cultured tones of Milton Cross on Saturday afternoons, as he recounted all the ridiculous plots for the Metropolitan Opera broadcasts.

Through our radio we heard about a wonderful new electric record player that would bring the very best of classical music into our home on demand, and could supplement our cherished Stromberg-Carlson. RCA Victor offered a new series of vinyl records by the magnificent NBC Symphony Orchestra, under the baton of their conductor, Arturo Toscanini. What an unbelievable feast was now set before me: Haydn symphonies like the Clock, the Surprise, and the Drum-roll, Beethoven's 5th, Mozart's 40th, and many others were on the list.

We snapped up all the records they offered, and I was soon busy wearing out the grooves of these masterworks, storing them mentally as I flailed away in front of the imaginary orchestra that filled my ears. I might kvetch today about some of Maestro Toscanini's overly-brisk tempi in Mozart's Symphony

No. 40, but then, in my blissful ignorance, I was in musical heaven.

Apropos of Toscanini, I certainly would have scoffed if someone had told me that, some eight years later, I would be studying violin at the Juilliard School of Music with Mischa Mischakoff, concertmaster of this very orchestra. Specially created by NBC's David Sarnoff in 1937 for Maestro Toscanini, the NBC Symphony Orchestra was the crown jewel of U.S. orchestras, until it officially disbanded in 1954. Many musicians decided to remain together as a cooperative after the orchestra was dissolved, and they called themselves the Symphony of the Air.

My father told us that a Mr. Sarnoff (General Sarnoff during World War II) once showed up at the plumbing supply store and offered to sell him shares of stock in the newly-created Radio Corporation of America. What business person in his right mind would buy shares of stock in a newfangled radio company if he could invest in safe and solid things like toilets and bathtubs? Ridiculous! Mr. Sarnoff was politely shown the door.

When I graduated from P.S. 208 in January of 1940, a chum, who knew about my ambition to be a conductor, wrote on a leaf of my yearbook, "Look out, Toscanini." While Toscanini didn't need to worry about competition from me, he and members of his NBC orchestra were about to figure importantly in my future.

High School Pals:
David Jackier, Bernard Zaslav and Herbert Handt

CHAPTER II
Samuel J. Tilden High School:
Istruzione Scolastica

I wanted to try out for the new High School for Music and Art in Manhattan, but my neurotically-overprotective mother was against the idea. "It's too long a ride," she told me. "You'd have to take the Utica Avenue trolley *and* the IRT subway to get there." She read the papers, you see, and she knew all the dangers. Her helpless little Buddy might get himself electrocuted, or somebody might push him onto the subway's third rail.

I don't know why I didn't have the gumption to stand up for myself; other kids my age rode the subway all the time. Subway murders weren't making the headlines in 1940, and the drug-related crime problems of the 1960s had yet to defile the Brooklyn that I grew up in. My patient mother had certainly seen me through some scary illnesses, but her over-coddling left me without a clue about how to not give in to her anxieties. I had to settle for the high school closest to home.

Samuel J. Tilden High School, like the other high schools in Brooklyn during those happy years, was blessed with a hard working and highly dedicated faculty. It was due, in large part, to the expanded funding for education provided by our feisty little Italian mayor, Fiorello H. LaGuardia. He was affectionately known to us as the "Little Flower," who, during a newspaper strike, went on the radio to read the comics to the kids.

Tilden High had a very good orchestra. Our conductor Ralph Satz (we called him Uncle Ruby) had some connection to Am-Rus, the Russian music publisher, so we got to play works by contemporary composers like Dmitri Shostakovich, Béla Bartók, and Paul Hindemith. "Uncle Ruby" selected me to play in the violin section of the prestigious New York All-City High School Orchestra during my junior year, and I gave my first-ever violin recital (accompanied by my mother) in our large assembly hall. The program included Vittorio Monti's ever-popular Csardas, and Béla Bartók's folksy Rumanian Dances.

My Spanish teacher at Tilden High was the well-known writer Sam Levinson. He supplemented his high school teacher's income by working in the summer as a comedian and a story teller in the Catskill Mountains, and his success there led him to a career as an ethnic (i.e., Jewish) humorist. His early life in Brooklyn supplied him with an abundance of material. He dismissed his family's poverty as being relatively unimportant, because his family and his street life was so rich and joyful. This healthy point of view is certainly much better than kvetching about not having enough money.

Sam brought his sense of humor to the classroom, and would teach us faux-Spanish history with a Yiddish slant, like "The Journey and Travails of Don Juan, *y su meshpucha*" (and his family). He was also an amateur violinist, and one day he sat me down to play through a string quartet for the very first time. In later years he followed my career, and would sometimes show up at my concerts.

Quite a few of my Tilden friends went on to careers in music. Alla Goldberg became a free-lance cellist, Avron Coleman joined the cello section of the New York Philharmonic, and his red-haired brother Shepard Coleman, who was also a cellist, became a Broadway conductor and arranger. Chauncey Welsch, who abandoned the violin to become a trombonist, joined the Glenn Miller band, and Howard (Howie) Weiss, an excellent pianist, changed his name to Peter Howard, and wrote arrangements for Broadway shows like *My Fair Lady* and *Hello Dolly*, *Chicago*, and *Annie*.

In my second year at Tilden High, I met a richly talented pianist named Leonard Rosenman who composed his own music. He was skinny, intense, almost two years older than me, and far more sophisticated, especially concerning contemporary music. He introduced me to the music of the German-born composer Lukas Fuchs (now known as Lukas Foss), and we shared a mutual passion for Paul Hindemith.

Hindemith was a brilliant innovator, and one of the most forward-thinking German composers of the twentieth century (as well as a highly-respected violist who wrote so much music for the instrument). The first piece of Hindemith I heard was the spine-chilling overture to *Mathis der Maler*, an opera about the life of the Reformation-era painter Matthias Grünewald.

Lennie and I enjoyed reading through the violin and piano repertoire and improvising in the style of Hindemith. After studying composition with Hindemith at Yale, Lennie continued his studies with Arnold Schoenberg and Roger Sessions, and became a prolific film composer. I still get tiny residual checks from the Musician's Union for playing the recording session for *East of Eden*, his 101st film score.

David Jackier, an art student (who became a sculptor and painter), was my closest friend at Tilden. We still remain close in spite of the three thousand miles that separate us. We would spend hours discussing the all and everything of life; the ways and the absurdities of the cosmos, and more importantly, which girl had the best looking legs. Along with Herbert Handt, another Tilden friend (who had a melting tenor voice, and went on to have an international career), David and I would ride the New York subways (unaccompanied by my mother) to the fabled isle of Manhattan.

It was with David and Herbie in Greenwich Village that I consumed my very first non-kosher hot dog (strangely, I was not struck dead on the spot). On Saturdays, the three of us became keen observers of the Village's exotic life styles; its coffee bars, and the local artists' sidewalk displays, not to mention the as-yet-untasted-but-nonetheless-fascinating parade of femininity. Our Brooklyn girls were nothing like those we could ogle in Walt Whitman's "Mannahatta."

During our senior year David and I were enrolled in Mrs. Marjorie Dycke's drama class, and we shared an intense crush on our teacher. Combine the ethereal looks and perfect diction of 1930s film star Loretta Young, if you will, with your basic Aphrodite, and you're still not even close. Mrs. Dycke was tall and lithe in figure, always modestly attired, and wore her long dark hair in a bun (hot). We quivered in unison when we saw her unpin it at the end of the day. We found ourselves vying for her favor, and as her devoted and enamored servants, we would invent needless errands to run for her. As far as the age difference was concerned, we felt that the prevailing paradigm was manifestly unfair to such younger (and clearly more virile) males as ourselves. We were obviously more appreciative of mature feminine beauty than the more doddering class. We wondered why our adored Mrs. Marjorie Dycke had to go home each and every night to that mysterious husband who could not have been worthy of her. Was there no justice?

Taking this drama class helped me to lose some of my feelings of physical and social inferiority. Before taking the class, if I spied a girl coming down the sidewalk I would usually cross to the other side of the street, while my supremely self-confident friend David bestrode any arena like a conquering hero (sort of like Burt Lancaster in the 1962 film *Birdman of Alcatraz*).

I played the role of Georges Clemenceau, the Tiger of France, one of the leading roles in a play concerning Woodrow Wilson's "Fourteen Points" speech and the League of Nations. My big scene had Clemenceau fervently arguing the cause of freedom before the entire assembly, and I goofed big-time. Girding myself to my full height, I declaimed, "I must warn you, gentlemen, that . . . er . . . democracy . . . er. . . leads inevitably to . . . er . . . facism." Curtain.This was not my best moment! David may have recalled my foolish misstep in the oil painting he gave us as wedding gift: a Picasso-like stunned-looking, close-eyed male, reposing in the arms of his patient inamorata. He titled the painting "Luv, Luv," and it's been hanging at our bedside ever since we got married.

After graduation I planned on going to college to major in English, science, or both, though I was still wondering where my love of music might lead. A fast-talking clarinetist named Richard Etlinger, a friend who lived down the block, told me about a terrific music camp in the wilds of northern Michigan. I knew my mother would never let me go to this camp (there were, you see, wolves that far north), but slippery Dick made an instant hit with my mother, and I was enrolled for the summer session at the Interlochen Music Camp.

The director of the camp was Dr. Joseph E. Maddy, a faculty member of the University of Michigan, and the camp faculty included the Australian pianist Percy Grainger, the composer Howard Hanson, and the conductor Guy Fraser Harrison. The latter two were on the faculty of the Eastman School of Music in Rochester, New York.

Dick and I eagerly boarded the train for Traverse City, Michigan. When we arrived at Interlochen, we found our bunks in

Boys' Camp: boys and girls were segregated (and for obvious good reason). I soon began to get the hang of camp life. When I first showed up at mealtime, the head counselor took one look at my skinny frame, and immediately put me on extra milk rations. I hated plain milk, and that's what I was getting, not chocolate milk, or even the Ovaltine that my mother forced into me (sometimes slipping in an egg when I wasn't looking). I thought myself to be rather stoic about the whole experience.

Mail call for me usually meant a package from home containing an extra sweater and a few handkerchiefs, but the "care packages" that Dick received every week (and shared rather reluctantly with me) had the goodies I really craved. Those cookies, candy bars (especially the Baby Ruths), kosher salami, and bologna, saved me from utter starvation, possibly even death.

Learning a new orchestral program every week, playing chamber music, and taking conducting classes was the perfect entree to the serious study of music. I thrived on it. There was a weekly competition for the concertmaster's seat of the student orchestra. This was my first entry into any sort of musical competition, and it forced me to practice a lot more seriously. I alternated the concertmaster seat that summer with Richard Ferrin, a violinist who later spent many years in the Chicago Symphony's viola section.

I became friends with Seymour Lipkin, a pianist from Detroit. He was two years younger than me, quite studious in demeanor, and studied with Rudolf Serkin at the Curtis Institute of Music in Philadelphia. We shared a love for Haydn symphonies, and were soon competing in our made-up game of identifying their themes. We also used silly names for each other, inspired by Russian literature. I was Rodion Romanovitch Raskolnikov (from Feodor Dostoevsky's *Crime and Punishment*), and I named Seymour Paskudnyak (a horrible person) Pashaslavnyik (just too silly.)*

Percy Grainger had a private studio at Interlochen, and it was furnished with an especially fine piano. One afternoon he generously made it available to me and Seymour, so that we could

---

* Many decades later, Seymour and I played together and taught chamber music together at the Kneisel Hall Music Festival in Blue Hill, Maine.

read our way through some Beethoven Violin Sonatas. While we were playing we noticed that Mr. Grainger quietly slipped to the back of the studio. When we took a break between movements Mr. Grainger remarked, "I never really liked Beethoven," and walked out! From what I have read about Beethoven's sloppy living habits, his many landlords might have shared Grainger's feelings.

Percy Grainger was well past middle age, but he was in excellent physical condition. He was strong, muscular, and never one to miss his early morning plunges into Interlochen's icy-cold lake. He was reportedly a rather colorful character who sometimes rode the rails on boxcars, like a hobo, to reach his destination, much to the chagrin of his managers.

Our concerts were held in Interlochen's huge outdoor music bowl, which was raked downward rather sharply so that the stage rose about three feet from the low end. One day Guy Fraser Harrison was conducting a rehearsal of the orchestra for a piano concerto that Mr. Grainger was going to play with us. Out of the corners of our eyes we could see Mr. Grainger standing quietly at the back of the bowl, listening intently as the orchestra approached his entrance point. He decided right then, as a lark, that he would attempt to run down an aisle from the back of the bowl to the stage to make his entrance. While we played, goggle-eyed, he ran like a shot. When he reached the stage, he hauled himself up, and seated himself at the piano bench just in time for his entrance. Percy Grainger was sixty-two years old at the time.

Ferde Grofé (who was also a violist) guest-conducted our performance of his "Grand Canyon Suite." Our conductors normally sat at the podium on a high wooden stool, so that they might command the eyes of the strings and woodwinds, as well as the brass and percussion players who were seated farther back. Mr. Grofé was quite overweight at the time, and his buttocks hung over the stool-seat edges very noticeably.

Our concerts were broadcast on Michigan radio, and my friend David Krupp, a baritone with a rich speaking voice, had been chosen to do the announcing for the concerts. David was obviously entranced by the spectacle before his eyes, because that night Michigan radio listeners were informed that the work they were about to hear was the "Grand Canyon *Seat*." David and I later attended Juilliard together, and we have remained close friends. He became a Chicago attorney, and refers to himself as a "failed baritone."

Aaron Copland dedicated "An Outdoor Overture" to the Interlochen orchestra. It was the custom to perform this work along with Howard Hanson's Second Symphony (the Romantic, in all its richness) for the last concert of the season, and it always evoked a lot of emotion from the students and the audience.

Howard Hanson, who was born in Nebraska to Swedish parents (and indeed looked most Scandinavian), was one of the warmest and most engaging people it has been my good fortune to meet. His luscious harmonies stirred my inner composer. When I finally got up the nerve to show him a few things I had written, he surprised me by saying that after I graduated from high school he could offer me a scholarship to the Eastman School of Music. Guy Fraser Harrison also confirmed that possibility. I was overjoyed.

I couldn't have imagined such an opportunity when I arrived at Interlochen only two months earlier, and I came to realize that science and English, much as I loved them, were going to take second place to music. Dedicating myself to composing and conducting had only been a dream, but that offer from Eastman suddenly made it seem possible after all.

CHAPTER III
"My" Juilliard:
Gradus ad Parnassum

Shakespeare says, "What's in a name?"
With him we disagree
Names like Sammy, Max, or Moe
Never bring the heavy dough
Like Mischa, Jascha, Toscha, Sascha—
Fiddle-le, diddle-le, dee.*

I was bursting with the news about Eastman when I returned from Interlochen, and I was proud of what I accomplished my first time away from home. My experiences at Interlochen convinced me that I was headed in the right direction. Eastman's offer of a scholarship in both composition and conducting, a gift out of the blue, was proof enough that music would be my true calling. I naturally expected my parents to be equally overjoyed (such things don't happen every day), but I was absolutely flummoxed by their response. For my own parents to nix the idea of my accepting this offer seemed absolutely unbelievable. Their line of obsessive reasoning was that the Eastman School of Music, a division of the University of Rochester, located in upstate New York, was too far away from home to be considered, no matter how many scholarships I was offered.

How could they not understand what a golden opportunity this was for me? I was almost eighteen years old now, nearly all grown up, by my reckoning. When the heck would *they* grow up? I felt that their eternal overprotectiveness was unjust and humiliating. Lots of youngsters who were my age were leaving home for college or getting jobs to support themselves, but my

---

* Mischa Mischakoff's daughter, Anne Mischakoff Heiles, believes that Mischa Mischakoff might have been the "Mischa" referred to by Ira Gershwin, since he played many premiere performances of George Gershwin's music. Some believe the "Mischa" would be Mischa Elman. The others are probably Jascha Heifetz, Toscha Seidel, and Sascha Jacobsen, my first teacher at Juilliard.

closeted upbringing left me without any real life experience to find my own way.

Unlike David Jackier, my best friend at Tilden High, I never had to look for summer jobs. I bet he would have figured out what to do in this situation. His parents hadn't babied him. Through working at his father's shoe store, he knew way more about the real world than I did. I still speculate (pointlessly, I know) about the turn my life might have taken if my parents had supported my musical development at that important juncture, allowing their "sickly child" to follow his dreams.

My hopes were dashed for the Eastman School of Music, but I wondered if Juilliard might be in the cards. Besides being one of the most highly-respected conservatories in the world, it had the added virtue (to my parents) of being located right across the East River in New York City, and was, thereby, less threatening to life and limb (at least to my life and my limbs). I didn't have an entrée to its conducting or composition departments, and I wondered if Juilliard would accept me, considering my relatively few years of training on the violin. I listed my meager qualifications on the Juilliard application, and put the completed form in the mail. I was encouraged when an invitation to audition came the next week. Perhaps things were looking up.

On a cold winter morning in February 1944 (all by myself this time, not a threatening wolf in sight), I waited for the streetcar at the corner of Avenue D and Utica Avenue in East Flatbush with my violin case in hand. The old unheated rattletraps that called themselves trolley cars must have stopped at every block, and this one took over half an hour to reach the Eastern Parkway subway station of the Interborough Rapid Transit. I dropped my nickel into the turnstile slot, and waited on the platform to catch the New Lots Avenue train, which would take me to the 116th Street station in Manhattan, a ride that could last another hour or more. From there it was a short walk up Broadway to the corner of 122nd Street and Claremont Avenue.

When The Juilliard School of Music was founded in 1905 as the Institute of Musical Art, it was located at Fifth Avenue and

12th Street, and in 1910 it moved to 1910 Claremont Avenue, in Morningside Heights. The attractive old building that I call "my" Juilliard became the current home of the Manhattan School of Music when the Juilliard School moved to Lincoln Center in 1969.

I signed in for my audition along with the other hopefuls, and was directed to the green room (the traditional designation of the performer's waiting room in theaters and concert halls) to warm up for the juried selection process. I found myself surrounded on all sides by frighteningly sophisticated geniuses who were blithely tossing off dazzling roulades from the violin concerto repertoire. With my past regimen of on-again off-again violin lessons, I knew I was outclassed by these would-be Heifetzes, who never seemed to falter when they performed their finger-busting routines. They reminded me of a famous circus troupe of the day called the Flying Wallendas, who performed their daring high wire act many feet above the ground without a safety net. My secret hope was that the jury might be willing, in my case, to settle for a warm body with a modicum of musical talent.

Perhaps I wasn't all that bad, because my audition went surprisingly well. The jury accepted me and awarded me a partial scholarship to study with Sascha Jacobsen, the first violinist of the Musical Arts String Quartet.

The Second World War was raging, and hundreds of thousands of young men were serving in the armed forces. Perhaps my being three months too young for the draft was a factor in the jury's decision. Before I reached the draft age of eighteen in April of 1944, an Army recruiter who was visiting Juilliard told me that after I was inducted and had done my basic training, I would most likely be assigned to an Army Orchestra in Washington, D.C. I was rejected for military service, and given 4-F status because of a previously-undetected minor heart problem and poor vision. My flat feet probably sealed the bargain.

Most Americans believed, after the bombing of Pearl Harbor in 1941, they had no choice but to join the war effort against the Axis powers. Any young man who walked the streets in civilian clothes was met with baleful looks from passersby. I could see the unspoken question, "Why my son (or husband or father), and not you" in their eyes. Johnny Gallo, a public school friend who lived right across from me on East 49th Street, died in action as a tail gunner in a B-17 bomber somewhere over the North Atlantic. His death brought the war very close to home for me. Like all those who had received deferments, I felt guilty for not serving my country.

There were others at Juilliard who had been found physically unfit for military service and given similar deferments. My friend Arnold Black had been afflicted with cerebral palsy as a child, but through incredibly strong will and determination he was able to play the violin. He was an amazing guy in every sense, beloved by all who knew him (years later we played together on his Mohawk Trail concert series in Shelburne Falls, Mass).

Arnie was later regarded as the unofficial mayor of New York City's Upper West Side musical community. He was a brilliant composer, with a long list of works for theater, a string quartet, and music for television commercials to his credit. In addition to writing scores for the Circle in the Square Theater in the early 1950s (including *Ulysses in Nighttown*, a playlet based on the James Joyce novel, that starred Zero Mostel), Arnie also wrote a whimsical number for the dancer and comedian Ray Bolger called "I'll Never Forget What's-Her-Name." James Ringo, another Juilliard composer friend, did get drafted. He wrote us postcards with amusing tales of riding a mule for miles to play (he was an army organist) for church services in the Philippine Islands.

Sascha Jacobsen chose the fairly simple (but lovely) Kreisler transcription of the flute solo from Gluck's opera *Orpheus and Eurydice* for my first violin lesson at Juilliard. After I played it through, Mr. Jacobsen picked up his beautiful reddish violin and demonstrated what this music could sound like in the hands of a master. The most exquisite sounds poured forth from his violin, and what a violin it was: the so-called Red Diamond Stradivarius, made in Cremona, Italy in 1732. I had heard a few great violinists like Heifetz and Elman on our

Victrola at home, but I was simply bowled over by the liquidity of Jacobsen's sound.

Almost everyone smoked in those days, and my wonderful violin teacher was not one of the exceptions. I will never erase the vivid mental picture I have of Sascha holding his magnificent instrument under his chin with the ever-present cigarette dangling from his lips. He continued to smoke all through our lessons: I can still see the curling plume as it closed one of his eyes, and the white ash that dribbled down (with fatal accuracy) into one of the f-holes of his magnificent violin. I was shaken, not stirred.

Considering my level of technical skill at the time, I thought it was rather generous of Sasha to give me a B for my first semester at Juilliard. I studied conducting (my first love) with Fritz Mahler (a cousin of Gustav Mahler) at Juilliard's summer session, and when I returned for the fall semester I learned that Sasha had moved to California to become the concertmaster of the Los Angeles Philharmonic, where he and his instrument would embark on an oceanic adventure.

Sasha was driving along the Pacific Coast Highway during a severe rainstorm on January 16, 1953, when he and his instrument were nearly submerged in rising water from an overflowing stream. He tried to hold onto his violin case, but it was swept out of his hand and into the ocean. He barely made it safely to dry land. The next day, by pure coincidence, a friend of the Los Angeles Philharmonic's music director found Sasha's case with salt- and water-damaged violin parts on the beach. It took the outstanding luthier Hans Weisshaar nine months to restore the instrument. Experts agree that the Red Diamond still sounds as good as ever (perhaps even better) after its ocean voyage, destruction, and resurrection. It now belongs to a friend of mine, and it remains in daily use.

I was thrilled to learn that my new teacher would be Mischa Mischakoff, the concertmaster of Arturo Toscanini's NBC Symphony Orchestra. Mischa was short in stature, only one inch over five feet tall, and strongly built, with short, stubby fingers. He was very proud of his full head of curly hair (which he kept well into his eighties), and would often comb it vigorously with a pocket comb. I knew, from the photos of him huddling over a score with Maestro Toscanini, that his normally reserved facial expression could sometimes break out into an impish smile. I wondered if I would see that smile when he heard me play.

Toscanini and Mischakoff

I felt a bit uncertain as I entered his studio. I opened my violin case, applied a bit of rosin to the hairs of my bow, and tuned up quickly, hoping that my bow arm wouldn't tremble from nervousness. But my trepidation was unwarranted. Mischa stood nearby, fiddle in hand, looking pleasant, and not at all intimidating.

I began playing the Gluck piece that I'd studied with my former teacher, and after a few bars, Mischa came nearer to observe me more closely. He raised his eyeglasses to his forehead, and stared fixedly at the fingers of my left hand. I felt his hand on my bow arm, signaling me to stop, and heard his crushing pronouncement, "*You hev puysoned fingerz! You never play wioleen!*"

Mischa noticed right away that my joints could collapse far too easily. Actually, all of my joints were extremely loose, most notably the middle joints of my fingers (the proximal phalanx, in anatomical terms) and they tended to collapse when I pressed too hard against the fingerboard. This is not uncommon in youngsters, and I thought I had corrected this problem with the strengthening exercises I learned from my former teachers.

My heart sank. "YOU NEVER PLAY WIOLEEN?" I imagined that this would be the end of the line for me and my musical ambitions. Years later I discovered that I had been born with a connective-tissue disorder called Ehlers-Danlos Syndrome. In some medical textbooks this syndrome is termed "India Rubber Man." During my public school days, kids liked to make fun of my "freaky fingers." As a joke (or more likely, as a defense mechanism), I would make tiny paper spitballs, and insert them into the grooves of my middle finger joints. When I popped these joints, the spitballs would shoot out like tiny bullets. My hope was to annoy (or possibly attract the attention of) the girls sitting nearby. I was already considered freaky, so my display was met with either sneers or giggles.

It took Mischa Mischakoff, the distinguished violinist and concertmaster for Arturo Toscanini, to sort out my finger problems. If he had not done so, I doubt that I would be writing this memoir. Mischa Mischakoff, like Jascha Heifetz and Nathan Milstein, was a product of Leopold Auer's St. Petersburg school of violin playing. That school believes that the fingers of the left hand ought to be regarded as levers rather than be made into arches, and while the fleshy pad of the fingertip (rather than only the tip) should make contact with the strings, the base joints (knuckles) should initiate the finger movement, This technique serves to reduce excess hand tension, and results in surer intonation and better control of the vibrato, which is something that all string players strive for.

In their intensity, some players will mistakenly squeeze the fingerboard of the violin in a death grip, their fingers curved claw-like into arches, so that it is only the very tip of the finger that actually makes contact with the string. Mischa showed me that he flattened these arches in his hand position, which allowed him to use as much of the finger pad as possible to stop the string. Perhaps this was the most significant bit of wisdom I learned from any teacher. It allowed me to find my own sound on the instrument, and it also allowed me to show my own students how to produce their own individual sounds. People may joke unfairly that Mischa was inarticulate in three languages, but he didn't issue pat streams of dialogue when it came to teaching the fiddle. He played, you observed, you listened, you learned, and you never forgot.

In *Mischa Mischakoff: Journeys of a Concertmaster*, Anne Mischakoff Heiles tells the story of her father's remarkable journey from Poland and Russia to become concertmaster of several top American orchestras. The Ukrainian town of his birth, Proskurov (now Khmelnitsky) was, as his daughter writes, "known for manufacturing chocolates and pogroms against its Jewish population." During the early part of his life, Mischa used several different names to hide his Jewish origins. He, who is generally considered the finest concertmaster of the mid-twentieth century, was often called "Toscanini's third hand." The Maestro was notoriously nearsighted (he memorized all of his scores), and relied on his concertmaster to convey his instructions to the orchestra. What a stroke of luck it was to have such a master of the instrument as my teacher!

Toscanini and Mischakoff discuss a point.

Mischa's teaching and rehearsal schedule was so hectic that I would sometimes take my lessons downtown at Rockefeller Center, where the NBC orchestra rehearsed. Finding my way around that massive complex was quite confusing. I once found myself riding on an elevator with the superb violinist Nathan

Milstein, one of my all-time idols. I tried unsuccessfully not to stare at him: he was, as always, impeccably dressed, though surprisingly short in stature. One day when I arrived a bit early for my lesson, I accidentally stumbled into NBC's Studio 8H while the orchestra was rehearsing Beethoven's violin concerto with Fritz Kreisler as the soloist. Kreisler had been struck down some weeks earlier by a New York taxi while crossing a street, but there he stood, exuding his inimitable Viennese style, charm, and nobility. Everyone who knew him, had seen him play, or had heard recordings of his playing, simply adored Kreisler. We all breathed a collective sigh of relief upon his recovery. He died in 1962, but the adoration of his inimitable *gemütlich* style of music making continues. Great violinists still play and record his *Liebesleid* and *Liebesfreud*.

Kreisler would perform delicious little pieces in his recitals that he would pass off as "discoveries," written by seventeenth and eighteenth-century composers like Vivaldi, Pugnani, and Tartini. Skeptical critics took him to task, so when Kreisler finally let it be known, in 1935, that he was indeed the author of these tasty pastiches, he calmly responded to complaints about the subterfuge by saying, "The name changes, the value remains."

Mischa was extremely generous with his students, but he was rather "sentimental" about money. Colleagues and students exchanged humorous anecdotes about his frugality. One colorful story concerns the journey from his apartment to Rockefeller Center. Mischa had the option of taking the Sixth Avenue bus, which cost five cents in those days, or taking the Fifth Avenue double-decker bus for ten cents. He solved the problem rather neatly. Instead of parting with good money for bus fare, he chose to walk down Fifth Avenue (which was the longer route) instead of Sixth Avenue, and saved himself ten cents rather than only five. I once saw him bend down to pick up a piece of string, roll it up, and put it in his pocket, while strolling through the halls of Juilliard. Good habits die hard.

Following the custom of his teacher, Leopold Auer, Mischa held weekly open sessions for his students. These master classes gave us the opportunity to play for each other, and to work through our nervousness, and to size up the competition. Somehow I had become part of a three-person clique with fellow violin students Gerald Gelbloom and Arnold Black. I wouldn't classify us as "smart-asses," but Gerry came closer to fitting that description then either Arnie or me.

One of the bow strokes used by string players is the staccato, a rather flashy one that string players often employ to "wow" the audience. You could call it a useful arrow to carry in your quiver. The basics of the stroke can be taught, but the best practitioners of the staccato seem to be born with a natural gift. The staccato involves a specific coordination of finger, wrist, and arm musculature used to draw the bow across the string (under continuous pressure) in such way that the bow hairs alternately bite and release the string extremely quickly. The resulting effect is like the popping of a (musical) machine gun. It's usually reserved for flashier passagework. I would call Jascha Heifetz's performance of Grigoras Dinicu's "Hora staccato" the *ne plus ultra* of staccato. At the end of the 1939 film *They Shall Have Music*, he coolly gives an amazing display of up-bow and down-bow staccato, and at one point, he even seems to be doing this stroke sideways, if that's at all possible. Heifetz said that Dinicu was the greatest violinist he had ever heard, quite a statement considering its source. Practitioners of early music are somewhat contemptuous of the modern-day staccato, regarding the stroke as mere glitz. Their disrespect might be due to the fact that music of the Baroque era regarded the staccato stroke quite differently. Ah well: different strokes for different folks.

As for our teacher's staccato, Gerry, our rather fiendish friend, began to wonder openly whether (heh, heh) Mischa didn't actually *have* a natural staccato in his arsenal; after all, we'd never seen him use it in class. We warned Gerry about making such a *tzimmes*. We told him that he was skating on thin ice here, and tried (halfheartedly) to talk him out of putting our teacher on the spot.

Sure enough, at our next session, Gerry just had to open his big yap. He asked Mischa, ever so innocently, why he had never shown us his staccato. In reply, Mischa simply put bow to fiddle and the show began. Violinistic fireworks burst out all over the place: rockets, pinwheels, and cherry bombs, you name it. Our teacher's staccato, both up-bow and down-bow, simply blew us away. For my money he rivaled Heifetz and anyone else on the concert stage with that particular stroke. After his spectacular performance, our modest and ever-patient mentor put down his bow and, referring to Toscanini, explained, "Mayestro dusn't like: I dun't play." At least Arnie Black and I, as Gerry's associates, had the decency to blush in unison, while we pinched a crestfallen and unresisting Gerry repeatedly. *Quel ensemble*!

As I worked through my shyness, I was finally able to converse with Eiko Yoshizato, one of the few females in Mischa's violin class at Juilliard. She and her Japanese-American family had been interned in one of the shameful prison camps that were created during World War II. Eiko later married Edoardo DiBiase, who was a fellow violin student and a composer. Eddie and James Ringo, another composer friend, performed my music and encouraged me to keep writing, even though everything that came from my pen, including a set of piano variations and a string trio, sounded like imitation Howard Hanson.

Eddie was poor but steadfast, and he had a fine hand for copying music scores. He spent what little money he earned from copying to buy the best quality olive oil for his father's special spaghetti sauce recipe. He was a copyist for Virgil Thomson, the well-known music critic and the composer of the American opera *Four Saints in Three Acts*, with a libretto by Gertrude Stein. Eiko recalls that when Virgil visited their tiny 125th Street apartment, he would loll on their couch and talk about his studies in Paris with Nadia Boulanger. While they all dined on Eddie's excellent spaghetti, Virgil would talk about the performer he intended to pan the next day in a review. Perhaps this was when he wrote about Heifetz's playing as "silk underwear music."

Eiko remains a dear friend, and writes about her life experiences; but, because of her gender, she missed out a singularly unusual one. Due to his crowded schedule, Mischa was sometimes was forced to employ a particularly novel way to optimize the use of his teaching time. Briefly stated, when he was required to answer a call of nature during a lesson at Rockefeller Center, we were required to continue playing our assigned pieces as we followed him into the NBC men's room, while he made use of one of the stalls. Only his male students were *privy* to that special experience.

In 1927 Mischa became concertmaster of the Philadelphia Orchestra under Leopold Stokowski. It seems that Stoky, as he was generally known, was conducting a rehearsal of Claude Debussy's *La Mer*, an ethereal three-part tone poem about the sea. One movement contains a quietly shimmering duo passage for oboe and violin. When they reached the passage in question, Mischa, impeccable concertmaster that he was, played his part in his accustomed forthright manner.

Stoky, always the exhibitionist, stopped Mischa in mid-stroke and began a long harangue, describing to his concertmaster the essence of the work. Instead of the vague gestures that were Stoky's forte, he used high-flown words to relate what the piece was about, how, in this case, the music must evoke the mystique of *la belle France*, its *je ne sais quoi*, and how it must exude the very aroma of Paris. "Tell me, Mischa," inquired Stoky from his mighty perch, "Have you ever toured the French countryside, Provençal, Marseilles, the wine country? Ah, have you ever been to *Paris*, Mischa?" Mischa simply smiled up at him and answered, "No, maestro. I came right from Russia to this country."

Because of complications from having her gall bladder removed, my mother was never able to taste the food that she cooked for our family, so the idea of "home cooking" doesn't inspire me the way it seems to inspire others. She often complained about a mysterious pressure in her chest, and when she died in her eighties, it was loosely described as "congestive heart failure."

She listened regularly to the reigning medical radio pooh-bah, Dr. Carlton Fredericks, Ph.D. (he always attached his title to his name). On his weekly radio program he advocated special dairy products, such as acidophilus milk, and low-fat everything. Using a sumptuous voice that resembled Vincent Price, he had completely convinced my mother of their benefits. Since our regular milkman didn't handle these products, they were delivered to us semi-weekly by a likable bear of a man, who also was a member of the Polar Bear Club. These (fool) hardy souls were famous for swimming and cavorting in the Atlantic's icy waters off Coney Island during the winter for supposed health benefits. This man watched me grow up, and was aware of my love for music and the violin. One morning someone else brought my mother's special dairy products to our door, and he told us that our old milkman had become a policeman.

In April, 1944, I turned eighteen, the legal driving age in New York State, and my parents finally allowed me to drive our dark green Packard sedan by myself. The 1941 Packard Clipper was the first American production car with fadeaway fenders that blended smoothly into the body of the car. It simply blew the minds of every car lover, and harked back to the ground-breaking streamlining of the 1934 Chrysler Airflow. I chose the nearby section of Brooklyn's Belt Parkway for my first solo excursion. I had driven that stretch as a student driver, and thought it was the perfect place to see what that great eight-cylinder Packard engine could do.

I was speeding along the Belt Parkway, feeling excited and liberated, when I saw red lights flashing in my rear view mirror. Those elated feelings were dashed in a hurry, and my heart began to thump to the tempo of the flashing lights. I pulled over and stopped in the breakdown lane as soon as I could. A patrol car stopped behind me, and a policeman asked me to step out of my car. I was shaking somewhat as I followed his instructions.

A second large and burly officer wearing dark sunglasses emerged from the patrol car. He took a good look at me and, without saying a word, he lifted me off the ground in a crushing embrace. It was none other than our former milkman, who was now asking me, "Buddy, how the devil are you? How're you doing with your music?" I told him all about my mother's health, and that I'd just finished my first semester at Juilliard, which delighted him. After finishing my news report, I didn't know what to say to this police officer who had loved me and *kitzeled* me all through my childhood, and had now caught me speeding on my first time out. Before I could come up with anything to say, he gripped me by the shoulders and said sternly, "Buddy, I want you to know that this ticket I'm about to give you is for your own good. I want you to have a long life, so you have to promise me you'll never speed again. Okay?" This act of generosity set a precedent that I hope to topple some day, but I've never yet been stopped by a police officer without receiving a ticket. Some people get off with a warning: I always get stuck with the real damned thing.

Because my daily commute by subway and trolley from Brooklyn to Manhattan took so much time, I rented a room for seven dollars a week in an apartment located at 550 Riverside Drive, just down the street from Juilliard. The owner of the apartment, Count Lurton Blassingame, was a kind of outdoorsy type who wrote for *Field and Stream* Magazine. My allotted space was a tiny maid's room with a tiny window, that was furnished with a dresser and a folding cot. The best part of the deal was that the Blassingames allowed me to practice until 6:00 p.m. Their annoying wire-haired terrier put up with it at first, but eventually he would nip me without apparent cause (or maybe he didn't like my playing). I schlepped my dirty laundry back to Brooklyn for refills on weekends, but living away from my parents seemed to be making me into somewhat more of a mensch.

For reasons having to do with my physiognomy and natural coloration, whenever I would walk by people from India, on the sidewalk or at a shop, they would scan my face quickly, and then do a double take that seemed to say, "Nope, he's not really one of us." I began to wonder if the source of my genetic material was limited to Odessa and Rumania.

Hoping to strike up a conversation with the occasional pretty girl at the nearby International House of New York, which housed hundreds of students from all over the world, I worked up a fair imitation of a Peter Sellers-style Indian accent. Plucking up my courage one day, I strolled through the marble-floored entrance of International House, and gave it a whirl. I must have looked both half-Indian and totally nuts. Sometimes I'll still try out the remnant of the accent at an Indian restaurant, but I make sure to let others select the curry, while I bury my face in the menu.

The old Juilliard building on Claremont Avenue was certainly much more intimate than the school's current huge installation at Lincoln Center, which some people call the "Juilliard Hilton." The old building had a common room at the head of the staircase which was just the right size for meeting fellow students on a break, or for kibitzing around the "bridge majors" who played cards most of the day. When the devil did they find the time to practice? We lived in a relaxed atmosphere compared to the intensely competitive atmosphere that students must surely experience at Juilliard today.

There always seemed to be time for a few words of guidance and encouragement at the ends of our lessons. Vittorio Giannini, our theory teacher, would often go a bit overtime to explain something about sonata form to a still-puzzled student, which was a special privilege. We were fortunate to study our craft in this amazing city, where we could enjoy eating at a cheap Chinese restaurant upstairs on Broadway and 118th Street, or have the occasional brat and ale at the nearby Golden Rail.

Student passes to concerts and recitals at Town Hall, Carnegie Hall, and other New York performance sites made a significant contribution to our musical education. We had the privilege and the pleasure of hearing a great many of the important artists of our day. In addition to my own teacher, the Juilliard faculty included violinists Louis Persinger, Edouard Dethier, and Joseph Fuchs. There was also the British cellist Felix Salmond, who I heard play all five of the Beethoven cello sonatas in one concert, a bit nervously, but with elegant style. The piano faculty boasted Rosina Lhevinne, a legendary pedagogue, and a classic example of the Russian *grande dame*.

A pianist and I were awarded a dual coaching on Mozart's

Sonata, K. 302 from Mme. Lhévinne and Mischa Mischakoff. Their teaching schedules usually kept them from having much contact, and so these two Russian artists were obviously delighted to have the opportunity to work together. They babbled in their native language to each other and to us throughout the entire session. My pianist and I could barely catch the gist of the musical gems they were imparting, so their gestures and facial expressions had to suffice. We struggled to keep straight faces, but we did make sure to nod sagely at each of their suggestions. Our resulting performance of the piece went well, and we both received extra credit. We were left with some happy memories from the experience, and I'm sure that whatever they said to us must have been pure gold.

I struck up a friendship at the Juilliard Cafeteria with Joel Rosen, a rather sophisticated pianist from Cleveland, who was a private student of Sascha Gorodnitsky. Joel and I hit it off immediately, and we talked at length about music and life. But we mostly spoke about his impressive roster of girl friends who pursued him because of his dashing, Paul Henreid-type looks.

For the benefit of non-moviegoers, Paul Georg Julius Henreid Ritter von Wassel-Waldingau was an Austrian actor and film director born in 1905 in Trieste, which was then part of the Austro-Hungarian Empire. He was the son of an aristocratic banker and studied theater in Vienna under Max Reinhardt, gracing American movie screens from the 1940s until his death in 1977. He starred with Bette Davis in the 1942 film *Now, Voyager*, where the two played a much-imitated scene where Henreid lights two cigarettes in his mouth at once, and then coolly hands one of them to Davis, whose already huge eyes enlarge significantly as she takes her first puff. I guess this phallic metaphor had somehow slipped by Hollywood's rigid production code.

Joel was at his best when holding court with a group of musician friends at his apartment. For us it was a *salon*, since it boasted a grand piano that his father, who was a doctor in Cleveland, rented for him. Everyone who knew him agreed that nobody could look sexier than Joel as he lit up cigarettes for himself and/or his girlfriend. To our lower caste of starving students, his apartment seemed posh indeed. It was a cheerful place to gather and talk with fellow music students, many of whom were pianists.

Naomi Civkin at age 17

I hold Joel's apartment responsible in large part for what followed. During one of his musical séances, I found myself staring at a dark-haired, extremely pretty, though rather shy, first-year piano student from Winnipeg, Manitoba. Naomi Civkin was Canadian all right. You could hear it in everything she said. Naomi rested upon a "chesterfield," not on a sofa, like the rest of us. She wiped her pretty lips with a "serviette," not a napkin, and I was smitten! Perhaps it was the accent, a far cry from typical Brooklyn girls, whose voices could grate jarringly on your ears. Or perhaps it was her dark eyes, her modest demeanor, her interest in Russian poetry and literature, and her natural sweetness and innocence. You think?

Nah, I'd call it lust, pure and simple, and I was a goner. With my nerdy lack of social graces, I hadn't ever dared to ask a girl out on an actual date, but this lovely girl's shy demeanor, together with her physical presence, was driving me up the wall. I was desperate to meet her, so I sloped over in my usual clumsy fashion to introduce myself. She clearly found me ridiculous, and I guess my puerile intensity must have scared her. As I came nearer she called out, "Vivi, he's crazy!" to Joel's current girlfriend.

Eros was in the ascendant! I dreamed about this entrancing Canadian girl that night and every subsequent night for the next two weeks. I had noticed her at Juilliard before this gathering. I took note of her as she walked down the halls to her classes, or chatted unconcernedly with a particular male pianist friend as they stepped off the elevator (this with the faint glimmerings of jealousy), or with friends in the school cafeteria. That cafeteria! You could hear forks drop when she entered wearing one of her homemade sweaters. You see, Naomi had come from modest circumstances back in Winnipeg, and so her mother had to knit all of her sweaters. And, if the wool she used happened to be too expensive, or in short supply, those sweaters might turn out to be a little too . . . oh, forget it!

After my boorish behavior at Joel's, I was far too shy to approach her directly. Joel came to the rescue by casually inviting both Naomi and me to come to his place one afternoon. At last I was able to speak to her in normal tones, rather than slavering helplessly.

Naomi was an absolute natural as a pianist. She started playing the piano at three, and her first teacher was her sister. She seemed to play as if there were no bones in her fingers, and she poured out her natural warmth and musical sensitivity into the instrument. We read through some sonatas for violin and piano, and before we knew it, our musical selves became entwined with our physical selves. On a fair New York evening we would stroll hand in hand past General Grant's Tomb in Riverside Park, without a care in the world. We were eager to learn absolutely everything about one another, our similarities, our differences, and our feelings about life and music.

Juilliard's 1945 spring semester ended in June, and Naomi

returned to Winnipeg for the summer. Fritz Mahler accepted me again for Juilliard's summer conducting course. I really loved studying with him, but reading the tiny print in my pocket orchestra scores began to exacerbate my eye problems. I required increasingly stronger eyeglass prescriptions, so I doubted that conducting would ever be my calling. Naomi (whom I thereafter called "Nomi," thus saving countless syllables for decades to come) and I poured out our hearts to each other in smoldering letters and expensive long-distance phone calls that summer. We hadn't the faintest idea where our unexpected emotional attachment was going, but we chafed at the slow passage of time until we would next see one another.

When Nomi flew back to New York that September, Joel picked her up at the airport in a friend's borrowed car, and the three of us met at his apartment. Greeting each other with no more than a brief kiss in Joel's presence, hearts pounding, we were frightened by the intensity of our feelings, uncertain, and yet too embarrassed to speak openly about where they were leading. All we knew was that Nomi would be studying again with Mme. Lhévinne, and I would be working extra hard with Mischa on his prescribed basic scales, arpeggios, and études, especially on holding down those "flat fingers" that he espoused.

Receiving a diploma in violin from Juilliard required a passing grade from a faculty jury for a full recital program. Nomi agreed to accompany me in a Vivaldi Sonata in A major, the Brahms Sonata No. 2, Op. 100 in A major, the Mozart Violin Concerto No. 5, K. 219, in A major, and two short pieces in, you guessed it, A major. Even though every single piece on the program was in the same key, all went well, and I received my diploma in May of 1946.

In addition to my parents' continued support, that summer gig with Raymond Scott put a few extra shekels in my pocket, so I was able, at last, to reciprocate (in a very small way) for Nomi having accompanied me in my recital. The best I could afford was lunch at the Dutch Mill, a tiny basement restaurant on Claremont Avenue (just around the corner from Juilliard). The Dutch Mill offered students a very modest three-course meal for only 35 cents. The three-course menu offered a salad (presented as a side dish), a bit of what the cook dignified as their daily entrée, and a hot beverage, but, as advertised, at least three plates graced the table. More opulent dining, like hummingbirds' tongues under glass, would have to wait until I was no longer dependent on my parents.

I needed a proper viola teacher in order to make the switch from violin to viola, so I reapplied to Juilliard in September of 1946. George Wedge, the dean of the school, told me that I would have to sign up for a full academic program in order to be eligible for study with Milton Katims, the school's viola teacher. A full academic program didn't fit my needs. I was only interested in studying viola.

I felt that there was still a great deal to learn from my violin teacher, so I asked Mischa if I could study viola privately with him. Happily he agreed to take me on. He found me a very nice, though somewhat large (seventeen-and-a-quarter inch), modern Italian viola that was made in Padua by Gaetano Chiocci, and the money I saved from the Scott gig was sufficient for the down payment. I was able to produce a robust and pleasing tone with this new instrument, so I retired Mike's forty-dollar wreck to the back of *my* closet, to sell to the next impatient viola wannabe.

The Graduating Class of the Institute of Musical Art, May, 1946
Bernard Zaslav is in the back row at the extreme left, and Eiko Yoshizato is the eighth from the left of the middle row. WWII was the reason for the disproportionately small number of men in the class.

CHAPTER IV
The Chautauqua Symphony:
Learning the Ropes

Studying viola privately with Mischa was just what the doctor ordered. In fact, this turned out to be a dream year, thanks to the (slightly illegal) generosity of some of the Juilliard faculty members who already knew me. I was permitted to sit in on the classes that I truly wanted, like advanced theory, composition, and chamber music. In this fashion I "ghosted" my way through that wonderful year. I was seated first chair in the viola section of the junior school orchestra, which was conducted by the cellist Willem Willecke, and I even had time to continue composing.

It happened that Toscanini's NBC Symphony needed to enlarge their string section for a particular piece, so along with a few of Mischa's other favored pupils, I was asked to play. Unfortunately, fate chose this time to bring me down with one of my frequently recurring septic sore throats, so I had to miss the opportunity to play under Toscanini. Sheesh, I was but a cough away from being a contendah!

Mischa spent his summers as the concertmaster of the Chautauqua Symphony Orchestra at the Chautauqua Music Festival, which took place near the city of Jamestown, New York. Founded in 1874, it was a rural center for education, lectures and artistic performances. It was at Chautauqua that Franklin D. Roosevelt gave his famous 1936 "I Hate War" speech. The Chautauqua Symphony, conducted by Franco Autori, was largely made up of members of the Pittsburgh Symphony, but when vacancies in the string sections occurred, Mischa sometimes offered them to his advanced pupils.

I had been making good progress on the viola, so Mischa engaged me to play their six-week season, which started on July 10th, and ran through August 20th. This would be my first professional orchestral job, playing viola at a salary of $80 a week. Not bad for 1947!

Morris Stonzak, a commercial contractor, occasionally called me to sub for one of his Broadway shows. At $25 per job, it reduced my financial dependence on my parents. In March of 1947 Stonzak surprised me with a call. I expected that he wanted me to sub again, but what he had to say was completely unexpected. "Hey, kid," he said, the telephone voice reflecting his gruff personality. "You wanna play an audition for George Szell? Tell me quick, yes or no." I was 21, and he was still calling me "kid." He's certainly got a lot of brass (yeah, and lots of woodwinds, too).

I wondered if I had heard correctly that Maestro George Szell, the brilliant new conductor of the Cleveland Orchestra, was here in New York, and was looking for someone to fill a vacancy in his viola section. This was exactly what I had been hoping for: the chance to play in a great symphony orchestra under a major conductor.

When Stonzak repeated, "So waddaya say. You gonna take the audition or not?" it was like an echo of that other life-changing phone call from Hugh Brown only a year earlier, the one that resulted in my switch from violin to viola. But why would a big-time commercial contractor be calling me about an opening in a symphony orchestra? The two worlds are poles apart, but perhaps someone with Stonzak's connections would be just the guy to track down candidates for a symphony orchestra's string section. With many musicians still in uniform, perhaps civilian viola players were thin on the ground. Certainly, working under Szell, one of the most highly acclaimed conductors of the time, would be the best possible education for me. I knew by way of the musician's grapevine that Szell was a tough taskmaster, but I thought I could use a little scar tissue at this stage of the game. With nothing to lose, I told Stonzak I was up for the audition.

I only had two days to get ready, so I practiced the most often demanded orchestral excerpts, and a few of my own solo pieces, in case Szell should want them. I was under no illusions as I stepped off the elevator and knocked meekly on the door of his hotel room. I froze momentarily when George Szell opened the door to greet me with his oft-photographed scowl. The photos of him on his record jackets tell all. Those eyes, staring at you

THE CHAUTAUQUA SYMPHONY

through the ubiquitous horn-rimmed glasses, seemed to scoop you in, while, at the same time, they dared you to fail.

Toscanini's extreme nearsightedness kept people from entering into his private space, but George Szell's glare could stop you in your tracks. He made a noncommittal nod in my general direction, so I tuned up quickly and got down to business. "Business" consisted of me playing through a few of the selections he placed on a folding music stand, like the tricky opening to Mozart's Overture to the *Marriage of Figaro,* and a few passages from Beethoven's Fifth Symphony. Szell waved his baton just inches away from my bow, and he watched, eagle-eyed, for the least bit of faltering as I followed his beat.

George Szell

Naked fear has mercifully blacked out the rest of that afternoon. I can't even remember if we said our proper good-byes, or if any words were spoken at all, though I might have heard a gruff "we'll see," as I slouched out the door. Thinking it had all been for naught, I was surprised and elated when a contract came in the mail for me. It was dated April 7th (my birthday), and it specified a term of employment of thirty weeks at a salary of $85 per week, beginning on September 29, 1947. I couldn't believe my sudden good fortune. After six weeks at Chautauqua, I would be heading to Cleveland!

I arrived at Chautauqua a day before the first rehearsal, and after settling into my room, which I shared with another player, I checked out the huge amphitheater where the concerts were given. As a neophyte among mostly veteran Pittsburgh Symphony members, I was in for some good-natured ribbing, especially when word got around that I was soon to enter George Szell's domain. The order of seating is normally determined by the conductor and the leader of the section. In a string section, two players share a music stand so that the player sitting inside can stop to turn a page without the entire section dropping out simultaneously. Since Mischa had me seated on the third stand outside of the violas (more easily seen by the audience as well), my colleagues must have thought me pretty special.

At the first rehearsal I found Richard Strauss' tone poem *Don Juan* awaiting me on the music stand. It's one of the more treacherous staples of the orchestral repertoire, and, because of some tricky passagework, is always included in collections of orchestral excerpts. Anyone trying for an orchestra position had better know this one cold. I had done my woodshedding on the piece, and had the notes securely in my fingers. Even though Fritz Mahler, my conducting teacher, tried to give me some notion of what to expect from conductors in the real world, I guess I was still raw, as evidenced by my failure to scope out the difference quickly enough between conductor Franco Autori's upbeat (the get-ready, get-set signal) and his downbeat (go).

Conducting styles and gestures are not set in stone, and they will naturally vary to some degree from one conductor to another, but I goofed here big time. In the opening bars of this brilliant score, the entire string section of the orchestra enters with an arpeggio figure, an up-rushing swirl of rapid sixteenth notes in unison, which produces a startling effect when it comes off properly. I was all primed to go (and secretly hoping to show everybody in the section that I could cut the mustard), but in my nervousness, I misinterpreted our conductor's upbeat for his downbeat. As a result, like a highly strung racehorse shooting out of the stall too soon, I came in half a bar earlier than everybody else: I did play every note in tune, exactly as written, but I did it all by myself. The entire orchestra of pros hooted at my gaffe. I *had* made quite a splash, though not the sort I was hoping for, but it was a learning experience not to be forgotten, and nobody let me forget it.

The six weeks at Chautauqua brought me new friends. It also gave me the opportunity to learn some staples of the repertoire, as well as few new orchestral works. Mischa was the concertmaster of the orchestra and also led the Mischakoff String Quartet, where he played with his violist son-in-law, Nathan Gordon. Occasionally he allowed me to sit in with the group (as second viola) to play string quintets.

My accommodations consisted of a crummy little room, which I shared with a marvelous oboist named Marc Lifschey. His father, Samuel Lifschey, had played principal viola in the Philadelphia Orchestra under Stokowski. In 1950 Marc become the principal oboist of the Cleveland Orchestra under George Szell, and he remained in that spot for 15 years. Oboists everywhere still speak of Marc Lifschey's oboe playing. He was universally admired for his jewel-like tone and the perfection of his phrasing.

Marc was irrepressible outside of the concert hall. He, Arnie Black, my violinist pal from Juilliard (another Mischa recruit), and I tried to outdo each other in zaniness. As a smart-alecky trio, we did little damage in our clowning, except to our image. Marc, who had played in the Buffalo Symphony, told us a hilarious story about one of the orchestra's performances.

It's probably unnecessary to mention that not all the orchestra members are playing all the time during a piece of music. An overeager efficiency expert might see this as wasteful, but there are, of course, times when a musician is inactive and counting measures of rest. An oboe player, for example, will often fuss with a reed while waiting for the arrival of the next entrance. Those players of "the ill wind that no one blows good" are noted for being rather odd ducks. Some think it's because these poor souls are often forced to hold their breath without fully letting it out, but more sensible people know that their insanity stems from their quest for the perfect reed, the holy grail of oboists. They spend much of their lives hoping that the ideal piece of French cane might possibly exist, all the while knowing full well that it never will. Any double reed player—oboist, bassoonist, or English horn player—will be happy to explain it all in about five tedious hours. And be sure to keep away from that razor-sharp reed knife!

During this performance, Marc was sitting behind his music stand, wetting his reed in his mouth. Since there were quite a few bars of rest before his next entrance, there was no need to look up at the conductor until just before his cue. Oboe players really only look up to reassure the conductor that they're both at the same spot in the score. Right before his entrance approached, Marc inhaled and looked up at the podium for the (basically unnecessary) cue from the conductor, but there was nobody there. He could only see the top of an empty podium, and he watched in disbelief as a cuff-linked hand attempted to claw its way over the top. And then a second hand, and an arm, followed. Finally, all of the humiliated conductor could be seen climbing back red-faced onto the podium from which he'd obviously toppled. While watching this spectacle, Marc had to enter with his solo without cracking up!

Symphony orchestra salaries were generally low in 1947, even allowing for inflation, and the playing season was sometimes less than thirty weeks long. Cities that could sustain a major orchestra, like New York, Boston, Philadelphia, or Los Angeles, were able to extend their seasons, but only a very few could sustain the cost of a summer season. Musicians' salaries for the major orchestras generally ran parallel, but members of orchestras in smaller cities often earned about half of what their counterparts in the major orchestras earned.

It was at Chautauqua that I first understood the all-important orchestral musicians' pecking order. Their status, and often their remuneration, correlated directly to how close to the podium each player in a string section was seated. Every decision about the orchestra members hung on the whim of the almighty conductor. It was left solely to him (always a *him*, in those days) to decide who sat closest to the sacred podium. A conductor might consult his concertmaster about a candidate's qualifications for a position, but it was usually the conductor who had the last word in personnel decisions. Seating was ascertained through audition for the conductor, with the concertmaster's assent, though a musician's reputation played a part. There was no such thing as seating rotation back in 1947. The seating order in a section, once established, was usually fixed, until someone in the section either died or was replaced.

The concertmaster sits directly under the conductor's nose, and relays instructions to the players behind him, either orally, or by gesture. He is responsible for inserting bowings into the violin part before rehearsal begins. As the leader of the section, he (and often nowadays, she) normally commands the highest salary, and is usually granted the opportunity to play a solo concerto every season. The principal players of the second violin, viola, cello, and double-bass sections have likewise come to expect relatively similar benefits, and some of them may occasionally be offered the opportunity to perform as a concerto soloist.

The traditional sovereignty of the conductor has yielded to the power of orchestra committees and the musician's union. Committees made up of elected orchestral members have shifted the balance of power, and have a much larger say in hiring. Nevertheless, among the 90 or more members of a symphony orchestra, order must reign if it is to function, and that order is established and maintained by the conductor. Musicians in both amateur and professional orchestras respect their art and take enormous pride in what they do. They're hardworking devotees of their chosen instruments and, as the interface between audience and composer, they are the ones that make the air column move.

I haven't been a member of a professional orchestra since 1968, so I can only portray today's orchestral model as I observe it through colleagues and former students in the orchestral world. In my freelance days in New York during the 1960s, Local 802 of the American Federation of Musicians set the musicians' fees at a rate that is proportionally far lower than they are today. Except for the concertmaster and a few principal wind players, everyone received union scale, which was approximately 12 dollars for a three-hour rehearsal, and 24 dollars for the concert (before taxes and travel expenses). After I achieved some degree of recognition in New York music circles, I attempted to bring the pay scale for the principal viola a little closer to that of the concertmaster, but it was tough going with many of New York's contractors.

My six weeks with the Chautauqua Symphony Orchestra gave me with my first inside taste of professional orchestral playing, and I was about to join a major symphony orchestra, to learn my craft under one of the finest conductors ever to mount a podium.

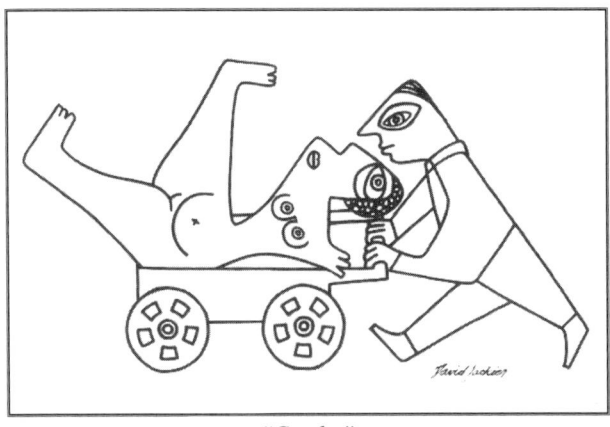

"Gotcha"
by David Jackier

CHAPTER V
The Cleveland Orchestra:
Szell's Magnificent Instrument

My musical career was taking off, but I realized that my relationship with that Canadian pianist was just as important to me. What began two years earlier as a case of romantic I-can't-live-without-you love, had become a firm resolve to share our futures and our love of music as one. Mme. Lhévinne told Naomi's mother, Celia Civkin, that Naomi definitely belonged in music, which was quite a compliment when you consider her teacher's high standards. I wondered if I was in any kind of position to ask Nomi for her hand in marriage, together with all the other lovely bits attached thereto.

We hadn't thought through the logistics when I signed my contract with the Cleveland Orchestra, and in addition to objections by both our families to marriage (they said that we were too young and inexperienced), Nomi had her own musical future to consider. Mme. Lhévinne said it was fine for us to marry, as long as Nomi could continue to study at Juilliard. She recommended that I should go to Cleveland on my own, and I could visit Nomi in New York. Giving up the opportunity to get a degree from Juilliard was asking a lot of Nomi. Few of Mme. Lhévinne's students would have given that up.

After more hot and heavy letters and humid long-distance phone calls through the summer months, true love won out. Nomi would come with me to Cleveland, and we set our wedding date for September 7, 1947. Our decision to marry over the protestations of our parents impressed our Juilliard friends, although a few of them thought that leaving the Big Apple for Cleveland was a bit nutty and lightheaded. We were on our way, scared but happy, wondering all the while whether my orchestra salary would be sufficient for the two of us to live on.

Our modest wedding ceremony took place in a rabbi's rather frowsy apartment on Brooklyn's Eastern Parkway. In attendance

Wedding Photo
September 7, 1947

were Nomi's parents, who came in from Winnipeg, my parents, and two of our closest friends and supporters, Joel Rosen and David Jackier. We had an equally modest reception at Dubrow's Cafeteria nearby on Utica Avenue. Dubrow's was a Jewish approximation of Swedish smorgasbord on steroids. It was like one of those cafeterias on New York's Lower East Side where Isaac Bashevis Singer and his literary set noshed the night away, while discussing the direction the world was headed. Our guests could select their personal favorites from the overabundant display, and their heaping plates proved that the restaurant's reputation was well deserved. Nomi looked like a truly beautiful innocent angel, in a satin gown "of the period," and a satin hat, "just the thing," found by my Aunt Minnie, who worked at the upscale Molla Shop on Flatbush Avenue.

THE CLEVELAND ORCHESTRA

After saying our goodbyes to the assembled guests, we drove off happily to the Nevele Hotel in the Catskills for our projected two-day honeymoon in our wedding present from my parents, my father's 1941 dark green Packard Clipper. The happy and still dazed groom, managed to come down with one of his untimely septic sore throats on the wedding night, generating a temperature of 105 degrees. The bride, not to be outdone, proved equally indisposed, due to the stage of the lunar cycle, so the expected marital rites were put on hold, though not for very long.

After our honeymoon, Nomi and I drove Andor Toth, who was joining the first violin section of the Cleveland Orchestra, his wife Louise, and their newborn son, Andor Jr., to Cleveland in our Packard. The heater of our heretofore wonderful car chose to fail somewhere near Harrisburg on the Pennsylvania Turnpike. We feared that Andor Jr. might freeze in the back seat, but he survived, and he grew up to become a respected cellist and a professor at Oberlin College.

Finding an apartment in Cleveland was no picnic. Housing was scarce in those postwar days, rents were high, and my salary was looking smaller and smaller. We finally rented a very tiny room with an even tinier bathroom, that was walking distance from Severance Hall, where the orchestra rehearsed and performed.

To call the tiny space that we rented a "room" was an overstatement. It was really just a small vestibule (with an unusable fireplace) that led to a glass-paned greenhouse. This forsaken greenhouse looked gap-toothed because of its missing panes. It was attached to the back of a dilapidated old mansion right out of a Charles Addams cartoon. This once grand home had been reduced to a mere rooming house with Addams-like characters sloping about its halls. A ghostly old woman, almost slave-like in her behavior, would slither silently up and down the curving stairway outside our door in the evenings, scaring the bejesus out of my new bride. I hated to leave Nomi there alone when I went out to rehearse or to play concerts.

In order to keep us from freezing to death, and to prevent snow from covering us as we slept in our folding cot, I had to stuff whole Sunday editions of the *Cleveland Plain Dealer* into the cracks between the walls of our vestibule and the greenhouse. Nomi cooked our meals on a small electric hot plate in the tiny bathroom (when it wasn't being used for other purposes). When we held parties with other orchestra members, we filled the claw-foot bathtub with ice and used it to keep the beer cold. We were poor, but happy: think *La Bohème*, minus the coughing soprano.

After my audition George Szell mentioned, in passing, that I might wind up on the first stand, next to the principal violist. Given my lack of experience, that was patent nonsense, which I should have known. I was seated (once again) at the third stand outside seat of the viola section, next to a grizzled, slightly dotty but pleasant old-timer, who doubled on percussion when needed. Szell's biography makes fascinating reading. He was born in Budapest in 1897, and grew up in Vienna. He toured Europe, and made his London debut as a pianist and composer at the age of 11, and was thought of as the next Mozart. He turned to conducting at sixteen, and began his association with Berlin's Staatsoper at 18 as an assistant to its conductor, Richard Strauss. It happened that the composer overslept on the morning of the first (already-paid-for) recording session of his *Don Juan*, so Szell conducted parts of the first recording of the piece.

Though he was born partially of Jewish parentage, Szell kept it quiet. He conducted various symphony and opera orchestras in Europe during the 1920s and 1930s, and in 1939 he settled in New York, where he was a guest conductor for the NBC Symphony Orchestra. He spent four years conducting at the Metropolitan Opera, and made his debut with the New York Philharmonic in 1943. In 1946 he accepted the position of Music Director of the Cleveland Orchestra, with the understanding that he would have total control of the hiring and firing of the players.

During his 24-year leadership of the orchestra, Szell transformed the Cleveland Orchestra into one of the world's top ensembles. When Szell died in 1970, critic Donal Henahan credited him with having built the orchestra into what many critics regarded as the "world's keenest symphonic instrument." I heard that Szell's rehearsals were legendary for their intensity. He demanded absolute perfection from every player, and would dismiss musicians on the spot for making too many mistakes, or simply for questioning his authority. He was not alone in this practice. Arturo Toscanini was equally dictatorial, and both conductors were able to retain total control of their orchestras.

Szell was an excellent pianist, and his 1946 recording with the Budapest Quartet of Mozart's two piano quartets continues to be highly regarded. His ability to sight-read orchestral scores at the piano was legendary. If Szell heard a player practicing backstage before a concert and wasn't pleased with what he heard, he would not hesitate to give detailed notes on just how the music should be played, even if the concert was only minutes away. His autocratic style extended as far as giving suggestions to the Severance Hall janitorial staff concerning mopping techniques, and what brand of toilet paper to use in the restrooms. I must admit the toilet paper bit was news to me.

There's a story about a well-known pianist who was being considered to play a concerto with the orchestra. Before a contract could be offered, he was asked to run through the work for Mr. Szell, which was Szell's standard procedure for less-well-known soloists. Our mystery pianist was instructed by his manager to go directly to Szell's hotel room for the audition. One would naturally have expected to see a piano of some kind there, but our auditionee was surprised to find none in sight. Mystified, he asked Szell how they could possibly communicate their conceptions of the work to each other without a piano.

Szell response was, "Oh, don't let that bother you. I'm sure we both know the concerto very well, so it won't present any problem. Please seat yourself right here in front of this telephone table and imagine it as your keyboard. I'll conduct while I watch your hands very closely, and see how we're getting along musically." Our hapless pianist didn't know what to make of this mad idea, but a chance to play as a soloist with the great Szell was not to be missed. He sat down dutifully and, crazy as it sounds, began tapping out the first movement of the concerto on the table with the fingers of both hands, as requested. Szell halted the proceedings after a few bars to complain. "I'm afraid, my friend," he said, "that I'm not happy with your tempo." To which our frustrated pianist responded, "Well, Mr. Szell, I'm afraid I'm not happy with your goddam piano, either," and stalked out.

Coming from Vienna, Szell obviously felt some loyalty to the musicians he had known there, so Marcel Dick, the former principal violist of the Vienna Philharmonic, became the principal violist of the Cleveland Orchestra. Unfortunately his big solo turn in Richard Strauss's *Salome* showed very clearly that he was well past his prime. Ernst Silberstein, Szell's choice as first cellist, was also from Szell's Vienna. Although he sounded better than the first violist, he was not the kind of cellist one would expect to be principal in such a fine orchestra. Silberstein would be called upon to play "The Swan" by Camille Saint-Saëns, for children's concerts. His playing style was dated, but he was masterful at lifting his bow off the string after the last note and looking raptly heavenward, as many cellists are wont to do. Szell kept both Dick and Silberstein in their positions during my first year, but he soon found replacements who were far more suitable.

Our concertmaster, Josef Gingold (1909–1995), was born in Russia, and came to the United States in 1920. In 1927 he went to Belgium to study with Eugène Ysaÿe, and he joined the NBC Symphony in 1937 where, by the mid 1940s, he had moved up to the position of assistant concertmaster. In 1944 he became the concertmaster of the Detroit Symphony, and in 1947 Szell lured him to Cleveland. He left Cleveland in 1960 to joined the faculty of Indiana University where he remained for the rest of his life. While he was in Detroit he taught Joseph Silverstein, who went on to become the concertmaster of the Boston Symphony Orchestra. Some of the students who studied with Gingold at Indiana University, like Jaime Laredo, Joshua Bell, and Miriam Fried, continue to teach there.

Josef Gingold

Gingold was a beautifully sensitive player, and was one of the most dedicated concertmasters imaginable. He practiced his orchestra parts as if they were concerti, and he never permitted a word to be said against Szell. He was an inspiration to all the string players, and gave generously of his time to anyone who requested his help. His solo performances with orchestra of Roy Harris's Violin Concerto and Édouard Lalo's *Symphonie Espagnole* were absolutely gorgeous.

One night three orchestra buddies and I got together backstage to sight-read string quartets.* Jacob Krachmalnick, the assistant concertmaster of the orchestra, was a close friend who often showed up for breakfast. He played first violin for this ad-hoc get-together, Kurt Loebel played the second violin part, I played viola, and Avram Lavin, who later became a member of the New York Philharmonic for donkey's years, played cello. We had been playing for a while, when Joe Gingold happened by, and stopped to listen. After we finished a movement, Joe gave us his wonderful

---

* "Playing a part" implies that the musician has put in some practice before a performance of a piece. If musicians are sight-reading for a performance in front of an audience, they announce it before beginning to play. It's a way of warning the audience; making excuses beforehand for any mistakes that might be made. Musicians usually sight-read music for commercial recording sessions, but that's a well kept secret.

smile and growled, "Hey *bouyess*, maybe I could sit in with you for a little bit?" Sit in? Was he kidding? Was our beloved concertmaster offering to join the orchestral proletariat and play with us, solely for our collective enjoyment? He was. Jake, who had been playing first violin, quickly stood up to hand over his fiddle, but Joe said that he preferred to play the second fiddle part.

We happened to be playing one of the Op. 18 quartets by Beethoven. While they are not nearly as complex as his later works, many experienced quartet players find these "simpler" compositions extremely tricky, style-wise, to pull off in concert. Joe borrowed our second fiddler's instrument, sat down, *closed the music*, and played through the next movements of that quartet by memory! I later learned that while he was in the NBC Symphony, Joe played second violin in the Primrose Quartet, with Oscar Shumsky playing first violin, William Primrose playing viola, and Harvey Shapiro playing cello. What a stellar group that must have been!

Joe sat right under Szell's nose, and Jacob Krachmalnick sat next to Joe. A strong and solid violinist, Jake later became concertmaster, successively, of the Philadelphia, the Concertgebouw, and the San Francisco Symphony Orchestras. It was obvious to all (or at least it was obvious to me) that Szell, for whatever personal reasons, was unfairly harsh in his treatment of Joe. Joe was kindly in nature; always the gentleman, and incredibly diligent in his role as concertmaster. Jake's *modus operandi* was quite the opposite, and when Jake played the "tough cop," Szell practically fawned on him. The injustice and lack of sensitivity on Szell's part really bothered the heck out of me, but I guess it is the case that power respects only power.

In *Violin Dreams,* Arnold Steinhardt, who replaced Jake as the assistant concertmaster (before he left Cleveland to join the Guarneri Quartet), describes his days in the Orchestra. He mentions that Szell sent him to study with Joseph Szigeti in Switzerland for several summers, which demonstrates that Szell was most eager to support talent where he saw it.

After a performance in Chicago, during an Orchestra tour, Joe took a few of us to a Hungarian nightclub called The Blue Lantern, where we were enraptured by a truly incredible Gypsy fiddler named Béla Babai. He dazzled us with his purity of sound, his lightening-like finger-work and bowing skills, and the streams of notes, harmonics, and stratospheric birdcalls that issued so effortlessly from his violin.

Joe invited Béla to sit at our table so that we might express our appreciation of his artistry. Pretty soon some wise guy among us had the chutzpah to ask Béla if he had ever played any music by Bach. In response, Béla picked up his fiddle, and he tossed off a florid sort of Gypsy nosegay (a little arpeggio direct from Budapest) before beginning Bach's G minor Solo Sonata. Béla doused his Bach liberally throughout with paprika, and made it all the tastier.

The Cleveland Orchestra, then as now, was widely known for its one hundred-plus musicians' ability to play together as one. Critics have often compared it to the finest of chamber groups. When Szell accepted the post, he made it clear to the trustees that he needed to have total artistic control of the orchestra: he alone would decide whom to hire and whom to fire. The quality of the orchestra had much to do with the musicians Szell chose, because we all know that the baton by itself makes no sound (except when it breaks). Using his remarkable ear, Szell did an extraordinary job of balancing and tuning the woodwind and brass sections. Every rehearsal required absolute perfection from all of us. There as no goofing off, even for a second. You couldn't "phone in" your part for Mr. Szell.

Veteran members of a professional symphony orchestra can size up a conductor as soon as he or she mounts the podium. If the conductor is faking, incapable, or isn't a decent sort of human being, they can, figuratively speaking, chew him up and spit him out. If they see sincerity, wisdom, clarity of beat, and musical knowledge, the conductor has a chance, but only time will tell how long the romance lasts.

Neither Leonard Bernstein nor Seiji Ozawa had totally mastered his craft until after being hired to direct a professional orchestra. There's a conundrum here: If conductors can't master their trade until they have the opportunity to stand on that glorified upside-down box, and if they can't really be hired to direct an orchestra until they have a track record, how does anybody ever get to be the conductor of a professional symphony orchestra?

There is no hard-and-fast answer to the question of how a conductor-in-training can become a conductor-in-fact. In Bernstein's case, there was the not-so-rare opportunity of stepping in when the New York Philharmonic's conductor, Bruno Walter, suddenly became indisposed. For a fortunate few, simple politics has a way of greasing the skids before said conductors-in-waiting have fully proven their mettle.

A large part of Szell's reputation was due to his penchant for solid and innovative programming. It was bold of him to program six of Mozart's twenty-seven piano concertos (two per program) during the 1947 season. The soloists were the French pianist Robert Casadesus, Rudolf Serkin, Szell's lifelong friend and fellow piano student in Vienna, and Artur Schnabel, an eminence whom Szell revered.

Schnabel, who was born in Austria in 1882, was universally admired during the 1940s as the grand old man among pianists. He was best known for his edition of the Beethoven Piano Sonatas, and his superb recordings of them. Schnabel was also a composer, and he wrote using Schoenberg's twelve-tone system.*

On February 19, 1948, it was Schnabel's turn to play the first of his two scheduled Mozart concerti. Since a normal rehearsal lasts three hours, a conductor needs to get the most out of every minute. Skipping the cadenza when rehearsing a concerto saves precious rehearsal time for the orchestra. We always enjoyed guessing which cadenza a soloist might play. Sometimes it would be one supplied by the composer of the piece, sometimes it would be a flashy one by another virtuoso of the instrument, and sometimes the soloist would improvise a cadenza on the spot (following Mozart's custom). Soloists would sometimes tease us by

---

* Szell programmed Schnabel's Rhapsody for Orchestra, one of his more severe atonal pieces, at the end of my first season.

playing a snippet of the chosen cadenza, but not Mr. Schnabel. We would learn why at the performance.

When we halted at the customary place for his cadenza, all musical hell broke loose. Schnabel had the unbelievable temerity to insert his own twelve-tone cadenza into the perfect fabric of this Mozart concerto. The more musically sophisticated members of the audience just about swallowed their chewing gum at the stylistic affront that Schnabel stuffed into this elegant jewel of a work, while Szell contentedly beamed his evil smile, clearly enjoying the moment. We wondered what he knew, and when he knew it.

As a longtime fan of these delicious Mozart piano concerti (and being married to a pianist), I knew most of the solo piano lines very well. Too well, as it turned out. We were rehearsing one of these concerti prior to another guest soloist's arrival in Cleveland, and Szell, in his usual manner, had the orchestra play up until the end of the tutti, and then stop. In an imprudent effort to impress my fellow musicians with my knowledge of the piano literature, I quietly noodled the upcoming piano entrance. It was not quietly enough to escape Szell's all-encompassing ear. He immediately seized upon my display of effrontery, and skewered me with his murderous glare. I also got a good tongue lashing after the rehearsal. Jake, big shot that he was, enjoyed seeing me get chewed out royally. He reveled in my bit of *mishigas,* and even encouraged me to commit more folly, but I wisely resisted his goading.*

The orchestra performed two of the three movements from Claude Debussy's Nocturnes during that first season. The first, *Nuages,* has some very quiet sections, where all the strings are muted. The mute of a string instrument is placed on the bridge to act as a damper to alter the tone and soften the sound. String mutes were usually made of ebony in 1947, and though they take a bit more time to attach and remove, many players still prefer them to the newer and more easily-applied mutes that are made of

---

* In his later years, Jake and I performed and taught together in Maine at Kneisel Hall, and we remained friends until his death in 2001.

plastic or rubber. Larger instruments require larger and heavier mutes, which is the unsubtle point of my story. Sure enough, during a very quiet spot during a performance of the Debussy, one of the bass players sitting on the back risers (the customary placement of the orchestra's bassists is on the last of a series of ascending risers at the rear of the orchestra) accidentally dropped his mute. The ebony monster began its maddeningly slow (and noisy) descent, bouncing off each of the risers until it landed not far from the podium, adding its own percussion part to Debussy's ethereal wisps of sound. Horrified, we all watched Szell's face change from its normal sandstone to solid granite, although the motion of his baton didn't show what he was thinking. After the concert there was a special call posted for a rehearsal the next morning. We showed up at our places for the rehearsal, and we all found rubber mutes sitting on our music stands. Szell summarily dismissed us without saying a word.

Another sad but true tale demonstrates Mr. Szell's notorious emotional coldness in a situation where you would expect at least a modicum of human sympathy. A veteran member of the first violin section had been saving his pennies for many years to purchase the instrument of his dreams, a fine violin made by Jean-Baptiste Vuillaume. A comparable instrument sold for $95,000 in 1999, so in 1947 it probably would have gone for around $10,000; but $10,000 was a fortune in those days for a member of the Cleveland Orchestra, and banks weren't making loans for the purchase of rare instruments. We were happy for him, and one would have thought Szell would also have been delighted to raise the overall quality of his string section.

In order to get onto the stage from the musician's quarters, it was necessary for the string players to walk down a short, curving flight of stairs that passed right by Szell's dressing room door. As the inspired owner of the newly-acquired Vuillaume passed by the door of Szell's room one night, violin in hand, he tripped on a step and fell, smashing his precious violin to pieces. Hearing the clatter outside the door, Szell opened it to see the dazed violinist sitting among the debris. Szell's curt response upon seeing the catastrophic scene before him was, "Can you find another violin in time for the opening number?"

Once a famous pianist came to Cleveland to play a big Romantic concerto with us, and it became clear that this choice of soloist hadn't been Szell's. At the first rehearsal the pianist repeated sections of the work to Szell's dissatisfaction, and our maestro adopted his Darth Vader visage, eyeglasses pushed far back on his forehead. Finally, pulling down his famous red rehearsal sweater in exasperation, Szell mercifully called for a break. As we were rising from our chairs, he practically shoved the soloist off the piano bench, and launched into the solo part himself (he played it brilliantly, of course), in order to demonstrate how it really should be played. Our guest pianist was destroyed, and his subsequent performances were among the most painful experiences imaginable.

Pianists like Paderewski and Rubinstein, and violinists like Szigeti and Heifetz were willing to travel by train to the boonies during the 1930s and 40s. Nomi heard all four of them play in Winnipeg when she was growing up. Kreisler seemed to come every year, and she cried when she heard him. Nomi's sister took her to a recital played by the above-mentioned unnamed pianist back in Winnipeg when she was a teenager. She went backstage afterwards to compliment him, and asked if she might play for him. While listening to her play at his hotel the following day, he began to stroke her hands "to make a point" as they moved over the piano keys. His behavior frightened her, and she made haste to leave. As she ran out the door, he begged her not to tell her father. As an aside, Nomi confesses that at the time our pianist looked quite old to her, perhaps as much as thirty-five!

Szell's innate rigidity could be somewhat painful to observe. He certainly looked awkward when it came to conducting a *rubato*, an Italian term that literally means "stolen," (stolen from Peter to put into Paul's pocket). In music, it means stealing a tiny bit of time from one note, and adding it to another, a kind of metronomic spice added to enrich the interpretation. Instead of employing subtler gestures to achieve his ends in a performance of Schumann's First Symphony, for example, Szell would actually divide the written pulse of four beats into six stiff wrist-snaps of his baton, which had the effect of putting a romantic passage into a kind of aesthetic straightjacket, at the expense of Schumann's rhythmic freedom.

Perhaps Szell's towering intellect wouldn't allow him to trust such a large number of orchestral musicians to integrate their sensibilities with his own. He had something of a bull-in-the-china-shop approach to romantic music. And yet, while he couldn't be accused of exhibiting much personal warmth, Szell was undoubtedly one of the musical giants of his time, and he deserved the enormous admiration and respect that he received.

I feel extremely fortunate to have played my first concert in Carnegie Hall with Szell. I'll never forget the thrill I had sitting on the stage of Carnegie Hall on February 8, 1948 for a concert of Hindemith's *Symphonic Metamorphoses*, Schumann's Fourth Symphony, Smetana's "The Moldau," and Beethoven's Fourth Piano Concerto with Artur Schnabel.

Szell led the orchestra through staples of the repertoire for 35 concerts during the 1947-48 season, and while the fox (Szell) was away, we (chickens) played with a few excellent guest conductors. When the French conductor Charles Munch, came to conduct Berlioz, Joe Gingold, who was fluent in French, served as his translator. Munch spoke little (if any) English, so Joe wasn't above injecting some mischievous Yiddish humor into his translation. We watched Munch's eyebrows reach to his hairline; our esteemed guest conductor must have thought that the much-lauded Cleveland Orchestra was out of its collective mind as we tried vainly to suppress our giggles. But everything came right in the end: Munch's famous interpretations of the music of Hector Berlioz were more than on the mark. His baton transcended all spoken languages!

Another notable guest that season was the Swiss conductor Ernest Ansermet. The clarity and precision of his beat were a definite treat. Years later, visiting a conductor friend in Geneva, I had the good fortune to attend Ansermet's performance of Alban

Berg's opera, *Lulu*, with Rita Shane, a wonderful soprano and a compatriot (she came from Brooklyn like me) in the starring role.

Georges Enescu, the much beloved Romanian violinist and composer, came to Cleveland to guest-conduct. By 1948 he was already crippled with arthritis and severely bent over, but he was still a magical presence on the podium. Playing under him was like being invited into the living room of a master musician and philosopher. How I wished then for the chance to play the famous viola solo in his Second Rumanian Rhapsody, but when I finally did many years later, it was, sadly, not under the baton of the composer.

Some of the less sophisticated (or less open-minded) members of the audience were known to walk out of the hall when we performed music by Mahler, Bruckner, Olivier Messiaen, or even the relatively tame Peter Mennin.*

While my viola chops were developing, something else of even greater import in our life was growing apace within my dear spouse. In November 1947, we learned from Joel Rosen's father, a Cleveland doctor, that our attempts at birth control had been futile, and that our first child was due to arrive around the first week of July. We certainly hadn't counted on such an early addition to our family, but Nomi was in good health, and we were told that she could count on a normal birth.

With additional medical expenses in the offing (there no such thing as health insurance in the 1940s) we had to figure out how to secure sufficient income. Cleveland didn't have a summer season, so my meager paychecks would stop during the summer. Luckily, Chautauqua came to my rescue for the second time with a six-week season that began on July 15. Nomi and I headed back east, and our son Mark was born on July 5, 1948 in Brooklyn. Nomi did go to the hospital on July 4, but was sent back home because as-yet-unborn Mark, not yet secure in his lines, dawdled

---

* Some people still found such music controversial in the late 1960s. In March of 1971, when the Fine Arts Quartet, performed Bartók's six string Quartets in three concerts in London's Wigmore Hall (adding one quartet by Joseph Haydn to each program), there were complaints about programming such dissonant and hard-to-understand music. Today it is not uncommon for all six of Bartók's Quartets to be played in a single concert, and music by Mahler, Bruckner, and Shostakovich are part of the standard orchestral repertoire.

in the wings before making his entrance. If he had come on stage sooner, we might have been tempted to call him Yankee Doodle Zaslav, but that name doesn't trip lightly off the tongue. Dr. Mark Richard Zaslav sounds much more impressive.

Nomi with Mark

This should have been the happiest of times for us, but we both felt awful about my having to leave Nomi and our new infant with my parents. Nomi also required further hospitalization for some rather serious post-birth complications while I was away working in Chautauqua, and I was immensely relieved when I heard the news of her recovery. It had been a traumatic time for her without me at her side. It took a while for Nomi to regain her strength, but she did, and could once again care properly for our healthy, beautiful boy.

Towards the end of my first season in Cleveland I found an affordable third-floor attic apartment, and I prepared and painted it myself before going back to Brooklyn for Mark's birth. We were all set to move into the apartment in September, when the landlord informed us, at that late date, that infants weren't permitted to live on the attic floor. I lost three months of rent, plus the paint, and all the time I spent fixing up the apartment. We finally found another place to live. It was far from ideal, but rentals were still scarce in those years, and we considered ourselves lucky.

The repertoire for the 1948-49 season was even richer and more varied. We played loads of Wagner and Strauss (including *Till Eulenspiegel* and *Don Quixote*), Berlioz, Smetana, Ravel, William Schuman, Howard Hanson, and Harold Shapero. We performed the Grieg Piano Concerto with Menahem Pressler, and Chopin Piano Concertos with Guiomar Novaes. For me the most memorable works were Bruckner's Seventh Symphony, Mahler's Ninth Symphony, and Hindemith's tone poem *Mathis der Maler* (the work that opened my ears back in high school). The feast continued with Beethoven's Fifth, Sixth, and Eighth Symphonies, all four of Schumann's Symphonies and the Manfred Overture, Brahms' Third and Fourth Symphonies, Haydn's 86th, 88th, and 99th Symphonies, Schubert's Ninth, Mozart's 40th, and Tchaikovsky's Fourth Symphony.

We were blessed with an array of distinguished guest violin soloists, including our own concertmaster, Josef Gingold, who gave a brilliant performance of Roy Harris's Violin Concerto. Jacob Krachmalnick played Mozart's Fourth Violin concerto, Erika Morini performed the Tchaikovsky Violin Concerto, and Zino Francescatti performed Saint-Saëns's Third Violin Concerto. Ginette Neveu, the fiery young French violinist, offered her rapt audience an intensely muscular interpretation of Beethoven's Violin Concerto. She was only twenty-eight when she performed with us, and already at the height of a brilliant career. The following year both she and her brother Jean-Paul, who was her pianist, died in an Air France plane crash in the Azores.

Rudolf Serkin gave two memorable performances of the Brahms D minor Piano Concerto, a towering work that lasts between forty and fifty minutes. It takes the measure of any pianist, with its crashing chords and its portentous thundering trills. It had already been made clear to the public that in his heart-of-hearts, Szell held some contempt for Brahms' indulgent use of Gypsy themes (which delighted audiences). Szell was known to have dismissed Brahms as a "café composer," but he still programmed all four of the Brahms symphonies and the *Variations on a Theme of Haydn* during my two seasons with the orchestra.

Szell let it be known which side he took in the famous Brahms vs. Wagner debate of the late nineteenth century. Argument waxed hot and heavy between the votaries of Wagner, who praised his ideal of the *Gesamtkunstwerk*, a synthesis of poetry, epic drama, music, and the visual, and adherents to the "pure music" of Brahms. In hindsight, these were merely two loud-mouthed armies fighting a pointless battle. Both flavors exist to be enjoyed, as pianist and conductor Daniel Barenboim maintains.

In hindsight, I might compare Szell with Sergiu Celibidache, who was known for his intensity in the rehearsal process. It was said that Celibidache once cancelled a concert after having already held ten rehearsals with the orchestra because he felt that "they weren't ready." Szell liked to say that our rehearsals were even better than our performances, for he spared no one, including himself, in his attempt to reach his personal conception of perfection. In precision of beat, shaping of phrase, balancing the second trombone perfectly in a chord, and selecting exactly the proper tempo for each passage, he was an acknowledged master. He could be insufferable at times, but it was always the music that was of paramount importance. As a quartet player, I learned to become more severe as a taskmaster myself (my spouse and duo partner claims that I often go too far), so I don't see all that much wrong with a conductor being a severe taskmaster, as long as truth and humility are uppermost. After all, the conductor's task is to mold the members of the orchestra into a finely-tuned instrument, with which he can bring highly complex musical works to life. I certainly received an enviable education as a youthful member of this remarkable ensemble.

Playing in the viola section of an orchestra, even one as fine as this, was gradually losing its luster. I was given a meager ten-dollar-a-week raise for the second season, but without a summer season, my salary still fell short of what was required for the three of us to make it. Many orchestra members were forced to sell shoes or insurance during the summer in order to make ends meet. To make our ends meet, I had to sell my lovely Joseph Gagliano violin to Jake, who needed a better fiddle.

When I learned, toward the end of the season, that Szell was planning to replace his principal viola, I decided to take an audition merely as a lark; I knew that I would hardly be in the running for the position. I played quite a good audition this time, but all Szell offered me was an additional five-dollar raise if I would remain with the orchestra.

Nomi did some teaching at the Cleveland Conservatory, and she accompanied Jake Krachmalnick in a few recitals, but we both agreed that our Cleveland experience was a dead end. When I refused Szell's offer to stay on, he angrily told me I could go to hell. I guess I was no longer of interest to him. I later discovered that Abraham Skernick, an excellent violist with far more orchestral experience than me, had already been hired for the spot. Abe remained the principal violist of the orchestra for the next 27 years, until he retired in 1976.

As a section player in an orchestra, my voice was only one of approximately 99 others, and I was ready to go on to other musical challenges. I learned a lot about my craft in Cleveland, and gave it a good try, but the city had nothing more to hold us. Without other offers from the music world, it seemed that my only option was to head back to New York, where we could stay with my parents, and I could look for a way for the three of us to go forward with our lives.

CHAPTER VI
Plumbing the Depths:
Miserere

"Into each life a little rain must fall." HENRY WADSWORTH LONGFELLOW
"Oh yeah, and gimme a length of half-inch galvanized pipe and a dozen elbows." JOE, THE (BROOKLYN) PLUMBER

After two years of George Szell's impeccable European-inflected English, I now found myself responding to every rich flavor of Brooklynese on tap, as I stood behind the zinc-lined counter of my father's plumbing and heating supply business. Rather than taking my cues from a maestro's baton, I was being paid, meagerly at best, to fill out orders from plumbers and contractors for the kitchen sinks, bathroom basins, and toilets they needed for their daily work.

How I got into this fix had much to do with the financial pickle Nomi and I found ourselves in after the arrival of our first child. We thought of our move back to Brooklyn as a stop-off on my way to finding employment as a violist, but my parents (mainly my mother) suggested that I should go to work with my father, and eventually become a partner in the business.

The three Zaslav brothers, who had been delivering their bathtubs and boilers in their sturdy old Mack trucks since the 1920s, decided to separate while I was in Cleveland. The two older brothers, together with their sons, immediately opened plumbing supply businesses in different sections of Brooklyn, and after twiddling his thumbs at home for a while, my father opened his own business on Flatbush Avenue. He was trying to run the store with only a truck driver and a part-time secretary, so it was clear why my mother suggested that I should join him. It opened for business at 6:30 a.m., six days a week, and we closed up shop at around 6 or 7 p.m., depending on what was needed by which customer, and when.

Competition from larger firms made it well nigh impossible for us to continue in the same fashion as the old Zaslav Brothers, which had been strictly wholesale. There was a gray area between selling at wholesale, which sold only to the trade, and retail, which sold directly to the public. I knew that our only option was to expand the business by adding display areas for the retail trade, but my father strongly resisted any change to his entrenched method of doing business.

Nevertheless, after making the change, it didn't take very long for the newly-expanded business to prosper, and after a year my father bought an entire building located nearby on Flatbush Avenue to use for our large showrooms. Rather than sorting through a grimy plumber's catalog, customers could see the newest items on offer. They could browse at their own pace through displays of the latest steel kitchens by Youngstown, and look at modern bathroom fixtures by Kohler, Eljer, and American Standard.

Our newly-purchased two-story building had once been a Studebaker dealership. In order to install an elevator for the upstairs storage of heavy items, like sinks, cabinets, bathtubs, oil tanks and boilers, we had to chop through a thick concrete floor that had been strengthened with steel rebars. We also had carpenters install over 200 bins on the ground floor for various types of pipefittings. I had to clamber up those bins, pail-in-hand, to fill plumbers' orders, which was not the best thing for my ex-fiddle fingers.

Since copper pipe and tubing prices were always changing, I had to compile new price lists almost daily. Buying, billing, and phone calls were all part of my job. I scheduled truck deliveries and walked customers patiently through showrooms. My father gave every new secretary we hired a hard time (many soon left in frustration), so I was constantly breaking in someone new.

Within a year in the new place we tripled our volume and our profits. You'd think that my dad would have been pleased. Think again! Samuel Zaslav was not only stubborn, he was downright hostile to new ideas. He was happiest when he could act like the Jimmy Cagney tough-guy, telling his plumber cronies "where to get off." Since we couldn't really compete in price with the big guys, his plumber cronies soon dwindled to a very few. I understood his frustration, but the business model had changed, and he refused to change with it.

For our first four years, Nomi and I rented the small, one-bedroom apartment in the basement of of my parents' small house, a place that had been my hidey-hole for late night reading while I was growing up. My folks bought a much larger new two-family home in East Flatbush after our retail expansion, and we rented the three-bedroom apartment upstairs. We finally had a decent place to raise our family.

My mother, who was naturally outgoing and sociable, remained close to her four sisters and her brother throughout her life, but my father eschewed any friendships beyond his business. He was short, slim and sinewy; sharp in mind and body, and a natural at mental arithmetic. For all that, there was the aspect of the dray horse about him, schlepping the cart that was his plumbing supply business behind him. We rarely interacted during my childhood because his old-country Russian background (he went to work at the age of ten) hadn't provided him with much of a model for fathering.

I could just about make ends meet on my so-called starting salary. When our profits went up, I expected to earn a bit more to better support my family, but that was never the case. As for that promised partnership, my folks were always on the cusp of "calling in the lawyer" to make it happen, but it was obvious that my father wasn't going to let loose of the reins, no matter what had been said. I attended evening classes to learn how to design heating and air conditioning systems with the hope we might attract some wholesale business from commercial builders and contractors, but due to our relatively small size, we simply couldn't compete in price with the big boys. I still keep the certificate I earned from the Institute of Boiler Research in remembrance of that futile effort.

While I was stuck behind that bloody counter, I would often find myself staring enviously through our storefront windows at the strangers who walked about freely in their daily lives. The store became a hell of my own choosing. My health suffered from the daily tension, and I returned home exhausted every night, falling asleep after supper, and cheating my loving partner out of the life we had expected to make together. I rarely saw my father when I was a child, and there we were, the two of us arguing endlessly over every little business matter. I tried to find the odd moment to practice the viola, and Nomi and I occasionally played chamber music with friends who were willing to make the trip to Brooklyn on a Sunday, but this offered little hope for the future. My situation reminded me of the cartoon that shows father and son standing outside of their shop. Both windows are bedecked with signs that read, "Closing soon. Everything must go," while the caption reads, "Someday my son, this will all be yours."

Our daughter Claudia came into the world on June 6, 1953, and we became a family of four. Mark was introspective and loved to play in his room with his homemade inventions like "Robby, the Robot," but Claudl (as we liked to call her privately) was a *ketzele* (a kitten). She was clever, cuddly, and born with the gift of gab. As a tiny tot in arms, she would amaze strangers by spouting the names of dinosaurs (like pithecanthropus erectus), that she had learned from her brother. Claudia first learned to play piano from her mother and continued her piano studies at the Chatham Square Music School in Manhattan. She fell in love with the flute in her teens, studied in New York with

Mark and Nomi at the beach

Thomas Nyfenger and Paula Robison, and later studied in Nice.

Nomi and I knew Ernest Bright when he was a clarinet student at Juilliard. Ernie was a busy freelancer who rarely permitted work to keep him away from the golf links. He would sometimes come to Brooklyn to rehearse the Mozart Trio in E-flat Major, K. 498, the so-called *Kegelstatt* Trio with us. At two years of age, Claudl was used to hearing our viola and piano duo, but she was fascinated by the sound of the clarinet. During our trio rehearsals she would sit at our feet, staring raptly at Ernie and that black wooden thing he was playing. Perhaps in her subconscious effort to connect with that beautiful sound, she held his clarinet case in a death grip. After we were done, Ernie took his instrument apart, and was ready to pack it up, but when he removed his clarinet case from Claudia's clutching hands, he was surprised to find the canvas case cover suspiciously damp. When Ernie leaned down to our little daughter and gently questioned her whether she might have had an accident, Claudl broke us up by looking up at him and saying, ever so innocently, that he had done it himself! Talk about a river named "de Nile."

There were occasional moments at the store that lightened up those seemingly desolate years. One surprise "walk-in" customer was Duke Snider, the center fielder of our hallowed baseball team, the Brooklyn Dodgers. Our beloved "Duke of Flatbush," a Baseball Hall-of Famer, came in to buy a few plumbing supplies for his own home repairs. There were also a few customers I called "wealthy schleppers" (cheapskates), who looked as if they could do with a handout, while in reality they were the landlords who owned the multi-dwelling apartment houses that were scattered all over town. These greedy characters would never loosen their purse strings to hire a real plumber; they hung on to every penny by doing their own repairs. They weren't below crawling under a tenant's dirty kitchen sink or a filthy bathroom basin to replace the odd piece of worn-out drainage pipe, or replace the broken ballcock of a tenant's leaking toilet. We regularly sold colorfully-named items like ballcocks for toilet tanks, and the metal files known to the trade as "flat bastards."

One day a man and his two sons came to the store, and asked me to design and furnish materials for a heating system they wanted to install in their New Jersey chicken farm. It turned out that the two brothers were Seymour and Maynard Solomon, founders of Vanguard Records. They started their rather elite catalogue in 1953 by recording Bach cantatas and then, during the blues and folk era, they added The Weavers, Phil Ochs, Judy Collins, Bob Dylan, Paul Robeson, and Joan Baez.

The musicologist Maynard Solomon is highly respected in his field, and his books on Mozart, Beethoven, and Schubert are important contributions to the literature. In 1985, when I was a member of the Stanford String Quartet, Stanford University's musicology department invited Maynard for a symposium on Mozart. I was already seated in the lecture room when Maynard entered, and he rushed up to embrace me. I observed the puzzled faces of my academic colleagues. I'm sure they wondered what I, a mere violist, might have in common with such a distinguished musical scholar, but I held my tongue. Why should I divulge my tale of Maynard Solomon's chickens coming home to roost to those academics?

An amateur violinist named Peter Ostwald became another contributor to literature about musicians. While he was studying at Bellevue Hospital in Brooklyn, he sometimes parked his bright red Triumph TR2 roadster in front of our house and played chamber music with Nomi and me. Peter became a leading psychiatrist in San Francisco, and was the founding director of the Health Program for Performing Artists at UCSF, a program that treats over-use injuries that often plague orchestral musicians. In his book, *Schumann: The Inner Voices of a Musical Genius*, Peter attempts to find a more exact diagnosis of Robert Schumann's mental disorders, and he and his wife, Lise, who is an excellent pianist, would give lecture recitals about Schumann's piano music. In *Glenn Gould: The Ecstasy and Tragedy of Genius*, Peter explores the complicated psyche of this unique Canadian pianist, and in *Vaslav Nijinsky: A Leap into Madness*, he examines the difficult life and colorful career of the famous Russian ballet dancer. Nomi and I played chamber music on New Year's Eve at Peter's home until his untimely death in 1996.

Back in 1952, in an effort to escape my servitude, I thought about calling Morris Stonzak, the contractor who told me about the Cleveland Orchestra audition five years earlier. Swallowing the small amount of pride I had left, I phoned him to say that I was once again (how do you say?) "available." Stonzak mentioned that he had a Broadway show based on a Truman Capote novel called *The Grass Harp* that was opening at the Martin Beck Theatre on March 27. He told me that if a big-shot ex-symphony orchestra member like me might deign to lower myself, he would give me a shot. I jumped at the chance, and was just about kissing his hand through the phone.

The Grass Harp tells the story of an orphaned boy (perhaps Capote himself) and two elderly ladies who observed life while nonchalantly sitting up in the branches of a Chinaberry tree. It starred Sterling Holloway and Mildred Natwick, was directed by Robert Lewis, and had scenic and costume design by Cecil Beaton. Virgil Thomson wrote the music (mostly hymn tunes) for flute, violin, viola, cello, and harp. The flutist Claude Monteux, son of the famous French conductor Pierre Monteux, was our leader and conductor. Rather than sitting in a pit, our little band sat backstage in the dark behind a curtain. We followed the onstage dialogue, and relied on a small work-light to signal our cues.

The scenery consisted solely of an enormous tree house that dominated the stage. It was taken apart and pushed together in sections as required by grunting stagehands, and the actors would sit up in the branches for many of their lines. The play called for only ten minutes of music, which came only in the last act, so our first cue wasn't until about 10:15 p.m., enough time for me to close the store, grab a bite, and drive to Manhattan to search for a parking space close to the theater. I recall that union scale for my first well-paying Broadway show was about $110 per week. Sadly, the show closed after only thirty-six performances, but that was long enough for romance to flower between the cellist and the harpist, who had been sitting next to each other in the dark for thirty-six nights. Claude and I merely remained close friends.

My next Broadway outing was the long-awaited revival of George Gershwin's brilliant *Porgy and Bess*, an American folk-opera that first appeared on Broadway in 1935. It opened on March 9, 1953, at the Ziegfeld Theatre on Sixth Avenue and West 54th Street. Much of the music that had been cut from the premiere of *Porgy and Bess* was restored for this production, and we performed it under Alexander Smallens, the opera's original conductor. Every lush harmony of the original score, every one of Gershwin's thrilling songs like "Summertime" and "It Ain't Necessarily So," actually did leave the audience humming as they left the theater. The reviews in the *New York Times*, the *Tribune*, the *Telegram*, and the *Mirror*, were long and ecstatic. Walter Kerr in the *Times* said, "For this is surely the most restless, urgent and shatteringly explosive production of the Gershwin masterwork we have yet had." An astonishing young soprano named Leontyne Price burst into the limelight on opening night, singing the part of Bess. William Warfield played a marvelously touching Porgy, and Cab Calloway was Sportin' Life, a role that was conceived with him in mind. The poet Maya Angelou played Ruby.*

The musician's union rules allowed management to hire a full complement of musicians for the first six weeks, and then, to reduce costs, management could fire those players whose names were on the cut list. The Ziegfeld Theater's orchestra pit was unusually large for Broadway. It held a complete orchestra with full string sections, including six violas. I sat on the second stand of the viola section along with Theodore Israel, a violist who was able to extract the most naturally rich sound from any viola he picked up, so we weren't in danger of being cut.

---

* In 1927 Florenz "Flo" Ziegfeld, Jr. built the theater in such a way that he could observe what was happening on the stage from a window of his living room (so the story goes). In 1944 it was bought by the veteran showman, Billy Rose.

In order to park my car near the theater by 7:30 p.m., I had to leave directly from the store for the six evening performances, as well as the Wednesday and Saturday matinees. A day job and a night job made for a grueling schedule. I was feeling a real sleep deficit because of my dual life, and one night, three weeks into the run, I simply dozed off while holding on to the final note of a song. I only awoke when I felt Teddy grab my bow arm and whisper urgently into my ear, "Stop playing, Bernie." I had fallen into a dead sleep in the pit while playing a whole note! Everyone else had stopped at the conductor's cutoff, but I continued to play that stupid note in my sleep.

It was abundantly clear that I could no longer do my day job and moonlight in the pit for three and a half hours every night, so I offered to place my name on the cut list in place of Al Brown, the violist sitting behind me. Al later became a contractor, and hired me for gigs.

After I quit *Porgy and Bess*, the company began a national tour, and Price and Warfield married shortly before beginning a State-Department-sponsored tour to Europe and the Soviet Union. *The New Yorker* asked Truman Capote, who traveled with the cast, to write an article about the tour, and he expanded it into *The Muses Are Heard: An Account*. Rather than only painting a positive picture, he wrote about the cultural differences, surveillance by the K. G. B. and the Russian Ministry Staff, and how the Soviets secretly yearned for world approval.

A member of the musical grapevine suggested that I should contact the celebrated violinist Mishel Piastro to get some work. Piastro was a pupil of Leopold Auer (like Mischa Mischakoff and Jascha Heifetz), and became the concertmaster of the New York Philharmonic in 1931 under Toscanini. He was the assistant conductor of the Philharmonic under John Barbirolli, and left the Philharmonic in the 1943 to become the conductor of the Longines Symphonette, a radio broadcasting orchestra that played on WOR. For years they had a morning show of short classical pieces beginning at 7:00 (with the last movement of Beethoven's Fifth Symphony as its introductory theme) but by the 1960s they seemed to be a collection of old-timers who were reduced to playing whatever sort of gigs they were offered.

Mishel Piastro, a warm, and distinguished gentleman, invited me to audition for him at his home. When he asked me to join the group, he warned that they no longer had their radio connection, and that any of their upcoming gigs would be strictly in the nature of a cooperative venture. The players agreed to rehearse programs as often as needed, without payment, and split concert fees equally. Accordingly, about a dozen of us held rehearsals three times a week for several weeks, without knowing exactly what we were rehearsing for.

Surprisingly it turned out to be a single afternoon performance at Grossinger's, one of the largest hotels in the Catskills, whose patrons naturally expected more of a Yiddish flavor to the proceedings than we had prepared. Since we had taken the bus up and back from the city at our own expense, they gave us a bite of food after the concert as a sop for our efforts. When we split the pot, we each came out with about seven dollars, net. Not much for our two weeks of work, but at least I made a few new friends, including Richard Kay, the cellist of the Kohon Quartet.

Claude Monteux (the flutist and conductor for *The Grass Harp*) asked me to play some summer concerts in Maine for a festival he was starting with a clarinetist named Emery Davis. Emery was the son of Meyer Davis, a popular society-band leader who contracted me to play a New Year's Eve show at the Hotel Waldorf (once again I played viola with a jazz band).*

For this new concert series, Emery hired me, Nomi, a brilliant violinist with a droll sense of humor named Matthew Raimondi, cellist Philip Cherry, and soprano Virginia Davis, who was Emery's sister. He couldn't afford to pay us in actual hard cash for his new festival, but we received food allowances, and shared basic accommodations at the Cove Cottage, on the shore of a tidal pool in Hancock, where our son Mark could collect tiny shrimp in the shallows. It wasn't grand, but Maine in the summer can't be beat. We shared automobile lifts to and from New York, and were

---

* Emery's brother Garry Davis is famous for renouncing his American citizenship and declaring himself a "citizen of the world."

pretty much singing for our supper, but it allowed us to escape New York's heat and humidity, play the chamber music we loved, and eat our fill of lobsters, clams, mussels, and all the wild blueberries we could pick.

For our first concert in Hancock's Forest Studio we played a Beethoven Piano Quartet, a group of songs by Jean Françaix, a clarinet trio, and the Serenade for String Trio by Ernst von Dohnányi. I thought it went fine, but the reviewer of our local newspaper, the *Ellsworth American*, absolutely gushed, writing, "It was, in a word, delightful. In spite of Sunday's rain, more than three hundred people came to hear a program of unusual charm and diversity." We were "performers of the highest accomplishment and sincerity," we had "dash and style," we even had "*gemutlichkeit*," so who were we to argue? They simply loved us in Hancock, and we loved the tasty lobster rolls at Tidal Falls Lobster Pound after the concert.

Claude Monteux, an inveterate "gadget gorger" by nature, adored anything mechanical. He was one of the foolish purchasers of that hopeless French automotive flop known as the Renault Dauphine, and was inordinately proud of his latest acquisition, a new Jaeger-Lecoultre alarm wrist watch. In one memorable performance of Beethoven's Op. 25 Serenade for Flute, Violin, and Viola, that I played with him and violinist Matthew Raimondi, Claude's prized new possession chose to go off during a slow movement, while he was holding a long note. He was, of course, unable to turn the damned thing off while he was playing, so we (and the audience) watched in stunned disbelief as he kept his embouchure intact, with his eyes just about popping out of his head, until it finished telling us all to wake up.

I had obviously reached my nadir in plumbing-supply-land. I knew the bogus promise of a partnership in the business, part of what lured me back to Brooklyn, would never happen. The business had become quite profitable due to our retail trade, but to remain open an extra two nights a week along with our regular store hours was untenable. As for the wholesale end, a few of my father's plumber cronies turned out to be deadbeats. Some of them owned nothing more than a few tools and a broken-down truck. We extended credit to a few of them, and hired a lawyer to collect their unpaid debts. In one case, the lawyer searched for months until he discovered that one particular character was already serving time in jail, for exactly the same offense.

After paying rent to my parents, my salary left us with just enough to get by, and through all those years, my only bonus was a two-tone blue 1955 Pontiac Chieftain sedan. My father and I were always at loggerheads, and working with him started to take a real toll in my health. I felt guilty about leaving my father alone when I ran out for a quick lunch, and the only nearby place to eat was a delicatessen, which was no help to my cholesterol level. I developed an ulcer, and had an ankle problem from being on my feet all day (I had to use crutches for a week or two).

My brother Billy turned 24 in 1957. He hadn't gone to college after graduating from Tilden High School, and with nothing else on the horizon, he helped out at the store occasionally. I tried everything I could think of during those difficult years to work alongside my father, but it was finally no longer possible, so I started showing Billy the ropes so that he could take my place in the business. With Nomi's love, support, and fortitude, I finally got up the gumption, at the age of 31, to try to make my livelihood in music.

While I keenly regret the waste of those nine precious years, perhaps they weren't a total loss. Our two children were able to grow up in a safe environment, and attend good local schools, and I may have learned more of the real world than I would have with only my conservatory background. The irony is that with even a short-term loan from my parents, something they could well have afforded, I would have been able to join the ranks of New York's freelancers nine years sooner than I did.

PLUMBING THE DEPTHS

If I goofed when I was playing stoop-ball in Brooklyn, I could ask for a "do-over," but real life rarely offers such luxuries. An extra-sharp marksman might hit a "Pensy Pinky" off the edge of the top step to make the ball soar, but I had to make due with the cards I had drawn.

As I grow older, and perhaps mellower, it has become easier for me to respect my father's strength of character and his dedication to his family. Sam Zaslav remained the little tough guy to the last. He spent his last years in a retirement home in Florida, and died at the age of 95 (or perhaps 97 – the records are inaccurate), and outlived my mother by nearly ten years. My brother lived nearby, but my father remained reclusive. I offered my father a private phone so we could speak more often, but he refused. He never had an education, he had gone through hell in WWI, and he could never figure out why I wanted to be a musician. He loved boxing and enjoyed watching Lawrence Welk on TV, and I regret that he never shared my interest in classical music.

My nine pointless years in the plumbing supply business bring to mind a story about a *yeshiva bochur* who wakes up to find himself in a dark coffin. Confused, he asks himself, "If . . . I'm alive, why is it so dark in here? Or, on the other hand," he muses, "If . . . I'm dead, why do I have to pee?" Life goes on, and I suffered from making the proverbial Hobson's choice. I have repeatedly asked myself why I remained in such a state of limbo for so long, and why I had even entertained the proposition that my father and I might have reached an agreement on anything. But it's from our mistakes that we learn how to cherish the better times to come.

CHAPTER VII
Nu, Phoenix, Rise Already?
Ad Astra

When I was a teenager my mother took me to Carnegie Hall. We sat high up in the balcony to hear William Primrose, the best known violist of the day, play an entire recital of music for viola and piano. Such things were a *rara avis* in the 1930s and 40s. Among his other virtues, Mr. Primrose was responsible for commissioning Béla Bartók to write the Viola Concerto, but Bartók was unfortunately unable to complete the manuscript before his death in 1945.*

My viola "chops" were rather rusty after my long and misguided hiatus, so I thought of William Primrose as a possible teacher to remedy the situation. Mr. Primrose taught at the University of Utah in Ogden, but moving there with my family (and my near-empty pockets) was not an option. I learned through the music grapevine (the musician's vine of choice) that during the summer of 1957 Lillian Fuchs was teaching viola and chamber music at Yale University's Norfolk Music School in Connecticut.

Most of the other Norfolk applicants were quite young, and I feared I was a bit long in the tooth to be accepted, especially with my family in tow. It's my guess that Ms. Fuchs took me on as a special challenge. I wasn't in terrible shape as a violist, but I was slightly rusty, and I needed to spend time working on the basics. Lillian was sometimes heard to say that she had "rescued" this so-called "ex-plumber," though, in my defense, I had never handled a pipe wrench professionally.

---

* William Primrose gave the premiere performance of the incomplete Concerto in 1949 with the Minneapolis Symphony under Antal Dorati. Tibor Serly completed the piece in 1950, and it was published in various editions, including one by Bartók's own son, Peter Bartók. Bartók originally intended the Concerto to have four movements rather than the three that make up the various versions of the work.

Lillian Fuchs

Lillian Fuchs, born in 1902, was the younger sister of violinist Joseph Fuchs and cellist Harry Fuchs. She began her musical training as a pianist and a composer, learned to play the violin, and switched to the viola when she was presented with the opportunity to play in an all-female string quartet. She was an intensely hard worker with a huge talent, and had the ability to cultivate people of means among New York's music lovers. Some of them supported her various string quartets and chamber music groups, and one very generous person saw fit to loan her a marvelous small viola made in the sixteenth century by Gasparo da Salo.

Lillian Fuchs was the first American woman to make a name for herself as a viola soloist. She was the first violist to record the six Bach Cello Suites, and her recordings are still considered among the best viola recordings ever made. She and her violinist-brother Joseph were famous for their many performances of Mozart's Sinfonia Concertante, K. 364 for violin and viola. Though Lillian was barely five feet in height, she stands tall in the viola firmament because of the intensity and power of her sound, her superb technique, and the honesty of her phrasing.

The four of us drove from Brooklyn to Norfolk in July of 1957. My viola lessons and chamber music coaching were free, but I was required, like the other students (some of them half my age) to do kitchen duty at mealtimes. Nomi and the kids had a ball watching me dishing out food from behind the steam tables. The kids had never seen me in the kitchen at home, since their father (like his father) was always "at the store." Norfolk and the surrounding countryside featured a swimming hole called Toby Pond, had many historic towns for us to visit, and provided some well-needed relief from New York's summer heat.

My lessons began with the Bach Cello Suites. We used the

Schirmer edition, and Lillian inserted her own fingerings and bowings. We began with the First Suite, her starting point for any new student, and then we jumped far ahead to the Sixth Suite, the most technically difficult of the bunch. It was originally written for a five-string cello, and Lillian's transcription for viola (which has but four strings) ascends into the stratospheric regions of the instrument, where the air is rather thin.

In our lessons I was able to observe how Lillian pulled a rich tone from her fifteen-and-a-half-inch Gasparo da Salo viola. Considered small in viola terms, it fit her five-foot frame very naturally. She used a bow that was nearly half an inch shorter than normal, a specimen made by the important early English maker John Dodd, which suited her natural arm length.

As a rule, viola bows are somewhat longer and heavier than violin bows. I've even seen viola bows made by Nicholas Maire that were too long to fit into a normal viola case. I own one of his normal-length bows, a beautiful specimen that has been my "workhorse" bow, one" that I could use for everything. It handles very evenly, both at the frog and at the tip, and it has been broken seven times during its lifetime. My contribution to its history of injury happened on stage while I was playing a piece by Bartók. It was repaired by a specialist, and plays as well as ever, rising like the Phoenix.

A large part of Lillian's secret for producing such a rich sound was her special attention to bow pressure. She liked to position her bow a bit closer to the bridge than normal, but not so close as to cause the tone to break. Even to a novice, relating bow pressure to speed hardly qualifies as rocket science. Many teachers concentrate on arm weight, wrist angles, pronation versus supination, and the proper grip, but Lillian's method of teaching bow pressure, a most important factor, was unique. She asked her pupils to draw the bow across the string while pressing sufficiently hard to produce scratching (it can sound like a feline's death throes), and then gradually attenuate the bow pressure, while increasing the speed at which the bow is being drawn. After a lot of patience and practice, this produces the loudest possible sound from the instrument, without breaking the tone.

The next (and far more difficult) step is to incorporate this technique into everyday use. It seems so obvious that any fiddler would ask, "What's so new about that?" There is nothing new about it, but it can be easily overlooked, since while we draw our hank of horse hair over what once were the guts of sheep, we direct most of our attention to the black squiggles on the page.

Lillian was a kind of "Unsinkable Molly Brown" (a famous survivor of the RMS Titanic). She would not be diverted. To use the words of Oscar Wilde, "she had a whim of iron." She seemed to be in competition with her often-overbearing brother, Joseph, who was one heck of a fiddler. He had a sterling technique, total control, pure intonation, a rich sound, and what critics used to call a strong musical "profile."

During the late 1960s, when I was a member of the Musica Aeterna orchestra, Joseph Fuchs played Vaughan Williams' "The Lark Ascending" (with its incredibly high tessitura) and the luscious Mozart Rondo for violin on a program at New York's Metropolitan Museum of Art. It was a veritable lecture in pure violin sound. Lillian had all of that, in spades. Strong profiles seemed to be the Fuchs trademark.

Joe and Lillian recorded the Mozart Sinfonia Concertante with the Musica Aeterna Orchestra under conductor Frederick Waldman, a member of the Juilliard faculty who had the favor of Alice Tully, a great patron of Lincoln Center. It would be a stretch to describe Mr. Waldman as a really capable conductor. His nerves often got the best of him, with disastrous (though sometimes amusing) results. During the recording sessions, the soloists vied constantly with one another for control of subtle changes of tempo; it was a classic example of two strong wills in conflict. Lillian would have her way no matter what, stamping her foot if things were not right.

There is a treacherous moment at the end of the cadenza in the second movement. The orchestra has to enter right after the soloists finish playing the *Nachschlagen* (it's a kind of yodel, a veritable "yoo-hoo") attached to the ends of their trills. Dealing with this common musical device had our conductor completely stumped. Mr. Waldman stood frozen in place during the trills, unsure of where or when to make a gesture for our re-entry. We had to rely on the totally unshakeable Gerald Tarack, our-rock solid concertmaster, for the necessary help.

Joe and Lillian had to play the entire cadenza section over and over for the recording session, and they were both getting highly irritated. In what turned out to be the final take, Mr. Waldman was reduced to standing immobile while we came in (as one) at Gerry's cue. I must, add in all pride, that New York's vaunted free-lancers specialized in saving the *tuchas* of many a conductor. We were absolutely conductor-proof.

Even though he was certainly less than sure-footed on the podium, Frederic Waldman deserves credit for bringing many rarely heard works to New York audiences. In another Metropolitan Museum Musica Aeterna concert, we were playing a String Symphony by the young Felix Mendelssohn. Many classical works finish up with the traditional ending of chord, rest, a second chord, rest, and then the final chord. Mendelssohn, the smarty-pants (he was the child genius of his era), went tradition one better here. Instead of the usual number of chords and, ta-da, the end, the boy wonder decided to throw in one more of the same at no extra charge, to show that he could outdo the big boys. Our maestro beat out both of those two accustomed deals, and then turned around to face the audience for his applause. But the musicians had been engaged to play all of the notes, so our bemused conductor found himself standing with his back to the orchestra in red-faced disbelief, while we played the final widget, as written, behind him!

One of the heroic New York freelancers was June Rotenburg, a rather jolly and rotund bass player, who amused us with tales of her travails schlepping her fine instrument around town. Some of the busier commercial bassists would leave an instrument in each of the studios they frequented, but concert bassists like June, Julie Levine, or Alvin Brehm had to cope with the problem of carting their basses to every rehearsal and concert. Brehm carried his bass around town in a little Citroën 2CV Deux Chevaux, a weird little monstrosity that was designed for French farmers. Alvin poked the scroll of his fine old instrument through its sliding canvas top, and successfully diverted the attention of fellow drivers who might have been vying for the same parking space. Like most of her colleagues, June used cabs to get to her dates in town, and after a Waldman rehearsal at the Met Museum one rainy day, she tried to hail one. After she flagged one down, June struggled to get both the bass and herself into the taxi. A watchful kibitzer stood by and asked her, "Lady, tell me. Whaddaya need it for?"

Malcom Gladwell asserts that along with being talented and being born in the right place at the right time, a person must put in minimum of at least ten thousand hours of study in order to achieve success in a given field. This is probably less time than today's solo musicians put in. They also need to have the right equipment.

The tonal quality of a string instrument depends a lot on its age. An instrument with years, perhaps centuries, of having been "played in," will generally allow a player to position the bow somewhat closer to the bridge, and play with more than normal pressure without "crushing" the tone. Comparing old and new instruments makes that abundantly clear. I was fortunate later in my career to have owned two extraordinary violas made in the eighteenth century, one by Michelangelo Bergonzi, and a world-famous instrument made in 1781 by G.B. Guadagnini. Both of these instruments were slightly small in body length, but they projected into the concert hall amazingly well, as long as I heeded Lillian's important lesson about bow pressure and speed.

I crossed paths once again with Matthew Raimondi in 1958, and we worked up an unusual program for a summer concert at the piano-less Boothbay Playhouse in the town of Boothbay, Maine. Matthew, cellist Philip Cherry, oboist Henry Schuman, and I called ourselves the "Mt. Desert Chamber Players." Our program had a Mozart Duo for violin and viola, a Beethoven string trio, Benjamin Britten's "Fantasie Quartet," and Mozart's Oboe Quartet. I was able to return to Norfolk that summer, and took chamber music classes together with Lillian's twin daughters, Barbara, a cellist, and Carol, a violinist. Ms. Fuchs spared no one in her quest for exactitude, family member or not. At one point she reduced Carol to tears over a relatively small point in the Debussy String Quartet. In Lillian's mind it was a case of music above all!

The Italian cellist Luigi Silva taught at Norfolk, and one of his students that summer was the fifteen-year-old Joel Krosnick, who later became the cellist of the Juilliard String Quartet. After playing together in one of the weekly concerts in Norfolk's Music Shed, Joel and I decided that for the next concert we would try Beethoven's duo for viola and cello *mit zwei obligaten Augengläsern* (with two eyeglasses obbligato). Beethoven places a *fermata* at a cadence point in the first movement to indicate an unmeasured resting place, so I decided to write a cadenza for the two of us to play. In order to keep my bit of compositional license a surprise, we made sure not to play the cadenza during our rehearsals with Lillian. She was *not* amused when we sprung it on her at the concert. It was *nicht echt*, but we enjoyed strutting our stuff before all the serious faces in the audience.

Lillian's brother Joseph called her from London that summer to tell her he was bringing a small 17th-century Brescian viola back to the States for her. The instrument was made by Giovanni Paolo Maggini, an apprentice of Gasparo da Salo, the maker of the instrument that she used. When the viola arrived, Lillian invited me to her cottage to compare the Maggini to her current instrument. She wanted to judge the Maggini's ability to project, and the only way to know this is to hear it played at a distance by someone else. It was quite an honor to be asked to help.

I arrived a little early, and noticed a stack of the latest Hollywood movie magazines on a table. A taste for movie glitz is something that I never would have suspected from Lillian. She brought in both viola cases, and we opened them. I stood at the far end of the room while she played, and they both sounded rich and powerful in her hands. She then asked me to play both instruments. What a treat it was to be allowed to play such marvelous instruments made by two of the earliest known Italian makers, side by side. The Maggini had more of an edge to the sound; I preferred the richer quality of the Gasparo under my ear. Lillian felt the same way, even at a distance. The Maggini was a fine instrument, but she continued to favor the richer and more complex sound of the Gasparo for the rest of her career.

After Lillian's death in 1995, Nomi and I visited her daughter Barbara and her architect husband Don Mallow (he designed and built their summer home in Blue Hill, Maine).* There, on a table, sat Lillian's Gasparo. Although it had been repaired after suffering a grievous accident, it was still a treasure to behold.

Barbara asked me to play her mother's Gasparo for her. I picked it up readily, though gingerly, because of its tender condition, and as I recognized its magical quality and its presence, it began to speak memories to me. I gradually got into it, and played some well-known viola passages, but after only a few minutes, Barbara, who had tears in her eyes, called out for me to stop. Hearing the sound of her mother's Gasparo surely must have have tweaked her memories (I can only imagine her emotions). For me it was a moment of homage to this great lady and the voice that she had throughout her career. Jeanne Mallow, the daughter of Barbara and Don, is a fine violist who carries on the Fuchs tradition. She performs on her grandmother's instrument.

I had always dreamed of being accepted to study at the Marlboro Music Festival, in Marlboro, Vermont. Pianist Rudolf Serkin and the brothers Adolf and Hermann Busch started the festival in 1951 as a seven-week retreat for advanced musical training. It has since become a world-famous musical oasis for generations of renowned concert artists, including Pablo Casals, Felix Galimir, Mieczyslaw Horszowski, Madeleine Foley, Sandor Vegh, members of the Budapest, Galimir, Guarneri and Juilliard String Quartets, and the Beaux Arts Trio.

When I mentioned my desire to study at Marlboro to Lillian, her recommendation was sufficient for them to accept me for the

---

* Barbara and I remained very close friends, and played chamber music together at Kneisel Hall in Blue Hill for many years.

last two weeks of the 1958 season. My family and I drove back home after Norfolk was over, and I took off solo (no family this time) for Marlboro, to play chamber music by Beethoven, Mozart and Dvořák, and to spend two weeks being coached by several of the world's best musicians. I was inspired by the unique spirit of Marlboro, where great musicians come together in the summer to make music for the pure joy of it. Since I arrived at Marlboro at the end of the summer session, I had little time to engage personally with many other students or faculty members, but I did get to know my fellow violists Philipp Naegele, Karen Tuttle, and Harry Zaratzian.

Things were looking up back in New York. I started getting called for more freelance work, so I joined Radio Registry, the telephone answering service that most musicians used (so I wouldn't miss hoped-for calls from contractors), and bought my first real date book, just like the regulars. It was unsettling to be utterly dependent on whatever voice might be on other end of the phone, but I wondered if that long-dormant Phoenix was about to to stretch its wings and rise from its mythical ashes.

I began to sub with the New York City Center Ballet, and played record dates with Mishel Piastro's group. I got my first chance to be part of an established string quartet when I met Richard Kay, the cellist of the Kohon Quartet, at one Piastro's gigs. He told me that the Quartet was looking for a new violist, and invited me to "do a few exploratory rehearsals." As a result, I became the new violist of the Kohon String Quartet in the fall of 1958, a decisive step (without a salary) that would set me on my true course in music.

My little black datebook was filled with lots of quickly pencilled scrawls. There was an orchestral concert with pianist Van Cliburn as soloist at the Newark Mosque Theater, some viola lessons at home, a concert at the United Nations, another at Carnegie Hall with the Symphony of the Air conducted by Fritz Reiner, and a concert with Newell Jenkins' Clarion Concerts at Town Hall.

On December 21 I played Vivian Fine's "Capriccio for Oboe and String Trio" with oboist Lois Wann, violinist Lilla Kalman, and cellist Sterling Hunkins for an all-Fine Composers' Showcase concert at the Nonagon on Second Avenue. This was a free concert, one of many I was called for, but I was happy to play without a fee for such a "fine" composer. Later that December, some friends and I decided to organize our own chamber music concert at Carnegie Recital Hall. Renting the hall was quite inexpensive at the time. By papering the house with freebies, and inviting a few dozen paying relatives, it was possible to break even. My flutist pal Claude Monteux played a Carnegie Recital Hall concert the year before as part of a group he called the "New Century Chamber Players," so we decided to use that name for this concert. Our program had to be interesting, and we needed a new work or two in order to attract an audience and a music critic (hopefully, one from the *New York Times*).

You've probably heard the story about the overbooked freelance musician who was available for all the rehearsals but couldn't make the concert. I've been told that this was often the case in French orchestras, and was something that drove conductors to distraction. This happened with our clarinetist, Ernie Bright. He fell ill after we had worked together for some time, so on February 8, 1959, The New Century Chamber Players played the Carnegie Recital Hall concert as planned, but with clarinetist Jack Huggler (who was also a composer) instead of Ernie.

Nomi, Jack, and I played the Mozart *Kegelstadt* trio, and Claude, Sterling Hunkins and trombonist Gilbert Cohen gave the premiere performance of Elias Tannenbaum's Trio for Flute, Tenor violin, and Trombone. We also played the difficult Roussel Trio, Op. 40 for Flute, Viola, and Cello, Schubert's rarely-heard Quartet in G for Flute, Guitar, Viola, and Cello, with guitarist Leonid Bolotine, and Henry Brant's *Music for an Imaginary Ballet or Lightweight for Three*, for piccolo, cello and piano, with three movements called, "My Marionettes," "The Theme (That Tango)," and "Ten Years Later (Can-Can)." Ross Parmenter, a critic of the *Times*, found the Schubert "easily the most charming part of the program," and found "wit and humor" in Henry Brant's piece. Sadly, due to legal complications concerning his divorce proceedings, Henry couldn't attend the concert. The *Times* reviewer sized up Henry's piece this way: "In the 'Lightweight,' Mr. Monteux played the piccolo, while Mr. Zaslav both turned pages for his wife, Naomi Zaslav, and helped her to play the piano part by dampening (*his* word) the strings and occasionally whacking at its woodwork."

The reviewer would probably have been more accurate to use the word "damping" here. I can assure the reader that no fluids (of any sort) were involved. He also mentioned that playing with a substitute clarinetist in the Mozart "might have accounted for its hesitancy, but the others were [sic.] not noticeable for their ensemble either." That was my very first review in the *Times,* and it stung.

An aphorism by the Greek physician Hippocrates reads *Ars longa, vita brevis* (Art is long, life is short), but while I was enjoying the artistry of my new chamber music life, the grocer still demanded ready cash, so I was back to "bowing for dollars" again (credit for that phrase must go to Jerry Grossman, the principal cellist of the Metropolitan Opera Orchestra, who has it inscribed on his license plate).

In 1959 I was called to play in *Juno,* a Broadway show based on Sean O'Casey's 1924 play *Juno and the Paycock,* with music and lyrics by Marc Blitzstein and book by Joseph Stein. The stellar cast included Shirley Booth, Melvyn Douglas, Jock MacGowran, Jean Stapleton, and Sada Thompson. The choreography was by Agnes de Mille, and the show was directed by José Ferrer. It opened at the Winter Garden Theater on March 9 of that year. The show began with a chorus number called "We're Alive." As the curtain rose, gunshots rang out all over the place, and after the smoke cleared, there were corpses strewn about the stage. My stand partner, who was a houseman (one who is paid whether or not there is any music to be played) whispered, "We're dead." The show closed after sixteen performances.

With inflation and constantly rising stagehand salaries, opening a show on the Great White Way or even Off-Broadway was starting to cost producers millions instead of the many thousands they had been willing to gamble on getting a hit. For this reason Off-Off-Broadway shows were beginning to catch on with the public and the press.

Once Upon a Mattress, an adaptation of Hans Christian Andersen's fairy tale "The Princess and the Pea," opened Off-Off-Broadway at the Phoenix Theater (on 11th Street and 2nd Avenue) on May 11, 1959. The production featured a fresh-faced and hugely-talented newcomer named Carol Burnett, who brought the house down when she made her entrance as Princess Winnifred the Woebegone. The music was by Mary Rodgers, the daughter of Richard Rodgers, and the cast included Joe Bova as Prince Dauntless the Drab, Jack Gilford as King Sextimus the Silent (his facial imitation of pea soup was priceless), and Jane White as Queen Aggravaine. Jane sang a witty number written in 5/8 time called "Sensitivity," which proved a bit difficult at first for a few of the woodwind players.

The band rehearsals took place at Carrol's 48th Street studio, a nonstop beehive of rehearsal studios rented out by the hour (usually for three-hour sessions) day and night, for everything under the sun. An opera rehearsal might be happening next door to a rock band, alongside the studio of Dr. Robert Moog, the inventor of the Moog Synthesizer.

I remember showing up at Carrol's early one morning for an American Opera Society rehearsal. Allen Sven Oxenberg, the Opera Society's director, was able to attract singers like Maria Callas, Elizabeth Schwartzkopf, Joan Sutherland (known as *La Stupenda*), and basso George London, for a series of semi-staged operas in Carnegie Hall. While I was waiting for the other musicians to arrive, I quietly opened the door of the near-empty studio, and saw the marvelous Spanish soprano, Teresa Berganza (known as "the ideal Rossini singer") sitting in a corner of the studio and singing a Spanish lullaby very softly to the baby she held in her arms. It was a moment never to be forgotten.

At the first dress rehearsal we found it wasn't possible to fit all the strings for "Mattress" into the Phoenix Theater's small orchestra pit. You couldn't sneeze, much less draw a bow, without taking your neighbor's eye out. Mary Rodgers noting the problem, kept her cool, and ordered everyone *except* the violins to come back the next day for the dress. The next day we found that the string parts had been rewritten, and the violin parts were given to the violas. Since I was the first chair violist, I became the official concertmaster of the show. I also got to play few solo licks in a dance number called "Very Soft Shoes."

"Mattress" was a palpable hit: it was a big break for Carol, and they say it's still performed somewhere in the world almost continuously. It got wonderful reviews in all the papers, and then it went uptown for a total of four hundred and sixty Broadway performances. I maintained my "top dog" position for the downtown run of the show as violist/concertmaster, if only as a Chihuahua, but the producers demanded the return of the violin section to sex up the sound of the cast album.

A major perk of working in that downtown location was the old-style soda fountain next door. Between the acts we could partake liberally of artfully-concocted, but now hard-to-find, egg creams. The name may confuse the uninitiated, since this by-gone delicacy employs neither eggs nor cream in its manufacture. It must be constructed in a genuine slim-waisted Coca-Cola glass, using a *bissel* milk (maybe half an inch, at most) and a full inch of *Fox's U-bet* chocolate syrup (none other will do!). Next, ice-cold seltzer must be spritzed into the above ingredients by means of a high-powered jet, for the full effect. The nectar of the gods is then consumed in as few gulps as humanly possible. Houyhnhnms (pronounced "whinnems") have been known to sip it, causing it to lose the delicate head (its crowning glory), and insulting a legendary drink of my youth.

My bowing for dollars delivered me into the pit of the Shubert Theater for *Take Me Along*, a show based on Eugene O'Neill's *Ah, Wilderness!* It starred Jackie Gleason, and was another palpable hit. The show opened October 22, 1959, and closed after 448 performances. I didn't play all of them, but some nights (and matinees) it felt like I had.

Along with Jackie, the cast included Walter Pidgeon, Una Merkel, Eileen Herlie, Robert Morse, and Arlene Golonka. Bob Merrill's music was decent enough, and our conductor, Lehman Engel, was an accomplished composer and opera conductor. I suppose they needed someone as dependable as Engel in the pit because Gleason was a big name, and he drew big box office numbers. For some reason, Lehman Engel took a shine to me. During performances he would occasionally pass notes to me, addressed to "Primrose," concerning what he heard happening in the band, or about the general state of the world. It was a nice touch from a really intelligent and charming conductor.

The audiences for the Wednesday and Saturday afternoon matinees on Broadway were usually filled with people from various show parties. I have always suffered from allergies, but I was particularly miserable on afternoons when the many varieties of perfume worn by hundreds of women would meld and waft their way down into the pit. Playing the same damned show tunes eight times a week gets awfully boring, so eventually I memorized my part and put a book on my lighted music stand to read during the long pauses. Quite often some kindly lady sitting in the first row would peer down into the pit and warn me that I'd be "ruining my eyes" by reading the book on my stand without enough light. Shades of my mother.

Jackie was simply dazzling on stage. He was incredibly light on his feet, but being "on the sauce" took its toll. A few weeks into the run, he had some bad moments on stage, and occasionally he fell asleep while mumbling his lines. I saw Walter Pidgeon try to save the situation by improvising, while Jackie's head sank ever lower onto the table.

During one afternoon performance, a man in the balcony perched himself on the rim of a row of box seats high above the stage. While Gleason was strutting his stuff, this man threw his eyeglasses down to the stage, and called out, "Here I come Jackie!" The musicians in the pit could see that this person was prepared to jump, but some people in the audience might have thought that this "stunt" was part of the show. Gleason immediately started a dialogue with this clearly disturbed individual, and attempted to talk him down. The two of them bandied nonsense back and forth for nearly five minutes, by which time a few stagehands were able to get up behind the attempted suicide (it was that high up), and drag him down successfully from his perch. Jackie's quick wit in this situation earned him a round of applause, and the story made it into the evening papers.

This episode was especially dangerous for the percussionist Richard Kopf, my good pal and Brooklyn neighbor (we often drove to the theater together). The box seat from which the potential jumper was about to do his thing was located directly over the place Dick stood, hemmed in by all of his drums and equipment. He would have had a good chance of being killed by this nut.

Another time during the run of the show, the dreaded call of "fire" was heard, and our conductor gave the cue for the obligatory National Anthem, in order to calm the audience. When it proved to be a false alarm, the panic died down, and we continued with the show.

A busy week for me in the 1960s involved ten or more dates, if I was lucky. One week during the run of *Take Me Along*, (which had eight performances), I had three rehearsals, two recording sessions, and a private concert at the East 77th Street home of a wealthy patron of the arts (their home boasted two of the twelve El Greco paintings known to be in private collections). Among the guests that Sunday were William Kroll, the leader of the Kroll Quartet, and the conductor Leopold Stokowski.

After a show or a concert (I would get back home around 11:30 p.m.), Nomi and I would sometimes drive down to Brooklyn's Sheepshead Bay for a late supper together at Lundy's Restaurant on Emmons Avenue. It was a huge seafood restaurant, famous for its enormous Shore Dinners, which offered a bowl of clam chowder, steamed clams, half a chicken *and* a "chicken" lobster (meaning a lobster that weighed less than a pound) for less than ten bucks. You couldn't beat it anywhere.

Long are the tendrils of the musical grapevine. Word quickly gets around town about a player's ability or lack of ability. You are known (and hope to get called for work) because of how you sounded the last time out, and not merely by your bio or your reputation. The life of a freelancer involves waiting for phone calls from contractors, and managing schedule conflicts. Telling a contractor about a particular conflicting commitment might mean that contractor will never call again. My colleagues in the Hollywood circuit tell me, perhaps sneeringly, that what counts in their world is how you're *perceived* to play by the contractor alone.

In New York, we were always under the gun. One might hear things like, he's a top-notch player, she's okay but hard to get along with, he's often late, she doesn't follow the bowings set by the section leader, he plays out of tune, she doesn't turn pages fast enough, he hogs the music stand, or she's a "good friend" of the contractor. Still, getting work in the New York of the 1960s had more to do with how you played than whom you knew.

Colleagues told me not to be embarrassed about visiting the United States Unemployment Office when things were slow. Once, when I didn't have anything forthcoming in my date-book for a few weeks, I swallowed my pride and walked up to the Unemployment Office window to request my legal handout. When the clerk asked me about my current financial situation (i.e. exactly how much I had made during the previous week), I had to be honest. My previous week's take came to nearly $500 (it had been an unusually busy week). I got a scathing look from the clerk, scathing looks from the people in line behind me, and a check for $37.50. I never had the gall to show my face there again.

Although I had made a modest reputation in New York circles as a quartet player and as a section leader in chamber orchestras, there were definite class distinctions to be observed in the music world, and I hadn't cracked the big-time recording crowd by any means. It is common to add extra strings to the orchestra for the official cast recording of a Broadway show, and the big-money commercial players who always get first call for these high paying dates, naturally expect their status to be recognized in the seating.

Whenever one of our freelance buddies would run off mysteriously, we'd wink knowingly and say, "Oh, oh, I guess Katz is playing tonight." Here's the story: So this amateur violinist gets a call from his friend, another avid aficionado of the art, who tells him that he's stuck with an extra ticket for tonight's Carnegie Hall recital by Nathan Milstein. Somebody couldn't make it, so would he care to come along? "Sorry," says his pal, "Katz is playing tonight." "Oh," says his friend, "this guy must be pretty good for you to pass up Milstein, but I'll call you again if something pops up."

A few weeks later comes another call, and this time his friend can't wait to blurt out the good news. "You're not gonna believe this," he says, "but I have this extra ticket, front row center, for Heifetz tonight at Carnegie, and I'd love for you to be my guest." "Oh heck, what a drag," says his friend. "I really hate to miss Heifetz, but you see, Katz is playing tonight."

"Are you nuts? What's with this Katz?," asks his friend. "For this guy you'd miss Heifetz? How come nobody's ever heard of him? What is he, some kind of unknown genius, another Michael Rabin, maybe?"

"Well, no," comes the response. "He's actually a pretty lousy fiddle player; sits in the back of the seconds in the community orchestra. But when Katz is playing, his wife sits home alone."

In March of 1961 I played principal viola in a run of *The Happiest Girl in the World*, a show that starred Janice Rule, and used music by Jacques Offenbach. The conductor for the show was Robert DeCormier, a Greenwich Village Renaissance kind of guy, a scholar, an experienced choral conductor, and an arranger. DeCormier, ever loyal to the players in his pit band, insisted that I should sit as principal violist for the recording sessions, just as I did in the show. The score of "Happiest Girl" happened to contain a few solo viola licks, so when I took the principal viola seat for the first recording session, some eyebrows among the heavy-hitters headed skyward.

I was a bit nervous at first, but my solos went well, and I was pleased to hear some complimentary bow-tapping on music stands from my colleagues. During the break, Walter Trampler, a well known solo violist, a fabulous dresser, and a totally classy guy, came up to me and shook my hand. Usually expensive cigars were broken out during the breaks, but Walter offered me my first ever *Gauloises* cigarette, and my day was made. Soon after that recording session I started getting calls from contractors I never heard of, but best of all, Walter and I became colleagues and close friends.

It is actually a much better deal for a freelancer, or even for the occasional Broadway pit player, if a show folds quickly. That way musicians get to record the original cast album at recording scale, which is top money, and then they are free to accept a call for the next show.

At the end of the summer of 1962, I played in a production of the operetta *Die Fledermaus* by Johann Strauss under the Czech conductor Franz Allers. Allers loved this repertoire. It was his meat, and he conducted it seriously and fastidiously. Rather than keeping the beat regular for the *um, pah-pah* after-beats in the viola part, the Viennese tradition is to rush the first of the two *pahs* the slightest bit, and then delay the second one. It comes out something like um, *pah* . . . *pah, um, pah* . . . *pah*, and continues until nausea sets in. Franz made quite a deal of this dizzying and highly-exaggerated rubato, causing members of his echt Viennese audiences to swoon in old-world ecstasy.

Allers hand-picked the musicians he wanted for this production, and he insisted that I play principal viola for the show. I still had a few summer concerts to play in Maine, and I couldn't make the first rehearsal because of the airplane connections. In order to get to the second rehearsal on time, I had to take a helicopter to the Manhattan Sky-port roof. I thought that arriving by helicopter for a mere rehearsal was living high, but Mr. Allers was satisfied that I was able to play the run of the show.

After *Fledermaus*, I played *Tovarich*, a comedy based on a play by Jacques Deval and Robert E. Sherwood and starred Vivian Leigh and Jean Pierre Aumont. It opened on March 18, 1963, and was fraught with problems from the beginning. Ms. Leigh won a Tony Award as Best Leading Actress for her role, but her mental situation made it necessary, one evening, to hold the curtain for the second act, and her understudy had to take over. Her career gradually came to an end.

In 1964 I subbed occasionally for *Fiddler on the Roof*. It was nearly impossible to take my eyes off Zero Mostel when he played Tevye der Milchiker (the milkman). Zero, a great character actor as well as a comedian, was born Sam Mostel, and he lived in the Brownsville section of Brooklyn for a while. He enjoyed painting (I had occasion to see a few of his paintings), and had a great love for James Joyce. Nomi and I saw him play the character of Leopold Bloom in *Ulysses in Nighttown* at the Houston Street Theater. The music for the playlet was by Arnold Black, my violinist pal from Juilliard, who had overcome cerebral palsy.

Zero was also famous for playing the part of Pseudolus in *A Funny Thing Happened on the Way to the Forum*. His shenanigans with comedian Phil Silvers recalled vaudeville, especially the way Zero played tic-tac-toe so leeringly on the shapely back of a statuesque chorus girl. Stephen Sondheim's wonderful opening song "Comedy Tonight" was apparently written just before the show opened in New York. This show, like *Once Upon a Mattress*, seems to have been playing constantly here and there, all over the world, since it opened on Broadway.

I Had a Ball opened at the Martin Beck on December 15, 1964, and it starred Buddy Hackett. The script was dreadful, but, in spite of all the critics dumping on it, it ran for almost two hundred performances. This was Hackett's first show on Broadway, and he wisely chose to ignore the script and insert his own off-color comic routines as he saw fit.

Very soon into the run he started coming out for personal curtain calls, and he began to deliver riotous comic monologues while sitting comfortably on the edge of the stage, and dangling his feet into the pit. Since his routines were the *filet mignon* of the evening, audiences often didn't show up until the second act, coming mainly for what the critics termed "smutty," hilariously unprintable "blue" stories.

The management was faced with a problem. The union rules stated that the band's exit music couldn't be played until the audience started to file out of the theater, and since Buddy's spiel often went past 11:00 p.m., the management was forced to pay us overtime. Watching Buddy's face crease up like a satyr while he delivered the dirty bits was worth the price of admission. Feelthy story, anyone?

Alan Alda and Barbara Harris played Adam and Eve in a real gem of a show called *The Apple Tree* which opened in October 18, 1966 at the Shubert. When the script called for Adam to ask Eve how she knows the names of all the animals in the Garden of Eden, Harris batted her big blues and replied, "Silly, what else could it be but a giraffe?" Her performance won her a Tony award for best actress in a musical that year.

Nomi and I met Alan and Arlene, his clarinetist wife, at the home of the violinist Marvin Morgenstern and his violinist wife, Vera. We knew the Morgensterns from Juilliard, and during the early 1960s Marvin and I played in a short-lived string trio with cellist John Goberman, who later became a TV producer for *Live from Lincoln Center*. One morning, Marvin left his apartment on the West Side, saying he was going to the store, and was never heard from again. The police investigated the case for months, but never had any results. A group of musicians hired a detective to help solve his mysterious disappearance, but to no avail. Friends, relatives, and generations of musicians still speculate about the strange disappearance of Marvin Morgenstern.

Cabaret opened at the Broadhurst on November 20, 1966. It is based on *I am a Camera,* a 1951 play by John Van Druten, that is, in turn, based on Christopher Isherwood's novel *Goodbye to*

Berlin. Cabaret starred Joel Gray, Lotte Lenya (wife of Kurt Weill), Jill Haworth, and Jack Gilford, and featured an onstage, scantily-clad female German jazz band. I don't believe anyone ever sang *"Willkomen,"* the opening song, as well (and as evil-sounding) as Joel Gray. Elliot Lawrence, our totally-dedicated conductor, was a sweetheart; he gave a custom-made coffee mug as a Christmas gift to everyone in the pit. The assistant conductor for the show was Freddie Vogelgesang, a graduate of the Curtis Institute of Music, and a "triple threat." He played violin, piano, and French horn, and would step in whenever any of these parts was required. His crowning achievement was making a "solo" recording of the Brahms Horn Trio, Op. 40, playing all three parts on separate tracks, and combining them.

I played in the pit for *Golden Boy*, a musical based on the play by the same name that Clifford Odets wrote for John Garfield (born Jacob Julius Garfinkle). The main character is faced with a choice between being a violinist or a boxer (I doubt that my mother ever thought about such a choice for me). Charles Strouse's music for this production was specifically tailored for Sammy Davis Jr.'s special singing and dancing talents. Sammy was "on" all the time, and was simply a ball of fire. He enjoyed the company of beautiful women and (ordinary looking) musicians, in that order. He liked to sit in for a couple of hands of our between-the-acts poker game, betting wildly, but willing to lose gracefully, even intentionally.

The Broadway theatre is an essential part of the American musical heritage. Many of the shows I played to earn my daily bread could be considered national treasures, and I have deeply-etched memories of their easily-singable songs and lovely, haunting melodies. Many shows had clever lyrics, sparkling rhythms, wonderful dance numbers, timeless messages, and believable plots. Sadly, the musicals of the 21st century seem to be tailored more to the eye than the mind's ear, and that is a loss.

When I recall the number of years I played in Broadway pits, I think of that old saw about the guy whose job at the circus is to follow the elephants and shovel their dung. When the guy is asked whether he ever thought about quitting, he looks up amazed and replies, "What, and leave show business?"

I hope I don't sound condescending towards Broadway: I'm speaking purely from the perspective of someone who had to play the same unchallenging parts eight times a week, while being squeezed into a theater pit, which is a rather unaesthetic place to be. There were pit musicians who did their jobs extremely well; dependable "doublers" like Cal Opperman, who played flute, clarinet, saxophones, and I don't know how many other instruments. Sitting with these experienced Broadway musical legends, there were so-called classical musicians like me, who were lucky to have this work for sustenance, while hoping to make a career in another musical arena. I've heard it said that working for money is, at best, an artificial construct, but I knew very clearly what I was doing, and exactly why and for whom I was doing it. My goal in life was to play string quartets, but Broadway kept me going while I was on that path.

The Carnegie Tavern

Before it closed and left a gaping hole in the memory of many musicians, the Carnegie Tavern at 156 West 56th Street sat for many years right next to the stage door of Carnegie Hall. It was the hangout, watering hole, and eatery for the New York Philharmonic, major visiting orchestras like the Boston Symphony, and Philadelphia Orchestra, the Symphony of the Air, folks working down the street at City Center, and members of the Arts Students League on West 57th. The proximity of hall to tavern gave us musicians an advantage over the tavern's other customers. We could pass back and forth with such ease that you could sometimes see the odd tuba player with two hundred bars of rest in his part as he nursed his beer and silently counted measures before sneaking back into the hall just in time to make his entrance.

Perhaps Lew Waldeck (now sadly deceased), tuba player and the author of this elegy, may have sipped his pint while standing next to me at the bar on occasion without my knowing. As a poet, he certainly caught the pulse of the joint. You can just smell the food and the funk as you read his words. A bassoonist friend passed this evocative elegy on to me, and I have tried, with no success, to locate Lew's flutist wife to get her permission to include his poem in this book. If there is a Lew Waldeck estate, I apologize for printing Lew's magnificent poem without permission. Get in touch with me and I'll request it.

The Carnegie Tavern

Proust like,
I taste one note
Of Mahler's Resurrection,
And all the smells of the
Carnegie Tavern live again,
As pungent as yesterday,
In my mind's nose.

Breakfast.
Frying onions
For Salisbury Steak Lunch.
La Touraine coffee waiting
For the first sleepy musicians,
Returning after a short doze,
For the morning rehearsal.
Coming in with them,
Faint whiffs of
Instrument case leather and velvet plush
And cork grease, rosin, and valve oil,
Mixed with Listerine.

Yeasty Gnome bakery rolls
Cardboard and wax coffeetogo cups
Sometimes even friedeggonnaroll.
All this tinged
With last night's beer and smoke
Stale in the air
Despite the doors, open to 56th Street.

The sun tries to sneak in
Through the vestibule
While old Louis
(Who must have come with the place)
In his best NY waiter's manner
Slowly grumbles at the sunshine

FERMATA: THE CARNEGIE TAVERN

For tracking in the dry, nose wrinkling
Dust and exhaust.

He vainly swats at it with his broom,
Succeeding only in raising the
Whole city scent high into the air
Intermingling it with the dancing motes.

Now add Seagrams and Prior chaser
As Emil automatically
Serves the first drinker of the day.

The musicians move off to their
Musty locker room to warm up.
New playing card fragrance
As Pinochle games resume.
Camels, Balkan Sobranie, and
The first of many Bock Panatellas.
Rotten egg farts and garlic belches
Meld with some violinist's Mennen's
And the urinal's deodorant block
Floating in from the doorless tile toilet.

Meanwhile in the Tavern
Anticipating lunch,
Smell mashed potatoes with milk and butter,
Overcooking creamed spinach, string beans
Carrots and peas, red cabbage, and sauerkraut.
Boiling oil for chunky fries and
Steamy salt water for spaetzle.
John and Bill contribute a
Clean starchy comfort to the mixture
By flapping fresh tablecloths and napkins.
Old Louis sweeps again
Raising more street fragrance
Emil squeezes lemons.

Lunch
Oil paint, charcoal, and lithograph crayon
Precede the entree of the artists.
From the League, across the street,
They come, at twelve sharp,
Released from their dusty
Turps saturated studios
And their unwashed, longhaired,
Mostly talentless, students.
Free for one hour to inhale
Their own fame.

All at one big table
They argue endlessly
No one so great as they,
Always excepting
John Singer Sargent.
On that they all agree.

Rising from the table
Wafts fragrant restorant.
Consomme and fruit cups
Blended with herring in sour cream and
Chopped liver.
Beer.
Seidel light,
Seidel dark and
Half and half.
Cold, foamy , and redolent of barrels.
Yeasty crumbs of rolls, rye bread, and pumpernickel
Salt horns with carroway seeds, and
Bread sticks for the constant dieters.

Now smell Bacon Lettuce and Tomato on toast
No mayo.
Picasso, impasto,
Giotto, and gesso,

FERMATA: THE CARNEGIE TAVERN

Mixed with Roast Beef,
Corn beef, and Club.
The Carnegie Special
Ham, bacon, and turkey.
Smell the white toast.
Commissions, omissions,
Matrons and patrons
Bratwurst and Knackwurst,
Capers and Klops
Piquant in their hour of freedom.

Three conductors,
You would recognize them,
All expert in producing
Musician's dyspepsia,
Huddle in the corner of this
Musician's sanctuary
Aware of their invasion
But drawn by
The remembrance of
Hot roast beef sandwiches past,
Bruckner, Berlin,
Managers, and agents
Blended with acerbic house wine.

A singing teacher, a theoretician, an editor
All treat their ulcers with
Cheese sandwiches and milk.
Schenker mixed with Titralac
Polite responses to the conductors' nods
But still sitting between them and the players.
Preserving their neutrality,
One of them experiments with
A half-sour pickle.

Raw meat,
Said to be raised and aged on Paul's farm,
Delivered right through the front door
Followed by the faintest scent of the abattoir
Stimulates the salivary glands
As surely as a musky hint stimulates others.

The musicians return from rehearsal.
Louie, Bill, and John
Confer, without asking,
Everyone's daily desires.
The fragrances of onions,
Of meat, of fried potatoes
Reassured everyone.
Their security revived
They begin the never-ending critique.
The conductor, the soloist
The chairs, the repertoire,
The condition of the parts.
None of which was as good as last week's,
Last year's, or perhaps,
Last decade's.
The only sure things in their lives,
The enmity of conductors
And the comforting aroma of their lunch.

Emil soothes them with beer, bourbon,
Presbyterians, and Manhattans.
Pipes of all shape bellow pungent vapors,
Mingling with Cuban cigars and oval cigarettes.
The musicians move on to
Record dates,
Teaching duties or
Afternoon dalliances,
The tobacco fog trailing them
Into the street.

FERMATA: THE CARNEGIE TAVERN

The Tavern is quiet now,
Gently belching from time to time.
Expelling through the open doors
The fumes of lunch.

The waiters eat their lunches
Trading the latest gossip and jokes.
John calls his bookie.
A gentle rain falls,
Raising a coppery,
Back of the mouth,
Cement breath of spring in the city.

The evening shift,
Harry, Bill the waiter, and Bill the bartender
Join the others for lunch.
Paul waddles in,
Dons his gray host's jacket,
Counts the lunch take,
Prepares a deposit and talks with the chef,
Who, after all these years needs no reminder.
He cooks his repertoire as surely as a musician plays
Mozart Forty or Beethoven Five.

Now, with Louie gone,
The setting sun,
Still just rising from winter's nap
Projects a shaft
Through the stained glass windows
Glinting on the dark, crazed varnish of the booths
Applying a strip of orange and blue and green
Across the gleaming, white tablecloths.
The cunningly folded, triple peaked napkins,
Casting hard black shadows
Across waiting baskets of yeasty rolls
Raising a floury, dusty sniff,

Across salt and pepper shakers, and
Gleaming silverware.
(Paul says "The secret of a good restaurant is
Sharp knives and good rolls.")

The moment is lost.
Dark wood,
Smoky paintings,
Wooden chairs with
Red, oilcloth covered pads
Remain.
Waiting.

Dinner
"Hello, how are ya"
In his high tenor,
Paul greets the first diners.
He in a suit, if possible,
More formal than the one at work.
She introduced by sweet, flowery gusts,
Soon to be melded with other colognes
Into a more general melange.
Blue haired,
Hippo butted,
Brunhilda bosomed,
She moves to the chair held for her.
They sit and order.
Miraculously,
They replicate themselves,
Filling all the tables.
Differing only in origin and accent,
They find common ground amidst the
Emanations of Weiner Schnitzel und Sauerbraten.
Paul pipes, "Enchoyit"
(In all these years he has not mastered the J)

FERMATA: THE CARNEGIE TAVERN

Behind the counter,
My nose sees Bill slicing apple strudel.
The bar is quiet now,
No one wanting to fall asleep at the concert.
Food unalloyed with drink,
Perfumes the air.
If you sniff closely
You can divine the Sauerbraten's secret.

. . . Ginger snaps.
For dessert,
Recites Max,
Apple Strudel,
Cheese strudel,
Chocolate or Vanilla.

Deserted.
Paul puts up his feet
(Normally a sin)
In a back booth.
Harry opens the door for a little air
Bill the waiter sips lemon water
Bill the bartender
Sleepily polishes glasses.

Startled from his doze,
Bill serves
The low brass,
From the ballet down the block,
Slipped out during a tacet,
For a small libation.
They drink, look at their watches
And hurry back to announce Katchei.

Now breathe in alcohol.
An olfactory cacophony of brew.
Bright eyed,
Thrilled by the emotion of the performance,
The whole audience,
It seems,
Fills the Tavern.
All sizes,
All shapes,
All ages,
Crowd to drink.

Crowded into every possible space,
Barely able to bend elbows,
They drink,
They talk,
They marvel at what they have heard.
The musicians wisely,
Change slowly,
Trying to prolong the
Timeless,
Egoless feeling of a
Great performance.
Anyway, they know,
Soon there will be plenty of room.

The fresh green scent of grasshoppers
Mixes with dark musty scotch
At a corner booth where two ladies,
Just friends in Dubuque,
Dare to hold hands openly.

Beer and sherry smolder
While two lovebirds
Drink each other,
Disapproving Paul,
Standing over them

FERMATA: THE CARNEGIE TAVERN

Sweetly inquires
"Hows da vife?"
(T and W are difficult also.)

Whisky, sherry, and mixed drink potpourri
Begins to give in to the sweetness of beer.
The tavern belongs to the musicians now,
Instruments piled in the corner,
Tuba in purple corduroy making a phone call,
Cello in soft case
Joining the conversation at the three seat table.

At the bar,
Loving students surround an old master
Who utters an amazing, long
Shostakovich-sounding belch.
All laugh and admire.
He smiles slyly,
Twiddling his thumbs
Which rest comfortably
On his great stomach.

After an hour of steady beer
He rises, saying,
"Tut-a-ka-tut, old thing" and
Walks, stately as the Queen Mary,
To the men's.

The ballet orchestra comes in,
They joke and needle.
All is relaxed now,
Winding down after a hard nights work.
Bad phrases and
Conductor's death rays forgotten.
Colleague with colleague,
Warm, friendly.
The familiar late hour essence
Quiets and soothes them.

One by one they drift out.
Glasses washed,
Chairs up,
Lights out.
The only smell now,
Ozone, as the air freshener starts.

Lew Waldeck March 22, 1995

CHAPTER VIII
My Lance is Free:
Scorrevole

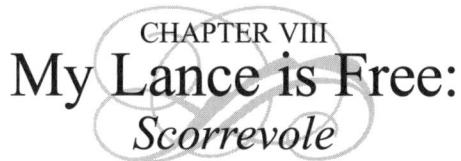

"All art constantly aspires to the condition of music."
WALTER PATER

I was walking east between gigs on West 56th Street one cold New York winter afternoon, and had just reached the stage door of Carnegie Hall, gloved and shivering, with my viola case in hand, when a voice down the street called out to me, "Hey, Bernie Zaslav! It's Isidor." Isidor Saslav's last name is one of the many variants of the rather common Russian name of Zaslavsky. Isidor Saslav and I knew of each other by reputation (he was a past concertmaster of the New Zealand Symphony and made a fine edition of Haydn's string quartets), but before this moment we had never actually met.*

As Isidor and I approached one another for our first face-to-face meeting, my viola case slipped from my hand, and fell right to the concrete sidewalk. It couldn't have fallen more than a foot, and it probably wouldn't have been noticeable to anyone else amidst New York's constant traffic noise, but to me it sounded like the crack of doom. With trembling hands and fluttering heart, I opened the case and saw, to my horror, that my viola sustained an ugly crack along the grain of the belly (the top plate). It didn't look like total destruction, but it was bad enough to make me want to strangle myself right on the spot. I childishly wanted to blame it on my heavy gloves. String players are neurotic about their instruments; they care for them and fret about them during every waking moment. How could I have done this incredibly stupid thing?

After rushing through a hurried greeting, my face beet red in shame, and my heart fearful of what other damage my viola might have sustained, I said a hurried goodbye to Isidor, and ran around the corner to my beloved luthier. The handsome brass nameplate

---

* In 1966, when Isidor was the concertmaster of the Rochester Philharmonic, he received a letter from Juilliard's placement office announcing an audition for the position of concertmaster in Minneapolis. He could not understand why Juilliard would contact him, since he had gone to Curtis. It seemed that they were looking for a guy named "Bernard Zaslav." Isidor took the audition, and got the job. I guess I inadvertently had something to do with his career!

attached to the doorway of the old Steinway Building on West 57th Street (and polished daily), proclaimed to the public at large that the Stradivarius Studios, and its proprietor, Vahakn Nigogosian (1910–1977), could be found within. Born in Istanbul, Nigo, as everybody called him, studied in Paris with the famed French luthier and bow-maker Marcel Vatelot. He came to New York in 1958 to work as an assistant to the highly-respected Italian violin maker Simone Sacconi at the House of Wurlitzer on West 42nd Street.

Nigo was one of the world's most admired restorers and tonal adjusters of fine string instruments. Not one to suffer fools, Nigo was was known to be quite impatient, even irascible, when he came across poor workmanship. He was an intense and insatiable artist, and his results bespoke a manic attention to detail. Nigo would spend inordinate amounts of time cutting a bridge or adjusting a sound-post, those parts of a string instrument that rock ever so minutely as they transmit the energy of a bow stroke from the belly of an instrument to its back. These adjustments are central to the instrument's sound quality and its response to the player's needs. He could bring out all of an instrument's latent possibilities, and he strove to find the innate richness and subtle beauty of an instrument, rather than its sheer power. Nigo attended some of my concerts in order to confirm (and report to me) if his latest attentions enabled me to project the voice of my relatively small viola to the back of a concert hall without forcing its tone.

I would hang out at his shop between gigs, sometimes chatting with his wife Alice, who was often there to help him through his trying, overworked days. I recall seeing Nigo at his bench next to Sacconi, working on the cello that belonged to Pablo Casals (I believe it was a Matteo Goffriller). There it sat, with its belly plate off, and lying beside it; its insides open to the world. Nigo pointed out to me how its maker had made the ribs (the sides) very thin, and how they had been lined with linen for added strength. What a feeling to peer into the innards of Pablo Casals' voice, the same cello that he used for his daily traversal of the Bach Cello Suites.*

---

* In the December 1943 issue of *Violins* and *Violinists*, the cellist Maurice Eisenberg credits Pablo Casals as the first performing artist to play an entire unaccompanied Bach suite in public, and, in doing so, Casals opened new horizons for all string players.

Nigo once made an exact copy of a Stradivari cello, which remained in a glass case in his studio for about twenty years. It was still "in the white" (unvarnished), naked as a jay bird, and strangely beautiful.

Charles Rufino and Carlos Arcieri apprenticed under Nigo. Usually one of them would be at work by his side, but sometimes I would find Nigo alone in the shop, and immersed in some delicate project. When this was the case, I would answer the door to sell some violinist the odd E string, so Nigo could remain at work at his bench.

The best part of hanging out at Nigo's was when he decided to take a break, put up his glasses, and place a *firkin* of Armenian coffee on the Bunsen burner that heated the rabbit-hide glue used to close the seams of string instruments. Nigo's *firkin* would began to froth up, and some of Alice's sweets, like sweet and squishy *lokoum* (Turkish Delight) would magically appear on his bench. Then Nigo would impart some of his fiddle "secrets" to me, and we would talk for many happy hours about sound quality and the artists who were "the fairest of them all." He was my mentor of sound, and my savior in time of need.

When I showed up at Nigo's shop with my damaged viola still in its case, he knew from the look on my face not to ask the obvious. It was embarrassing to ask how badly it had been damaged, and or how long it would take for repairs. I watched his face as I stuttered sheepishly, "Er, . . . when, Nigo?" I was relieved but daunted by his response, "Oh, if not too busy . . . maybe a *month!*"

After my years of plumbing supply and free-lance life, and Nomi's many child-rearing years, we badly needed some time together. Rather than trying to borrow an instrument of sufficient quality to use for recording dates, Nomi and I decided to visit Europe (for the first time in either of our lives). We left our children with my parents (who lived downstairs), I asked the Radio Registry to inform contractors they could call back in a month, and Nomi and I went off on our first carefree jaunt together.

Arthur Frommer's *Europe on Five Dollars a Day* was the ultimate travel authority in the 1960s, but we weren't thrilled about his first suggested "canal house" in Amsterdam (no room to make decent love in those bunks). We continued southward to Venice and surprised my old high school chum Herbert Handt with a phone call. Herbert was an "expat," who had been living in Lucca for years. A Monteverdi specialist with many honors to his credit, including being officially named an Honored Citizen of Lucca (he sent me an engraved announcement), he enjoyed a great vocal career at La Scala, Covent Garden, and many European opera houses and concert halls. His voice is meltingly beautiful, with a tasteful Italianized *kvetch*, when it's called for.

There was no "Hello, how are you" on the phone from Herbie. I tried to explain patiently that we were larking about the Continent for the first time in our lives, and the first thing that erupted from the receiver was his roar, "Never mind that shit, just tell me where the heck you are right now."

"Why, we're enjoying your beautiful city of Venice. It's so quaint, the canals and the . . . "

"Okay Buddy, just cut the crap. I happen to know those canals stink. Now listen carefully, and don't say a word. Pack up your stuff right away and catch the next train to Rome, and then get the train to Civitavecchia. It's very simple, even for a dummy like you. From there take the overnight boat to the port of Cagliari in Sardegna, and make sure you get an inside cabin, 'cause it gets cold as Baba Yaga's *tuchas* on the water."

"Look Buddy," he continued, a little more patiently, "I'm taking my chamber orchestra on a tour of Sardegna and you're gonna play first viola for some concerts I'm conducting in Cagliari, Alghero, Sassari, Olbia and a few other places. You'll visit the relics of the Nuragi people, you'll eat roast suckling wild boar (even if it ain't kosher) you'll eat roasted cheese and visit a famous costume museum in Nuoro, you'll see the palace of the Aga Khan, and you'll both have a great time, Buddy. Would I kid you?"

Evidently his years of dealing with musicians and being an expert on the music of Monteverdi and Rossini hadn't softened any of Herbie's Brooklyn edges, so I hollered back into this Italian version of a telephone. "Hold on a minute, Herbie," I said. "What the hell are you talking about? We're here in Italy for our first vacation in years, I don't have a viola with me and you're an. . ."

"*Pace, mio dio*," he replied. "Look Buddy, my schmuck of a first viola player broke his wrist playing soccer yesterday, and he can't make the tour. I'll get you a viola, and we'll have a short rehearsal when you arrive. No problem."

"Sure, it's no problem for you, but I don't speak any Italian!"

"So what, my musicians don't speak any English either, but you'll catch on quick. Hasn't anyone ever told you that music is the universal language?"

"Yeah sure, but Herbie, we just . . ."

"Don't worry, okay? I'll make all the reservations for both of you by train, boat and every little thing. Just tell me you'll be there, okay?"

So I did, and we did, and that wonderful time, as promised, was had by all. The viola he found for me was passable, but I have to say that Herbie was a far better tenor than he was a conductor. We saw and experienced all of the wonders he mentioned, and more. Sardegna seemed to exist in an historic time warp. Women covered their heads, men sat outside playing cards, drinking and talking politics. Whenever our antiquated tour bus got too hot for comfort, the driver would simply pull over to stretch or eat a sandwich whenever and wherever he felt like it. There seemed not to be any schedules to be concerned about while we were drinking in the wild scenery and the remarkable ancient stone huts that were put up centuries ago by shepherds. Nomi recalls one bus trip where members of the orchestra serenaded her in what they took to be English. "Oh Susanna" has to be heard when sung with Tuscan fervor in order to be truly appreciated.

When we returned to their home at San Michelle in Eschetto outside of Lucca, Herbie and his wife Laura Ziegler, an acclaimed sculptor from Columbus, Ohio, graciously offered us a guest room on the top floor of their historic house, which adjoined a tiny historic church. We thought it was all so romantic, until 6:00 the next morning, when the ear-splitting infernal bells of the bloody historic church rang out. Literally yards from our pillows, they blasted us out of bed. Herbie drove us along the circular road atop the wall that surrounds Lucca's old town, and we admired the barbershop-pole style of decoration on the pillars of its churches. All in all it was a memorable trip.

Back in New York, Nigo had taken every pain to accomplish his hoped-for magic in time for our arrival home from Italy. There wasn't any sign of the belly crack to be seen on my viola; in fact, my viola sounded even better than it did before the accident. My colleagues praised my chutzpah for taking a whole month off, but I hoped that in my absence all the blessed New York contractors hadn't erased my name from their lists.

In addition to hanging out in Nigo's shop between gigs, I enjoyed haunting Schlieps' shop. George Schlieps (1894–1977) came from Russia (he was a nephew of the composer Alexander Glazunov) and rode a motorcycle through the New York traffic, even at an advanced age. He and his bow-maker son Armin occupied one of those fragrant shops tucked away in the old Carnegie Hall before its restoration, where you might come across a dance studio, a swami, maybe a fortune teller, and the office of Richard and Theodora Schulze's Telemann Society.

My friend Werner Torkanowsky was a real Renaissance man. He was a remarkable person: a fine violinist and a composer, as well as a conductor (he conducted the New Orleans Symphony and later conducted the Bangor Symphony in Maine, where he spent the remainder of his life). Werner once borrowed a very rare seventeenth century Italian viola from a generous New York musical family for a few concerts in Hancock, Maine. While hurriedly loading up his car after one of the concerts, he placed the viola case on the top of his car, and drove off, forgetting it was there. The police found it some time later along the side of the road, smashed into zillions of pieces. Werner walked shamefacedly into George Schlieps' shop to deliver the news, and show what was left of this ravaged bit of Italian history. Schlieps apparently regarded restoring this rare instrument as the challenge *par excellence*, the feat that would establish his reputation in the restorer's firmament. He worked on the instrument for several years, and took photos of the work in progress. In one photo you can see him picking out the tiniest shards of varnish from a small wood fragment. He eventually was able to restore this rare instrument, bringing it back from almost total destruction. I had the opportunity to play the instrument after its miraculous restoration. You could barely see where Schlieps made his repairs, even with a magnifying glass.

A far more splendid, high-ceilinged atelier run by Jacques Francais was around the corner at 140 West 57th Street. It was *the* place. You could see many of the big shots of the string world there, and you could hear less-celebrated fiddlers try out instruments made by Stradivari and Guarneri del Jesu, even though few of them could come up with the necessary *gelt* to buy one. I hung out at Jacques' shop between gigs too.

I happened to be at Jacques' place one day when a violinist, who is best left unnamed, rushed in to the shop, looking for a laugh. Although he was missing an index finger on his left hand, this fiddler did very well in the commercial music world. With all eyes on him, our hero yelled, "Jacques, I'm begging you. Please sell me anything you have in the shop. Anything at all. I don't care what it is. I'll make a fortune on it." He got the laugh he was after, and he turned out to have been absolutely right. He did make a minor fortune.

In the words of another of my New York colleagues, you met a better crowd at Schlieps. You would often see artists like the wonderfully gifted violinist David Nadien in deep discussion with Armin Schlieps, not about violins, but about the virtues of natural foods. We all expected David, with his wonderful facility and elegant style, to have a highly-successful solo career, but for some reason, only a few people knew what a marvelous fiddler he was. Luckily his solo recordings have been reissued, so we can all enjoy his playing in perpetuity.

George Schlieps once promised to hold a particularly fine French viola bow for me until I could pay for it, but through some miscommunication between father and son, David (the rat) had gotten his mitts on it the day before I showed up with the down payment. It was a rare specimen by the French maker Maire, and it worked perfectly with my viola. Viola bows are somewhat longer and a bit heavier than violin bows, so I wondered why David would want one. Perhaps he enjoyed those few extra grams of weight on the violin. But David (still, the rat), who had become the concertmaster of the New York Philharmonic shortly after he bought the bow, somehow managed to break the bow at the tip (a bow's weakest and most vulnerable part). He then sold the bow to my violist friend Teddy Israel for its insurance value. Teddy had the tip repaired, and then he sold the bow to me, minus the original frog. Nicholas Maire left his imprint on bow-making with a particular part of the frog, so Teddy decided to keep the original frog for its rarity. I asked Emile Ouchard, an excellent French maker, who was living in New York, to make a replacement frog for the bow. I broke the Maire again (several times) in the exactly the same place, including once while performing a piece by Bartók. It has since been well repaired and remains a favorite of mine.

Hank Sylvern wrote the music for a David Susskind TV show called "Emanuel," and scored it for the unusual combination of viola, electronic organ, and French horn. I played viola, Hank played the organ, and the great John Barrows played horn. The call was for about three hours, but we got started late, and due to a combination of technical difficulties (and Hank's insistence on perfection), the session kept running later and later. John paused to call for a sub to play his early morning rehearsal with Leopold Stokowski, and we said goodnight at about 4:00 that morning. Union scale, with overtime, for that gig was obscene, but Hank was obsessive about his product.

I got home really bushed. When I mentioned this recording session to a colleague, he told me that Johnnie showed up at that Stokowski rehearsal as planned! He was heroic: playing all those long, beautiful horn calls over and over, and still showing up for a gig the next morning. I caught the show on TV some months later, and loved hearing Johnnie's pure sound. Playing gigs like this one, and especially finding a piece for organ, viola, and French horn, made my freelancing days challenging and worthwhile.

I got a call from a contractor to play a midnight record date (midnight recording dates were not unusual) at the old Pythian Temple on West 70th Street, a building that Columbia Records converted into a recording studio. I entered the lobby of the building carrying my viola, and rang for the elevator. Four rather burly and unshaven men walked in, and they surrounded me as we waited. We got on the elevator together, and I selected my floor. They made no move to select another.

It was late night in a relatively deserted part of town, and with nobody else around, and not a word being spoken, I felt a bit of trepidation. When the elevator reached my floor (I think it was the eighth), I walked out quickly into a large recording studio that was nearly empty, and the four men followed right behind me. Not knowing what to do, I stood there until somebody wearing headphones rushed up to these guys and gave them a warm hello. Whew! It turned out that these people I was concerned about were "Jay and the Americans," a rock group that my young daughter was crazy about. They were the talent for the recording session. My daughter couldn't believe I hadn't gotten her an autograph.

The conductor, Max Goberman hired New York's top freelance musicians at a special union "symphonic scale" rate to record all of the known works of Antonio Vivaldi. Since most of the musicians he called were busy during the day playing regular union-scale jobs, and many played Broadway shows that closed around 11:00 p.m., the recordings had to be made at midnight. I had worked with Goberman on Broadway in the show *Milk and Honey*, so I was called to play these recording sessions.

One night, when I was scheduled to play some of the solo viola parts in a few Vivaldi concerti, an infamous snowstorm shut down the transit system in our fair city. Nothing moved at all, except the underground subways. All the street traffic ground to a halt, and it looked spooky out there. It was February 3, 1961, and

I was at home in Brooklyn with nothing else in my book for that day, so I figured the odds. Yes, there was a snow storm, but a recording session with a solo part in a Vivaldi concerto with New York's finest didn't happen that often. I could stay home and watch the television show me how awful it was out in the snow, or I could swaddle myself to the hilt like an Arctic explorer, schlep my viola, walk the bus route (since the busses weren't running), and reach the IRT subway station on foot. That is what I did.

When I arrived at the studio, I was dumfounded to find every single person sitting in place. This was just another New York catastrophe that we musicians weathered heroically. We did our darnedest, but the recordings were never released. The following year Goberman was found dead in his Vienna hotel room, while in the process of recording all of the Haydn Symphonies with a group of Viennese musicians.

The bassoonist Loren Glickman called me to record all of the Mozart piano concerti with Rudolf Serkin and his son Peter, who joined him to record the concerto for two pianos. Alexander (Sasha) Schneider, the former second violinist of the Budapest String Quartet, was the conductor. After leaving the Budapest Quartet, he began his own "Schneider Quartet," and performed all of Haydn's 84 Quartets (including some we now know were not written by Haydn), and all seven of the *Seven Last Words*. Sasha took a leading part in the Casals Festival in Prades with Pablo Casals, and he loved to conduct. Love is sometimes not enough to get the job done properly.*

Sasha was lionized by many of the New York ladies, but he was rather hopeless as a conductor. He sang every phrase to us using his personal brand of *rubato* and inflection, and kvetched and complained about everything we did. Loren put together a wonderful group of musicians, but nothing we did pleased Sasha. He was sincere about his musical intent, but many of his requests were outlandishly exaggerated. He was a fine fiddler, but he was

---

* Loren once told me a story about Sasha's love life. Once he was forced to call Sasha late one night about some problem or other. He said that after hearing the phone ring, Sasha picked it up and growled, "Not now, I'm f…ing," and slammed down the phone.

his own worst enemy holding a baton.

Everybody looked up to Rudolf Serkin, a celebrated pianist and a dedicated musician, so we humored our conductor (or semi-conductor, in the opinion of many) through the many takes that each session required. Loren played second bassoon, and he hired Eli Carman to play principal. At one point Sasha became red in the face during a disagreement with Eli concerning the way he played a particular phrase. Eli simply had it. He got up from his chair and walked towards Sasha with the bassoon in his hands, saying he was about to insert (shove, was the word he actually used) this four-foot long wind instrument up his fundament. Sasha cringed and cried out, *"Vat I said, vat I said?"* as he cowered away from the equally red-faced Eli. I must apologize for reporting this indelicacy in such detail, but it really was Sasha's fault. Peace was eventually restored, they both apologized, and Sasha didn't have any more complaints that day. An unfortunate postscript goes with this story: Eli's life ended tragically when he was accidentally run over by his wife backing out of their driveway. Both of these colorful gentlemen are no longer alive, but a lot of good music happened on their watch.

Fritz Kreisler, the most beloved of all violinists, passed away in January of 1962. I was one of the members of the chamber orchestra called to play a Fritz Kreisler Memorial Concert at Carnegie on December 26 of that year. The orchestra personnel (I believe we volunteered our services that night) was a "Who's Who" of New York's top players from the quartet, free-lance, and concert world; with concertmasters elbowing other concertmasters in the first violin section. The soloists that night were Zino Francescatti, Nathan Milstein, Erika Morini, and Isaac Stern, an all-star line-up, never to be equalled. The impish Nathan Milstein broke the solemnity of the occasion with some clowning during one of the rehearsals. His schtick was to play holding his 1716 ex-Goldman Strad either on top of his head or at chest level (he sounded just fine either way).

The concert opened with the Juilliard String Quartet playing Beethoven's Quartet Op. 59, No. 3. They took that last movement at a breakneck tempo, which they claimed to be Beethoven's original tempo marking (though nobody could really have known the condition of his metronome). The tempo of this movement is always under discussion, since the violist starts the ball rolling with the first statement of the theme, and controls the throttle. Some more somber fireworks followed, with concerti for two violins by Bach and Vivaldi, and another for four violins, also by Vivaldi, played by various configurations of our star violinists, each of them politely taking turns at the first or second part.

Topping them all with her technical perfection and purity of tone, the great, though less-often heard Erika Morini, played a movement from a concerto by Louis Spohr (I believe it was his *Gesangsszene*, though it was not indicated as such on the program). As a former student of Ševčík, her bow hair never seemed to leave the string. I was sitting next to Arthur Granik, who was the principal violist, and we both were entranced.

David Oistrakh came from Russia during the 1960s to play a few concerts at Carnegie Hall with the Symphony of the Air, an orchestra conducted by Alfred Wallenstein. I knew his recordings (he plays the cadenza of the Shostakovich first concerto like no one else), but this was the first time I had the opportunity to see and hear him up close and in person. We were all truly taken by the honesty and power of his playing, and the human openness of the man. He looked more like a Russian shopkeeper than the great artist he was. We repeated the concert somewhere in New Jersey, and then we all repaired to a nearby dive for a late night nosh. We sort of took over the place; there were so many of us that we had to be seated at separate tables. David was seated at a table with the conductor and a pair of Soviet thugs, and he looked very lonely with only Wally and said thugs to keep him company. We tutti players weren't allowed to talk to him, but he smiled over at us and sent a bottle of wine over to our table, which was very moving. I understand he used the fees from that trip to buy a Strad from Rembert Wurlitzer.

I own a wonderful LP recording of David and his son Igor playing the Mozart Sinfonia Concertante for violin and viola. Igor played the violin part and David had the best viola sound imaginable. The French horn players of the Russian orchestra accompanying them produced some very odd-sounding vibrato. Perhaps they were frustrated violinists at heart.

I played quite often with the Symphony of the Air, and when Arthur Granik, their regular principal viola was unavailable, I had the opportunity to play first chair. Once, when Jacob Avshalomov conducted a performance of the Brahms A-Major Serenade, a work that doesn't use violins, I enjoyed the thrill of walking out onto the stage of Carnegie Hall and tuning the orchestra, normally the concertmaster's job. He was me, I was he, that night.

The Swiss Music Library sponsored a special chamber music concert at Carnegie Recital Hall on April 2, 1963, that featured Heinz Holliger, the brilliant young Swiss oboist and composer. He looked like an adolescent Peter Pan, but he already had an international reputation as one of the most celebrated players of his instrument. Buzz had gone around town, and New York oboists like Leonard Arner, Henry Schuman, Ronald Roseman, and Albert and Doris Goltzer were there to hear him. We even heard that the British oboist Leon Goossens, the brother of conductor Eugene Goossens, was in the audience.

The program included music by Klaus Huber and Holliger's own duo for oboe and harp, which he performed with his wife Ursula Haeneggi Holliger. Matthew Raimondi, cellist David Soyer, and I joined Holliger for the Mozart Oboe Quartet. Rehearsals were a great Swiss-Italian blend: Matthew had a rare Carlo Bergonzi fiddle to match my Italian viola, and Soyer alternated between his Amati and his Guarnerius. You can imagine our collective surprise as we crowded into the Carnegie Recital Hall's tiny backstage area, and saw David take a brand new cello, covered with bright shiny orange varnish, out of his case.

Considering all the hours we spent on balance and on matching tone quality with our star oboe player (who had the lightest, most melting tone imaginable), Matthew, a hot-blooded Sicilian by nature, was aghast. He asked David if one of his Italian cellos had sustained an accident, and David simply shrugged and said that he had just decided to give this one a try for the evening. I guess we were the only ones to notice the difference, because the audience's response was tumultuous. They wouldn't let us leave the stage until we repeated the last movement.

I worked with David on various recording dates in New York, and later, when the Stanford and Guarneri String Quartets played the Mendelssohn Octet together, I came to know this as typical of him. David was a no-nonsense guy, and one of the finest quartet cellists ever.

A recording session for a silly tune called "How Much is that Doggie in the Window" was running into far too many takes. The advertiser's vice president sitting behind the glass wall of the recording studio was giving the rest of the merchandising talent a hard time, and the recording engineer, the singer, and the well-paid commercial musicians sitting outside in the real world in front of the microphones were totally bored.

The singer and the band began take 15, and after the words "in the window," a bored-out-of-his-gourd Jazz violinist from Paducah, Kentucky named Harry Lookofsky had the temerity to bark the two immortal words into his microphone that turned the silly tune into a hit. Those words were, "Woof, Woof." Harry's colleagues thought that Harry had just committed financial suicide, but when they all heard, "That's *it*! That's *just* what we needed," history was made. Harry Lookofsky became first call on every contractor's list, and wound up with a Stradivarius in his fiddle case.

Cellist Maurice Bialkin (known as "Moe") was called for a "jingle" (studio gigs were called "jingles," but you never knew what a gig actually was until your showed up). Moe was surprised to find that he was the only musician there, but it didn't make any difference. Jingles were mostly background for some kind of product, and, as it turned out this one was for a popular laxative called ExLax.

After recording the usual safe 10 or 15 takes of boredom, the advertising executive in charge had the brilliant idea of trying to give the project some class. He decided to show an honest-to-god cellist playing a beautiful instrument in the ad rather than merely relegating him to producing background music. They put Moe on a platform, and they asked him to play something for the cameras, whatever he wanted, so he played a couple of measures from one of Bach cello suites (you can't expose the lowbrow public to too much of this stuff, right?). Since this was video and not just audio, the residuals paid enough for Moe to take his family on a European vacation. He boasted about it to me later, and warned me not to turn down anything I get called for.

As free-lancers, we were understandably reluctant to turn down any work offered to us. We lived from job to job in order to keep afloat, and I was quite happy to be in this varied and competitive musical arena, but I began to pay a physical price for taking on such a large workload.

In 1966, when a painful left-hand finger joint put me out of commission for a while, I phoned around to a few colleagues (including a member of the Guarneri Quartet), and was told about a highly regarded "finger doctor" who was known for treating musicians. I made an appointment with Dr. Grokest, who diagnosed me with a condition called Ehlers/Danlos syndrome, a hyper-extensibility of joints and connective tissues. I remember that when playing sports as a youngster, (when they'd let me), I would often end up with severe muscle trauma, while the other kids merely suffered the occasional "charley horse."

Dr. Grokest mentioned that this syndrome could be hereditary. When I told him that our son Mark was nearing the age when he could be drafted into the army and sent to Vietnam, Dr. Grokest examined Mark, and it turned out that he had indeed inherited this syndrome. When Mark was called up for the draft, he was declared unfit for Army service. Amen!

I played a concert with the New York Pick-up Ensemble for a

"An Evening with P.D.Q. (pretty damned quick) Bach" (1807–1742, yes, I know) at Lincoln Center's Philharmonic Hall on December 2, 1967. After making his entrance by swinging down to the stage on a rope, our conductor, Professor Peter Schickele, from the University of Southern North Dakota at Hoople, informed the audience that the young P.D.Q. Bach was taken to a concert that included a concerto for two violins by Vivaldi. He and his father arrived late, and could only hear the concert from behind closed doors. Even though he hadn't actually seen the performance, the young P.D.Q. was inspired to write his own concerto for the same number of human hands, but he wrote it for just one instrument to be played simultaneously by two players, one holding the viola under his chin, and his partner standing at the other end of the instrument. He called the piece "Sonata for Viola, Four Hands." Both players finger different strings of the fingerboard (yes, it can be done), and they bow across the strings in opposite directions. A surprising amount of rehearsal is required for the two players to manage this complex feat. Because of the intimacy involved, it is suggested that both players should shower before and after each rehearsal.

The first two movements are marked "Andanteeny," and "Allegro Liberace,' and the slow (and hilariously boring) third movement, which uses only the viola's open C string, is marked "1 lb. Ground." It requires one player to hold the instrument at the proper angle so that a thirty-foot length of well-rosined nylon fish-line can be drawn across the open string by two stagehands. Instead of using a normal bow for the last movement, marked "Allah Breve," another length of prepared fish-line is substituted for the blade of a hacksaw, which is energetically drawn back and forth across the strings by one player, who employs suitable facial grimaces.

I played the premiere of the P.D.Q. Sonata (edited by Professor Peter Schickele) with Jorge Mester. We returned to the stage to wild applause, and engaged in mock-dueling (using our cheapest bows) for comedic effect. During the course of this silliness, Jorge knocked my glasses off my face, and they fell into the audience (they thought it was part of the show). The concert was televised, and Nomi told me that my mother watched it on our television set at home in Brooklyn. 1960s color television sets had knobs to adjust the red and green tints, and it seems that when I came on stage my mother turned up the red tint so that I would have "a little color in my cheeks."

After the release of the Disney film *Fantasia*, Leopold Stokowski became very popular, and when he came to conduct the Symphony of the Air, he would fill the hall. I played for quite a few of his concerts, and can assure you that Stokowski's vaunted sumptuous sound had more to do with the quality of his players than the otherworldly motions of his hands. One of his noted failures was to mess with the normal seating of the orchestra. In an attempt to make the orchestra's tone more homogenous, he would reseat players as he saw fit; placing a lonely cellist between two trombones, or dumping an oboe player in the middle of the viola section!

The Symphony of the Air normally engaged conducting stalwarts like Fritz Reiner and Alfred Wallenstein, but it was also available for hire to the various neophytes who were trying to make a career in New York. In an attempt to make the orchestra a more viable entity, the members held a meeting in the mid 1960s to decide whom they should invite to be their permanent conductor.

None of the players could stand Stoky's tyrannical ways and general phoniness (he used lines like, "A painter paints his pictures on canvas. But musicians paint their pictures on silence. We provide the music, and you provide the silence"). I was told that he put the moves on some of the young women who came to his apartment to audition, but his popularity with the public still made him a strong candidate for the job. He was eventually rejected because of his age, since he was around 83, and we feared that he might die quite soon. The joke was on us, because Stoky continued to be active until the age of 95, while the Symphony of the Air died shortly after our meeting.

Stoky could act like a slave-master in rehearsal. He would often pick on the older players at the back of the sections (veterans of the old NBC orchestra) by making them stand up and play their parts all alone. He kept a list of names on his stand and, with a stony stare, would openly erase the names of those who displeased him. Sitting through this cruelty made my skin crawl.

I played for many of his recording sessions, including one for a 1967 Vanguard Records release made under the auspices of The Bach Guild called "In Dulci Jubilo, a Baroque Concert." A note on the album cover called the orchestra "a virtuoso orchestra," and it listed the players: violinists Gerald Tarack, Lamar Alsop, Matthew Raimondi, Charles Libove, John Pintavalle, Joseph Shot, Sidney Kaufman, Arthur Bogin, Saul Ovcharov, and Alan Grishman; violists Walter Trampler, Al Brown, Theodore Israel, and me; cellists Charles McCracken, Harvey Shapiro, and Seymour Barab; bass player Alvin Brehm; flutists Gerardo Levy and Paula Robison, oboists Leonard Arner, Henry Schuman, and Bert Lucarelli; English horn players Sampson Giat, and Charles Kuskin; bassoonist Loren Glickman, and harpsichordist Igor Kipnis.

I played music by Virgil Thomson for Stoky in the recording sessions for *The Plow That Broke the Plains,* a documentary about the Great Depression. One *molto adagio* episode of Virgil's religious-type Americana is written in three quarter time, and, whether he was looking at the score or not, Stoky was beating it in four quarter time, i.e., four unremitting swipes of his arm to the bar (he avoided using a baton so that he could gesticulate exaggeratedly for the "benefit" of the audience).

We had to rely on the concertmaster (it might have been Jake Krachmalnik) as our lifeline to sanity, so we kept going by extending the last quarter note in the measure to make Virgil's cadences work, all the while bursting at the seams with suppressed laughter. We knew from experience to avoid speaking to Stoky directly because of his tantrums, so Jake just smiled affectedly (albeit somewhat vacantly) at our conductor. Virgil, who was in the recording booth, kept his silence out of sheer cowardice, and we recorded the whole damn movement like that! I sometimes wonder what it sounded like, but I don't really want to know. I am aware of how many have come to praise Caesar, but I was there.

I wasn't there for this story: it comes indirectly from Cyrus Segal, my bassoonist pal of many years, who has been with the New York City Opera for what seems like forever. Apparently Stoky had asked his contractor to call his usual list of players for a series of recording sessions, but Stoky accepted an engagement in Europe instead and decided to postpone. When he returned to do the series a few months later, many of his regulars had been booked for other sessions in his absence. When he mounted the podium to begin the first session, he looked around, mystified by all the new faces sitting in front of him and asked, "Who are all you people?" Upon which, before anyone was ready (this was his favorite shtick) he gave his usual rushed downbeat, only to be amazed as the entire orchestra came in as one. Now even more mystified, Stoky stopped for a moment to gaze upon Matthew Raimondi, his new concertmaster (not his regular choice for this important seat), and asked him, "How is it that *you people* are able to play this music so perfectly?" Without missing a beat, Matt beamed up at him angelically and said, "You see, Maestro, we've all been practicing our parts like mad while you were away in Europe."

Cy Segal also told me a story about James Politi, the venerable and much-loved first flutist of the Metropolitan Opera Orchestra for many years. It seems that a certain nasty German guest conductor was giving Mr. Politi a hard time about a particular spot in the music. This conductor asked him to repeat his solo over and over again. He complied through many repetitions, and then Politi, grizzled veteran that he was, simply put his flute down on his lap and responded, "Sir, I've played this solo much worse, more than a hundred times, for much better conductors than you."

The Kohon String Quartet
Harold Kohon, Raymond Kunicki, Richard Kay, and Bernard Zaslav

CHAPTER IX
The Kohon String Quartet

"What's in a name?
That which we call a rose by any other name would smell as sweet."
WILLIAM SHAKESPEARE, *Romeo and Juliet*

When a newborn string quartet searches for a name to distinguish itself from the rest of the pack, one of the members is bound to mention the Schuppanzigh Quartet, one of the most celebrated groups of the past. The first violinist of that group bore the name of Ignaz Schuppanzigh. After the giggles subside, someone reminds the other members that Schuppanzigh was officially known as the "leader" of the quartet, which involves further comment about such old-fashioned things as rank in a string quartet. Modern string quartets decry the idea of a "leader," since we now accept the idea of equality as central to our egos, musical and otherwise.

The Schuppanzigh Quartet began its career by playing informal Friday morning concerts in Prince Lichnowsky's Vienna apartments, and during the 1804–1805 season the Quartet presented the first known series of public quartet concerts in Vienna. At the request of Count Razumovsky, Schuppanzigh put together the finest string quartet in Europe, and in 1807 that quartet (with the Count playing second violin) played the first performances of Beethoven's three Op. 59 Quartets. The group remained together until 1814, when a fire destroyed the count's palace.

Schuppanzigh left Vienna for St. Petersburg, where he promoted Beethoven's music. When he returned to Vienna in 1823, having probably influenced the commission for Beethoven's late quartets, he joined the Quartet again. All the premieres were successful except for Op. 127, and Beethoven, who seemed to be the person truly in charge of the quartet at this time, was furious. He fired Schuppanzigh, and replaced him with Joseph Boehm, who had played with the Quartet during Schuppanzigh's absence. Eventually Schuppanzigh got back into Beethoven's good graces, and played the first performances of all the Quartets written after Op. 127 except for Op. 131. Schuppanzigh's famous complaint to Beethoven about a particularly difficult passage that earned the reply, "Do you believe that I think about your miserable fiddle when the muse strikes me?" makes sense in the grand scheme of things. While Beethoven was acting like a conductor or a contractor, the Quartet still went by the name of its first violinist.

This hoary tradition of using the name of the first violinist for the group continued to survive through the ages with the advent of the Rosé, the Joachim, the Capet, the Kneisel, the Kolisch, the Suk, the Griller, the Kroll, the Végh, the Brosa, the Galimir, the Schneider, the Chilingirian and the Arditti String Quartets, all of which were content to accept the last name of the first violinist as their own. One quartet, the Primrose Quartet, is a rare instance of a group with two star violinists, Oscar Shumsky and Josef Gingold, and the equally prestigious cellist, Harvey Shapiro, taking its name from their star violist, William Primrose. Things began to change as benefactors (people we called "angels") arrived on the scene. For example, the Coolidge Quartet took their name from Elizabeth Sprague Coolidge, and other groups followed. There was the Perole Quartet (my teacher Lillian Fuchs was their violist), and the Musical Arts Quartet (my teacher Sasha Jacobson was their first violinist). From 1917 to 1967, the Budapest Quartet was our standard of excellence. They actually began with three Hungarians and a Dutchman, who were eventually supplanted by four Russians, but the group still bore the name of Hungary's capital.

Quartet nomenclature took another turn with the emergence of the Curtis, the Hollywood, the Juilliard, the La Salle and the Claremont Quartets. The La Salle and Claremont quartets took their names from streets surrounding their members' alma mater, the old Juilliard School of Music. The next wave took on a host of composers' names, from the Amadeus and the Alban Berg, to the Smetana and the Ysaÿe Quartets, with lots of others, like Beethoven and Shostakovich, in between. A few settled for cities or states of the Union like the Philadelphia, the Los Angeles, and the Iowa, or countries, like the Hungarian, the New Hellenic, the American, and the Quartettto Italiano. A few even named themselves after famous luthiers like the Amati, the Stradivari. In the case of the Guarneri Quartet, their cellist David Soyer, claims that the name was derived, not from the esteemed family of violin makers, but instead from David's barber.

Nowadays, all bets are off, and we have quartets with names like the Carpe Diem String Quartet, the Bolshoi Theatre Quartet, the Kronos Quartet, and unconventional names in all capital letters like FLUX, JACK, and the ETHEL (no, not the alcohol), who perform standard repertoire and neglected music, and enlarge the already vast quartet literature by commissioning and recording new works.

String quartet players must first learn the "book," meaning

they must become well acquainted with Quartets by Haydn, Mozart, Beethoven, and Schubert. Learning this repertoire serves to sharpen their musical intelligence, and hone their technical chops, intonation (no end to that), phrasing, attention to balance, and ensemble skills.

Without the luxury of a college residency or a patron to provide a stable financial base, string quartet life involves a delicate balance between musical gratification and the struggle to survive. Much of the string quartet repertoire was (and is being) written by highly-skilled and introspective composers, and much of it represents a depth of feeling that, unlike symphonic or operatic music, is not intended for "playing to the crowd." Composers' goals in string quartet writing are often lofty and ambitious, and learning to perform these works, especially those by the best contemporary composers, is like money in the bank, right next to the account that has accumulated daily deposits of technique from years of practicing.

An important first step to string quartet happiness is to learn the importance of decorum (hopefully, not the hard way). Quartet decorum involves both psychology and teamwork. A college course in psychology might help, but perhaps not as much as a degree from the college of hard knocks. Part of a quartet's "chemistry" involves being able to offer musical suggestions respectfully. I have found that the best way to offer suggestions is by simply playing a phrase in question in various ways, as opposed to than talking about it endlessly. Equally important is the ability to accept criticism positively, while still asserting your personality. The repertoire you are privileged to play will become your undying passion. If you are lucky, and if all goes well, it might become your life's work.

When I first sat down to play with Harold Kohon, the first violinist of the Kohon Quartet, I found him to be such a natural on the instrument, that he almost seemed to be the product of some mad geneticist commissioned to create the most efficient violin-playing unit ever. He was physically gifted with a short, powerful physique (he was once an amateur wrestler), long arms, strong hands and fingers, and a warm smile. Sharp-as-a tack mentally, his one certifiable crime was being an incurable punster: off to the punitentiary with him, I say!

Harold studied with Mishel Piastro in New York, went to Curtis, and continued his studies in Paris with Georges Enescu. Harold was a soloist with the National Symphony Orchestra under Leon Barzin in Carnegie Hall, and with the Royal Philharmonic in London. He was concertmaster of the NBC Opera Orchestra, and later became the concertmaster of the Baltimore Symphony.

The Kohon Quartet had been together for a number of years before I joined, and I knew that I had chosen well for my first chamber music group. My first run-through with the quartet brought smiles all around, so we put our heads together to plan our first program, and then settled into some serious rehearsing. I was flattered when Richard Kay asked if I might like to sit in with the Quartet, but I had no idea about the degree of commitment that playing in a string quartet required.

Initially we rehearsed at Richard's home on Bedford Avenue in Brooklyn, which was very close to where I lived, but since most of us freelanced in Manhattan during the day, we agreed to move our rehearsals to Harold's inexpensive ($65 a month, I believe) rent-controlled apartment in the Bronx, near Mt. Eden Avenue and the Grand Concourse. This was in the colorful neighborhood of Molly Picon, when she became famous on radio and TV with her leaning-out-of-the-window call of "Yoohoo, Mrs. Bloom."

There were many new pieces to learn, so we usually had five three-hour rehearsals a week. Sometimes we rehearsed even longer. Rehearsing in the Bronx worked out well for the other members, but attempting to commute by subway and bus, especially after my late night gigs and Broadway shows didn't work for me. My only option was to drive from Brooklyn to the Bronx (and everywhere else). New York drivers are unquestionably the best in the land, the ultimate drivers (BMW take note), since Darwin's law clearly states that only the fittest may survive going cross-town at rush hour.

Harold was a committed collector of fine violins and bows. At one point he played a rare violin by Guarneri del Jesu, and one by Jean-Baptiste Vuillaume. He also owned two very rare violin bows made by Nicholas Kittel, a Russian bow maker of German origin. Harold was soft spoken and openly warm, though he continued to be a wrestling devotee. He lived modestly with his devoted wife Pauline, and his violinist daughter Isadora, and lots of wrestling magazines, that were strewn about the apartment along with all of his precious instruments.

Our second violinist Raymond Kunicki, was a friendly, tall, and well-dressed guy of Ukrainian origin. He was a solid, dependable player, and the owner of a fine violin made by a member of the Guadagnini family. Ray was "skinny as a rail," one of those rare metabolically-anointed types that you read about. He could eat all of us under the table easily in any Greek diner. I was impressed by his old white Ford Falcon; a terrible car, but he kept it running forever. Our cellist, Dick Kay, was a bit of a character. His normal voice was a low-pitched growl, and he bore an unnerving resemblance to your basic Chicago mobster straight out of *Guy and Dolls*, but he was a gentleman to a fare-thee-well, in both his style of dress and his manners. He appeared to be driven by a father who pushed him to be a soloist, and he once played a solo cello tour in Asia for the State Department. He owned a fine old cello made by Matteo Goffriller.

Almost all of Goffriller's cellos were cut down in size after the 18th century. They were made to be used as church basses, and hung by a string around the player's neck while he walked down the aisles. Goffriller's instruments normally feature wide-grained wood and a dark brown varnish. Pablo Casals , Mischa Maisky, and many other cellists favor Goffriller's cellos for their dark and mellow sound.*

---

* George Sopkin, the cellist of the Fine Arts Quartet, owned a lovely, rich-sounding Goffriller, and in the 1970s, a few years after I joined, he traded it for another Goffriller that had a darker and even more powerful sound. I began playing a very rare viola made by Johannes Baptiste Guadagnini in order to better match the vibrant sound of George's new Goffriller.

Dick's Goffriller had lived a long and eventful life. It had sustained many repairs, and it wasn't in top condition, but it did have the tone quality for which Goffriller is justly famous. Dick bought his cello from Rembert Wurlitzer (of the House of Wurlitzer) and was looking to improve himself with a yet finer instrument (weren't we all?). One day he had the *chutzpah* to show up at our rehearsal with Gregor Piatigorsky's famous Domenico Montagnana cello, made in 1739 in Venice. It was a magnificent large instrument that Grisha had named the "Sleeping Beauty." It surely must have been worth a fortune, so who did Dick think he was kidding? Our eyes bugged out when Dick pulled it from the case, but as soon as he put a bow to this raging beast, it simply drowned out the entire quartet. Back to Wurlitzer it went (just think of the money he saved).

We were beginning to make a name for ourselves in the New York scene, but our concert fees alone hardly sufficed, and the salaries from the residencies mentioned in our publicity were non-existent. It was still financially necessary for me to continue freelancing, so my life remained varied and quite challenging. The IRS was very fussy about certain musicians' falsely-claimed expenses, so I was obliged to keep detailed records of every little item in case of an audit. At this remove, I'm having lots of giggles looking through them, thinking about the amount of trouble I went through for so little.

A story went around town about a fiddle player who was audited by the IRS because he had claimed a deduction of almost $1,000 for strings. The auditor, who was a violinist himself, knew this claim was pure BS, because nobody could possibly go through that many violin strings in one year. But since the claim was so audacious (I've refrained from using a stronger word here), the IRS auditor let him get away with it (just this one time).

I had to fight the daily rush hour traffic driving from East Flatbush, through the Brooklyn Battery Tunnel, over to East River Drive and Bruckner Boulevard (you wouldn't go that way today) all the way up to the Bronx for morning quartet rehearsals at Harold's apartment. Then I would drive back to Manhattan to search for a parking space, on the street if possible, or perhaps in a lot that wasn't too far from my last gig. I would get to my first city gig on foot, by bus, or by subway, schlepping my viola case, a music bag, and, if I had a concert to play that night, a garment bag containing my tails or tuxedo.

If I had a concert at night, I would wear my satin-striped black formal trousers and what passed for concert shoes during the day to save weight in that darned bag. If I happened to have a session with the highly-paid recording crowd, someone would inevitably razz me for being a mere peasant, i.e. one of those low-paid serfs who depended on playing classical concerts for their sustenance. Leonard Arner, equally famous for his pure, beautiful oboe sound, and his acid tongue, was one of my more frequent hecklers. The class system in this crowd was evident, but in Arner's defense, I probably did look like an overworked gypsy when I tried to hail a cab.

Since Harold Kohon was a steady customer at Wurlitzer, and I had joined Harold's quartet, Rembert Wurlitzer found a viola that he thought would work in the quartet. It was a lovely sounding instrument, with a light gold varnish, that was easy to play. Its maker was an early Dutch (or Flemish) maker named Jan van Jacobus, whose work was often mistaken for something made by the Italian Amati family. I enjoyed playing it for a few weeks, both at home and in the quartet, but its price of three thousand dollars was more than we could afford (my total earnings for that year amounted to a little over ten thousand dollars before taxes). After my quick fling with the lovely Jacobus viola, I had to return it. The instrument was subsequently sold to my good friend Harold Coletta, an excellent violist. It became a genuine Amati, according to another expert, following Rembert Wurlitzer's death. As to who the maker really was, I recall the words of the Jewish radio comedian Jack Pearl, who got a laugh by rebutting his straight man, Ben Bard, in his famous "Baron Munchausen" "routine in a pseudo-German accent, "Vas you dere, Shaarrlie?"

Harold Kohon was one of the busiest freelancers in town. He would often be called to play concertmaster for every sort of gig, from concerts to film scores, TV shows, and jingles. He was the sole violinist with Joseph Gallichio's band for John Gambling's 6:00 a.m. show on WOR radio called "Rambling with Gambling." Harold once got called for a week's worth of very lucrative recording sessions that conflicted with Gambling's morning show, so rather than calling in a regular violinist to sub for him (one who might barge in on his territory), he loaned me a violin, and asked me to fill in for him for that week. It turned out to be quite an enlivening (and scary) experience.

Joe Gallicio's band played its own arrangements of "The Light Cavalry Overture" and Rossini's "William Tell Overture" (shades of the Lone Ranger) between announcements, and they also played back-up under John's talking throughout the show. When I arrived at the studio the first morning (there was no rehearsal) I found some semi-classical fiddle parts and some pop tunes in manuscript sitting on my stand for me to sight read. The handwritten parts were full of slightly-familiar and barely-legible music symbols that indicated where to start, to stop, and where to repeat from the beginning. Joe directed the band with signals, raising one, two, or three fingers to show how many times to repeat a section underscoring John's weather reports, ads, or late breaking news spots. We had to start and stop on a dime without goofing. The six or so members of this small band all knew the pop routines by heart, but I was playing a slightly-foreign instrument and hanging on for dear life.

I got very little sleep that week. I had to leave Brooklyn at 4:30 a.m in order to make it to Manhattan's garment district for the 6:00 a.m. broadcasts, and I got stuck in the early morning traffic jams while looking for parking spaces. After my scary two-hour stint was over, I'd hang around town for hours (the show ended at 8:00 a.m.) and wait until it was time to play the rest of my gigs for the day and the evening, on viola.

I was getting better known in town as a quartet player (my name was even mentioned occasionally in the papers) and there were new opportunities for me in New York's music world. The Quartet was becoming known for playing worthwhile music by contemporary composers, which might have been one reason why Columbia University asked us to be their string quartet in residence (an appointment without a salary). A string quartet in residence on the faculty of a university is considered to be a feather in its academic cap. It's often a major part of their student music program, and it serves the school's local mission by performing concerts for the community.

Our first official concert at Columbia took place at their McMillan Theater on April 18, 1959. Howard Shanet conducted the university orchestra for a performance of Ludwig Spohr's Concerto for String Quartet and Orchestra, Op. 131. The rarely-performed Spohr is quite dated in style, and is a real bear technically. It offers ample opportunity for each member of the quartet to play exposed three-octave arpeggios up and down the fingerboard. We also gave the premiere of "Fantasia for String Quartet and Orchestra," by Columbia's faculty composer Otto Luening, a work specially commissioned for us. Though the concert gave us some prestige, Columbia's administration seemed to have little reason for our presence. The only money we received for the two years we spent there was when one of the professors paid us out of pocket to play for his wedding ceremony at Low Library. It was not difficult for New York University to lure us downtown with a rather minor position, because their residency came with a bit of remuneration for the five concerts we played in our first season.

As part of the New York chamber music scene we found ourselves performing alongside the prestigious Budapest and Kroll String Quartets, and the legendary pianist Mieczslaw Horszowski. There were at least five newspapers in New York at the time, and their music critics took the Kohon Quartet seriously.

A reviewer at the *Herald-Tribune* wrote about our "solid performances" and "innate musicality." We seemed to be ahead of the curve in our choice of repertoire, playing less-often-heard staples of the literature and premieres of new compositions.

During the 1950s and 60s record shops carried many recorded versions of standard orchestral repertoire, but there weren't many recorded versions of non-standard repertoire (like the Mahler symphonies) in their stacks. There were adventurous record companies like Vox, Vanguard, Nonesuch, and CRI, who were on the lookout for well-regarded performers to record less-often recorded music. After hearing the Kohon Quartet play a concert, George H. de Mendelssohn-Bartholdy, one of the founders of Vox Records (and a fourth-generation descendent of composer Felix Mendelssohn), asked us to make some recordings for his budget-priced Vox Boxes.

There's a wonderful story about George Mendelssohn-Bartholdy and the German conductor Otto Klemperer. While they were visiting a record store together, Klemperer asked the clerk, "Do you have Klemperer conducting Beethoven's Fifth?" "No," the clerk replied. "We only have it conducted by Ormandy and Toscanini. Why do you want it by Klemperer?" "Because I am Klemperer," the conductor replied indignantly. "Right," the clerk said sarcastically, nodding at his companion. "And that, I suppose, is Beethoven?" "No," Klemperer said with a smile. "That's Mendelssohn."

During the 1962–1963 season we played nine Dvořák quartets on a three-concert series at the 92nd Street YMHA, the first all-Dvořák quartet cycle to be performed in America. We also performed his mature and gorgeous Seventh Quartet, Op. 105, at a special concert sponsored by the Czechoslovak National Council, in celebration of the unveiling of a Dvořák statue at Lincoln Center.

Only seven of Dvořák's quartets were in print at the time, and our performances of the "new" quartets were listed on the program as "world premieres." The scores and parts for three previously-unknown works (Op. 16 in A minor, Op. 34 in D minor, and Op. 2 in A major) were provided to us by Dvořák's official State Biographer. The A-major Quartet is an extremely long work with a very strong Wagnerian imprint, and we didn't dare to make cuts in it for its first outing.

After our Dvořák concerts at the 92nd Street Y, Mendelssohn asked us to record the nine Dvořák quartets we played for a series of three Vox Boxes. A reviewer for *High Fidelity* Magazine wrote in the February 1963 issue that, "Listening to this [first] album is a voyage of real discovery." The reviewer lauded the superior stereo quality of the recordings, and said he "looked forward with pleasure to the release of its two sequels."*

The Kohons played a concert for recorder and strings at the 92nd Street Y with Theodora and Richard Schulze's Telemann Society, and then we recorded the program on a Vox album. After a concert we played with clarinetist David Glazer (whom I had known from my days in the Cleveland Orchestra), we made a Vox album of the Hummel and Weber Clarinet Quintets. We offered our Carnegie Recital Hall audience the three emotionally-charged string quartets of Robert Schumann in one sitting, and the *New York Times*' music critic Howard Taubman wrote such a highly favorable review that we were engaged to repeat the program at the National Gallery in Washington, D.C. As a result, Vox engaged us to record all three Schumann Quartets and the three Brahms Quartets (six quartets on three LPs) in a single Vox Box: quite a bargain.

We recorded at a studio in Englewood Cliffs, New Jersey that Rudy van Gelder built in 1959. Inspired by the work of Frank Lloyd Wright, with high ceilings with long supporting wooden arches, it was an acoustical dream. After a busy day of freelancing, we would cross the George Washington Bridge (using the lower level, snidely called the "Martha Washington") to reach New Jersey for our many sessions.

These were magical nights of intense music making, and we got back home late, bushed but happy. Vox paid us pitiably little for recordings, and we didn't get any residual payments, regardless of how many albums were sold. A typical five-hour recording session, that resulted in recording a single Brahms Quartet (that took months of rehearsals and performances to season to our satisfaction), would net each of us exactly $42.57

---

* People still seem to remember these recordings. During the summer of 2009, Masumi Per Rostad, the violist of the Pacifica Quartet, came to visit me at my home in Stanford. Imagine my surprise and delight when he told me, while we were standing in my garage and looking at my Vox Box collection of Kohon LP recordings, that he had grown up with these Dvořák Vox Boxes, and that he still enjoyed listening to them.

(in 1962 dollars), but it was an important way to further our career. When word got around about the sound quality of van Gelder's studio, we found ourselves in competition for session time with the likes of Miles Davis, Django Reinhardt, Sonny Rollins, John Coltrane, Stan Getz, Herbie Hancock, Cannonball Adderley, Hank Mobley, and Gil Evans. We also made commercial recordings in New York for Vanguard, the company started by Maynard and Seymour Solomon, my former plumbing supply customers. One was with Joan Baez, one was an album of Yiddish folk songs with folk singer and actor Theo Bickel, and another had arrangements by Peter Schickele (of P.D.Q. Bach fame).

Due to the efforts of pianist John Kirkpatrick (not to be confused with the harpsichordist Ralph Kirkpatrick) and Bruce Shepherd, the Librarian for the Ives Collection at Yale University, the music of Charles Ives was finally being played in New York. "The Unanswered Question," and "Central Park in the Dark," his first two symphonies, and the huge "Concord Sonata" for solo piano were being performed by a few hardy souls, and the public was learning to acquire a taste for Ives' brand of odd and folksy Americana.

The Cooper Union held a series of contemporary music concerts on the very stage where Abraham Lincoln addressed the issue of slavery in 1860. These chamber orchestra concerts were free to the public, and featured commentary by the conductor, and a discussion that followed each work. Since the area was in the East Village, between Sixth and Seventh streets, the concerts attracted a few homeless people who simply wanted to come in from the cold.

On January 15, 1960 I took part in a Cooper Union performance of Charles Ives' "The Unanswered Question" for strings, trumpet and four flutes. The strings were seated on stage, and the flutes and trumpet were strategically placed in the doorways at the back of the hall and behind the boxes. The strings played a slow hymn in one meter, while the four flutes screamed their occasional shrill outbursts in another meter. Every so often the trumpet would enter with a five-note motif that

Ives describes in the score as "the eternal question of existence."

Following some scattered applause, our conductor turned to the audience for their reaction. One member of the audience, who was seated toward the back of the hall, rose shakily to his feet and said that he hated it. When asked if that were the case, why he didn't he simply get up and leave the hall, he responded, "Well, I tried to git the heck outta there, but there was always some idiot playing some goddam instrument or other blocking the exit doors."

The Kohons had the honor of playing the American premiere (the first performance to be documented) of Ives' complete First Quartet on April 24, 1957, at New York's Museum of Modern Art. Vox asked us to record both of the Ives Quartets, and since there wasn't yet a recording to be had on the shelves of record shops, we decided to jump into the breach. In 1957 the only available parts for the highly-programmatic Second Quartet were barely decipherable, and they didn't have any dynamics. Yale University's Ives Collection finally provided usable parts for us, and we were able to release the first recording of both works in 1963. The notes were written by Dr. William B. Ober, and they included portions of the manuscript with comments by the composer. The folks at Vox had the wisdom to place a reproduction of Grant Wood's iconic painting "American Gothic" on the record jacket, which may have helped to sell out the first pressing. They quickly released a second printing on their "cheapie" Vox Turnabout label, but we never got an extra penny for the reissue: we were regarded monetarily as the hired help.

In the first of the two quartets, "A Revival Service," Ives quotes liberally from a variety of popular 19th-century American church hymns. Each of the four movements has a subtitle: "Chorale," "Prelude," "Offertory" and "Postlude." Near the close of the Postlude, the first violin and the viola play together in 3/4 time against the second violin and cello in 4/4 time; quite forward-thinking for a piece written in 1896 by a 21-year-old!

Ives started sketching his Second Quartet in 1907, and he completed it in 1913. The three movements have purely programmatic titles: "Discussions," "Arguments," and "The Call of the Mountains." The manuscript has a pencilled-in annotation from Ives that reads, "From the Salvation Army, NOT QUITE, and the old green anthem book." It's a different cup of New England tea, often dissonant and blustery, where four men (in the composer's words) "converse, discuss, argue (in re 'Politick'), fight, shake hands, shut upthen walk up the mountain side to view the firmament."

Ives created a foil named "Rollo" who is played by the quartet's second violinist. Rollo gets little tunes to play. One is called "Andante emasculata." (Ives was fond of calling music that was too consonant or too classical "emasculated" music). Rollo tries futilely to reconcile his three disputatious friends, while Ives offers sarcastic remarks in the manuscript like, "Cut it Out, Rollo!" and "Too hard to play—so it just can't be good music, Rollo." He later says, "Beat time, Rollo!" After he plays a rather florid passage, Ives tells Rollo to "Join in again, Professor, all in the key of C. You can do that nice and pretty."*

We had beaten the excellent Juilliard Quartet to the punch, so to speak, since our Ives Quartet recording was released before their recording came out. Irving Kolodin of *Harper's* gave us a good review, and compared our recording with the Juilliard's. In the *All Music Guide*, Uncle Dave Lewis wrote, "Experienced ears are starved for more "love" in this music—a case of point would be the old Vox LP of the First Quartet by the Kohon String Quartet, where the music is handled lovingly, and not in a winking, tongue-in-cheek manner."

Richard Kay left the Kohon Quartet in 1962 to try for a solo cello career. Eventually he joined the Metropolitan Opera Orchestra, where he remained for many years. Ray Schweitzer, a very busy session player at one of the big radio networks, became

---

* The idea of a program being written into a piece of absolute music can be "geared for failure," as Harold Kohon used to say. In his Second Quartet, Ives uses American band tunes he heard during his childhood—people marching every which way—as a metaphor for "demos," the essence of the American democracy that infused him. Here, after two movements of discussion and argument, four protagonists come together to shake hands, and find existential peace. One of Mahler's tortured *sturm und drang* movements, with their thematic contrasts, may finally resolve in peaceful harmony, but it took Charles Ives to employ easily recognizable tunes from his New England childhood to resolve the eternal conflict of man.

The Kohon String Quartet
Harold Kohon, Raymond Kunicki, Raymond Schweitzer, and Bernard Zaslav

the Quartet's new cellist. He performed Alban Berg's rarely-heard Op. 3 Quartet with us in Carnegie Recital Hall, and is on our recording of the Berg that Vox released in 1962 (the Ramor Quartet's recording of Schoenberg's Second Quartet is on the other side). Ray was pink-cheeked and hearty looking, but very shortly after he joined the quartet, he died of a sudden heart attack. We were stunned. He was so young and in his prime.

Our recording of the Berg was awarded the *Academie Charles Gros Grand Prix du Disque* in 1964. Irving Kolodin remarked, in the *Saturday Review*, that we "command the razor-sharp intonation and the precise rhythmic control to give Berg's patterns their due in both indispensable respects," and there were similarly complimentary reviews from *High Fidelity* and *Hi Fi Stereo Review*. Harold, who is living in a retirement home, told me that he still keeps the gold-mounted trophy on his shelf as a memento of our wonderful times together.

I met our next cellist, Robert Sylvester, while I was playing a trio concert at the Museum of Modern Art with Isidore Cohen, the second violinist of the Juilliard Quartet. Bobbie was an excellent cellist who had studied with Harvey Shapiro at Juilliard. He was richly talented, but he kept mum about his age. He actually turned out to be even younger than his claimed age of eighteen, something I discovered only later, when we became closer friends. Our hot-shot new cellist had chops to burn and a beautiful warm sound, and we all were happy to be playing concerts and making recordings with him. I hope it wasn't a case of bad breath on our part, but he also left the Quartet to pursue a solo career, and then he joined the faculty of the Eastman School of Music. He was married to a wonderful flutist named Paula Robison, who was making a career of her own. Nomi and I became very close with both of them. They shared our passion for antiques, and seemed to regard our relationship as some sort of a model for happy marriage, although their marriage didn't last very long. When our daughter Claudia became interested in playing the flute, she studied with Paula.

Aaron Shapinsky was the next (and my last) Kohon cellist. He was a serious, thoughtful person and a dedicated performer. He owned a remarkably rich-sounding Goffriller cello that produced a dark, powerful tone. Though his cello was in unusually fine condition, Aaron was incredibly fussy with it, and actually changed bridges between movements when we recorded the Ives Quartets at van Gelder's studio. Aaron was exceedingly proud of his pianist son Ian, who grew up to have a brilliant career.

Aaron's brother played the bass in the Pittsburgh Symphony under Fritz Reiner. The bass section stood at the back of the orchestra at some distance from the conductor, and since Reiner had a notoriously small beat, the story goes that, in jest, his brother once brought a telescope to rehearsal, for a better view of the conductor's "vest-pocket" beat. He was, of course, summarily fired. This sad tale seems to have gotten around to so many musicians that I imagine that there might be some truth to it.

After my fling with the Jacobus-turned-Amati viola from Wurlitzer, it became clear that the seventeen-and-a-quarter-inch Gaetano Chiocci viola that Mischa Mischakoff found for me was simply too cumbersome, so I traded it for a sixteen-and-five-eighths-inch instrument made by Frederick Haenel, a Saxony-born maker who moved to Winnipeg and settled in Toronto. I used that Haenel viola for all the recordings I made with the Kohons.

Harold was smiling mysteriously when I arrived at his apartment for a rehearsal one day. He opened a small case that was sitting on his couch and said, "Look what I found for you." I lifted a beautiful old viola out of the case, but because of its small size, I smirked the usual violist's smirk. "Harold, how come you're showing me this ladies' size viola?" (There was a tradition among instrument makers to make slightly smaller-than-full-size violins and cellos for use by women, hence the term.) Violists have this perennial neurosis that they won't be heard in competition with fiddles and cellos if they play a smaller instrument, and some conductors seem to believe that size equals volume. Consequently, many players and even a few of my students, continue to harm themselves by playing overly large instruments, hoping to show the boss how much sound he can produce for the salary the boss is willing to pay. Harold's response was curt, "Bernie, just shut up and play it."

I did as he asked, and was immediately knocked out by its quality of sound. Though it was almost an inch shorter in body length than my Haenel, I was amazed at how much pure viola tone issued from its f-holes, and how quickly I was able to adjust to it. I guess the usual violist's prejudice was uncalled for, especially taking Lillian Fuchs' fifteen-and-a-half-inch Gasparo viola into consideration. This viola, that was the same length as Lillian's, had a tone of pure gold, and it was a cinch to play, right off the bat.

Harold said he learned about the instrument from a violinist that he worked with on a recording date. This guy said he knew the woman who owned it (see?), and that she wanted X amount of dollars for it. The person from Harold's recording date turned out to be that same violinist who ran into Jacques Francais's shop, yelling, "Sell me anything." This remarkable instrument bore a label that said it had been made by Giuseppe Odoardi (1685–1750) in Ascoli Piceno, but genuine or not, it was the epitome of true viola sound for me. I played its lovely heart out from that day forward, until another wonderful day in 1974 when an even greater instrument became available.

While I may have thought of myself as a promising artist, money-wise I was still a poor schnook. We haggled, and finally agreed on a price of somewhat less than the X number of dollars, plus a bow made in 1926 (my birth year). My new instrument really was a rarity, and musicians always commented about how much sound and projection was possible from such a small viola. I learned from the seller that it had come through Joseph Settin's shop on West 57th Street. Joe was famous for gabbing all day long with his clients, and then getting to the actual repairs rather hurriedly after he closed the shop. I once gave him a fine French bow to re-hair, and when it came back I saw that he had somehow split the silver ferrule (the part that holds the ribbon of hair flat at the frog) by inserting too thick a wedge into it. He didn't tell me what happened, and simply re-soldered the ferrule. I did notice it later, so that was the last re-hair I had done by him.

Since Settin had known my new instrument's previous owner, I dropped into his shop between gigs, where I was startled to see Mischa Elman, one of the greatest violinists of the century. He was waiting for Joe to finish his bridge adjustment. Hearing Mischa Elman and Jascha Heifetz records on our old Victrola had changed my life, and seeing this idol of mine standing right there in front of me rendered me practically speechless. I meekly greeted Mr. Elman.

Joe was taking quite a bit of time with that bridge, so Mr. Elman looked at the viola that I removed from my case and in that famously (and surprisingly) squeaky voice of his, he asked me about it, and asked me to play a few notes for him. He listened to it for a bit, and then he asked if I would be so kind as to let him try it. I was thrilled. But a sudden horrifying thought hit me just as he was putting it under his chin. In those years the parking meters in front of his building on West 57th had to be plugged with quarters, and meter maids and tow trucks did a good business on that busy thoroughfare. I had been lucky enough to find a meter right in front of Settin's building, but I suddenly realized that while I was waiting for him to finish up with Elman, the meter must have run out.

Petrified (my livelihood depended on being able to use my car), I stammered shamefacedly that I had to run for an appointment and couldn't accept his generous offer to play my instrument. Imagine how stupid I felt in rebuffing this idol of my youth, by plucking my viola out of his hands only to feed a meter. I didn't have the nerve to watch his face as I closed the door behind me, and I cringed in shame all the way to my still un-ticketed car.

Elman's father was vest-button-popping proud of his famous son, and he boasted to all and sundry that no fiddle player alive could top his boy. Mischa usually played his yearly Carnegie Hall recital to full houses, but things were changing in the violin world. He was getting older, and playing concertos with orchestras drew larger fees. There was less to be risked playing a concerto than in playing a recital to a less-than-full house.

There's a story about an old crony of Elman's father meeting him on the street one day and asking, "How is it I don't see your Mischa playing recitals lately? Isn't he feeling well? Is it maybe he doesn't like us any more? What's going on?" The response came, "Well, I'll tell you how it is. Mischa himself is just fine, but lately it seems that Fritz (Kreisler) isn't playing much, Jascha (Heifetz) you rarely see nowadays, Nathan (Milstein) hasn't been around lately, and from Menuhin you don't hear. Erika Morini and Enescu, they're mostly playing in Europe and, just between you and me (don't let it get around I said it), it seems that Szigeti, bless his heart, is past it. So tell me, my friend, against *whom* shall he play?"

For another tall tale, you must provide the imaginary locale: it could be Vermont's Marlboro Festival, or Music Mountain in Connecticut, or any summer music camp (gulag) of your choice. Here, the eager and overambitious students (inmates) are required to spend at least eight to ten hours a day practicing, till the blood seeps from their fingertips. But, by golly, they're gonna get to Carnegie Hall or bust.

It's usual for all these insanely competitive wannabes to meet weekly in the dining hall, conference area, or concert space, where the grand eminence himself holds court. Here you may select from a menu of celebrated violin pedagogues of the past: Eugène Ysaÿe, Otakar Ševčík, Joseph Fuchs, Raphael Bronstein (who taught over a thousand students during his 65-year career), Ivan Galamian, Josef Gingold, or perhaps even have the ghost of Leopold Auer, as the lead villain. Imagine further that the grand pooh-bah sits in state, like George Lucas' Jabba the Hut, and rummages around in his fast-becoming-senile brain to tell his favorite *geschichten* about the good old days: who envied whom, who despised whom, who stole fingerings from him, who wished that the concert manager Sol Hurok should only *plotz*, or what good are conductors, anyway.

The subject for his spiel tonight veers from the usual blather about vibrato, bowing, and phrasing, to an entirely new subject, namely, how limiting it can be for these inmates to practice their études endlessly, without a thought about improving their minds.

So, he begins, "Sure, from Kreutzer, from Paganini, from Vieuxtemps, from these guys, you know already. But tell me (he asks archly), does any one of you know the least little bit about history, about art, literature, or science? While you *kratz* on those *farkakte* fiddles of yours, don't you realize there's a whole *world* out there? Has any one of you ever sat down to read a *book*? Is there nothing else in your life except the *farshtunkene* fiddle?"

A small hand rises timidly from the back: it's (no surprise) the pale, bespectacled Melvin. "Maestro" he says. "I read books, I read them all the time." To which the maestro thunders, "Yes Melvin, I know that you read. *You* should practice!"

Modern technology has changed some things for the better, but lots of the above-mentioned woodshedding is still needed to compete in today's world of incredibly high technical achievement. Of course, a pianist deals with the entirety of a musical work, and can perform alone, but players of other instruments must decide how they will pursue their careers. Qualified instrumentalists can opt to join an orchestra (if they are fortunate enough to be chosen) or pursue solo careers (if they are blazingly talented, well-supported, *and* extremely lucky).

One can reach ever higher, in the mind of many, for the supreme luxury of pursuing chamber music as a way of life. Such an ambition must surely lurk in the heart of every string player who has ever played a quartet by Haydn or Schubert, but along with that luxury comes the high price of total dedication. In effect, you must pledge your troth to your chosen colleagues, knowing that such a commitment will demand your trust, your respect, your allegiance, and most of your time. It will affect every personal and familial decision you make, even more so if you should go on to achieve success. Playing a gig, a recording, a show, or a jingle, is normally a one time deal; you do your job and it's over—goodbye Chaarrlie. If you did it well, there could possibly be a reengagement (or not). But the many hours spent in rehearsing as a quartet will serve to hone your technical skill and improve your ability to play your own part while you interact with three other contrapuntal lines. It stretches your mind as no other endeavor possibly can.

Since the grocer demands hard cash, a steady symphony orchestra position is far more secure. The biggest downside of playing in a full-time orchestra used to be getting "stuck" playing Beethoven's Fifth some twenty times a year, but things have changed for the better. Conductors now tend to perform more contemporary music, and they vary their programs in order to fill halls and keep audiences awake.

Four accomplished musicians from within the string section of an orchestra might share a common point of view and decide to form a string quartet. This was the case with the Fine Arts Quartet in 1946, whose original members came from the string section of the Chicago Symphony under conductor Frederick Stock, when they began playing concerts on radio station WFMT in Chicago. Today, we see the emergence of graduate string quartet programs at many universities and conservatories, hiring prominent quartets-in-residence to coach new crops of student quartets. It is interesting to consider how those quartets-in-residence learned their stuff. Musical tradition has its value, but with the Kohons in the 1950s, and the other quartets I joined thereafter, we invented our own wheel, so to speak. Each Quartet created its individual profile, and learned, through years of collective experience, what worked and what didn't. Quartets are blessed with an enormous repertoire (most every composer has taken up the challenge), and this perfectly-evolved form continues to invite the most innovative minds to the party.

The Kohon Quartet was making an enviable place for itself in the chamber music world, and we felt lucky to be able to fill a particular niche in New York with our choice of repertoire (the Budapest could only play so many concerts). As for an income stream, Papa Haydn got his support from the Esterhazy family, and the Berkshire String Quartet derived theirs from Mrs. Elizabeth Sprague Coolidge, but our financial sustenance depended on freelance gigs and Broadway. Because we didn't have a sustainable financial base, three of our four cellists left the quartet (sadly the second one died). Dick Kay left for the Metropolitan Opera Orchestra, and Bobby Sylvester had joined the faculty of the Eastman School of Music.

Violinist Kenneth Gordon, a protégé of Mishel Piastro, tried to keep alive his solo aspirations alive while sitting in the first violin section of the New York Philharmonic, so I considered joining the New York Philharmonic at one time. But after being in the viola section of the Cleveland Orchestra under Szell, I knew that the quartet experience, and its repertoire, was far preferable. I decided to continue freelancing until a sustainable quartet residency became a reality.

Freelancing put me in contact with many supremely competent and like-minded performers (and composers) of the day. I was often called for recording sessions with people who went on to truly successful careers as quartet players. Cellist David Soyer joined the Guarneri Quartet, and Allen Ohmes inspired us all by leaving town to join the faculty of the University of Iowa as first violinist of the Stradivari Quartet.

I had played a few contemporary music concerts with Matthew Raimondi, and felt that the music coming out of the current crop of contemporary composers (like Milton Babbitt, Elliot Carter, Roger Sessions, and Gunther Schuller), was interesting and challenging. Since I had been looking at a few other chamber music possibilities in town with various groups, and felt there were other options I wished to pursue, I told Harold that he might think about replacing me. Violist Eugenie Dengel had worked with him previously, and after I left, she rejoined the Kohon Quartet in time to record their album of quartets by early American composers, including Chadwick, Loeffler, Griffes and even old Benjamin Franklin.

I wasn't quite sure where the next road led, but in the meantime I had an even stronger and more personal challenge to explore: the special, but still rather meager repertoire for viola and piano. Happily I was able to explore it with the fleet-fingered Canadian pianist from Juilliard that I married back in 1947.

CHAPTER X
Set for Two

Violinists and cellists have vast oceans of recital repertoire from which to choose, and violists can only drool over their riches. A viola and piano recital was a relatively rare animal in the early 1960s, and it was like looking for hen's teeth to find them advertised in the newspapers. Nomi and I knew that if our duo was to succeed, it wasn't going to happen by playing the same-old, same-old. Since the Kohons had made much of their reputation by playing music by contemporary composers, Nomi and I decided to ask a few of those composers to write music for our duo.

The Kohon Quartet's connection with New York University offered us our first opportunity to play a duo recital at La Maison Française, New York University's charming nineteenth-century red-brick carriage house located at 16 Washington Mews. Our concert on October 24, 1961 included works for viola and piano by Antonio Vivaldi, Marin Marais, Johann Nepomuk Hummel, and Georges Enescu, and we invited composer Michael Colgrass, who was a fine percussionist, to perform his "Variations for Four Drums and Viola" with me. Mike wrote the piece originally for violist Emanuel Vardi, and I believe this may have been its second public performance. Mike agreed to incorporate a few small changes into the viola part that I suggested. Mike used adaptations of North Indian tabla-like instruments, and he tuned them softly to different pitches between movements. The rare sound produced by our dissimilar instruments was new to the ears of our audience.

Mike told me an amusing story from when he was in Europe playing percussion with the Seventh Army Symphony. Being anxious to know more about his Italian heritage (the name Colgrass was originally "Collagrassi" or something close), he made a side trip after the tour to the region of Italy from whence his parents had come. It proved to be a long and tough slog getting there, but he finally found the proper village, and he introduced himself to the family. They embraced Mike warmly and invited him to stay with them for a few days, eager to know how his folks were doing back in America. Since neither party spoke the other's language, communication was sketchy at best, but nonetheless, a grand reunion was had by all. On the day of his departure, while he was packing, the family again asked the exact name of his father, and it seemed that the ties that bind had missed their mark: Mike had been enjoying the hospitality of the wrong family.*

---

* In 1974 Mike moved to Toronto in order to enjoy Canadian support of the arts. After Nomi and I played at a Viola Congress in Toronto, we visited him and his fascinating wife, Ulna, who was writing for a journal about new music. In 1978 Mike won the Pulitzer Prize for Music for "Deja vu," a piece for four percussionists and orchestra, that the New York Philharmonic commissioned him to write. He has written a memoir called Adventures of an American Composer, and has a not-to-be missed website.

A woman who introduced herself as Nina Gordani came backstage after the concert Nomi and I played at La Maison Française. She told us that she was a personal representative and program advisor. After some conversation, we signed a contract with her. I offered her five sample programs, and hoped that she might help us make a dent as a duo. Unfortunately the only thing she ever produced was a single home concert in Larchmont, New York.

Her client brochure is really something for the ages. It features pictures of Henny Youngman, Humorist; Molly Picon, "The Darling of the World;" Tom Glazer, American Balladeer; Kajar, America's Most Televised Magician; and (best of all) Rickie Layne and Velvel, TV's most beloved ventriloquist. I think that nice lady sold us a piece of that famous bridge to Brooklyn.

Our friend Robert Parris, a fine composer (he actually wrote a really good viola concerto) and a music critic for a Washington, D.C. newspaper, arranged for Nomi and me to perform a recital at the Phillips Collection in Washington, D.C. on February 25, 1962. The program included his 1957 Sonata for Viola and Piano, a piece by Hummel, Darius Milhaud's First Sonata, and the premiere performance of the Sonata for Viola and Piano, Op. 49a, a work dedicated to us by our friend Jack Huggler. Mike and I also gave the first Washington D.C. performance of his Variations on that program. The concert garnered very favorable reviews, but our stage deportment left room for improvement. After we played Bob's piece, we blew it badly by forgetting to call our friend up for his deserved applause. We learned a never-to-be-forgotten lesson in manners. Sadly, Robert passed away while he was still quite young, and we still miss his bright warmth and musical talent.

Most artists make their official debuts when they are still young (Heifetz made his debut at age eleven). Nomi and I were both 36. We were a bit long in the tooth for a debut, but we decided that if we were ever going to make our long-delayed formal New York appearance, this was the time. Like many other impecunious would-be soloists, I gathered up the nerve to set up a meeting with Normie Seaman.

Norman J. Seaman, called a "niche impresario" in his 2009 *New York Times* obituary, was one of the most colorful and most generous of music's entrepreneurs. He was famous for producing modest "no frills" debut recitals in New York at a very affordable price. He would arrange for a performance space (usually Carnegie Recital Hall), place a small ad in the *New York Times*, and invite reviewers to the concerts. Norman's mother worked the box office, and his father took tickets at the door. Normie printed the programs, and made posters and fliers that he promised to distribute around town. Normie would split the profits from ticket sales (if there were any) with the performer after the concert.

Nomi and I posed for the usual brochure photo, handed over Normie's $180 fee, and waited in nervous anticipation for the half-inch ad to appear in the *New York Times*. Our debut took place on Saturday, October 27, 1962, at 5:30 p.m., and we performed the Hummel, the Parris, the Enescu, the Colgrass (with Mike), and closed with the viola transcription of the Brahms Sonata, Op. 120, No. 2.

Amazingly, the doors of Carnegie Recital Hall managed to withstand the onslaught of hoped-for throngs. There were some stray violists there, along with some of my colleagues who weren't working that night (I had not-so-secretly "papered" the house). My mother, who explained that my father was "at the store" that night (as usual) did not attend, but our 15-year-old son Mark came with a friend named Jay Paris, who had never heard a viola recital before. Note to Dear Herr Doktor Freud, N.B. under *Rejection*: Mommy and Daddy didn't even come to hear my debut (sob).

The *New York Times* reviewer dispatched one of their second-string reviewers, the one who was wont to fall asleep at many an avant-garde concert. He wrote of Enescu's "Concertpiece" (a really solid piece, by the way), "Why would anyone choose to program such an old potboiler?" I found out, after some research, that the piece had never been previously reviewed in New York. Now it's practically a staple of the viola literature.

My long-time violist colleague and good friend Jacob Glick was seated next to the reviewer, and Charlotte Moorman (of bare-chested avant-gardist-cello-performance fame) sat on the other side of our unnamed critic. The critic and Charlotte were deep in conversation throughout the concert, and he ended up substituting Charlotte's name for Naomi's in his review. The next day it was writ large that *Charlotte* Zaslav had proved to be quite an excellent pianist that afternoon.

Being officially "outed" as the Zaslav Duo, we sought new fields to conquer. A large part of our small niche consisted of newly commissioned music. We were invited to make our first recording as a Duo after giving the New York premiere of Wallace Berry's "Canto Lirico" at a Composer's Forum Concert at the Donnell Library on March 11, 1967. Mr. Berry then arranged for us to fly to Ann Arbor, Michigan to record the Canto on a CRI (Composers Recordings, Inc.) LP, along with some of his other works.

For one Carnegie Recital Hall concert on May 31, 1963 Nomi and I performed on a program with flutist Harvey Sollberger that included a flute and piano sonata by Howard Rovics, a work for two oboes by Sollberger, a piano trio by Charles Wuorinen, played by the composer, Sollberger, and cellist Joel Krosnick, a work for flute by Ursula Mamlok, a piano sonata by M. William Karlins, and the premiere of "Set for Two," a serial work that was written for Nomi and me in 1962 by the far-too-soon-deceased Charles Whittenberg.

We loved playing this technical romp, and showing off our new-music chops. Charles set high technical hurdles for both the viola and the piano in this spiky five-minute-long, 12-tone piece, and we would often play it twice in recitals in order to give the audience a second shot at hearing the idiom.

We got to know Charles, and his wife Mary, when we attended a few sessions of the Gurdjieff Society, a group that followed the teachings of the legendary Greek-Armenian mystic G.I. Gurdjieff. Gurdjieff, who became a minor fad in New York, wrote a series of books bearing the modest title *All and Everything*, and incorporated enchanted dancing to music by Thomas de Hartmann into his teachings.

In his wanderings, Gurdjieff learned the teachings of various Eastern religions, and he brought his own versions of those teachings to Paris during the 1920s. He died in 1949 after a spectacular automobile crash, but he remained quite popular internationally, especially among artists and musicians. Nomi and I wanted to know what the fuss was all about, and we read other books by him and his disciple P.D. Ouspensky, such as *The Fourth Way*, *In Search of the Miraculous*, and *Meetings with Remarkable Men*.

We played a duo recital at one of the Artist's Series Concerts at The New School for Social Research on December 13, 1963. Our program included Hindemith's Solo Viola Sonata, Op. 25, No. 1, the Whittenberg piece, and Roy Harris's "Soliloquy and Dance." Matt Raimondi and I played Bohuslav Martinu's "Three Madrigals" (a work written for Joe and Lillian Fuchs), and the clarinetist Arthur Bloom, and trombonist John Swallow joined me for the premiere performance of Robert Stewart's Trio No. 5, "Overture to *Doctor Faustus*" for viola, clarinet, and trombone.*

After Henry Schuman and I premiered Frank Wigglesworth's attractive, sprightly duo for oboe and viola at a contemporary music concert, Frank asked Nomi and me to present a pair of concerts at the New School for Social Research. Warren DeMotte wrote a review of the concert we played on March 12, 1965 in the April 1st issue of *The Villager*, a Greenwich Village paper. He mentioned that our duo was now "achieving a reputation for performances of contemporary music," but he had nevertheless enjoyed our playing of the Vivaldi Sonata No. 4, in an arrangement by Luigi Dallapiccola, as well as our playing of J.S. Bach's three viola da gamba sonatas (BWV 1027–9). I add blushingly that he also said, "Mr. Zaslav is a sensitive violist with a rich, dark tone that he produces with enviable ease from his splendid instrument. He played the sonatas with breadth and lyricism.

---

* After Bob Stewart joined the faculty of Washington-Lee University in Lexington, Virginia, he asked Nomi and me to play a recital at Lee Chapel. The concert on October 4, 1971 included the premiere of a viola and piano sonata that Bob wrote for us. Because of the odd angle at which the piano was situated in the hall, I was obliged to stand directly in front of Robert E. Lee's famous horse named "Traveler." It had been stuffed and mounted by an expert taxidermist, and it looked perfectly lifelike, as if Traveler were waiting for his long dead rider to appear. True tail . . . er, tale.

His intonation was secure and his musicianship stylish." As to our future, he continued, "I commend so destined a duo." It was encouraging.

Nomi and I played the premiere of a Duo for Viola and Piano written for us by Alvin Brehm for our second New School concert, on April 30, 1965. Alvin was a fabulous bass player, perhaps the best among New York's corps of excellent bassists, and he came to the concert with his pal Boris Ostrovsky, owner of the Ostrovsky Piano Company on West 56th Street, across from the Carnegie Hall stage door.

We opened the concert with Beethoven's D major Notturno, Op. 42, which is a viola and piano transcription of his Serenade for String Trio, Op. 8. A few measures into the piece, Nomi started to grimace in frustration because the middle (and very important D) key of the piano had jammed. We attempted to carry on bravely, but the situation was getting ludicrous, and we had to stop. In a trice, Boris came out of his seat and calmly walked up the steps to the stage. He leaned into the piano, fiddled around expertly with one of the hammers, and soon made everything right. He walked off, getting the hand he deserved, and we had no further piano trouble. Some years later Boris was badly injured in a motorcycle accident and we lost track of him.

I cooked up a program of duos for a Village Gate Sunday brunch concert on January 12, 1966 (viola and piano, viola and oboe, viola and violin, the Beethoven "Eyeglasses" duo for viola and cello, and Mike's Variations for viola and percussion). Carman Moore, the reviewer for the *Village Voice*, kvetched that "things are pretty dismal on the musical scene these days." He went even farther by adding, "over this scene hangs the smell of death, as the public worships everything that is old or stillborn." And then he cooled out a bit by admitting that, "The level of performance and the skill of performers on the New York stages today is incredibly high." Things were looking somewhat brighter when it came to our performance of Wilhelm Friedemann Bach's C minor Sonata, which Mr. Moore found to be "an absorbing piece." He said "the two performers, notably Mrs. Zaslav in some extremely rapid-fire passages, acquitted themselves with imagination and musical taste."

The soprano Montserrat Caballé had to cancel her February 11, 1966 recital in Lincoln Center's Philharmonic Hall, so Thomas Dunn, the conductor of the Festival Orchestra of New York (who later became the Music Director of Boston's Handel and Haydn Society) asked Nomi and me to take part in an ad-hoc chamber music program, on two day's notice.

Dunn played the harpsichord in a Bach Trio Sonata with flutist Gerardo Levy and violinist Gerald Tarack. Gerald then played the Bartók Contrasts with clarinetist George Silfies, and pianist Sue Thomas. Then cellist Fortunato Arico and pianist John Atkins played the Shostakovich Cello Sonata, Nomi and I played the W.F. Bach C minor Sonata, and finally the tenor Seth McCoy joined us for Vaughan Williams' "Four Hymns for Tenor, Viola and Piano." We received a highly favorable review in the *New York Times* for this unplanned outing.

I got another last-minute call to go somewhere in New Jersey to play a performance of the Verdi Requiem conducted by Eugene Ormandy, the conductor of the Philadelphia Orchestra. I was surprised to find myself seated at the first stand for this gig, and while I was packing up after the first rehearsal, I was told that Mr. Ormandy wanted to speak with me. I was even more surprised when Mr. Ormandy, whom I had never met, confided to me (I assume it was to be kept secret) that the Philadelphia Orchestra was seeking a principal violist for a one-year appointment. A number of string players, including their principal violist, had recently debarked from the Philadelphia Orchestra to the (rival) Boston Symphony, so I assumed they were holding the seat for someone who was not yet available.

Mr. Ormandy asked if I would like to audition for the position, right then and there. I didn't have any music with me, but I had the rather flashy Hindemith Solo Sonata in my fingers from playing it in recitals, so I gave it a go. Apparently Mr. Ormandy was sufficiently happy with what came out, so he asked me if I would accept the temporary position.

I was a little dazed by the suddenness of the offer. I considered my quartet obligations in New York and the chamber music career I was hoping to achieve. I also felt that it might be detrimental to my reputation if I were to accept such a responsible position as principal violist of the Philadelphia Orchestra and then leave after one year. I thanked him graciously and turned down the offer, but my good friend Harry Zaratzian felt differently. Harry, who is about as Armenian as one can be, affects an awful Scottish accent for his stale jokes, while wearing a rough approximation of a tam o'shanter on his head. He's a prince of a guy, and he filled in for the year with no ill consequences to his reputation as a freelancer.

Carnegie String Quartet
Lamar Alsop, Alan Martin, Ruth Alsop, and Bernard Zaslav

The name K. Lamar Alsop (I never found out what that K. was about) kept popping up among the fiddle players with whom I sloped about in my freelancing. Lamar was (and is) definitely a one-off with a wicked cool sense of humor with a remarkable background (including a Mormon mother). His foreground isn't exactly chopped liver either. He had played both violin and saxophone in Fred Waring's band, and was a professional whistler. He was the concertmaster of the New York City Ballet, a hugely responsible gig that involved standing up in the pit and playing violin concertos on demand, and he was the first violinist of the Carnegie String Quartet.

Their rather imposing name showed they had plenty of chutzpah for a group I hadn't heard of, but their *raison d'être* soon became clear. The group was a quartet of busy hotshot freelancers that participated in the work of Young Audiences, Inc., a far-thinking nonprofit organization designed to whet children's appetites for classical music. They worked with educational systems, the arts community, and organizations in the private and public sectors, to provide high-quality arts education in school classrooms. The aim of the organization was to motivate children who heard these in-school concerts to attend concerts on their own when they grew up. The Carnegie Quartet was one of Young Audiences' busiest groups.

During a recording session, Lamar mentioned that his Quartet was looking for a new violist, and he asked if I would be interested. "Dunno, already playing in a quartet." I replied, "tell me who's populating said bunch." The cellist was Lamar's wife Ruth (always Ruthie) Alsop, who also played in the Ballet orchestra. She was a strong player, and a sweet, sharp-tongued, strong-willed Irish lassie. Their second violinist, Alan Martin, also filled a responsible seat in the Ballet Orchestra. With his equally-sharp wit, there literally was never a dull moment with this quartet. His specialty (probably invented in the ballet pit to scare new conductors and new colleagues) was pretending to fall asleep. He would then wake up as if startled, and while attempting to put the violin under his chin, he would miss, slapping himself loudly in the face with his chinrest. It was always a hit the first time.

Our purpose certainly wasn't to compete with the likes of the hallowed Budapest Quartet, though we were damned good considering the little time we had for rehearsals. Our sole commitment was to rehearse enough so that we could play as many as three pairs of short public school concerts every week. Since I was still playing with the Kohon Quartet, we scheduled these concerts in the early mornings so that they wouldn't interfere with my afternoon rehearsals up in the Bronx.

Lamar had a natural eye for a bargain. He lucked into a genuine Stradivari violin for $10,000, a relative song, and he bought an entire service of Japanese Rose Medallion porcelain (sometimes called "famille rose") at a steal, even though there wasn't much food on the table at the time.

Lamar and Ruthie found a tiny inexpensive house in Dobbs Ferry, and they decided to add a huge room (the size of the house) to serve as a concert hall. Lamar and the dancer Jacques d'Ambrose, his friend from the ballet, haunted the roadsides of the Saw Mill Expressway in a pickup truck after work. The wooden light poles on the expressway were being replaced with metal poles, so by night, these two characters hauled off enough cut-down wooden light poles (10 x 10s, as long as the mast of a ship) as beams for the new addition to his home. Lamar would often show up for a Young Audience gig with his hands all messed up and spattered with paint, but when the project was finished, he had doubled the size of his formerly-tiny house with a usable concert hall.

The Alsops invited us over one evening to show us what they had done with the house, and we spent some time chatting about our respective families. Ruthie popped into a back bedroom, and reappeared in a few minutes with their daughter Marin, a sleepy, pajama-clad 5- or 6-year-old, who was holding a violin under her chin. After a little prodding, pretty little Marin obligingly played some Vivaldi for us, gave a little bow, and went back to sleep. This is the same Marin Alsop who become the conductor and music director of the Baltimore Symphony in 2007 (the first woman to be appointed as either conductor or music director of a major American symphony orchestra).*

Alan Martin lived in Manhattan, the Alsops lived in Westchester, and I would drive from my home in the Flatbush section of Brooklyn to, let's say, Chinatown on Monday, Staten Island on Wednesday, and way the heck up in the Bronx on Friday. Playing these gigs helped us grow as a quartet, add music

---

* On January 15, 2008 I saw Charlie Rose interview Marin on his television program. She was vital and articulate, and wrinkled her brow thoughtfully before responding to his questions. She has Ruthie's Irish smile, and her toughness of spirit, along with Lamar's wit and mental sharpness. In 1992 Marin began conducting a series of concerts at the Cabrillo Festival of Contemporary Music in Santa Cruz, California. In August, 2009 she invited Nomi and me as her guests, and I was thrilled by the quality of her orchestra, the quality of her conducting, and the amount of support she has been able to garner for new music. The apple clearly did not fall far from the tree!

to our repertoire, and supplement our freelance income to the tune of around $40 per morning for each of us. That was certainly better than slaving away in a pit for eight shows a week, and never having an evening at home.

Following directions to these various locations during early morning rush hour was challenging, and once we arrived we had to keep the attention of roomfulls of bright but often still-sleepy kids. We learned, after a few tries, that we would lose their attention if we opened our concert with a movement from a Haydn or Beethoven quartet, so we developed a new format. We would walk silently into a classroom, give a brief nod, open our music stands quietly, take up our instruments (with no introduction), and launch into the brisk third movement of Anton Webern's Five Movements for String Quartet, Op. 5. You might expect 12-tone music to sail right over these sleepy heads, but it was not at all the case. This was the 1960s, and these sophisticated kids had already been introduced to 12-tone and other varieties of new music in movies, television (*The Twilight Zone*), and radio, and they were actually quite into these sounds.

This brief, magical, quicksilver movement took only about forty-two seconds to unfold, and it captured the interest of our young audience from the start. Many of those notes are required to be played *ponticello* (at the bridge), employing a scratchy-sounding effect, and these young people had no trouble relating to it. After this short musical handshake, they were ready for the more conventional string quartet repertoire: a little Schubert, some Mendelssohn, and even a dash of Bartók at the end. We knew that we had offered something worthwhile to these youngsters.

After we finished playing, we would hold our instruments next to each other for comparison, and take questions. A few of the second and third graders would come up to touch our instruments and we would show them how they worked. When I mentioned the difference in size between my viola and the two violins, someone would invariably say, "Aw, that's just a big violin." I would respond by saying, "No. It's a *viola*," and then I would play a few notes to show them the difference (hoping to inspire a burgeoning violist in the audience).

Bernard Zaslav demonstrates the viola for a Young Audiences classroom concert.

The Young Audience people made it worthwhile financially for us to do some touring in upstate New York during the spring months. They supplied us with a rented station wagon, and we took to the hills (including a town by the name of Burnt Hills) for a few days at a time. Lamar and Ruthie were antique hounds, and I soon caught the bug myself. I lugged home some wonderful antiques (tied to the top of the station wagon) from those tours, including an antique chiming Gilbert mantel clock, a fine old Eastlake walnut hall tree (with four coats of paint that I patiently removed), and a delicate Shaker rocker with a woven bark seat. We passed on this rocker to Robert Sylvester and flutist Paula Robison when they married, and then it went to the Alsops. Years later Lamar and Ruthie bought a second home in Saratoga Springs, where the Ballet performed during the summers, and they discovered a treasure trove of antiques up in the attic that included a Tiffany chandelier. They used some of their attic treasures to open an antique shop.

Sigmund Levarie, the Dean of Music at Brooklyn College, became interested in the Carnegie Quartet. He offered us a small (but honest-to-god) residency, which meant that we actually got paid for teaching chamber music classes and performing regular concerts in their acoustically excellent George Gershwin auditorium. Nomi and I performed our W.F. Bach and J.S. Bach sonatas program there, and on October 15, 1966 she appeared as a guest artist with the Quartet.

While I was playing with the Carnegie Quartet I also played with a few other groups, like the Beaux Arts Quartet, which counted among its members (at various times) violinists Gerry Tarack, Alan Martin, Lamar Alsop, Charles Libove, and violist Carl Eberl. Later, with violist Nardo Poy, they held a residency at the Potsdam campus of New York State University. I also played in a quartet with cellist Sterling Hunkins and his violinist-wife Dorothy who lived out in Bayville, Long Island. We played some interesting quartet gigs, one of which involved driving directly from Long Island to a concert in North Carolina and back in order to make a recording date the following day. We put a mattress in the back of Sterling's little Nash Rambler station wagon and took turns driving and sleeping, stopping only for some delicious pecan pie with ice-cold buttermilk on the road. Sterling was an expert at enjoying the finer things in life, whether he could afford them or not. His second wife, also a violinist, was a *wunderkind* from Hungary named Lilla Kalman. After Sterling's untimely death, the Society of Friends gave him a moving memorial ceremony at St. George's Chapel at Rutherford Place.

The Kohon Quartet, the Zaslav Duo, the Carnegie Quartet, and my freelancing added more strings to my bow. I was excited that I had come this far, but I was still hankering for a more dedicated quartet life, and hoped that events would conspire to make such a thing possible.

New York: My Vienna

When it was time for an 18th or 19th-century composer to leave his garret, when it was time for a performer to say goodbye to his practice room, when the neophyte would-be conductor sought a podium, they hied themselves to Vienna, the big *Burg* where they might find wider exposure and a sympathetic ear. Haydn, Mozart, Beethoven, Schubert, and Brahms made their marks on this city; then came Mahler, Zemlinsky, and Schoenberg, along with Anton Webern and Alban Berg, the star students of his "Second Wiener School" of composition.

Gustave Eiffel's gift of the Statue of Liberty celebrated the United States as a "melting pot," a country where "huddled masses" might find relief from widespread religious intolerance, and brought so many of Europe's most talented artists (in every field) to her shores. Around the time of the *Anschluss* of Austria with Nazi Germany (1938), many successful Viennese composers like Arnold Schoenberg, Max Steiner, Eric Wolfgang Korngold, and Ernst Toch headed for Hollywood to write for films. Toch worked on more than 83 film scores, and Steiner worked on more than 500. Korngold, whose heart was really in "serious" music, recycled parts of his film scores (that backed up the derring-do of Errol Flynn), and made them into a luscious violin concerto.

More European musicians arrived between the *Anschluss* and the 1960s. Bela Bartók and the pianist Andor Foldes (who performed much of his music) came from Hungary, Paul Hindemith and Lukas Foss came from Germany, and Ernst Krenek, Karl Veigl, Fritz Mahler (my conducting teacher), George Szell, Fritz Kreisler, Rudolf Serkin, and Felix Galimir, came from Vienna. It seemed to me that New York was replacing Vienna as the musical center of the world.

In 1874 German Jewish immigrants built the 92nd Street YMHA on the Upper East Side of Manhattan as a cultural and community center, and many of these cultured people chose to live on the Upper West Side. I recall playing some *Hausmusik* (the Mozart "*Kegelstadt*" trio for clarinet, viola, and piano) for an intimate evening get-together at the apartment of clarinetist David and Mia Glazer somewhere in the West 90s. I happened to miss a page turn, and a few of the assembled guests, who were sitting around us, immediately responded by singing the notes I'd left out. Such had been the state of musical tradition in Europe.

Wherever you looked, new works and new people to perform them were practically on tap during this pregnant era of musical experimentation. There were also many places throughout New York to play new works, like Columbia's McMillan Theater on 122nd Street, the Symphony Space on Broadway at 95th Street, Carnegie Hall, Town Hall and the Donnell Library in mid-town, and the New School, Village Gate, and La Maison Francaise, downtown, just to name a few.

I would always take note of the people in the audience when I played or attended new music concerts. It was the best way to see the way the wind was blowing. Edgard Varèse (*le maître*), the white-haired French-born innovator and inventor of "organized sound" would often be in the audience for a premiere, surrounded by his acolytes like Chou Wen-Chung and Morton Feldman. I first heard Varèse's *Poéme électronique* for electronic tape in 1958, and the sound of the manipulated soprano voice reaching to etherial and impossible heights still haunts me. I recall seeing Varèse along with Morty Feldman and others of his coterie at the New Year's parties given at the Brooklyn Heights home of Eric Salzman. Eric was a composer, writer, and an important critic and advocate for new music. His composing career took off with a composition he called "Nude Paper Sermon," and it continued later with various academic appointments.

Early 20th-century Vienna offered its brand of 12-tone music (by Schoenberg, Berg and Webern) alongside kitsch by Strauss and Waldteufel, while mid-20th-century New York offered listeners premieres of works by Babbitt, Carter, and Sessions concurrently with jazz, night club standards, rock and roll, the pop music that filled the gaping maw of radio and television, and the Muzak that filled dentist offices and elevators. As a freelancer, I stood ready to supply New York's needs, and answered calls from contractors for music of both the classical and the other-than-classical variety. Many of New York's classical contractors were musicians themselves, like oboists Henry Schuman and Melvin Kaplan, bassoonist Loren Glickman, bassists Alvin Brehm and Sam Levitan, cellist Henry Aaron, and violinists Alex Cores and Eliot Rosoff. Those who handled the more commercial (and better paid) dates were Hank Sylvern, Artie Butler, Isidore Gusikoff, Morris Stonzak, Lou Shoobe, and George Duvivier. These gigs paid the bills, but my heart was in Quartet playing and new music.

Symphony Orchestra rehearsal time was so expensive that even a symphony the New York Philharmonic commissioned from Milton Babbitt was given pitiably little rehearsal time. Composers who wished to get their music performed wrote it for increasingly smaller ensembles and for string quartets. And why not? A string quartet would work for cheap, and could offer a composer all the rehearsal time it took to satisfy his or her demands. A quartet would even work for free, simply for the prestige and honor of presenting a new work to the public.

Composers were writing music to please themselves, each other, and the people performing their music. I feel extremely fortunate to have played premieres of string quartets and premiers of other pieces of chamber music by Elliott Carter, Milton Babbitt, Roger Sessions, Paul Lansky, Fred Lerdahl, Ezra Laderman, William Sydeman, Gunther Schuller, David Diamond, La Monte Young, Martin Boykan, Igor Stravinsky, Ben Weber, Billy Jim Layton, Ralph Shapey, Ursula Mamlok, Miriam Gideon, Jack Huggler, Ben Johnston, Henry Weinberg, Charles Wuorinen, Charles Whittenberg, as well as music by many others.

In addition to all the performances of new music, Baroque music was beginning to have a Renaissance in New York. Igor Kipnis, the harpsichordist and early music pioneer called me, Sterling, Lilla, Sonya Monosoff (a violinist who was a dear friend), and trumpet player Ronald Anderson to record an album of vocal works by Bach and Rameau in a small downtown cathedral with Eleanor Steber, a big-voiced soprano. The sound of her voice still gives me goosebumps. I also had the opportunity to record the Bach Orchestral Suites at Webster Hall on East 11th Street with the great Spanish cellist Pablo Casals conducting. Casals, who was already in his 80s (he died in 1973), was assisted by Sascha Schneider, his ever helpful colleague. Casals was vigorous and inspiring, in spite of his age. He used his cello to make musical points, and we played our hearts out for him.

Stanley Ritchie asked me to join a quartet that he was forming with his red-haired violinist spouse and with cellist Fortunato Arico, and we worked up a program that included one of Peter Mennin's string quartets. Stanley, who is recognized as one of the world's leading exponents of baroque and classical violin, joined the New York Philharmonic for a season (I knew he wouldn't last there, with his interests), and then he joined the faculty of Indiana University's Jacobs School as Professor of Early Music. In 2009 he was awarded the Howard Mayer Brown lifetime achievement award for his work in Baroque and Classical music.

CHAPTER XI
The Composers String Quartet

While still fresh from the composer's pen, the Schuppanzigh Quartet performed Beethoven's late quartets to bewildered audiences and hidebound critics. In 1927 the violinist Rudolph Kolisch (who held the violin with his right hand instead of his left) founded the Kolisch Quartet, which played works written for them by Alban Berg, Anton Webern, Arnold Schoenberg, and Béla Bartók. The Kolisch Quartet's dedication to music of the *Second Wiener Schule* continued with the LaSalle Quartet, which was founded in New York in 1946 by their 1st violinist Walter Levin.

During the 1960s, many of my colleagues seemed to be peeling off by fours to form new string quartets, hoping to grasp the golden ring and enjoy the *créme de la créme* of the string repertoire. The Guarneri Quartet, a group that began at Marlboro, burst onto the quartet scene in 1964. Under the aegis of Rudolf Serkin, Sascha Schneider, and Pablo Casals, heavy hitters in the classical music world, they were able to make their first recordings (Piano Quartets and Piano Quintets by Brahms and Dvořák with the world-famous pianist Artur Rubinstein) for RCA Victor. How could they miss? They were a beacon to all of us wannabes, like the Kohon Quartet, who were also traveling on that Yellow Brick Road to quartet heaven. We loved the Guarneri's playing, and we also envied their success.

A string quartet in the 1960s had a better than average chance of snaring the all-important notice in one of the city's five newspapers if, along with music by known, dead, white, male composers, it programmed a new work by a living composer. I felt that new music mattered, that it was important to hear new voices as they were emerging, and I felt that it was my mission (call it my holy grail) to do what I could to expand the literature for string quartet.

Freelance concert work in New York usually slowed down during the summer, so violinist Matthew Raimondi and I kept ourselves employed (and escaped the city heat) by playing summer concerts for the local gentry in "Down East" Maine. During the late 1920s, the Rockefellers had amassed large areas of scenic Mt. Desert Island from the state to create Acadia National Park. Other moguls of the time, like the Pierreponts, the Drexels, the Biddles, and Wells Fargo heiress, Mrs. Clara Fargo Thomas, built their "cottages" (often multi-roomed stone-walled mansions) on the pristine shores of Northeast Harbor and Seal Harbor.

In August of 1961 Matt and I played a concert in Hancock with Nomi, cellist Philip Cherry, and French horn player Joseph Eger; and in 1963 we played concerts in Wiscasset and Boothby with flutist Claude Monteux and oboist Henry Schuman. Mrs. Thomas, a past member of "the horsey set" during the Roaring Twenties, took note of our Maine activities, and on July 18, 1963 she invited Matt, Phil Cherry, pianist Fritz Jahoda (a longtime Maine resident), and me, to play a "trial balloon" house concert (as it was reviewed in the *Bar Harbor Times*). Her magnificent home, designed by the modernist architect, George Howe, was built atop Fortune Rock, at the point of the fjord known as Somes Sound. The room we played in was cantilevered right over the waters of the Sound, and the murmur of soft ripples accompanied the Mozart Divertimento, the Beethoven "Kreutzer" Sonata, and the Suite by Darius Milhaud that we offered to Mrs. Thomas' distinguished guests.

Matt, a dead lookalike for Al Pacino, had been the second violinist of the New Music Quartet, the Quartet in Residence at Yale University (along with first violinist Broadus Earle, violist Walter Trampler, and cellist Claus Adam). Matt and I first performed together in New York as members of string quartet (with violinist Joseph Schor and New York Philharmonic cellist Loren Bernsohn) on an International Society for Contemporary

Music concert at Carnegie Recital Hall on March 22, 1963. The program included the premiere performance of Ursula Mamlok's 1962 String Quartet, Elliott Carter's "Recitative and Improvisation for Four Kettledrums," Pozzi Escot's "Movimentos for Violin and Piano" (played by Matt and Paul Jacobs), and Miriam Gideon's "Sonnets from Shakespeare," sung by Shirley Sudock, and conducted by Gustave Meier.

The composer Gunther Schuller came up with the suggestion that Matt and I should form a string quartet dedicated solely to the performance of new music by American composers. He suggested that by offering composers the rehearsal time that was necessary to learn their music, we could become a platform for the vital new music that was being written. The thought of playing *only* works being written by the crop of contemporary composers who were working in the 1960s seemed like a bit of a gamble, considering the time and effort involved in navigating the hurdles new composers often put in their music. That time and effort would, however, hone a quartet's new-music chops, and could also help improve a quartet's cleanliness and accuracy in performances of the standard non-contemporary repertoire. Gunther's idea sounded good to us, so we searched for the other two members for this pie-in-the-sky quartet.

Anahid Ajemian, an excellent violinist who had been active in contemporary music since the 1940s, was a natural choice, as was cellist Seymour Barab, who, besides being one of the best (and busiest) cellists in town, was a superb composer (he continues to write chamber music, songs, and operas). Seymour, with his "iron rhythm," as Isaac Stern described it, helped me a great deal with his rigorous approach to playing whatever was thrown at us. Matt's mint-condition Carlo Bergonzi violin (which formerly belonged to John Pennington of the London String Quartet), Anahid's unusually powerful Amati violin, my Italian viola, and Seymour's fine Cuypers cello fitted wonderfully well together.

We rehearsed five days a week at Anahid's spacious apartment at the corner of Central Park West and 84th Street.

Gunther Schuller

Gunther Schuller was our manager and our guardian angel.* He drew upon his wide knowledge of contemporary music, his numerous contacts, and his understanding of what was new and worth being heard, to chose the music we performed (and slaved over).

Harold Kohon taught me (even if unconsciously), how to improve my playing skills, but what I learned from these three new colleagues went far beyond normal instrumental technique. Matt, with his years of experience playing in Yale's New Music Quartet, Anahid, with her background in varied musical styles, and Seymour, a composer who taught me how to subdivide quintuplets (into either three plus two, or two plus three) and how to deal with treacherous patches of complex polyrhythms, were my mentors during these years. Playing in the Composers Quartet is a sterling example of the benefits of working with musicians more experienced than you are.

We strove for rhythmic exactitude and true ensemble sound. We refined everything to the nth degree, putting every detail under our ensemble's microscope. "We're not together," was Matthew's frequent complaint, while "You're LATE, Zaslav,"was what I heard so often from Seymour. Contrary to her ready smile, Anahid's peacekeeping advice could be, "Oh, let's just try itagain—without talking this time."

At the beginnings of our rehearsals, Anahid's cat would curl up peacefully between the legs of our folding music stands, avoiding the hazardous end-pin of Seymour's cello, as well as our assorted feet. She would endure the screeching sounds we often produced for the first couple of minutes, but eventually, when

---

* Her husband George Avakian is a gentle and gracious man. He is also an important jazz critic and producer (he produced recordings by Louis Armstrong, Duke Ellington, Miles Davis, David Brubeck, and Charles Lloyd for Decca and Columbia Records).

some high passagework drove her nuts, she would dash out of the apartment door, where she would sit patiently, watching for a letter to drop down the glass-faced mailbox chute, so she could spring at it ferociously. If a poor put-upon feline couldn't learn to put up with the sounds we were producing, I wonder how some of our audience members managed to stay in their seats.

We played an important concert (or so it was deemed by the many composers in the audience) for the Friends of Music at Princeton University on December 2, 1964. This one was a bear of a program; perhaps not quite as adventuresome as what Kronos or the Arditti Quartets do today, but quite historic for its time.

We began with the premiere performance of the Quartet No. 1 by Steven D. Fisher, who later went on to write for the theater. Fisher's Quartet flitted around from one thing to another, and it gave the impression that he was trying to do everything in "one gulp." Perhaps everyone would have been happier if there were more of Stephen Foster in Steven Fisher's Quartet. We followed the Fischer with a Quartet that Ruth Crawford Seeger (stepmother of the folksinger Pete Seeger) wrote in 1931. It was groundbreaking at the time, and remains a masterpiece that still makes the jaws of contemporary composers drop. The piece is filled with intricacies and hidden compositional games, and it never fails to weave its magic with audiences.

The first haunting movement of this nearly-forgotten quartet, marked *Rubato assai*, is full of fragmented quirky little melodies in the twelve-tone idiom. The second, marked *Leggiero*, is a playful catch-me-if-you-can affair that is devilish to play. The third movement is like nothing else in the quartet repertoire. Simply marked *Andante*, it consists of a succession of single tones that expand and contract as sound masses (foreshadowing Varèse) alternately climax and retreat. It brings to mind the image of bubbles alternately enlarging, and then slowly bursting. The fourth movement, marked *Allegro possibile*, is written in retrograde inversion, a musical palindrome: think, "Able was I ere I saw Elba," or even the last name of our own cellist, Seymour Barab. The first violin begins with a very loud, short note, and the three other voices respond very softly with a timid-but-jazzy, unison note cluster (using a ten tone-row); it sounds almost as if they're quietly clearing their throats. Then, as if to say, "Oh, yeah, take *this*," the first fiddle plays *two* loud notes, while the nagging chorus mumbles its cluster a bit louder, but with one *fewer* note. The game continues in this fashion until it reaches a midpoint, and then turns around on itself, the ending being a mirror image of the opening. You might liken it to a snake swallowing its tail and then regurgitating.

We recorded the Crawford Quartet for two small record companies, but they both had financial difficulties (they went bust) and neither released it. A recording of the piece by the Composers Quartet finally came out on Nonesuch in 1973.*

After intermission we played Milton Babbitt's Second Quartet (which we called the "quartet with octaves"). In contrast to Morton Feldman, who is considered a "minimalist" because of his exceedingly spare use of notes and the importance he gives to silences in his music, Milton rightly could be considered a "maximalist" in every sense of the word. He controls (and carefully notates) every pitch, duration, rhythm, dynamic level (often one for every single note where deemed necessary), articulation, register, and timbre in his works. All this attention to detail gives a special clarity and beauty to Milton's music. Describing the amount of rehearsal time required to learn Milton's music could sound like boasting (or it could be perceived as a kind of sadistic addiction). Appreciating his music often requires more than one hearing, but it's well worth the effort.

Milton Babbitt

We ended the program with the premiere of Henry Weinberg's Second Quartet. Before studying with Babbitt, Henry studied

---

* Judith Tick's biography, Ruth Crawford Seeger: *A Composer's Search for American Music,* explores the life of this fascinating composer and the choices she made in her life.

with George Rochberg, Roger Sessions, and Luigi Dallapiccola. His piece seemed to me like an attempt to go Babbitt one better in matters of complexity. Weinberg's musical output has been said to deal with rhythmic structuring, high sonorities, and fluctuating textures. What I remember most are the work's hellish difficulties. We devoted almost a year of rehearsal time to make a performance of this monstrously difficult work possible, while making the life of Anahid's cat a living hell. Henry thought nothing of asking us to play triple or even quadruple stops that went so high up on the fingerboard that our fingers nearly scraped our noses. We had mixed feelings about his demands, but we suffered through them. We eventually recorded the Quartet for Columbia Records, and it won the 1967 Naumberg Foundation Award for Chamber Music.

The hot-blooded Sicilian genes embodied within Matt's DNA uncoiled themselves the night of the premiere. After the concert was over, the four of us entered the large green room (that had two entrances) through the left side nearest the stage, where we awaited the hoped-for plaudits from those (mostly composers) who were to be our mainstay during our *avant garde* career. We felt satisfied (as much as one can ever be) with our performances, especially our performance of the Weinberg, so we were eager to hear his reaction. When Henry rushed up from the other end of the room to grab Matt's hand, the very first words he spoke were, "Have you seen my hat?" We were aghast at such supreme tactlessness after all the work we put into learning his damned piece. Edgar Kennedy, a classic film comedian of the past, was known as the "master of the slow burn," but Matt ran him a close second that night.

We repeated this blockbuster of a program for our official New York debut at Carnegie Recital Hall on May 3, 1965. The concert was sponsored by Twentieth Century Innovations, an organization directed by Gunther Schuller. Gunther's program notes explained that the Quartet had been formed to fill a current void in the world of contemporary chamber music. He argued that there were literally hundreds of 20th-century compositions for string quartet that remained unperformed, and indicated that the Composers Quartet's express purpose was to devote its talents and energies to the performance of contemporary works, regardless of their complexity. The headline of Raymond Ericson's review in the next day's *New York Times* read, "Champions of Modern Composers Unite to Assure Contemporaries a Hearing." After noting that the members of the Quartet were familiar to him, he explained that the Composers Quartet was dedicated to the performance of difficult contemporary music that "other ensembles do not bother to perform." Ericson thought some of the playing was dazzling (he liked the brilliant scherzo-like section of the Babbitt), and thought we made "certain small phrases loom large in effect." It was pronounced in the *New York Times* that we were deserving of our name, and that composers were lucky to have us around.

We were pleased that it had all been worth our many months of effort. A historic figure in 20th-century music, Gunther Schuller's many-faceted career included conducting, writing, publishing, performing (he was a horn player in the Metropolitan Opera orchestra), teaching, and composing. The colorful sonorities in his first string quartet made this work a favorite of ours, and was highly acceptable to our audiences. Gunther became the president of New England Conservatory in the late 1960s (Harvey Phillips, the "Paganini of the Tuba" was his assistant), and the Composers Quartet became their quartet-in-residence, but this happened after I left the group.

As Gunther supplied us with more exciting new works, both the size of our audiences and the number of concerts we were asked to play increased. When a concert promoter timidly asked us to include a Bartók quartet in our program, Seymour immediately rebuffed him by saying that the Composers Quartet didn't play "old music." We declined to play a quartet written by Iannis Xenakis, because so much of the piece involved rapping on our beautiful old instruments, but some young 21st-century stalwarts have since recorded it.

We performed the Weinberg quartet along with Roger Sessions' Second Quartet at Boston's beautiful Isabella

Stewart Gardner Museum on January 26, 1966. We repeated the Sessions Quartet for an all-Sessions concert on January 31 at the Philadelphia Composers Forum, where pianist George Reeves also performed *From my Diary*, and Matthew performed Sessions' very demanding unaccompanied Violin Sonata.

In the winter of 1966 I had a chance to play some "old music" when I was invited to join the first Music from Marlboro tour. We traveled by car during that snowy New England winter, and made a stop in Brattleboro, Vermont to visit with Rudolf Serkin's son Peter, who was also a pianist. A good natured snowball fight ensued, and Peter scored a few hits on Felix Galimir and me. The tour ended on February 15th with a concert at New York's Town Hall with a program that included Arnold Schoenberg's lush string sextet, *Verklärte Nacht*, Op. 4. Samuel Rhodes (who later replaced Raphael Hillyer as the violist in the Juilliard String Quartet) played the first viola part, and I played the second. The four other players were violinists Felix Galimir and Ernestine Breismeister, and cellists Toby Saks and Jay Humeston.

Schoenberg wrote *Verklärte Nacht* in 1899, a number of years before he started using his twelve-tone method of composition, a technique for which he is famous (and occasionally deplored). This deeply-moving masterpiece incorporates a vocabulary of lush, chromatic harmonies. Schoenberg wrote the piece three weeks after meeting Mathilde von Zemlinsky, the daughter of his teacher, Alexander von Zemlinsky, and later he married the lady. *Verklärte Nacht,* written after a poem by Richard Dehmell, tells the story of a man and woman walking through a dark forest, and about the secret she shares with him about being pregnant with the child of a stranger. The five sections reflect the mood of each stage of the story, and the piece closes with the man's acceptance and forgiveness. The string parts are rich, and the part writing is demanding. It was especially involving to perform the piece with Felix Galimir, because of his personal acquaintance with Schoenberg, and because of his intimate knowledge of this repertoire.*

Verklärte Nacht is written as one continuous 30-minute-long movement. It has many moments of tension and release, so all of us were fixed on every gesture made by Felix, who was our first violinist and our virtual leader. Unfortunately, Felix had come down with a drippy nose cold after the snowball fight in Vermont, and it was in full bloom during this Town Hall concert. The piece did not leave him a moment to deal with his problem, handkerchief-wise, so we were obliged to watch his lovely Stradivarius violin, its tailpiece crowned with a diamond insert, being unsuitably anointed. Just as the imaginary hero of Richard Strauss' tone poem *Ein Heldenleben*, Felix's fortitude in the face of this embarrassment that night made him a hero in our eyes.

After hearing the Composers Quartet in concert, Elliot Carter (a two-time winner of the Pulitzer Prize in composition) and his charming wife Helen, invited us to their 8th floor apartment on West 12th Street so Elliott could give us performance suggestions for his First and Second String Quartets. In 1986 (long after I left the quartet), Carter dedicated his Fourth Quartet to the Composers Quartet. He continues to write new works well into the 21st century, after his own centenary (he was born in 1908).

We impressed the critics when we performed a quartet by Billy Jim Layton, the chair of the music department at the Stony Brook University on Long Island. Eric Salzman, the critic from the *New York Times*, found it to be "as vital, as startling, and as overwhelming as if nobody had ever written a quartet before."

Paul Lansky wrote a rich and complex work for us, and Ralph Shapey, a rather rebellious (and sometimes pugnacious) fiddler I knew from my Juilliard days, who was influenced by Edgar Varèse, graced us with his Sixth Quartet. We were asked to perform it at Town Hall. Town Hall has wonderful acoustics, and

---

* In 1927 Felix and his three sisters founded the Galimir Quartet in Vienna, where they played music by "Second Wiener School" composers. He eventually formed a second Galimir Quartet in New York with some excellent younger colleagues, at least two generations his junior, violinist Hiroko Yajima, violist Kim Kashkashian, and cellist Timothy Eddy, who became the cellist of the Orion Quartet.

a stage that is quite wide for its depth, so Ralph (ever the rebel) decided that it might be interesting for us to try something other than the usual quartet formation (shades of Stoky). He asked us to stand (except for the cello, who needed to sit) about four feet apart, with our four music stands spread across the width of the stage, for what he called "sonic effect." After rehearsing this way, inevitable ensemble problems made us realize that this hair-brained scheme was a lousy idea. Ralph showed up at the dress rehearsal and finally admitted his error. More specifically, his gracious words of apology were, "Aw, f--k it, just sit together."

Teresa (Tracy) Sterne, the bold Brooklyn-born pioneer of new music, is responsible for producing many recordings of important new works. With the help of audio engineer Marc J. Aubort, and his assistant Joanna Nickrenz, the Composers Quartet recorded Ben Johnston's microtonal Quartet No. 2 for Nonesuch Records. Tracy coupled it with a recorded performance of HPSCHD, a work by John Cage and Lejaren Hiller.

The piece was originally presented in 1969 as a multimedia 5-hour "happening" for an audience of 6000 at the University of Illinois in Champaign-Urbana. It featured seven harpsichordists playing seven amplified harpsichords, 208 tapes of computer-generated sound played through 52 monaural tape players, and hundreds of slides and films (some borrowed from NASA) projected on scores of screens. The 21-minute version of HPSCD on the Nonesuch recording used 51 electronic tapes, while the harpsichordists played randomly processed pieces by Mozart, Beethoven, Chopin, Schumann, Gottschalk, and Busoni, as well as pieces by Cage and Hiller. The LP album includes an accompanying printout instructing the listener how to adjust the knobs of a Hi-Fi rig, to get the most out of the eerie bunch of *ka-chungs* emitted by the speakers. There's a mass of numerical gobbledy-gook on the page, and the final words are, "Good luck."

The other side of the disc held the sweeter sounds of Ben Johnston's quartet. To indicate the tiny degrees of pitch alteration necessary to play this microtonal piece, Johnston placed plusses and minuses over each written note. Normally-sized human fingertips would benefit from the use of a pencil sharpener (with a bottle of anesthetic handy) to make Johnston's infinitesimal pitch adjustments. These early pieces point the way towards Johnston's later works which employ "just intonation," a method of tuning that requires musicians to adjust their pitches so that they adhere to a set frequency ratio (in contrast to the more-or-less equal temperament that is used to tune a piano).

Early in 1967, Jeunesses Musicales International asked the Composers Quartet to perform Martin Boykan's First String Quartet, which was America's string quartet entry (chosen by Gunther) for a composition competition in the "Man and Music Pavillion" at Montreal's Expo 67. They offered us an excellent fee, and the winner's first prize, as I recall, was 50 performances of the piece world-wide, and about $50,000, the largest award ever to be given at that time for a classical work.

A few weeks before our trip, while we were busy learning Marty's quartet, we got a call from JMI, asking if we could also perform a quartet by the Hungarian composer Josef Maria Horvath. The group originally scheduled to play the piece could not attend, and if we weren't able to play it, Horvath's entry, *Recordanz II*, would have to be withdrawn. They offered to double our fee, and, along with the international rivalry involved, it was just too rich to pass up. We spent the next two weeks working on the Horvath as well as the Boykan.

Around this time, I received an unexpected call from GeorgeSopkin, the cellist of the Fine Arts Quartet in Wisconsin. He said they were holding auditions to replace their current violist. He told me that my name had been mentioned, and asked if I would be willing to fly to Milwaukee (at their expense) to see if I would be interested.

After my return to New York from Cleveland, it never even crossed my mind to leave "the city that never sleeps" again. Our quartet stood firmly in the vanguard of new music in New York, and I felt that we had achieved something notable together. The rapport between Matt, Anahid, Seymour, and myself was warm and remarkable: we were at the same time good friends and devoted colleagues.

The Fine Arts Quartet had been around since 1946 and was widely acknowledged as a major chamber music entity. It was not as well known in New York as the Juilliard or the Guarneri, but New Yorkers can be rather provincial regarding the rest of their country. The Fine Arts Quartet performed the entire string quartet repertoire to critical acclaim, both in America and abroad. Their Beethoven and Bartók recordings had been mainstays for years by the time the Juilliard Quartet made their Beethoven and Bartók recordings. The position included a residency and a faculty appointment at the University of Wisconsin-Milwaukee, so joining this prestigious group would offer me financial security, something that freelancing in New York could never provide.

I mentioned the opening to my colleagues, and there were several raised eyebrows, but after some discussion, the consensus was that I should "go for it," as long as it wouldn't screw up our current obligations. I was gratified for their understanding, so I called George, and we set a date.

On July 1, 1967 we drove up to Maine to play for the Mt. Desert Concert Series at the Neighborhood House in Northeast Harbor, and then drove back to New York on the 9th for a week of rehearsals (as well as several commercial recording sessions for Murray Sandler and Abba Bogin). We drove North to Montreal on the 12th to prepare for the July 17th concert at Theatre Maisonneuve. Nomi came along, and we stayed for five days with her Montreal relatives. We had much more quality time there than we would have had staying at the Hotel Chateau Champlain with the rest of the Quartet.

For as far back in history as we can tell, strings had been made of twisted sheep gut, but when the intimate salons of royalty began to give way to concert halls, there was need for more projection. For this reason, string-makers responded by winding gut strings tightly with very thin metallic thread made of either silver or aluminum. To account for increased tension, the higher strings were often made of steel. Some stalwarts still preferred the warmer sound of gut, and since I studied with Lillian Fuchs, who used a "bare" (unwound) gut A string, I decided that I would use a bare gut A string on my viola. It did require extra time to keep in tune, but I preferred the warmth of its sound, in spite of its drawbacks.

The Horvath piece was first on the JMI program, and the very first note of the piece is played (or rather plucked) by the viola. It is marked *fortississimo*, and the composer directs the player to pluck the open A string as energetically as humanly possible. Sure enough, one of the dreaded weak points of using gut strings came into play on that fateful night. My string broke, and I was obliged to creep backstage with my tail between legs to put a new A string on my viola.

Since I had cast my lot with gut, I had not taken a backup steel A string along with me. I replaced the gut string, resumed my seat, and we began again (I plucked my opening note only *forte* this time). Gut takes some time to stretch, so I had to keep tuning the damned thing in between every tiny bit of rest. Matt's withering glance said it all, and I never again used a bare gut A in quartet playing.

By the time we got to the Boykan quartet, my viola (and my composure) had settled down, and the performance went without incident. We awaited the decision of the judges eagerly: Nomi and I both recall that the Horvath (embarrassedly) was awarded first prize, and that the Boykan received a commendation.

My audition date with the Fine Arts Quartet needed to be tucked into the space between concerts in the Composers Quartet's Mt. Desert Festival concert series, so I flew from Bangor, Maine, to Milwaukee, Wisconsin, on July 24th. This audition (my last one ever) was quite a "game changer." I arrived in Milwaukee, and spent the next day with the Quartet at cellist George Sopkin's rather luxurious home on North Wahl Avenue. We grazed on a little Mozart, some Haydn, a few of the Romantics like Schumann and Mendelssohn, and had a read-through of the Bartók First Quartet, a work that Seymour had called "old music."

THE COMPOSERS STRING QUARTET

It was clear to me that I was sitting in the middle of a really great string quartet. The Fine Arts Quartet had a definite sound, a personal style, and a warm, rich sound. They had an innate sense of ensemble, and picked exactly the right tempo for each movement. They also knew the repertoire cold. No matter which of the classic works a client might request, they had played it quite often, and had most likely recorded it.

When I drew my first bow together with George Sopkin, a magical something seemed to click to the "on" position. His solid rich bass sound reminded me of Mischa Schneider, the cellist of the Budapest Quartet. We instinctively shaped our phrases as one, while exchanging knowing smiles. George seemed to be the quartet soul-brother I always dreamed of, and I knew that if the Fine Arts Quartet asked me to join, the opportunity to play the quartet literature with this guy would be the deciding factor.

After saying our happy goodbyes, I flew back to Maine to rehearse for the remaining Composers Quartet concerts there. We were obliged to offer more balanced programs for the summer crowd, so one of the programs included Beethoven's Op. 127. As we were playing, I wondered how the Fine Arts Quartet would perform it, and whether the next time I played it might be as a member of their quartet.

A letter from the Fine Arts Quartet awaited me in New York. They said their timeframe had changed, and that their violist would be staying on for another year. They asked me if I would accept the position for the following year, 1968. The year's delay eased my conscience somewhat, because it would give my colleagues ample time to find my replacement.*

Nomi and I had to give this offer some long, hard thought. I was at the top of my game in New York, the Composers Quartet was on the cusp of a unique career, but we were still just about getting by financially. The members of the Fine Arts Quartet were between eight and twelve years older than me, and they played a good deal of the quartet repertoire that I had yet to learn.

---

* Jean Dupuoy, an excellent French violist took my place in the Composers Quartet, and he recorded the Elliott Carter Quartets (including the Fourth Quartet that Carter dedicated to the Composers Quartet) with them. They are very fine recordings, and were groundbreaking at the time. Jean returned to France, and was succeeded by Jean Dane, a violist who had played for me as a student.

I felt it would be a mistake to turn down such an opportunity, so Nomi and I agreed to make the move to Wisconsin. The Quartet responded by saying they were very excited about my coming, and asked if I might be able to hurry back to Milwaukee on the 25th of August to record with them. They were far behind in their schedule (they hadn't recorded all of the 30 Haydn Quartets that Vox requested), and hoped I would be available. These guys didn't kid around.

I was off again to Milwaukee, where we had three recording sessions per day in University of Wisconsin-Milwaukee's wonderful chamber music hall on campus. After nine intensive (and inspiring) days, we finished recording Haydn's Op.50 Quartets and his 1787 "Prussian" Quartets.

Before I had a steady job, I could never even be considered for a mortgage. George's wife Carol, who was a real estate agent, showed Nomi and me a few houses to consider buying. Our heads were in the clouds at the thought of buying our first house (the vaunted American dream) at the age of 41. One of the houses we looked at was an honest-to-god (though rather unremarkable) Frank Lloyd Wright house that was built around 1916. It cost around $35,000, but it was in questionable condition, so we passed on it. Carol said she would keep looking for something nice in our *price range*, words we had never heard uttered before.

We drove back to New York on September 6 (replacing two tires along the way). I made a recording for contractor Lou Shoobe at Fine Sound, and was invited for an evening of chamber music at the Park Avenue home of Daniel Saidenberg. Danny was a fine cellist and a conductor (he owned a gorgeous Stradivarius cello and had worked with Casals). He and his wife Eleanore were Pablo Picasso's New York agents, and they ran the Saidenberg Galleries. At least three small paintings by Picasso would stare you in the face when you visited their bathroom.*

People were already talking about a hot-shot youngster

---

* Daniel Saidenberg was a member of the Philadelphia Orchestra in 1926, and in 1929 he was the first cellist to win the Walter W. Naumburg International Competition. He joined the Chicago Symphony in 1930, and spent the remainder of his highly-impressive career in New York.

named Pinchas Zukerman, a hugely-talented Israeli violinist who Isaac Stern "discovered" and sent to Juilliard. To see what Pinky (as everyone called him) could do, Danny arranged a chamber music evening at his home. Pinky showed up late, with an adoring damsel clinging to his arm. While we played a Haydn quartet, this brash youngster fingered his fiddle like a toy. Perhaps he might have preferred toying with his lovely date for the evening.

The Composers Quartet continued its five-day-a-week rehearsal schedule at Ahahid's apartment, and I continued subbing on Broadway and playing in freelance chamber orchestra concerts with the Clarion, the Esterhazy, and the Festival Orchestras. I recorded film scores written by my friends David Amram (*Splendor in the Grass*) and Lawrence Rosenthal *(A Raisin in the Sun),* as well as film scores by other composers. I played many Young Audience school concerts with the Carnegie Quartet, and gave faculty concerts and coached chamber music groups at Brooklyn College.

In the midst of everything I was doing in town (and there was a lot happening), another long-distance call came from the Fine Arts Quartet. They asked if I would be free to fly back to Milwaukee on December 14 (during their academic break) to meet with Dean Adolph Suppan and the rest of the music faculty, and then spend ten days recording all six of Haydn's Op. 76 Quartets. Did they even have to ask?

*Fine Arts Quartet
George Sopkin (cello), Bernard Zaslav (viola),
Leonard Sorkin (violin 1), Abram Loft (violin 2)*

CHAPTER XII
The Fine Arts String Quartet (Part 1):
Gaudeamus Igitur

It was New Year's Day, 1968, and after playing a New Year's Eve P.D.Q. Bach concert at Lincoln Center with Peter Schickele, I had a rare day off. There was nothing penciled in my datebook (not even an unpaid rehearsal), so Nomi and I made plans for our upcoming move to Wisconsin. Claudia, who was 15, would begin high school in Wisconsin in the fall. Mark, who was 20, and in his junior year as a psychology major at Brooklyn College, would live in the basement of my parents' home. We decided that my brother and his family could take over our former apartment.

My little black book, the keeper of my every move, was crammed with commitments for January. In addition to weekly coaching sessions at Brooklyn College, there were seven Young Audiences gigs with the Carnegie Quartet, two concerts with the Composers Quartet (one at Hunter College and one at Princeton), and sessions to record Ben Johnston's Second Quartet for Nonesuch. I had two concerts to play with Newell Jenkins and the Clarion, one with Max Polikoff (at Town Hall), two with Thomas Dunn (at Philharmonic Hall), and I had two concerts with Frederick Waldman's series (one at Carnegie Hall and the other at the Met Museum). I had also accepted eight sub dates for various Broadway shows, and I was being called for recording sessions by contractors for whom I had never worked, like Joe Soldo, George Sawakis, Lou Haber, Irving Spice, and Bob Asher. I was finally a member of the "in crowd," and I wondered if it really was the time to leave New York.

Naturally, the grapevine, ever alert to climate changes, caught wind of my imminent departure. I would run into pals at gigs who would ask, "Bernie, are you nuts? Why would you leave for Minneapolis, or wherever it is you're going, just when you're getting so hot in town?" It was clear that Milwaukee simply wasn't within every New Yorker's ken. This, of course, brings to mind the famous New Yorker cover illustration by Saul Steinberg, "A New Yorker's View of the World," that points westward from New York, showing Chicago, and nothing until Los Angeles, the Pacific Ocean and far Cathay in the distance. (Nomi's family name was Civkin, and when she was growing up in Winnipeg, they called it the Pacivkin Ocean, though they had never seen it).

I bumped into Claus Adam, the cellist of the Juilliard Quartet (Joel Krosnick succeeded him in 1974) who mentioned that they had been seriously thinking of me as a replacement for their departing violist, Raphael Hillyer. Oh, really? After I'd signed on with the Fine Arts Quartet? Then I happened to share burgers with Sol Greitzer in a Greek joint across the street from Lincoln Center. Solly was a terrific violist who played in the New York Philharmonic (he was appointed principal under Pierre Boulez in

1972), and his wife, Shirley Aronoff, had been a piano student of Rosina Lhevinne. When we talked about my leaving town, Solly, who was kind of morose as he sat with me at the counter said, "Bernie, you lucky dog. I'd take that job in a heartbeat." That made me feel a little better.

Most of the others, certainly my colleagues in the Composers Quartet, thought I was out of my mind to leave the Big Apple. Even though people were always *kvetching* about New York's commercial recording business dying (along with Broadway), and observing that London's Abbey Road and Decca recording studios, along with the studios in Los Angeles and Nashville, were all gaining ground, Noo Yawk was where "it" was all happening. My plate was filling up nicely, but my personal "it" was, more or less, confined to playing music by contemporary composers and shlepping my viola case around town for everything else. "Out there" lay the entire canon of quartet literature, much of which I was still largely ignorant, and what I felt to be the highest calling in music.

This was really more about where I was going, and less about what I was leaving. My varied activities looked impressive on the page, but together they provided far less income than I would earn with my new position. As a member of a major string quartet there would be no more wasted hours commuting from Brooklyn to Manhattan, and no more "bowing for dollars" on Broadway. Rather than rushing from one one-time gig to another, every rehearsal with the Fine Arts would improve my playing and add to my knowledge of the repertoire.

Carol, George's wife, called us in New York to tell us about a house she particularly liked that was built in the style of a small Italian villa on an elm-lined street in the neighboring town of Shorewood. It was designed by David Adler, the architect who designed Milwaukee's Villa Terrace Decorative Arts Museum, and was made of Roman brick. It had a multicolored tile roof, Italian tile floors, a spiral staircase, and had a bas relief of Tintoretto's "The Last Supper" in the dining room; an optimistic effort to bring a bit of balmy Tuscany to frigid Wisconsin. Nomi and I flew out at the beginning of March for a look. We also looked at a more practical house in the town of Whitefish Bay. Opting for Shorewood's aesthetic beauty over practicality, we fell in love with our first "American dream" home (Italian though it was) at 2313 East Kensington Boulevard, across the street from Lake Michigan, and just a few blocks from Claudia's school.

With my new faculty status, I was now mortgageable, so the price of $45,000 for the house was within our realm. We made an offer, and flew back to New York so I could play a gaggle of concerts. We then flew to Chicago on May 18 for a dinner and reception given by the Fine Arts Foundation (to celebrate my joining the Quartet), had more meetings at the University of Wisconsin-Milwaukee, and closed on our new home. We flew back to New York two days later for more concerts, and then we packed up our *stuff* (anent George Carlin's spiel about everybody's *stuff*) for the movers to take to our "villa."

Nomi and I were given a heartfelt sendoff from my colleagues with a party at Anahid Ajemian's apartment that included delicious Armenian cuisine (Seymour wanted to engage the "Paganini of belly dancers" in our honor, but he was voted down) and on May 31, Nomi, Claudia, and I piled into my dark blue 1963 Cadillac Sedan de Ville, and drove to Milwaukee. We stayed with George and Carol for a week while I rehearsed with the Quartet. The movers arrived on June 7th, and we slept in our new home for the first time.

The next evening we explored Milwaukee's Downer Avenue, and decided to catch a film at a local movie house, named, not surprisingly, the "Downer." As we were waiting in line for tickets and gabbing away in our New York accents, some folks behind us caught the drift of our conversation. One of them turned to us and asked, in a rich Milwaukee accent (Claudl does a wonderful imitation), "So then, just what could it be that brings you big city folks to M'wahkee?" Here was one of those classic "I shoulda' said, I coulda' said" moments, where the proper comeback would have been something like, "We came to your fair city to play the greatest chamber music ever written with a famous string quartet." To avoid any further "downers," we did our habitual movie viewing at the Oriental Theater on Farwell Avenue thereafter, and tried eating our popcorn with chopsticks.

On June 11, only three days after moving into our new home, I was off to play my first official concert for the Fine Arts Quartet's new June Music Festival series in Albuquerque. Our program consisted of Haydn's "Sunrise" Quartet, Webern's Five Pieces for String Quartet, Stravinsky's Three Pieces for String Quartet (written in 1914), his 1920 Concertino, and the Brahms F minor Piano Quintet with Ralph Berkowitz, the pianist and music historian who organized the series. For the second concert we played the Mozart E flat Piano Quartet, the third Brahms String Quartet (which we were preparing to record) and Ralph joined us for the Shostakovich Piano Quintet.

Ralph was an old friend of my mentor Josef Gingold, and he persuaded Joe to take part in the series. Joe offered to play second viola in the Mozart G minor Viola Quintet for the third concert (using a small viola that I bought from Robertson's Violin shop in Albuquerque). The Fine Arts Quartet played the Berg Quartet, Op. 3, and then Joe and Ralph joined us for the Chausson Concerto for Violin, Piano, and String Quartet. After that summer, Joe and his wife Gladys became regular guests at the June Music Festival.

Josef Gingold and Bernard Zaslav after their Mozart Duo performance in Albuquerque

I was in heaven when I played the G major Mozart Duo with Joe. Hanging on my wall as I write is a treasured photo of the two of us (Joe with his impish, endearing smile) clasping hands after the performance. When we chatted about his studies with Ysaÿe, and tradition in music making, Joe growled in his bass clarinet voice, "*Bernaleh*, you'll make your own tradition."

After concerts, we repaired to the Albuquerque House of Pancakes, the only place open late in that part of town, for our requisite caloric infusions. Joe was a most delightful teller of tales, and he and Ralph Berkowitz, who was equally gifted in that department, made these evenings unforgettable.

Ralph toured extensively with the Russian cellist Gregor Piatigorsky, and held us in thrall with his unforgettable tales of "Grisha" (Gregor Piatigorsky) and "Natan" (Nathan Milstein). In these gabfests, the inflated egos and peccadillos of various soloists and conductors of note were regularly speared, not spared, though Joe, in his infinite loyalty, would never permit a single word to be spoken against Szell.

I believe it was in the House of Pancakes that I heard the story about Toscanini conducting the Verdi Requiem with the NBC Symphony and the four soloists, one of whom was noted for both her powerful voice, her copious feminine endowments, and her proportionately smaller intellect. Apparently, Toscanini, never one to suffer fools, became upset with her during rehearsal, and after stopping once too often to make his objections clear, he ran up to her, clasped her ample bosom in both hands, and cried out to the heavens (in Italian), "If only these were brains!"

The Composers Quartet's repertoire had taken a great deal of time and effort to learn, so I agreed to play the concerts we had booked before I left New York for Milwaukee. Accordingly, I flew to New York July 4th to rehearse at Anahid's apartment (her cat wondered where I had been), and we drove to Ipswich, Massachusetts the next day, to play for the Crane Estate's concert series at Castle Hill. Then I picked up my second car, a 1962 Pontiac Bonneville coupe, that I had left in Brooklyn, and drove back to Milwaukee for the Fine Arts Quartet's Summer Evenings of Music concert series. The series began on the 8th of July and included six weeks of Fine Arts Quartet concerts, chamber music coaching, and a weekly concert preview that attracted a large crowd of locals.

During my first year with the Quartet, we programmed around 24 quartets: works by Mozart, Piston, Barber, Britten, Schumann, Haydn, five of Beethoven's fifteen (in preparation for a complete cycle the following year), the Schubert A minor Quartet, and the Brahms Quartet, Op. 67. We also performed the Spohr Concerto for String Quartet and Orchestra with the University of Wisconsin-Milwaukee student orchestra.

After the summer series ended, we drove to Maine for a well-deserved vacation, stopping in Saratoga Springs, New York on the way to visit Lamar and Ruthie Alsop, and visiting George and Carol at Carol's family cottage in Round Pond, Maine. We returned to Wisconsin for my first faculty meeting of the semester, and the beginning of the school year for Claudia. After her first day at Shorewood High School, Claudia complained that, unlike her school in Brooklyn, every classmate seemed to have blond hair and blue eyes, and did a riotous imitation of the local Wisconsin accent (quite a shift from Brooklyn's ambience).

Our home, built in 1926, was designed for a small family with a live-in maid. The kitchen was badly in need of an upgrade, so I installed new kitchen and bathroom fixtures that were sent from the family business in Brooklyn. Interestingly, they were made by the Kohler Company in Kohler, Wisconsin, so, although new, they boasted plenty of mileage. I learned how to re-tile our kitchen floor and, more importantly, I learned never to try to do it again.

We were introduced to the Uihleins and Pabsts, known as the beer-baron families of Milwaukee. One of the family members gave a party at her magnificent mansion on Lake Drive: it housed a library that had been carted from England to Wisconsin, piece by piece. Mrs. Uihlein mentioned, in passing, about her son owning a new baseball team in Milwaukee "called either the 'Milwaukee Brewers' or the 'Milwaukee Braves,' something like that."

The first string quartet to have a university-sponsored chamber music residency in America was the Pro Arte Quartet. Founded in Belgium in 1912, they came to America in 1941 under the patronage of Mrs. Elizabeth Sprague Coolidge, and were given a residency at the University of Wisconsin in Madison. When cellist George Sopkin was in his late teens, and a neophyte in the quartet world, he was asked to sit in temporarily for the Pro Arte Quartet's cellist. When George showed up for his first rehearsal, three elderly Belgian gentlemen, formally attired in vests and jackets, entered the practice room, shook hands gravely all around, and introduced themselves. They sat down to rehearse, and after the first few bars, the first violinist stopped playing, turned to young George, and asked, "Would you please tell the second violinist that he's too loud?"

When he was 18 George joined the Chicago Symphony, and in 1939 he began playing quartets with Leonard Sorkin, a violinist in the orchestra.* In 1946, after their World War II military service, George and Leonard, along with second violinist Joseph Stepansky, and violist Shephard Lehnhoff, founded the Fine Arts Quartet (coincidentally the Juilliard Quartet and the Amadeus Quartet also began that year). For the next eight years they played weekly network broadcasts in Chicago's ABC studios, until recorded music replaced live performances on radio stations across the country.

In 1952 the Vienna-born violist Irving Ilmer replaced Lehnhoff, and in 1954 violinist Abram Loft replaced Stepansky. By the mid-1950s the Chicago-based Fine Arts Quartet had established itself as one of the country's foremost chamber ensembles. Ilmer played in the quartet for the next eleven years, and was replaced in 1963 by Canadian violist Gerald Stanick who stayed for five years until I replaced in him in 1968.

The Fine Arts Quartet had its first teaching residency from 1951 to 1954 at Northwestern University in Evanston, Illinois, just north

---

* What's in a name? In 1929 RCA's David Sarnoff employed Vladimir Zworykin, his top television scientist, to steal, reproduce, and thereby discredit Philo Farnsworth's invention of the first working electronic television.

of Chicago. At the invitation of the University of Wisconsin-Milwaukee's dean, they began their Summer Evenings of Music series on the Milwaukee campus. In 1963 the Fine Arts Quartet became the University of Wisconsin-Milwaukee's Quartet-in-Residence, and all the members were given positions on the faculty.

I was intrigued by the Quartet's dynamic, especially the rapport between George and Leonard, who had been working together for 22 years. Leonard was forthright in character, embodying the Yiddish expression *Tuhas offen tisch* (sitting with one's behind on the table, i.e., no nonsense), and that was his strength as an artist and as a player. George was primarily concerned with the Quartet's sound and phrasing.

Bernard Zaslav and George Sopkin in rehearsal

Once, during a rehearsal of the Debussy Quartet, George simply stopped and sighed. He looked down at the floor, then he stared long and hard at Len, saying nothing. When Len, who had become a little red in the face, asked him what the devil was the matter, George stammered, "Err, Leonard, uh . . . do you think you could play that phrase a little more . . . beautifully?" We all immediately riveted our eyes on our music at that point and, by gosh, Len played it again, and it was more beautiful. That was about as strained as things ever got between them.

George studied with Emanuel Feurmann (both in Germany

and in New York), and Leonard studied with Mischa Mischakoff, when Mischa was the concertmaster of the Chicago Symphony. Leonard reminded me of Mischa on stage: he was calm, solid, and absolutely unshakeable in both his playing and his demeanor. They also had similar bowing styles. Leonard would always suggest using a slower bow speed with more pressure in order to get the best out of the instrument, something that gave the Fine Arts Quartet its rich sound. Len took every violinistic difficulty in stride, even in the works of Babbitt, Johnston, Crawford, or Lutoslawski. His approach to everything we played was clear and honest (no Broadway there), and through the years I grew to admire him as a warm and gentle person and a heroic musical figure.

Before joining the Quartet in 1954, Abram Loft spent eight years studying musicology at Columbia University, and he spent another eight years there as a faculty member. He had been in the Fine Arts Quartet for 14 years and had seen the departure of two previous violists, so I guess that in 1968 he thought of me as the "new guy on the block." We were both New Yorkers, but our personal chemistry seemed to highlight our differences. Abe seemed a bit restive, considering his more cloistered (his own word) academic background. He played very well, and his musicological background was a huge asset. Abe was razor sharp. He always had a wisecrack on tap, and was prone to sharp, nervous yelps of laughter. He wrote excellent program notes, and in his 2003 book, *How to Succeed in an Ensemble*, he accurately documents the Quartet's history from its inception until his departure in 1979. He was a dedicated woodworking hobbyist, and his musical metaphors ran to armies colliding, bombs bursting, pots bubbling over, and the enemy waiting over the brow of the hill. Abe was a fine violinist, though perhaps the long-time lot of playing second violin in a string quartet may not have been an entirely happy one for him.

When the Fine Arts Quartet was based in Chicago, it established a recording company called Concertapes, Inc. and Concert-Disc (which later became Everest). Critics and sound engineers praised the Fine Arts Quartet's recordings, and considered the recorded sound some of the best of its time. Leonard was our in-house recording maven, and he dealt with all the equipment, chose and set up microphones, and would edit for untold hours, long after the rest of us had faded. When the product was ready for shipment, we stored it in George's garage. The Quartet also recorded for other labels (like Decca, Vox, Gasparo, and Vanguard), and by 1979 they had recorded entire cycles of chamber music by Haydn, Mozart, Beethoven, Schubert, Mendelssohn, Bartók, and Brahms. Eventually the Quartet sold the Everest label, and their Beethoven and Bartók recordings were re-released on other labels.

We commissioned, recorded, and performed many contemporary works (my experience with the Composers Quartet proved to be useful in many of our decisions), and I believe that we played a major role in making quartets by Bartók, Shostakovich, Bloch, Babbitt, Wuorinen, Martinon, Hindemith, Shifrin, Imbrie, Crawford-Seeger, Johnston, Britten, Lutoslawski, and Husa, better known and more accessible to the public.

The Fine Arts Quartet's ability to communicate the strength and intricacies of these works to their audiences made them powerful advocates of music that was new and less familiar. Their recording of the Bartók cycle is still considered a landmark. It grew into a television series that featured a complete performance of each work along with interviews and commentary (with musical illustrations) by the performers.

Before joining the Quartet I had performed more quartets by Carter than by Bartók, so it was a jolt when I sat down for my first Bartók rehearsal with my new colleagues. I played my first complete cycle of the six Bartók Quartets at the 92nd Street Y in New York, and critics, especially in those in Europe, would often remark that one could practically visualize the printed score from our performances. We repeated the Bartók cycle in Los Angeles, in London's Wigmore Hall, in Germany, and at the University of Puerto Rico, where the songs of birds through the hall's open windows competed with the sounds of Bartók, and students wandering in with portable radios raised even more auditory mayhem.

The Fine Arts was one of the first string quartets to appear regularly on network television. They appeared on the Ed Sullivan show, and Hugh Downs (an amateur bassoonist) featured us a number of times on NBC's *Today Show*. We also produced our own series of 20 hour-length programs about the string quartet repertoire for National Educational Television, the predecessor of PBS, and flutist Jean-Pierre Rampal joined us for several of them. The Fine Arts played many live concerts on WFMT radio in Chicago, and we had several on-air interviews with Studs Terkel, the well-known broadcaster, writer, historian, and actor. Studs was an iconic Chicago fixture (he lived to the age of 96, and died in 2008) who was a staunch fan of the Quartet. When we toured in Europe, we taped archival programs for radio stations in various countries.

Leonard owned violins made by Stradivari and G. B. Guadagnini before his teacher, Mischa Mischakoff sold him a powerful Guarneri del Jesu. Its varnish had been tampered with, so it was rather pale in color, but sound-wise it was a cannon. When I joined the Quartet, Abe was playing a fine violin made by Tommaso Balestrieri. Later, when he was in Switzerland, he found a violin made by Matteo Goffriller, which the Quartet preferred to his Balestrieri, and George played a rich sounding Matteo Goffriller cello.

We rehearsed for three hours at least five times a week, played our regular concerts and lecture previews, taught private lessons, coached chamber music, and did occasional run-outs on weekends. Because of our service to the university and the community, our teaching load was reduced accordingly to 12 hours. The biggest perk from the university was being able to take off two weeks every semester for European tours (as long as we made up our teaching responsibilities). We hit 21 cities in 27 days during one European tour that was scheduled adjacent to a semester break. Only madmen, such as the men in our

Quartet, would have taken on such an itinerary, and Europe's on-time trains were what made it possible (there were times when we had to take three trains plus taxis to get to an engagement). It took a bucket brigade to deal with all the luggage when our spouses travelled with us, and we sometimes had to pass items through the windows of a train that was about to leave, *on schedule*.

We taught and rehearsed in our individual studios, and we did our recording in the University's jewel of a recital hall (Leonard liked to use a pair of Schepps microphones for close up recording, and a pair of Neumanns for room sound). The Quartet had its own recording studio in a small room adjacent to the recital hall. It was fully equipped with state-of-the-art tape decks made by Ampex and Studer. We spent untold hours editing, which was not an easy task when four players needed to agree on which take to use. Len occasionally allowed our son Mark to run the tape machines during our recording sessions.

Our local concert season consisted of seven Sunday evening programs at the University of Wisconsin-Milwaukee, and going to the Fine Arts Quartet's lectures became *the* thing to do in town. Inspired by Abe's extensive musicological background, the four of us were very comfortable talking about the music we played in Milwaukee, on tour, and when we were on television.

On Mondays we would repeat the Sunday University program at the Goodman Theater (part of Chicago's Art Institute). On Tuesdays we would perform our program a third time at the Howard High School in Wilmette, where we had an audience of North Shore fans who preferred not to drive into town after a hard day clipping coupons or making their fortunes at the Chicago Mercantile Exchange. A wonderful group of four music-loving women (who named themselves "The Fine Tarts") worked heroically to make the Chicago series possible, and by the time I joined the Quartet, a spare ticket was hard to come by.

There were several well-heeled and influential Chicagoans who provided the funding required to commission new pieces by Milton Babbitt, Charles Wuorinen, Seymour Shifrin, Ben Johnston, and Karel Husa. Many of our fans played chamber music themselves and they "knew from good." Sometimes they would bring scores to follow during concerts. Call it what you will, the "Windy City," the "Second City," or the "City of Wide Shoulders," Chicago certainly did not take a back seat to New York in the realm of classical or contemporary music.

We spread our net and widened our repertoire by calling upon an impressive roster of guest artists. Some, like oboist Ray Still, clarinetist Larry Combs, French horn player Dale Clevenger, flutist Donald Peck, and harpist Eddie Druzinsky, were members of the Chicago Symphony. We also played with pianists John Browning, Lorin Hollander, and Richard Goode, flutists Jean-Pierre Rampal and Paula Robison, violist Francis Tursi, cellist Robert Sylvester, and bassist Gary Karr, and we collaborated with other ensembles like the Berkshire Quartet, the Pro Arte Quartet, the New York Woodwind Quintet, and the Modern Jazz Quartet.*

Nomi and I gave a party at our house for the members of the Modern Jazz Quartet (pianist John Lewis, piano, vibraphone player Milt Jackson, vibraphone, bassist Percy Heath, bass, and drummer Connie Kay) after a concert we played with them in Milwaukee. John Lewis came up with arrangements that allowed their ensemble to interact perfectly with our string quartet, and we made sounds that were totally new to the ears of Milwaukee's chamber music audience. Our concerts were usually reviewed in at least four newspapers (some of the critics were Robert C. Marsh, Bernard Jacobson, Linda Winer, Peter Gorner, and Arthur Darack).

Nomi and I became quite friendly with Eddie Druzinsky and his wife. Eddie was "Mr. Harp" in Chicago, because the Chicago-based harp-maker Lyon and Healy used his name for a special model that was made to his specifications. I subbed in a Broadway show with his father (who was a violist), and I knew his brother-in-law, the pianist Leon Fleisher. We enjoyed playing high stakes poker games with Eddie, his wife, and other members of the CSO, but I met my match when violinist Victor Aitay beat me with a higher full house.

* We often invited the New York-based bassoonist Mark Popkin, who was popular with our audiences, to play some rarely-heard Baroque works arranged for string quartet and bassoon. The names of Sorkin, Sopkin, and Popkin on the program made it look like we were a Russo-Jewish legal team.

THE FINE ARTS STRING QUARTET (PART 1)

Leonard Sorkin, Abram Loft, and Bernard Zaslav in rehearsal

During a break at a rehearsal of Ravel's "Introduction and Allegro" (for harp, flute, clarinet, and string quartet), Eddie sat in the audience while we string players struggled with a particular phrase. We had some intensive discussion about it. We played it one way, and then another way. When we asked Eddie for his considered opinion, he reflected for a moment, looked at us as if we were nuts, and said, "I don't know what the hell you guys are talking about: it sounds exactly the same to me!" The intricacies of string quartet rehearsals can be a mystery to the uninitiated.

George's wife Carol came to hear one of my first rehearsals with the quartet. She sat out in the recital hall, listened as we "discussed" a point, and suddenly burst into tears. When George hurried off the stage to ask what the matter was, she told him that she was afraid that this was going to be the end of the Quartet, and that their lives would be changed forever. "Don't be silly," he reassured her. "It's only a rehearsal."

My first appearance in Chicago with the Quartet was at the Goodman Theater on October 14, 1968. We opened the program with Haydn's final work, his 68th Quartet, Op. 103, and then we played the Chicago premiere of Karel Husa's Third Quartet. There's a real humdinger of a solo for the viola in the first movement of the Husa, as well as plenty for everyone else; quite a challenge for the new guy on the block. We finished the program with the Schubert Quartet No.15, Op.161. Robert C. Marsh, the reviewer for the *Chicago Sun-Times*, mentioned that the Husa "won an outburst of eager applause." Apparently, the Pulitzer Prize committee agreed, since his Third Quartet earned the 1969 Prize for Chamber Music the following year. As for my first outing with the Fine Arts Quartet, Mr. Marsh wrote, "One advantage of the work is that the opening movement gave prominence to Bernard Zaslav, who was making his first appearance as violist of the group. Judging from his contribution to the evening, he is an excellent chamber player and a new source of strength for the quartet."

During the beginning of my twelve years with the Fine Arts Quartet the Colbert-Laberge Management organized our domestic concert tours (they also handled the Juilliard Quartet's tours). My first domestic tour began in Salt Lake City on October 30th, 1968. We then played in Los Angeles on the 31st, Pasadena on November 2nd, Denver on November 3rd, and in Minneapolis on November 5th. We began our first winter concert series at University of Wisconsin-Milwaukee on December 1, and repeated the program on our Chicago series at the Goodman Theatre on December 2, at the Howard school the following evening, and ended the year of 1968 with a taping at Chicago's TV station WGN for NBC's "Sunday in Chicago." And I thought I had been busy in New York!

After the Christmas vacation was over, we began our regular three-concert series (at the University and in Chicago) on January 12th with Beethoven's Quartet Op. 18 No. 1 (not the breeze that one might think). We gave the premiere of Seymour Shifrin's Quartet No. 4 (commissioned by the Fine Arts Foundation) on that program, and ended the concert with Schumann's Third Quartet.

Allen Hughes of the *New York Times* regarded our New York premiere of the Shifrin in May, 1970 as only an "estimable example of academic craftsmanship . . . with hints of personal statement." On the other hand (said the one-armed lawyer), Robert P. Commanday, who later reviewed our recording of the piece in the *San Francisco Classical Voice*, wrote of Shifrin's "intense expressiveness," calling it "close-in music," and he said it was "inspired by a delicately worked lyricism, the fine and fanciful detail highly expressive, highly involved rhythmically, and involving."

This reminds me (stop me if you've heard . . .) about the rabbi who held court as two old-world plaintiffs related different stories about the same event. After hearing out the first, the Rabbi thoughtfully said, "You're right." The second told an entirely different version and was similarly rewarded with, "You're right." "Hold on there, rabbi," said an observer. "How the heck could both of them be right?" This gave the rabbi pause, so in his infinite wisdom he considered all sides and replied, "You're also right."

Nomi and I introduced ourselves to our new audience with a survey of music from the Baroque, Classical, and Romantic periods, in the form of a three-concert viola and piano recital series at the University of Wisconsin-Milwaukee's recital hall. We played our W.F. Bach Sonata and J.S. Bach Gamba Sonata program on February 9th, and on March 9th we played the Beethoven Notturno, Op. 42, the Mendelssohn Sonata in C minor (originally for clarinet), Schumann's *Marchenbilder* Op. 113, and the Brahms Sonata in E flat, Op.120, No. 2. Our third concert on April 28 had the *Canto Lirico* by Wallace Berry, the Sonata for Unaccompanied Viola by Paul Zonn (a former faculty member of the University of Illinois in Champaign-Urbana), "Set for Two" (the serial work that Charles Whittenberg wrote for Nomi and me), the short Duo for Viola and Cello by Paul Hindemith (with George Sopkin), and

A morning rehearsal of the Zaslav Duo

the Colgrass "Variations for Four Drums and Viola" (with Michael Rosen, a percussionist in the Milwaukee Symphony).

The eminent (and ever jovial) flutist Jean-Pierre Rampal came to town on February 12th to join the Quartet for the first of its three television shows on Chicago's WGN-TV. Nomi and I invited him to our home afterwards, and gave this tall, well rounded (in many ways) artist as much food as he could handle, which was plenty. Instead of relaxing after our meal, Jean-Pierre wanted to know if I had any violin and viola duos handy. I pulled out everything I owned, he pulled out his flute, and we had a ball playing for what must have been hours. He thanked us for the evening, and continued to call me "Bahhnie" whenever we saw one another.

After our February Milwaukee, Chicago, and Wilmette concerts, the Fine Arts Quartet flew to New York for the first of a three-concert Haydn series at Carnegie Recital Hall (we played Op. 33 No. 3, Op. 76, No. 4, Op. 20, No. 5, and Op. 76, No. 6). Theodore Strongin of the *New York Times*, called us "one of the more durable music groups around." He followed up by writing "The mark of the Fine Arts Quartet is ease and comfort, and a full, vibrant concerted sound. Each of its members is quickly responsive not only to the other's linear phrasing—but also to the densities of sound." Thus spake that particular rabbi, on that particular day.

The next day, February 21st, we "opened in New Haven" (shades of Broadway?), playing three of our Haydns at Yale, and returned to University of Wisconsin-Milwaukee to perform the Bloch Piano Quintet with Nomi as our guest pianist. Recording sessions for the Haydn filled up whatever free time was available.

A rapid succession of concerts followed. There were Quartet concerts, television tapings, Duo recitals, run-outs to New York, Detroit, Durham and Ashville, North Carolina, West Palm Beach, Pittsburgh, Rochester, Hamilton, Ontario, Oklahoma City, and back to Milwaukee and Chicago, and then back to New York.

In May we played in a Contemporary Festival at University of Wisconsin-Milwaukee, and played the Spohr Quartet Concerto with the Milwaukee Symphony under Kenneth Schermerhorn (look out for them trombone parts), and then we went off to Albuquerque, to play four concerts (in three weeks) for the June Music Festival, where we enjoyed hearing Gingold and Berkowitz tell more stories.

In between concerts and rehearsals, Joe would sit alone in his cheap, loudly-air-conditioned motel room, and practice while watching television. I've done that on tour myself. When your mind is on empty, your fingers can sometimes figure out what to do by themselves.

Albuquerque is located about ten miles of the majestic Sandia Mountains (Sandia Crest reaches 10,678 feet), and we enjoyed taking hikes in the surrounding countryside. I was one of two members of the Quartet who bought house lots in a development up high on the mountainside, and George and Carol found a house in a bit further north in Santa Fe that they shared with one of our hard working Fine Tarts. Like, why not, man? This was the 60s. With the Bomb and Vietnam era, the end of the world as we knew it didn't seem so far away, so perhaps we could choose to be incinerated in lovely surroundings.

We finished 1969 by recording Karel Husa's Second and Third Quartets, playing flutist Samuel Baron's arrangement of Bach's Art of Fugue at Eastman, with the original New York Woodwind Quintet, and giving concerts in Buffalo, Schenectady, and Boston. We also played on the South Mountain series in Massachusetts, St. Louis, and in Fargo (loved that movie), North Dakota.

Milwaukee, for all its supposed backwardness, is part of the America that many politicians idolize in their mind-numbing speeches about America's "heartland." We found generosity, honesty, a no-nonsense attitude, and an open-mindedness there that we never experienced in the "I'm-late-and-I'm-in-a-hurry" New York we left. After two years of working with the Quartet in this forward-thinking Midwestern university, I knew that I had come to a very welcoming place. My students were bright and hard-working (several went on to have solid careers), the majority of the other faculty members were courteous and helpful (though a few envied our perks), and the Dean was most attentive to our needs. Chicago's music critics supported our efforts, and our Chicago contingent of supporters was unusually helpful. Sometimes it felt that I had joined a large family, as well as a string quartet.

The winters could be harsh, but spring was welcomed with appropriate joy; we would store away our snow shovels and galoshes, and replace the huge eight-foot-high sash windows of our house with summer screens. In the fall we would go apple-knocking in Cedarburg. Mark transferred to the University of Wisconsin-Milwaukee to finish his degree, and a psychology professor set him on a career track immediately after graduation. Claudia also graduated from the University as a flute major, and wound up marrying a local math student from West Allis. I certainly shed my New York snobbery in Milwaukee.

Dennis Nahat of the American Ballet Theatre, choreographed a new ballet to the recording of the Brahms G major Quintet, Op. 111, made by the Budapest String Quartet with Milton Katims, and gave his work the appropriate title "Brahms Quintet." When the Fine Arts Quartet and Francis Tursi performed it with the American Ballet Theater, we were obliged, because of the timing of the choreography, to follow the Budapest Quartet's exact tempo choices. Dennis danced this *pas de deux* with Leonard's daughter, Naomi Sorkin, and we gave our first performance at the Brooklyn Academy of music on December 10, 1969. The success of "Brahms Quintet" inspired another ballet called "Ontogeny," which Dennis set to Karel Husa's prize-winning Third Quartet. We played four more New York performances of both ballets.

We repeated part of the "Brahms Quintet" on NBC's *Today Show* the following morning, and I observed Leonard wiping tears from his eyes as he watched his daughter dance. *The New Yorker's* dance critic called it "a personal, self-contained composition" and "a musical experience so absorbing that I could not keep my attention focussed on the stage."

In January of 1970 I began my very first European tour with the Fine Arts Quartet. Shlepping an indecent amount of repertoire in my music bag (in the early days the Fine Arts Quartet carried as many as 50 quartets), and dragging my small-but-heavy rolling suitcase that held my "soup and fish" (European audiences insisted on frock coat *mit* cummerbund, *es muss sein!*), shiny black patent leather slippers, a folding music stand, one drip-dry dress shirt, scratchy wash-and-wear undershorts, a small bottle of detergent, a passport, a Eurailpass, and my requisite viola case, I found my way, with some difficulty, out of London's Heathrow airport to begin my big adventure.

We gave two concerts in London, one at St. Johns and one for the BBC radio before leaving for the Netherlands. We went to Rotterdam and Hilversum (for another radio taping) and played a concert in the Kleine Saal of the Concertgebouw in Amsterdam, where members of an enthusiastic Dutch audience unfailingly rise to their feet as they applaud—if they like you.

German audiences loved chamber music, so a good portion of our commitments were in *Deutschland*. One fine day I was wandering through the park of a small German town, and I stopped for a bratwurst. The server noted my American English and asked me what I was doing in town. When I told her we were going to play an Op. 18 Beethoven quartet on our concert that night, she immediately asked which one of the six, and told me that she had just played some of those Op. 18 Quartets at home the night before.

The Quartet played its first two concerts in Germany for Radio Köln, and then we flew up to Sweden, and continued northward playing concerts in Sundsvall, Umea, Skelleftea, and Lulea. Our last concert was in Kiruna, which is north of the Arctic Circle, but it was nowhere as cold as Chicago. We played at the Bourse, the beautifully chandeliered home of Stockholm's old stock market, and we were introduced to *hjorton* (cloudberries) in Lyngby (outside of Copenhagen). We returned to Germany to play at *Amerika Haus* in Hannover, and then went to Hamburg, Berlin (where we played for Radio RIAS), and Baden Baden. Our next stop was Switzerland where we played in Zurich (psst . . . wanna open a bank account?), and Basle, and we returned to London on February 20th for some needed R&R at the Westbury Hotel. The Hotel was just around the corner from Hill and Sons, the violin dealer, and London's Saville Row, where I satisfied my craving for the perfect shoe, which can only be crafted by an English bootmaker.

We flew back by way of New York, and played a concert on March 1 in Essex, New Jersey (*Nu Joisey*), where our guests got lost finding the concert hall, and we flew west the next day for concerts in Milwaukee, Chicago, and Wilmette. The day after that we were back in the pit for three more "Brahms Quintet" performances with the American Ballet Theater.

I urged the Fine Arts Foundation to commission Milton Babbitt to write a new Quartet for us. Milton's serial idiom was not for everybody (especially at first hearing), but I had already performed his Second Quartet with the Composers Quartet, and Abe and I both knew his piece for viola and piano (Abe gave its premiere in 1950). Our amazingly brilliant plan was to include its New York premiere on a pair of concerts at Alice Tully Hall in Lincoln Center called "Commissions & Premieres," which included commissions from the past as well as from the present.

George and Carol Sopkin managed, during their travels, to acquire an ornate silver samovar reputed to had been owned by Prince Nikolas Galitzin of St. Petersburg, Russia, the same Prince Galitzin who commissioned Beethoven in 1822 to write his Op. 127, Op. 132, and Op. 130 Quartets. The three-color flyer for the concert has a picture of the four of us, with Leonard holding the samovar and pouring tea, "warming the rehearsal-break of four latter-day Beethoven enthusiasts." George smiled as he sipped his tea from an Imari famille Rose Japanese teacup. We were without shame.

We performed all three humongous Beethoven masterworks in a single concert on May 10th, 1970. An intermission was necessary between each piece to keep the blood flowing (our blood as well as the audience's blood). The second concert three days later (May 13th) featured New York premieres of recently-commissioned works by Seymour Shifrin, Karel Husa, and Milton Babbitt. We ended this concert with Ruth Crawford-Seeger's rarely-performed String Quartet, giving the audience a choice of tunes to whistle as they left Lincoln Center.

In the next morning's review in the *New York Post,* Harriett Johnson mentioned that our group interpretation had "the unified subtlety of a single, persuasive personality," and that we made these difficult works "immensely communicative." When she wrote about the Babbitt she noted, "at one point there was an evocative section for the sombre viola against considerable pizzicato and short bowing." There's that somber thing again. We violists have learned to live with it.

When Nomi and I played Erneest Bloch's 1919 Suite for Viola and Piano at the Albuquerque June Music Festival in 1970, Henry Roth, the writer of *Call it Sleep* and many other remarkable novels about growing up in New York, attended the concert with his wife, Mary. The two of them (Mary was a pianist) came backstage to congratulate Nomi for playing this rich music. The four of us remained friends, and spent enjoyable time together. Tom Perkinson, a young artist with a Christ-like beard and a beautiful face to match, came backstage with his wife after a quartet concert. He told us that this was his first time hearing a string quartet, and that it would inspire his future works. We remained fast friends with this wonderful young couple through our eleven Junes in Albuquerque. The eight of his mystical landscapes that hang on our walls keep his memory alive.

Bernard and Naomi Zaslav in Albuquerque

The prolific British composer Wilfred Josephs spent one summer as a composer-in-residence at the University of Wisconsin-Milwaukee. Wilf is a very warm and chatty Londoner, who wrote 12 symphonies, many works for BBC TV, and 22 concerti. I performed his Viola Concerto, "Meditatio de Beornmundo" Op. 30, with the University of Wisconsin-Milwaukee Orchestra (conducted by Leonard). The piece is well written and enjoyable to play, but it is a tad "somber" (that word again).

1971 marked the 25th anniversary of the founding of the Fine Arts Quartet, and my third year with the group. Francis Tursi joined us that year to perform all six of the Mozart String Quintets. Francis taught at Eastman, and his pupils all loved him so much that they referred to him as "Father Tursi." I thought the world of him as a person and as an artist. His fine large (seventeen-and-a-half-inch) Maggini viola and my smaller Italian viola sang sweetly together in these masterworks, perhaps the greatest of all Mozart's chamber music (Mozart was a violist too, after all).

In March of 1971 I had my first opportunity to perform the Bartok Quartet cycle in London's Wigmore Hall. I don't think there is a better hall in all of Europe for playing (or listening to) chamber music than Wigmore, although the marble-walled *Herkulesaal* in Munich's *Residenz* runs it a close second. The *Daily Telegraph* called us "one of the best international teams in existence, hitherto known mostly for their recordings." The reviewer thought our unanimity of attack was "astonishing," that we made a "stunning impression in wonderfully concentrated performances," and that we "achieved a depth and roundness of tone coupled with phrasing which had the flexibility of complete naturalness."

In the *Guardian*, Edward Greenfield wrote that "in the flesh they prove even more remarkable than on record." He was swept away by the "redbloodedness of our readings," and found "no concessions whatever in the direction of sentimentality or self-indulgent romanticism, their playing now has an extra breadth of phrase, an extra attention to delicate tonal contrasts which enhances interpretations which were already masterly." He ended the review by saying, "This is one of the great quartets of the world."

The rest of the tour took us to Oslo, Bergen, Berlin, Stuttgart, and we played our final Bartók concert (we played the First, Fourth, and Sixth Quartets) at Wigmore on April 7th, my 45th birthday. Martin Cooper wrote about the concert in *The Daily Telegraph* with the headline, "Penetrating Grasp of Bartók." He mentioned that our performances were "distinguished by an extraordinarily penetrating grasp, which enabled them to demonstrate, as it were, the structure of Bartók's thought and to make even his densest textures clear." He went on to write about the second movement of the Fourth Quartet as "a gossamer in which no filament was allowed to 'run' and an iron control was exercised over what appeared to have the effortless character of a natural phenomenon." Joan Chissel of the *Times* wrote, "It would be a very exacting musician indeed who could ever hope for more of the truth about Bartók than was given us last night by the Fine Arts Quartet. Criticism of the playing can only take the form of gratitude—for unfailing individual reliability and uncommonly close team spirit as well as what seemed like intuitive understanding of the Bartók message."

A surprising moment on this tour came when we heard part of a concert we recorded for the BBC on the cabbie's radio en route to Heathrow Airport (we had just recorded it the day before). After we returned home, Wallace Berry, the composer who dedicated his *Canto Lirico* to Nomi and me (we gave the premiere in New York), asked us to record the work on the CRI label, so we flew to Ann Arbor, Michigan to record the piece.

After the Fine Arts Quartet finished its concert series in Chicago, had played our June Music Festival in Albuquerque, and our Summer Evenings series in Milwaukee, we all scattered about the country for our short summer vacations. Our manager surprised us with a call asking us to substitute for the LaSalle Quartet for a few concerts in England and a pair of concerts at the Edinburgh Festival, so the four of us exchanged phone calls, and everybody happily changed their plans. Nomi and I were visiting with George and Carol at their cottage in Round Pond, Maine when we got the call, so Nomi and Carol drove back to Milwaukee (Nomi drove and Carol navigated), and George and I drove to Boston, and flew to London to meet up with the rest of the gang.

We took the British Railway from Heathrow to play at Cheltenham's annual Festival on August 22nd, and then went to Gloucester to play at the Three Choirs Festival on the 24th. We flew to Edinburgh the next day, where George and I settled in at the North British Hotel (which is now The Balmoral) and enjoyed their famous Scottish steaks in the hotel dining room. They literally overflowed our plates.

During a free day before our first concert at Freemason Hall, I was able to hear Pinky Zukerman and Daniel Barenboim play the best performance of the Schubert Fantasy I ever heard, and I got to hear Yehudi Menuhin, who was in top form, play the Alban Berg Violin Concerto in the Queen's Hall. For his encore, Menuhin played the first movement of the Bach G minor Sonata with melting beauty and passion.*

---

* We happened to meet up with Yehudi on the plane back to the States. He was off to Nebraska for something connected with the writer Willa Cather (perhaps festivities connected with her childhood home in Red Cloud being named a National Historic Landmark). He was open and very gracious, and we struck up warm conversations with him. He insisted on examining all of our precious instruments in detail, and took us us to his seat in first class to show us the two Strads, the "Soil," of 1714, and the "Khevenhüller," of 1733, that he carried in his double case.

THE FINE ARTS STRING QUARTET (PART 1) 267

We played Haydn's Op. 33, No. 3, Husa's Third, and the Ravel Quartet for our Freemason Hall concert; and four newspapers with reviews awaited me at the newsstand to next morning. A reviewer from the *Guardian* mentioned that the Ravel Quartet was beautifully played and noted that the viola "figures prominently and brilliantly in the first movement." The *Glasgow Herald's* headline read, "Chicago Fine Arts Quartet's spirited performance," and ended with, "The Ravel was played with breathtaking precision and beauty of tone; plucked notes varying between a savage attack and delicate arpeggios. After such performances it would be only justice if the Fine Arts Quartet were invited to participate at next year's festival." The headline in the *Scotsman* was more insistent: "Masterful quartet must return." The reviewer wrote, "Not all quartets live up to their recordings, but this is one that unquestionably does. Its tone is magnificently strong, resonant, richly coloured (the players all have priceless Italian instruments) yet by no means lacking in finesse. Each player pulls his full weight." While I should properly blush at the headline in *The Daily Telegraph*, "Violist's Distinction to Quartet," Martin Cooper wrote that the quartet "consists of four players, each of whom is a very fine instrumentalist in his own right. The violist, in particular, has a penetrating warmth and fullness of tone which lent distinction to the slow movement of Ravel's Quartet. In Karel Husa's Quartet No. 3, too, the first movement is largely built round the viola, whose rhapsodical figures play a large part in determining the movement's character."

I floated my way down Edinburgh's Prince Street that afternoon (feeling rather full of myself), when who should I bump into but fellow violist, Milton Katims. He had apparently read the papers too, because he greeted me with, "Hey Bernie, I see you're still playing too loud." I accepted Milton's wisecrack as the perennial inside joke. Violists often fret about being drowned out because of the pitch levels and the lower frequencies that we normally inhabit. I would like to believe that it's my playing, rather than my decibel level, that would entice the listener.

Playing too loudly in a string quartet is pointless and destructive. All four members strive eternally for proper balance. It's kind of like the story of Goldilocks: you try to play not too soft, and not too loud, but just right. I certainly didn't try to upstage my colleagues in any way. I simply enjoyed my part, and was happy that my efforts were appreciated. Usually the first violin or the cello carry the melodic burden, but there are wonderful opportunities for the viola to shine in the quartet literature. Some prime examples of important melodic viola material can be found in the Ravel Quartet, the Debussy Quartet, Hindemith's Third Quartet, the Dvořák "American" Quartet, Smetana's First Quartet, and the opening of Bartók's Sixth Quartet. And then we have the all six of the Mozart Quintets.

Once, when Francis Tursi wasn't available to perform the Mozart Quintets with us on tour, my good friend Walter Trampler came along as our guest violist. The headline for the review of our performance in UCLA's Schoenberg Hall read "Fine Arts Quartet Plus One Plays Mozart," and the reviewer wrote, "The only instances of tonal imbalance were those written into the music by violist [sic.] Mozart and unabashedly taken advantage of by violist Zaslav whose large, gloriously dark and suave tone makes such imbalance all the more welcome." The rest of the review used bloated phrases like, "indescribably affecting," "exquisitely floated," and "tonally resplendent exchanges of violinist Sorkin and violist Zaslav," but I got my comeuppance in another concert. There, the reviewer (note that I'm not calling this person a "critic"), confused about which violist was playing which part, gave similar raves about the playing of the first violist, calling him Trampler. Walter teased me about that for years.

We played the Mozart Quartet, K. 575, the Bartók Sixth Quartet, and the Mendelssohn Quartet, Op. 13 for our second Edinburgh concert. The next day's headline in *The Scotsman* read, "Fine Arts Quartet Confirm Ability." So everybody liked us. Even Peter Diamand, the Festival's director, was thankful that we were available to jump in at the last minute, but he never asked us back. We had a taping on the morning of the 30th for Scottish radio, and then it was back to reality and to Milwaukee to start the new semester.

In the 13-measure viola solo marked "Mesto" that opens Bartók's Sixth Quartet, the violist of a string quartet must paint a picture of inexpressible desolation. After playing it many times, I worked out my own expressive (and individual) fingerings to use for this haunting introduction, but the real challenge is creating a sense of quietude, in spite of the psychological tensions that arise while you're in the limelight, playing all alone, with each of your colleagues quietly observing you, while waiting for his or her turn to enter. I played it often, but there was one spot (and thankfully only one spot), that caused my head to play self-destructive tricks on me: "Yes, I'm in control now, but what if my bow should shake." I knew that "there be demons" if I didn't put a quick halt to this nonsense, but that's logic, and logic sometimes gives way to fear of the unknown. My solo went fine, almost ideally, at the Edinburgh performance.

Before I left New York there was a violist colleague who demonstrated New York's provinciality by suggesting that I was compromising myself by joining the Fine Arts Quartet. When the Fine Arts Quartet played the Sixth Quartet at Carnegie Recital Hall, said violist sat in the front row, and the demon had its way with me. I felt like my bow was trembling something awful during the opening solo, but the people I asked told me they never noticed. Of course, I simply couldn't believe those people, and I'm sure my colleagues must have noticed my discomfiture. I was able to face down that particular demon the next time I played the solo (and each time after that), but there's still a "what if" lurking somewhere.

I was granted tenure at the University of Wisconsin-Milwaukee in 1972. My colleagues, who had enjoyed five years of incremental merit increases in salary (they were given tenure in 1963), surprised me at the next faculty meeting by requesting that their portion of merit increase be adjusted so all of us would be at the same salary level. Now, that's real quartet loyalty!

We were very much in demand in Europe, so we had two separate tours in 1972. The oil shortage shook the carbon-burning world to its foundations, so our first 28-day tour had only 16 concerts. Autos were not allowed on the highways in Holland without a permit, so we had to travel by chartered taxi (permitted only by government order) to reach a concert venue outside of Amsterdam. Through the windows of the taxi we saw people happily walking along the deserted highways with their pets and horses.

London was having brownouts. We checked into the Westbury Hotel during one of their sporadic power-downs, and were given candles and matches. Nomi and I took the stairs up to our room. While I was unpacking my suitcase, I heard a kind of fizz combined with an awful stink, and I wondered what sort of accommodations the usually up-scale Westbury had given us. Then Nomi screamed, "Your hair's on fire!" Sure enough, she was right. My early 1970s-length hair had been singed, though without significant damage to my dated coiffeur. Sure enough, the word got out. The day after our first concert, Edward Greenfield, of the *Guardian* wrote, "Practicing by candlelight for this concert at the Law Society, one of the distinguished members of the Fine Arts Quartet (so it is reported) managed to set his hair on fire. With a quartet of so high a voltage it almost comes as a surprise

to find that even in a power cut their playing does not provide its own electric lighting. As last year—when they played Bartók at Wigmore Hall—it was a delight to hear four string players whose intonation matches so beautifully, take away the aural stresses which bedevil the sound of a string quartet."

We made a quick trip that winter to Fairbanks, Alaska, where an art gallery owner from the Bronx pressed some wonderful gifts of Eskimo art on us. We traveled to Princeton University to play a program of Babbitt, Schumann, and Beethoven at McCosh Hall (no unhatted Henry Weinberg on this occasion), and we played Irving Fine's String Quartet along with music by Babbitt and Shifrin for a Memorial Concert at Brandeis University in honor of Irving Fine. We played three concerts at Stanford University, one with clarinetist Mitchell Lurie, one with cellist Laszlo Varga, and the last with pianist Leonard Pennario, and we played Babbitt, Schuller, and Shostakovich for our first appearance at the Kennedy Center's Eisenhower Theater.

A few of our wives (though not Nomi) came along on our second 1972 tour, which began in Frankfurt where our German concert manager Fritz Dietrich lived. Fritz handled all of our German travel and hotel arrangements, and you would think that his home town would be the last place he would forget to make hotel reservations. Since Frankfurt is a busy financial and cultural center, the only last-minute rooms Fritz could find for us were on a *Tanzboot* that was moored on the Rhine River. This was a "dancing ship" where tourists (mostly from Scandinavia) paid good money to float down Germany's beautiful waterways and dance all day and all night wearing what sounded like hobnailed boots. We tried in vain to get some sleep but the steel floor of the boat was just two feet over our heads, and we were kept awake all night. We had better accommodations in Munich, where we played at the acoustically-excellent *Herkulesaal*.

I recall being warned by fellow Brooklynite Julius Levine (who played the bass part for just about every Schubert "Trout," including a recording with the Budapest Quartet) that touring in Germany would constitute a blot on my Jewish escutcheon. He said that, for a member of the normally circumcised tribe (and with three colleagues of the same persuasion), playing in Germany was a mortal sin, and would keep us awake nights (how right he was about Frankfurt).

Mrs. Bahlsen, of German cookie fame, gave us a reception after a concert we played in Hannover, and her home put me in mind of what Julie Levine said back in New York. There were many enormously-antlered deer heads mounted on the wall next to her, and her oppressive dining room was dimly lit by lamps with lampshades that might have been made from the skins of our tribe.

Our next German concerts took place in Herford and Mannheim, and we stayed for several nights at the Eden Hotel *Fruh am Dom* (near the great cathedral) in Cologne. We used it as our base for run-out concerts at Shlosshotel Burg Cleeberg, Geissen, and Mainz. During one free morning Nomi and I took the train to Aachen to explore the town. When we got back to the hotel, I realized that I had left my camera on the train. I was told to make a report at the train station, which I did, even though I thought of it as an exercise in futility. A package arrived a few weeks later at our home in Milwaukee that contained my camera along with a number of photographs of the entire staff of our hotel in Cologne standing behind the counter and waving. Imagine our surprise.

After playing concerts in Lausanne, Basle, Bordeaux, we made a recording in Paris for ORTF French radio, and played at the historic jewel-box of a hall known as the Théâtre des Champs-Élysées, the scene of the famous riot at the premiere of Stravinsky's *Rite of Spring* in 1913. We flew to London, and the British Railway delivered us to Kendall, located in England's peaceful Lake District.

Levens Hall, in Cumbria, is a castle from the days of the Norman conquest (its first occupant was Norman de Heiland, c. 1170), and we were there to play a concert that would be broadcast live on the BBC radio. The main residence was built in the 1590s, and its famous topiary gardens were designed by Guillaume Beaumont (1650–1729). Our host, Robert Bagot, the current owner of the house, showed us the great park with a herd of black fallow deer plus a smaller herd of "Bagot" goats named for his family. The lawns were a tribute to the well-known recipe for creating a respectable English lawn: one simply plants the best grass seed available, and mows it for five hundred years.

Our accommodations were understandably spectacular, as was the huge breakfast table where we ate our traditional English breakfasts. The great oak table supported a lavish display of historic silver pieces, and each piece was secretly wired to an alarm system. Apparently, someone had failed to disarm it; and when I reached for a magnificent saltcellar at breakfast, a deafening alarm went off and caused me to dislodge my kippers.

Abram Loft came down with a chill that was severe enough to send him to hospital for a checkup, so we arrived at Levens Hall minus one violinist. We made some frantic calls to the BBC in London, and they sent out a driver to bring us as much trio and duo music as they could collect on such short notice. Len, George, and I were obliged to sight-read (more or less) the live concert for BBC.

The following day the Bagots took us for an outing through the countryside in their huge Daimler saloon. We drove for a while, and then they turned off the road and opened the boot for a spot of nourishment. We made do by sitting on the cold ground and devouring a lavish (and cold) English lunch, quaffing sufficient champagne to ward off the Lake District chill. As we walked about afterwards, I pointed out some lovely hills over the horizon and wondered what they might be, to which Mrs. Bagot responded, "Well actually (*ectually!*), I believe they're still our land."

We finished up the tour with concerts in Liverpool, Oxford, Birmingham, Rotterdam, Utrecht, Leeds, Manchester, Nottingham, and finally made it back to Milwaukee on December 1st, when it was Len's turn to come down with the flu, so Abe, George, and I played trios for the University of Wisconsin-Milwaukee concert.

The pianist John Browning joined us for our 1973 season, and he played the Schumann Piano Quintet with us on our domestic tour. When we played in New York, the *New York Times* reviewer wrote of the "easy and immaculate ensemble," of our Mendelssohn Quartets, and of our pianist, he wrote, "Mr. Browning's clarity and dash were energetically matched by the string players; over-all rapport and precision never faltered." Translation: Mendelssohn, good; Schumann, better.

We continued to enlarge our repertoire with Benjamin Britten's three string quartets and quartets by Shostakovich, Walton, Alban Berg (the Lyric Suite), Lutoslawski, Lees, Carlstedt, Hindemith (the Op. 23a *Des Todes Tod* "The Death of Death" for two violas and two celli, that we performed with Jan DeGaetani), and the Elgar Piano Quintet, that we performed with Richard Goode.

When we played the six Bartók Quartets on a three-concert series at Carnegie Recital Hall in 1973, we added a contemporary work to each program. The first concert had Bartók's second and fifth Quartets, along with the New York premiere of Charles Wuorinen's First String Quartet, a piece we commissioned and first performed in 1971.*

Wuorinen's First String Quartet is haunting and exciting. He opens the work with twelve pizzicato "chimes" of a clock, an idea that fits with his general obsession with time (Wuorinen won his 1970 Pulitzer prize for "Time's Encomium," a work he wrote in 1969 that featured those same twelve chimes). We recorded Wuorinen's First Quartet for Vox Turnabout in 1972, and Music & Arts reissued it in 2005.

The New Yorker critic Desmond Shawe-Taylor called us an excellent quartet, and thought that we had a profound understanding of Bartók. He thought the Wuorinen was expertly written for the medium and "conveys the powerful thrust of a shaping intelligence." Music & Arts re-released our recording of the Wuorinen on CD, coupled with Babbitt's Third Quartet, another piece we commissioned.

We felt that the Colbert-Lafarge management wasn't doing its best for us, so we started looking for new management. The

---

* As an example of the vagaries of academe, Charles was let go from his faculty position at Columbia in 1970, the same year that he was awarded the Pulitzer Prize for Music.

THE FINE ARTS STRING QUARTET (PART 1)

*Leonard Sorkin, Abram Loft,
George Sopkin, and Bernard Zaslav*

pianist Menahem Pressler told me that his manager, Melvin Kaplan, was taking on quartets (like the newly-formed Emerson Quartet). I worked for Mel when he was an oboist and a contractor in New York, and I sat next to Ynez Lynch, his violist-wife, when I played the Frederick Waldman's series at the Met Museum. Mel, who no longer lived in New York, ran his management business from his home in Burlington, Vermont.

The Quartet drove to Mel's maple-tree-filled property in Vermont that spring to meet with him. During lunch he handed us each a small earthenware bottle of maple syrup, and after the end of our meeting, Mel had the unbelievable *chutzpah* to ask us each to pay him five dollars for what we had thought to be a sign of his generosity. Melvin Kaplan was truly and in every sense the sempiternal manager, and he proved it after we signed on with him. Every so often he would require us to play a "freebie" for one of his better clients. We soon learned to count our fingers after every handshake with him, but we still admired the way he coupled his *élan* with his sharp business sense.

Our 1974 Fine Arts Quartet tour was scheduled to begin in Frankfurt on January 8, so Nomi and I decided to use the Christmas recess to take our own holiday before joining up with the rest of the quartet. Our travel agent in Milwaukee was Turkish, and he suggested that his native country would be a fascinating place to visit, so on December 20th we took Pan Am's Flight #1 from Kennedy Airport to Istanbul. When we deplaned, the baggage claim area looked like a scene from Dante's *Inferno*. Hundreds of Turkish *Gastarbeiters* (guest workers) chose that exact time to return home from Germany, and it seemed that the big thing that year for many of them was to bring home three-foot-long, double-handed crosscut saws, loosely wrapped with paper and string, which they carried through the crowds on their shoulders. Since multiple decapitations seemed inevitable, the police employed truncheons liberally to the legs of the carriers in order to make a path for us, as well as for the other passengers.

We weren't able to make it to the baggage claim to pick up our luggage, so Pan Am's agents provided for our immediate needs, and told us to check into our hotel and come back the next day. When we returned to claim our bags the next morning, an agent showed us that our soft-sided suitcases had served a mattress for a person who had urinated in his sleep. Pan Am was most helpful in this emergency. They told us to replace our ruined items at their expense (luckily, I always kept my music and my viola in hand), and to enjoy ourselves, which is what we managed to do.

Nigo, my beloved Armenian luthier back in New York, told me not to miss the *Çiçek Pasaji* (the Flower Passage) in the old town, to make sure to visit the famous Blue Mosque, and especially, to enjoy the colorful *Büyük Tarabya* area. We savored the local-freshly caught red mullet from the Bosporus, and even though Nigo warned us about the nefarious Turkish carpet dealers (we were glad he did), we selected a few carpets, and had them shipped home.

We showed up at the Istanbul airport a few days later to continue our itinerary with a trip to the Efes Museum in Greece, and were told that even though we had reservations, our plane was already filled. We had checked out of our hotel, and were ready to leave Turkey, so I asked the agent behind the desk when we could get the next flight. He replied, "Oh, maybe in two weeks." Obviously, I had much to learn about the ancient art of *baksheesh* (tipping, charity, and/or bribery). We were eager to take the first plane out of there, so we found a direct flight on Alitalia to Rome.

We stayed at the Hotel Britannia (as recommended by our flight attendant) and had a marvelous time in Rome, eating the *Pesce de San Pietro* in Trastevere, and admiring the beautifully-dressed high-class whores in front of the Spanish Steps. We took a train to Paris where we ate the sweetest Belon oysters at a restaurant across the street from the Hotel Franklin Roosevelt. I visited the French luthier Etienne Vatelot, and purchased a fine Nicholas Maline viola bow to add to my collection. We spent five days in Paris, and then left for Frankfurt, where we checked in at Savigny Hotel, met the rest of the Quartet, and did some rehearsing for the upcoming tour.

Pssst, wanna join a string quartet?

My Peak Viola Experience: Performing Beethoven's
Grosse Fuga

In his 1963 *Dialogues and a Diary*, Igor Stravinsky calls the *Grosse Fuga* Op. 133, Beethoven's original final movement of his Op. 130 String Quartet, "a perfect miracle . . . an absolutely contemporary piece of music that will be contemporary forever." He goes on to write "I love it beyond any other." Having spent nearly fifty years performing the string quartet literature, I agree with Stravinsky: this movement overshadows every other piece in the genre. Schubert's G major Quartet, D 887, and the heartbreaking slow movement of his magnificent two-cello quintet may be its equal in emotional intensity, but the *Grosse Fuga* stands alone in every other way. In his book *Beethoven's Quartet*s Joseph de Marliave calls the *Grosse Fuga* "perhaps the greatest piece of chamber music ever written," suggesting that "the music here reaches an intensity of feeling that transcends all the agony of grief, all the depths of anguish that human grief could experience." This masterpiece exists on a different plane from Beethoven's earlier quartets, where his post-Haydn and post-Mozart sense of style simply spells genius. The *Grosse Fuga* is something of another realm.

Before they disbanded in 1967, the Budapest Quartet recorded this movement for the "golden record," a phonograph record containing a broad sample of planet Earth's common sounds, its languages, and its music, that was sent into outer space on board both of the Voyager spacecrafts, one of which has passed out of our solar system.

The *Grosse Fuga* comes after nearly thirty minutes of incredibly touching music. The movement that precedes it has the title "Cavatina," and is marked *Adagio molto espressivo*. A cavatina is commonly defined as a "short and simple song," so for Beethoven to call this movement a "cavatina" approaches the ironic, since so many musical scholars have waxed eloquent about this "simple song." Karl Holz, the second violinist of the Schuppanzigh Quartet, the group that gave the first performances of all but one of Beethoven's late quartets, and who was a personal friend and secretary to Beethoven, reports that Beethoven actually wrote this movement "with tears of sadness in his eyes and admitted to me that no other work of his own had ever made such an impression on him, and that even the remembered feelings aroused by this piece always cost him new tears."

After playing this heart-wrenching Cavatina, a quartet has two choices. They can finish with the light-hearted finale, which Artaria, Beethoven's Viennese publisher, implored him to substitute for the original final movement, or they can take on the 17-minute monster of a movement known as the *Grosse Fuga* that sits on the page, daring you to enter. Nowadays, most recordings will usually include both of these final movements, but for a performance, a concert manager needs to decide whether his audience can withstand hearing both finales in one sitting.

We exchange "good luck" smiles before we begin, and some of the more sophisticated audience members exchange expectant glances as well. We play the opening unison chord made only of the pitch of G, and then, still in unison, we state the eight-note subject, fortissimo. After a fermata, and still in unison, we play it twice as fast, and after another fermata, we play it twice as fast, but a sixth lower. The key changes to F major, and the first violin barely whispers the subject, which is answered by the cello and accompanied by the other voices. The key abruptly changes to B flat, and the first violinist states the subject all alone, on the weak beats of the measures, and even more softly.

The *Fuga* begins *subito fortissimo* with the first violinist's statement of the countersubject, and we're off to the races. There's no turning back, as we shift into the exalted, inexplicable state we recall so vividly from past performances. We don't look to some imagined supreme being on high, some metaphysical conductor of the universe for succor (even though Beethoven might have done so when writing it). The four of us have to make this treacherous journey without help.

Beethoven reveals his audacity, and we navigate his diabolic twists and turns of thematic counterpoint. He has created a work of infernal complexity and musical logic, something undreamed of by either his predecessors or his contemporaries. We seem to enter a time warp, and deliver our collective selves into the hands of the great, deaf magician who strode confidently ahead of Earth's mere mortals. The piece is replete with treacherous-yet-elegant passagework, yearning intervals, and highly-intricate cross-rhythms. On and on, this mad fugue careens, shifting the distribution of its varying densities among the four of us. There are many points of rest, of questioning, and of contemplation. Then it doubles back on itself again and again, and with every new page the players chuckle inwardly and wonder how the devil he got *there*. We play the eight-note subject for the very last time, and the piece is over.

But how can that be? When did it stop? We're still in shock, our hearts still pumping madly in our chests. We notice as we lower our instruments that those folks out in the audience seem to be taking a while to recover from the onslaught. There's some tentative applause. It strengthens and grows into a frantic roar of approval. But approval for whom? You know that they're not just clapping for your performance, no matter how well you may have played it. There aren't many really different ways to "cut the part." When you come down to it, this piece is crafted to be almost bulletproof, as long as you give this beast the clarity and the unstoppable energy that old Ludwig requires. We worked our tails off to rediscover the piece's inner logic, and have driven it to its mad, but inevitable conclusion.

Back on solid earth once more, we acknowledge the audience by taking our usual bows, and the four of us walk off the stage slowly, knowing that no encore could possibly follow the *Grosse Fuga*. The audience also knows instinctively that an encore would be redundant. After playing this work there is no more to be said.

We are all flooded with incoherent thoughts while we stand backstage, so we just stare at one another in dumb silence. In making Beethoven's *Grosse Fuga* come alive for ourselves and the audience, the four of us have come together as one, yet we are unable to communicate our innermost feelings to one another with words. So we shake our heads bemusedly, and dab at the bit of sweat on our instruments, those age-old devices that caused all that clamor. And then we think about the gift we have been offered. There's nothing else in the repertoire that allows a musician to scale such heights.

The Fine Arts Quartet's 30th Anniversary Album

CHAPTER XIII
The Fine Arts String Quartet (Part 2)

Fritz Dietrich booked 16 European concerts for us in 1974. We flew from Milwaukee to Chicago, boarded a direct Lufthansa flight to Frankfurt where we checked into our hotel to sleep off our invariable jet-lag before the first concert. When we arrived in Frankfurt I could feel a painful strep throat coming on (I had been having them since my teens, and I knew this one would be a dilly). Rather than attempting to sleep, I called Fritz's office and told them that if I were to make it to the concert I would need a doctor sent to my hotel. In short order (at about 2:00 a.m.) I answered a knock on the door and was greeted by an attractive redheaded American girl, who was smiling at my obvious consternation, while holding onto a set of bicycle handlebars.

I was certainly surprised. She explained that she was the doctor on call, and that she had come from Ohio to study holistic medicine in Germany (Germany makes both traditional pharmacies and organic *apothekes* available to the public). She noted that I was running a fever, and after examining my throat, she gave me a mysterious shot (she told me it was not an antibiotic), and gave me a number of easily-breakable liquid-filled vials to take. I slept well through the night, and was almost normal next day. I was in good enough shape to play the next three concerts and tapings in Frankfurt.

Our daily schedule on tour normally involves packing up early in the morning (is that drip-dry shirt really *dry*?), bolting down a *kleines Frühstück* (small breakfast), checking out of the hotel (which means becoming familiar with the currency), getting to that city's local *Bahnhof* (railway terminal) on time, and boarding the correct train (or trains, because some journeys involve several changes). After Frankfurt we planned to travel to Saarbrucken, Geissen, Sulzbach-Rosenberg, Linz, Salzburg (the Mozarteum), Leoben, Kempten, Baden Baden, Mainz, Detmold, and Nürnberg.

The European railway system is a blessing for any traveler. Compared to more expensive and sometimes chancy air travel, Europe's trains run on schedule, and the food is good. George and I once shared a compartment on a rather long train trip, and we bought bottles of beer from a vendor. We finished our beers, and both of us held our empty bottles and stared at the passing scenery, totally bored. George lifted the bottle to his lips after a while, and he blew a few honks across the top. I responded similarly (I'm an ensemble player, right?) and soon it was he, going "*oomp*" and me, going "*pah, pah*," in a lovely "*oomp, pah, pah*" waltz tempo. After a while, George took the bottle down from his lips to complain, "Bernie, your pacing sucks; could you play those "*pah, pahs*" a little sooner?"

After arriving at the next *Bahnhof*, we would check into the hotel (reserved by our manager), unpack, grab a few winks (and maybe a bratwurst), and dress for the concert. Local custom

THE FINE ARTS STRING QUARTET (PART 2)

Bernard Zaslav and Abram Loft

required full regalia, patent leather slippers and all. Then we would have to find the concert hall (a search that was sometimes more exciting than we had planned), greet the local agent, and collect our fee in U.S. dollars (with a few amusing exceptions).

We would then set up our folding music stands, arrange the music, tune and warm up backstage for a few moments, and, at the signal (and perhaps an introduction by the client that would make us grimace), we would walk on stage and do what we were paid to do. Following the concert, there would often be a huge dinner or a reception, where we would be encouraged to imbibe the local wines and delicacies (in Scandinavia, they use every herb on earth to vary their *aquavit*), and try to get back to our hotel before 1:00 to sleep off our huge meal. We would get a wake-up call at an ungodly hour the next morning, and pick up the local *Tagblatt* to see what the critics thought about our efforts, and repeat this routine every day for the next 15 days (or until the time came to grab our Lufthansa flight home). Touring isn't that bad a life if you can keep up your health and your enthusiasm, but it's not for the faint of heart.

European tours were especially enjoyable for me when Nomi came along. We would visit the marvelous German museums and watch the "blue" movies that the local populace seemed to enjoy. The biggest laughs in those movies invariably came from seeing an actor get kicked in the *tuchas*; that blew our minds. We ate delicious *spaetzle* (kreplach) on a castle top in Nürnberg, and when I forgot my encore music (the Gershwin "Lullaby," I believe) in Salzburg, Nomi ran from the *Mozarteum* to our hotel room during the intermission to get it. Best of all, the two of us were able to experience all this together.

Our Quartet once met up with the Canadian cellist Zara Nelsova on a German train platform. Nomi had known her as one of the Nelson sisters, a piano trio from Winnipeg. As Sarah (now "Zara") stood waiting with her tour assistant (who was shlepping her cello for her), her first words of greeting were, "Oh, you guys don't know how lucky you are to travel together as a quartet. It's so *lonely* being a soloist."

A chance meeting of three violists at Chicago's O'Hare Airport: Bernard Zaslav, Michael Tree, and Walter Trampler

Both of our children had grown up. Mark finished his Master of Science degree in Psychology in 1972, and was working towards his Ph.D. in Psychology at the University of Wisconsin-Milwaukee. Claudia, after graduating from the University of Wisconsin-Milwaukee (majoring in music, as a flutist), was engaged to marry her heartthrob, James Drosen, a mathematics student who was on the way to becoming a math professor. He played the horn and studied piano with Nomi, who was a member of the adjunct faculty at University of Wisconsin-Milwaukee.

The viola that Harold Kohon found for me in the 1950s was a treasure. Audiences and critics remarked about its warm tone, and luthiers and violists marveled at how such a true, round viola sound could emerge so easily from this relatively small viola. This viola had become my voice, and it was part of me, but I was unaware that it was made by an extremely important 18th-century Italian maker (this is the Michaelangelo Bergonzi viola I write about). I didn't learn its true identity until after I began playing my next (even better) instrument.

The label inside my viola read "Giuseppe Odoardi in Ascoli, Italy," and Joseph Settin certified it as an Odoardi when I bought it, but none of the other American or European luthiers or violin experts I showed it to believed the label belonged to the instrument. This is not uncommon: false labels are often inserted into instruments by unscrupulous dealers for their own nefarious motives. An expert's well trained eye can usually spot a fraudulent label, especially when it is inserted into the work of a known maker.

Some fiddle mavens claimed my viola to be the work of the brothers *Lorenzo* e *Tomasso Carcassi,* but none of the instruments I saw by the Carcassi brothers looked anything like it, including the choice of wood and the color of the varnish. I can't claim a high degree of expertise, but I did learn a lot from Nigo when I lived in New York.

I often dropped into Jacques Francais' shop when the Quartet played in New York. Jacques suggested that I might learn more about the Carcassi brothers by talking with his father, Émile

Français, who lived in Paris. Émile still kept up the historic shop that was home to Caressa and Français, a respected French firm of violin dealers. When the Fine Arts Quartet played in Paris in 1974, I asked George Sopkin to come along with me to *père* Émile's shop to see if any more light might be shed on my instrument's possible maker.

After struggling with Parisian street signs, we finally found the old shop tucked away in a colorful neighborhood. We climbed a dark stairway to enter a huge and dimly lit atelier, and we were greeted by the shop's truly ancient proprietor, Émile Français. He was a natural charmer, slight in build (like a character from an old French film). He was dressed very formally, and his "reconstruction" of the English language would put Maurice Chevalier to shame. When I mentioned my so-called Carcassi viola, his eyes instantly lit up, and he disappeared into a musty back room. He emerged, holding what he claimed was a genuine Carcassi viola. It looked unimpressive. It was puny, even smaller than my fifteen-and-a-half-inch-instrument, and it had a dingy greenish-looking varnish. Since I was there, I had no choice but to give it a good try. George stood nearby, and was alternately frowning and cringing at the sound coming out of that ugly thing, while *père* Émile went into what was obviously a well-practiced spiel. He rhapsodized (with a straight face, eyes pointed to the ceiling), "Ah, how beautiful the master makes it to sound. It is *Romeo*, come to wake his sleeping *Juliet* with a kiss!" Fade to black.

I could hardly contain myself, and George looked like he was about to explode. I didn't even bother showing *père* Émile my own viola. We counted ourselves lucky to be able to say our hurried goodbyes without breaking up. While we were leaving his shop I wondered if a touch of the father might have rubbed off on his far more debonair son. No, Jacques was far more subtle than his father in dealing with both his customers and his customers' angels. He had a trained eye, and years of experience (there were others in his family's 200-year line of luthiers who had more expertise and tact than Émile). Jacques and I always enjoyed each other's company through the years, and everyone was saddened by his passing away in 2004.

At some point in 1973, George found a Goffriller cello that he preferred to the one he had been playing. His new cello had an even richer and darker sound than his former instrument. Since it changed the balance between the lower voices of the Quartet, I considered looking for another instrument. I was still a member of Local 802, the New York branch of the Musician's Union (you never know), and saw an ad in the *International Musician* concerning a Guadagnini viola that was being offered for sale. I knew that Guadagnini was considered as next in rank to Stradivari and the Guarneri family, and I knew very well that his violas were extremely rare. In Ernest Doring's 1949 book on the Guadagnini family of makers, he lists the nine violas by Giovanni Baptiste Guadagnini that were considered authentic. I wondered if the ad could have been a misprint, confusing viola for violin, but I answered the ad, and I waited for a response.

Six months later, when I had already given up the ghost, I received a reply. The seller was a Mrs. P. from Michigan, the widow of the Guadagnini's previous owner, who claimed (falsely) that her husband had been a member of the Detroit Symphony. Mrs. P. was asking an outlandish amount for the instrument, but I wanted to have a chance at it, so I asked if she could bring it, at my expense, from her home in Detroit to Milwaukee, so I could try it in the quartet.

Mrs. P. said that without insurance on the instrument (?), she wouldn't let me play it unless she was sitting close by. She agreed to give me two days to play it, by myself (with her sitting beside me), and with the quartet (with her sitting in the front row of the hall), and then she would take it back home. I offered to put her up, but she refused, so I checked her in at a downtown hotel, and then brought her and the instrument to my home to run it through the wringer.

Meeting Mrs. P. in person was a shocker. She talked haltingly (when she talked at all), spoke with a nasal Midwest accent, and delivered her sentences as if she had memorized them from a script. She had a frog-like aura about her, and sat perched on our couch with the open viola case beside her (it looked to me as if she thought I was about to run off with the damned thing). She listened with downcast eyes as I wailed away on her gorgeous viola, and I realized that it was to be this one, and no other.

I handed the instrument back to her, and Mrs. P. finally spoke. Her measured words, in a tremulous falsetto were, "My, that's beautiful. It reminds me of my husband," whereupon she opened her purse and pulled out a color photograph. It showed a man, ruddy in complexion and fully dressed, lying in a silk-lined casket. "That's my husband," she said. I guess she was moved by her memories, but I wisely refrained from asking if his tan was the result of a pre-death trip to Miami. The entire episode was ghoulish and incongruous.

I took Mrs. P. and the viola back to the hotel, and the next day I brought Mrs. P. to our quartet rehearsal. Again, she watched my every move like a hawk, in case of some legerdemain on my part. We rehearsed for a half hour, and George's facial expression said it all; no more needed to be said.

After I returned to her hotel, I told her that I wanted to buy it and offered her X dollars, which was all that I could afford. She said that she wanted $5,000 more than X. I agreed immediately (not knowing how I would find the money). Then she said she would take the instrument home and think about it. The bait was deeply rooted in my gut, and she was reeling me in like a master. After she left, George suggested that I should seek a loan from one of our wealthy Chicago supporters, which I thought was an excellent idea. I contacted the patron who had commissioned Karel Husa's quartet, and he generously offered to loan me the major part of the instrument's cost. I lost no time. I called Mrs. P. back to say I agreed to her latest demand. It should not come as a surprise that she jerked the line once more, and raised the price by another $5,000.

Joseph Silverstein, the concertmaster of the Boston Symphony Orchestra (I first met him at a party at Curtis Institute many years before), happened to be in town to perform with the Milwaukee Symphony. Joey owned two gorgeous Guadagnini violins at the time, and he told me to simply pay whatever she wanted and be done with it, if only because of the instrument's rarity. I got on the phone with Jacques Français in New York, and he advised me to pay only so much and not a bit more. Sure. Mrs. P. was already asking over $10,000 more than the figure that Jacques suggested.

I called her again, and (you know it) she said it would now be another $5,000. Being firmly hooked, I called Nigo, the one person I trusted above all others. Nigo flew to Detroit to view the instrument at Mrs. P's bank. He spent nearly an hour examining it. He pushed back his glasses and said, "Bernie, it is what it is," meaning that he found it to be genuine in all its parts, *label included*. Those few words might seem merely theatrical or unnecessarily terse to some, but there was a lot riding on them. His real meaning was that, with his years of expertise in such matters, he truly believed in its authenticity. That was what convinced me to purchase the instrument I would hold in my hands for the next 33 years.

With only nine of G. B. Guadagnini's violas then known to be extant (11 are now claimed as original), there was little precedent to establish a proper price, but I finally agreed to pay what was the record price in 1974. Mrs. P. instructed me to meet with her and her attorney at her Detroit bank, and told me that payment for the instrument was to be made by a certified check made out to her. When I flew out to pay for the instrument, her lawyer (wearing a Sears Roebuck suit, bow tie, straw hat, and brown and white wingtip shoes), did all the talking. Mrs. P. opened the case to show me that the viola (and a bow) was in there, along with an appraisal from the London firm of Hill and Sons, and a bill of sale from the previous owner. She reached for the check and I reached for the viola case; the jockeying between us must have looked like a Laurel and Hardy skit.

I learned later that Mrs. P's husband had been a music copyist for the Detroit Symphony, but he was never *in* the Symphony. He had purchased the instrument from a Belgian violist of distinction named Émile Férir early in the 20th century. Férir, who had been the principal violist of both the Philadelphia Orchestra and the Boston Symphony during the 1890s, gave the first performance of Cecil Forsyth's G minor Viola Concerto at the 1903 London Proms, and received stunning reviews from music critics of the day. A pupil of Férir's from San Francisco gave me a copy of the Forsyth Concerto that had some of Férir's markings. He also gave me some of Férir's compositions, and a promotional brochure showing him as a soloist.

Describing this unbelievable instrument would exhaust all superlatives. I was bowled over by its beauty, its power, its playability, and its "mint" (pristine) condition. Everyone who examined the instrument (Walter Hamma in Stuttgart, John Beare in London, Max Möller and Zoon in Amsterdam, Roland Baumgartner in Basle, Switzerland, Jacques Francais in New York and both Robert Bein and Carl Becker, Jr., in Chicago) pronounced it to be the finest specimen that any of them had ever seen. For the record, it was made by Giovanni Batiste Guadagnini in Turin (his best and latest period) in 1781. The instrument is known as the "ex-Villa" (and now the "ex-Villa, ex- Zaslav"), and it has a distinguished history. I was only the fifth owner of this viola (perhaps, custodian is a better choice of word for an object that will continue to live long after I am gone), which accounts for its pristine condition.

Mrs. P. and I said our goodbyes at the Detroit bank. She was going off to live in Las Vegas because she liked gambling (yeah, especially when you're holding a winning hand, and you're playing a sucker like me). When I received my cancelled check from the bank, I discovered that she had somehow cashed the check without endorsing it. Nobody at the bank could understand how, but she *did,* and that two-bit lawyer in the Sears suit must have figured out how to do it!

Word was getting around Chicago (and it finally got back to me) that the person who had given me the loan had actually *bought* the instrument for me. That raised my hackles, so even though I had been given three years to pay off the loan, I decided to pay it off immediately. In order to raise the cash, I sold our lot in the Sandia Mountains of New Mexico (foolish), and put my previous viola up for sale with Carl Becker, Jr., the trusted violin maker and dealer in Chicago. When a prospective buyer appeared, Carl suggested that we send it to Dario D'Atilli in Florida for proper attribution. That's when I learned that my "Carcassi" was really the work of Michaelangelo Bergonzi.

The buyer, a Canadian amateur violinist, asked if I would accept gold coins instead of U.S. dollars, because of the difference in the exchange rate. Since I knew nothing about gold coins, I asked to be paid in U.S. dollars, so that I could repay my loan. I can't be certain of the numbers now, but I recall that the price of gold rose dramatically from the time we made that deal. So much for my business acumen; but I did save my pride by paying off the loan, for what that was worth.

One of the first recordings the Fine Arts Quartet made using my new Guadagnini and George's new Goffriller cello was of the Prokofiev Quartet No. 2 and the Shostakovich Quartet No. 3. It was an album in celebration of the Quartet's 30th anniversary that we released on Gasparo, a company founded in Nashville, Tennessee, by George's former cello student Roy Christensen. A reviewer in the chamber music magazine *Devotée* said, "The technical production capabilities shown on this album are as near perfect as one could wish for." (This was due in part to the acoustics of University of Wisconsin-Milwaukee's recital hall.) The reviewer went on to say, "If there is any one feature in these performances that might be singled out for special praise, it is the rich sound of Mr. Zaslav's viola. With it, he succeeds not only in creating solo passages of incredible beauty but also in enhancing the totality of the ensemble immeasurably." This was especially heartening since a few of my students told me that they missed the sound of my Bergonzi. I believe the Guadagnini *is* the ideal viola, in both size and tonal beauty, and I continued to play it for the rest of my career.

The composition department persuaded our dean to hire a "name" composer for the faculty. Someone suggested Ralph Shapey as a candidate. Ralph had achieved notoriety with his large body of work and his many awards, but I also knew him for his lavish use of gutter argot. After I played the premiere of his Sixth Quartet in New York with the Composers Quartet, I asked Ralph to write Nomi and me a new piece for viola and piano. Ralph's off-the-cuff response was, "Why the f--k don't you guys play the one I wrote?" (We never mentioned it to him, but his poorly-scrawled parts for that duo were basically illegible.)

He came to Milwaukee to meet with the faculty. After the general meeting was over, I was walking down the hall with him, George, and the dean, when a co-ed wearing a rather tight sweater walked by. True to type, Ralph sputtered gleefully, "Will ya look at the t--s on her." The Quartet might have lost a good deal of face with our red-faced dean that day, and Ralph's name never came up again.

The Fine Arts Quartet continued to win plaudits. In the February 17th, 1974 issue of the *New York Times* Raymond Ericson wrote a piece called "Most Influential Four," where he proclaimed the Fine Arts Quartet to be possibly more influential than the Juilliard Quartet. We were named Laureates of the Lincoln Academy of Illinois on April 20th of that year, and played a concert at Chicago's huge Orchestra Hall for the event.*

Our manager normally dissuaded the Fine Arts Quartet from accepting engagements in Spain during the post-Franco era, but we were advised that we might safely accept one in the Canary Islands. It was off the beaten track, but it was on the way home from a planned European tour, so we accepted.

---

* A few years later, on May 23, 1977, we were each awarded an Honorary Doctorate for our contributions to chamber music from Northland College in Ashland, Wisconsin. Even more honors were bestowed on us a few weeks later, on June 10, when all the members of the Quartet were awarded the rank of Distinguished Professor by the University of Wisconsin-Milwaukee's Board of Regents.

THE FINE ARTS STRING QUARTET (PART 2)

We began that foreign tour on New Year's Day of 1976 with a flight to Tel Aviv and a concert at the Mann Auditorium in Jerusalem. It was the first Jerusalem concert for the Fine Arts Quartet in 16 years, and the *Jerusalem Post* called us "one of the best." After concerts in Svensborg (south of Odense), Stockholm, Plon (in Schleswig-Holstein), Graz (Austria), Bischofshofen, Pforzheim, and in Queen Elizabeth Hall in Antwerp, Belgium, we flew to Las Palmas in the Canary Islands.

We checked into our hotel, and tried to reach the local concert manager, but the office seemed to have no idea of how to run things, and there was nothing about the concert in the local newspapers, or anywhere else. We finally learned that this concert was part of a private series, run mainly for the "in crowd." Since we heard nothing from the agent, we spent two days enjoying the sights, and seeing lots of British tourists who found the *Canarische Islas* to be quite a bargain (relative to the British pound) during the winter season. Aging sun-seekers were there in droves, and the restaurants were full of the most delicious seafood.

It wasn't until the morning of the concert that we were finally told that our concert was going to be in a very old Baroque church. It was rather decrepit looking on the outside, but had a richly-carved wooden interior. There was concern that this wonderful old church was marked for demolition, and I hope it is still standing. Acoustically it compared very favorably with London's Wigmore Hall, one of London's best concert halls for chamber music, which had also been a candidate for destruction until wiser heads finally prevailed.

We were told that the renowned opera star Madame Montserrat Caballé had often commented on the winning acoustics of this landmark building. People said that she had sung there quite often, which must have been a joy for them to hear. I heard her magnificent voice in New York when I played with her in a performance by the American Opera Society in Carnegie Hall during my freelance days.

Our contract clearly specified that we were to be paid in

advance for concerts abroad, and strictly in American currency. We arrived at the hall that evening, dressed in the required frock coat, looking like four slightly-sunburned Jewish penguins, and the local agent met us backstage. He opened a rather large leather satchel that was sitting on a table, and extracted a decidedly fragrant mountain of *pesetas*, the local currency. Noting our furrowed brows, he told us that his assistant hadn't been able to get to the bank in time (even though we had already been enjoying the Canary Island's sun and sea breezes for the past two days), but, not to worry: the bank already had instructions to exchange this funny, smelly money into U.S. dollars when it opened the next morning. (This proved to be completely untrue, and we ended up shlepping this Spanish *moola* all the way back to Chicago, muttering all the way).

As the agent divided this moth-eaten pile into four large bundles he warned us about the peril of leaving *anything* of value backstage. With show time coming up, we four frock-coated saps had no choice but to stuff all of these pesetas into any available pocket (or other orifice), before waddling on stage to play late Beethoven. Like sea tortoises squatting for the seasonal egg dropping, we lowered ourselves very carefully into our chairs. After most of our adjusting motions had subsided, I raised my bow for the opening notes. Then I noticed that Leonard was frantically motioning me to wait. Taking a leaf from Marcel Marceau, Len employed elaborately muted gestures to indicate that some of the loot was spilling out of my inside tailcoat pocket. It certainly was. While trying to look nonchalant, I put down my instrument and stuffed the loot back into my pockets. It wasn't my best moment, but *the show must go on*. And so it did, albeit with a lot of poorly-stifled hilarity exchanged among the four of us.

Another surprise awaited us at the airport the next day. As we passed through Customs, several grim-faced inspectors sporting impressive-looking *pistolas* on their hips, demanded that we open our instrument cases for their inspection. When my turn came, one of them, in his attempt to dig out the contents for a closer look, reached his huge paw roughly into the open case, where my precious Guadagnini viola slept, wrapped in its cloth bag. My natural instinct was to reach for it first, before he crushed it, whereupon *his* natural instinct was to unholster his weapon.

I'll never forget my naked fear during the resulting standoff, especially since I was still carrying all of those damned pesetas out of his country, perhaps illegally. But at last I was permitted to uncover my valuable instrument on my own while the inspector kept holding his gat. I guess my trembling hands were a tip-off that I wasn't a threat to the monarchy, so a potential shootout at the O.K. Corral was averted. We had plenty to chew on during our return flight, such as how and where to exchange our Spanish swag back in Chicago.

Bernard Zaslav in his studio

We played a concert in the Foyer of Chicago's Orchestra Hall on October 19, 1976 in honor of Carl G. Becker, one of the most important American string instrument makers. His prodigious career spanned 73 years, and his work was of the highest quality. Becker built 494 violins, violas, and celli by himself, and another

262 with his son and disciple, Carl F. Becker, Jr., who suggested certifying the identity of my former Bergonzi instrument. His instruments are prized, and have consequently held their value. Frank Miller, the principal cellist of the NBC Symphony and the Chicago Symphony, played a Carl G. Becker cello, and Craig Mumm, my former chamber music student, who sits on the first viola stand of the Metropolitan Opera Orchestra, plays a Carl G. Becker viola. Each member of the Fine Arts Quartet was given a Becker instrument to play for this concert; mine belonged to a violist in the Chicago Symphony. It was a delight to play, powerful and responsive, and only fifteen and a half inches long. Hurray for the smaller-size *Bratsche*.

Our European tour that began the following February took us to Germany (Limburg and Mainz), and to Venice where we played a concert at the magnificent *Palazzo Labia for Radiotelevisione Italiana*. Then it was on to Padua and Bordeaux, for concerts in March at the Grand-Theatre Municipal and the Bordeaux Hospice. George's bow arm began to bother him shortly after the tour, so we asked Michael Rudiakov, an excellent cellist from New York, with an Israeli no-nonsense air about him, to replace George in our regular Milwaukee-Chicago concert series.

Sam Adler, the longtime composer-in-residence at the Eastman School of Music, wrote his Quartet No. 8, "A Whitman Sampler," for the Fine Arts Quartet to play with mezzo-soprano Jan DeGaetani. We gave its premiere in Chicago on May 9, 1977.

Jan, whom I had worked with in New York, came to Milwaukee during my first year with the Quartet to sing Paul Hindemith's song cycle *Die junge Magd* for alto, flute, clarinet, and string quartet. When she returned the next year, I was especially pleased that she chose Hindemith's 1922 song cycle *Des Todes Tod* (The Death of Death), a rarely-performed lyric and tragic work, set to poetry by Eduard Reinmacher, that is scored for mezzo, two violas and two celli.

To know Jan was to love her. I loved her voice, her spirit (in the face of health problems), and her natural openness and warmth. In 1972 she married Philip West, an oboist and English horn player from New York, and they stayed with us when Jan sang concerts in Milwaukee and Chicago (and Nomi gave them a party at our house after a Milwaukee concert).

Thomas Willis, a Chicago critic and an avid Hindemith fan, understood the musical rapport I had with Jan. In his review he wrote, "Alternately led and followed by Bernard Zaslav's expertly inflected solo viola, she drew us in and thru the moving succession with the sensitivity of a fine actress." Both Jan and Phil went on to teach at Eastman, and many string players took Jan's classes to learn about phrasing. Jan died of leukemia in 1989 at the age of 56, and Phil died of leukemia 14 years later. The sound of Jan's lustrous voice remains in my ear.

My good friend, the violinist Aaron Rosand, stayed with us when he came to town to play an outdoor concert with the Milwaukee Symphony in one of the city's parks. Nomi and I attended the afternoon rehearsal, which was conducted by Alfredo Antonini. Aaron (his close friends usually called him Archie) stood holding his famous ex-Kochanski Guarneri del Jesu violin of 1741 in hand (perhaps the finest del Jesu of them all) on a platform with two enormous, eight-foot-high loudspeakers on either side of him. Before Archie played a note, the midwest summer breeze sharpened stiffly, and toppled one of the speakers, striking both Archie and Antonini. I ran to help Archie, and was able to grab the fiddle from him before he fell.

We followed the ambulance that carried the barely-conscious Archie and the slightly-injured Antonini to the hospital. When Archie opened his eyes, the first thing he asked was, "How's my fiddle?" (It was fine.) On the way back to our house, we passed a Kentucky Fried Chicken, and Archie had to stop and order a whole bucket after his ordeal.

Archie had indeed suffered some injury, and he lost a number of engagements as a result. He instituted a suit against the city for his loss of income, and asked me to be a friendly witness on his behalf. It so happened that the sitting judge on the case had been a poker pal of mine, and though Archie prevailed, his settlement barely covered the cost of his lost income. I heard a recording of him playing the Brahms Concerto with the Curtis Institute orchestra in a concert in celebration of his 80th birthday, and it sounded terrific. Archie is one of the best fiddle players ever, and his recordings prove my words.

George's arm problem eased up enough for him to tour with us in 1977, but he began having eye trouble during our four-week European tour in February and March of 1988, so Michael Rudiakov joined us for the tour, which took us through Holland, Germany, Switzerland, Austria, and France. Nomi came along with us, and I still tease her about the overly-loud stage-whispered remark she made while sitting at a table in a fine restaurant in Lausanne, "The frog's legs were *much* better in Montreux."

After 33 years of playing with the Quartet, George's arm and eye troubles finally made it too difficult for him to continue. His bow would occasionally drop from his fingers during concerts (Len would actually tie a string to George's hand so he could retrieve it). It was painful to see the public sufferings of my brave, beloved friend and musical soul brother.

Abe had been with the Quartet for 25 years, and was looking towards his own future. It was truly the end of an era when George and Abe played their last Chicago concert with the Quartet on May 8, 1979. George and Abe were still on board to perform for our newly-created Festival de Música de Cámara in San Miguel de Allende in Guanajuato, Mexico from May 28 to June 15 of 1979.

The town of San Miguel de Allende (founded in 1542) has been preserved by the Mexican government as a national monument of Spanish Colonial architecture, and attracts many visual artists from all over the world, including the American artist Leonard Brooke, who made it his home. Tom Sawyer, an amateur violinist who also lived there, helped sponsor the festival, along with the University of Wisconsin-Milwaukee and our own Fine Arts

Foundation of Chicago. The wife of the president of Mexico came to kick off this first session, and the Festival continues as a cultural treasure.

These were the last concerts that the four of us played together. Abe Loft had accepted a position as head of the chamber music department at the Eastman School of Music in Rochester, and George had "retired' to live in the beautiful home he built in Surry, Maine. George went on to create the New England Piano Quartet with pianist Frank Glazer, and later joined me on the faculty of Kneisel Hall in Blue Hill.

Was this the end of the Fine Arts Quartet? I loved playing chamber music, and was still at least a decade younger than George and Len. I had made several big changes in my life, and felt I was in top form on my instrument. I enjoyed my students, and felt I had much to give as a teacher. Some of my better students went on to join string quartets, like violist Matthew Michelic (who joined the DaVinci Quartet), violinist John Sherba (who joined the Kronos Quartet), and the entire Ying Quartet (I taught them in Winnetka, Illinois). Some became orchestral musicians, like Philip Rose who joined the New Zealand Symphony Orchestra, and Nancy Severance, who joined the San Francisco Symphony.

Replacing one quartet member is hard enough, but Len and I needed to find two replacements, which was a daunting task. We instituted a nationwide search, asking colleagues, like Bobby Mann of the Juilliard Quartet, for recommendations. One of the violinists Bobby suggested was Laurence "Larry" Shapiro. He was an excellent player and an all-around nice guy, with a wide background (including a professorship at Indiana University) and he joined us for the September 1979 season.

We had many fine cellists to choose from. One agreed to join, but then felt that the quartet repertoire would be too overwhelming to learn in so short a space of time. Our pianist colleague Menahem Pressler urged us to consider Wolfgang Laufer, the principal cellist of the Hamburg Philharmonic, who had already made a name for himself as a solo

The Fine Arts Quartet in 1979
Laurence Shapiro (violin 2), Wolfgang Laufer (cello),
Bernard Zaslav (viola), and Leonard Sorkin (violin 1)

recitalist. Wolfie had emigrated from his native Romania to Israel, and studied at the Tel Aviv Academy. Both his playing and his personality were strong and decisive, so we selected him as our cellist. Wolfie moved his wife and family from Europe in September of 1979.

We had many works to prepare with our new colleagues for three-concert series at University of Wisconsin-Milwaukee and Chicago. Critics gave our new configuration excellent reviews, and Nomi was praised in both Chicago and in Phoenix for her playing in the Dvořák Piano Quartet Op. 23 (Larry played the violin part). In early 1980 we made our first European tour with our two new members. This was my first time in Helsinki, Finland, and I enjoyed the hotel saunas and the proximity we felt to Russia (a few of the other quartet members squeezed in a quick visit).

Though it seemed we were still coalescing as a group, we had a shattering experience at a radio station in Stuttgart during a taping of the Cesar Franck String Quartet. We made repeated takes of the first measures, and then the *Tonmeister* walked out of her studio to suggest that, because of Leonard's intonation problems, it might be harmful to our reputation to continue. We packed up, and made a hasty retreat.

Len had always been a superb quartet player, but we had all gone through a stressful period, and none of us is immune to the consequences of age. Learning to play a string instrument obviously requires years of practice, but playing "in tune" involves a many-tentacled feedback loop between brain and fingertip (touch), hearing (memory) and instantaneous correction (muscle). These miniscule adjustments can occur so rapidly that they are barely noticeable, but they are nevertheless part and parcel of dependable intonation, both in solo playing and in adjusting one's own pitch to the other members of a string quartet. Bowing skills can suffer as we age, but intonation seems to be the thing that degrades first in people who play higher-pitched instruments. I heard William Primrose hit notes that were a full tone or two sharp in his later years. Isaac Stern, a wonderful fiddler, performed in public for far too long (as my students who accompanied him in concert can testify). I did hear Len play wonderful performances of the Brahms Violin and Piano Sonatas with James Tocco after he left the Quartet, and he played those well in tune.

A particular personal highlight of the 1980 season was playing three performances (the third was on May 11) of the Elgar Cello Concerto on the viola (Lionel Tertis had played it in 1920 with Elgar's blessing) with University of Wisconsin-Milwaukee's new conductor, Geoffrey Simon, in downtown Milwaukee's jewel-like Pabst Theater. On May 14th, the Quartet played Elgar's "Introduction and Allegro" with the Milwaukee Symphony Orchestra at Vogel Hall, and on the second half of the program, Len and I played Mozart's Sinfonia Concertante for violin and viola.

During the last days of May, and at the beginning of the second season of our Festival in San Miguel de Allende with our new lineup, I realized that I had been unsuccessful at trying to ignore the fact that if I remained with the group, it would have to be with another person in Len's chair. I was reluctant even to suggest such a thing, since Len had always been the leader of the

Fine Arts Quartet. It was extremely difficult to figure out what to do.

I had been particularly impressed by the impeccable artistry of Shmuel Ashkenasi, the first violinist of the Vermeer Quartet, a group that made its home in Chicago, and was the quartet-in-residence at Northern Illinois University in DeKalb. I knew there had been several changes in the group's personnel since I heard them last, and I wondered if a call to Shmuel might be in order. When I asked him about the possibility of him joining the Fine Arts Quartet, he suggested instead that I should join the Vermeer, since they were looking for a new violist. Now *there* was something to chew on.

Stage

A POEM BY CLAUDIA DROSEN, OUR DAUGHTER

He was onstage all the time. Or backstage performing his public smile for the nice people, the elderly blue-haired patrons of the arts, their pancake makeup clotting in their facial craters, the cloyingly sweet small talk, flowing like cider. "Oh, Mr. Z, you sounded so lovely this evening, you gave us such pleasure. We're so thrilled to have the opportunity to have such fine classical music in our town blah-blah."

Mr. Z is my father. Mine. To air out and exhibit to you people, blue-haired or otherwise. Mine. Yeah, right. Pardon me. He's about as mine as the Mona fucking Lisa. Mr. Z doesn't belong to me at all. His instrument's got his heart.

As he removes his bifocals, bends his neck to peer with naked, myopic eyes at the worm holes, the flecked patina of the wood of his (here's the spiel) 1781 G. B. Guadagnini viola crafted in Turin, Italy, one of only nine in the world, i.e., the equivalent of a Stradivarius in the violin world, (end spiel), he gives tender, unconditional love to his wooden baby. Like a kiss. Is it a son or a daughter? He must know.

Onstage, I watch my father, turning his musical insides out for me and the rest of the audience through the f-holes (that has always sounded obscene to me), of his rare instrument. I live with the guy, we sit on the same couch, eat from the same dishes, but I only know him up there, up the five or six steps to the stage, in his cummerbund and shiny black shoes, perched in front of the black Manhasset, playing another concert.

So it is, that I treasure one thing Mr. Z gave me personally, offstage, in my hot little hand, one summer day in our duplex in

Brooklyn back in the early sixties. It was the 1946 edition of the George Gershwin Original Songbook for piano, complete with lyrics, and Gershwin's own, virtually unplayable transcriptions immediately following the playable versions. Dad got it at Juilliard and since he knew I loved to play the piano and he was way too busy with his Guad, he passed its tattered contents over to me.

I have played it over and over again, performing for him, even when he's gone, pouring my love for him through the sounding board of the old upright into the air. I have hung on to this humble book of sheet music for 40-odd years. If I could, I'd have the burial guys bury it with me, against my chest under folded arms, King Tutlike, because Mr. Z gave me this gift not onstage, not backstage, not on any damn stage. He just gave it to me—his baby. Like a kiss. And I'm not even made of wood.

Vermeer Quartet 1980
Marc Johnson, Pierre Menard, Bernard Zaslav, and Shmuel Ashkenasi

CHAPTER XIV
The Vermeer String Quartet:
Ne Plus Ultra

"OUT OF THIS ALCHEMY IS BORN A THING OF BEAUTY WHICH ONE CAN DEFINE, WITHOUT HESITATION, AS PERFECTION." SWITZERLAND'S *SUISSE*

In the very early 1970s, Scott Nickrenz, my poker-playing violist pal from New York (who owned a large Gasparo da Salo viola) surprised me with a phone call. He told me he was now the violist of the Vermeer String Quartet, and that he and flutist Paula Robison (formerly Paula Sylvester) had gotten married and were living in Chicago. It seemed like a game of musical chairs: she and Bobby Sylvester, who idealized our marriage, had divorced. Scotty invited us to attend a concert by the Vermeer Quartet that featured Paula, as the guest artist, playing a Mozart flute Quartet. We drove from Milwaukee to Chicago and enjoyed what we heard.

The violist who succeeded Scott in the Vermeer was Nabuko Imai, an excellent violist from Japan, but she had left the Quartet after five years to pursue a solo career in Europe. Their interim violist wasn't working out, which left Shmuel Ashkenasi, the first violinist of the Quartet, in a bind. Rather than joining the Fine Arts Quartet, Shmuel was hoping to find an experienced violist for the Vermeer Quartet as soon as possible. He invited me to chat about it over an outdoor lunch at a Jewish deli on Halsted Street in hot, humid Chicago. I took Nomi along to check out the town. We found Shmuel naturally charming: his inviting smile and ready wit were seductive (the latest Yiddish or Israeli joke was always spilling out of him).

The Vermeer was founded in 1969 at the Marlboro Music Festival, and in 1970 they became quartet-in-residence at Northern Illinois University in DeKalb, Illinois. By 1980 they had achieved international stature as one of the most distinguished quartets on the concert stage, and critics all over the world were calling them one of the most technically-polished groups on the scene.

Shmuel was born in Tel Aviv and he studied violin with the legendary pedagogue Ilona Feher, the teacher of Pinchas Zukerman (his lifelong pal) and Shlomo Mintz. Shmuel went to Curtis, to study with Efrem Zimbalist, and at the age of 21 he received top prizes in both the Tchaikovsky Competition in Moscow and the Queen Elizabeth Music Competition in Belgium. He had started a promising solo career, recording the Paganini Concertos, the Beethoven Romances, and the Mozart A Major Concerto with the Vienna Symphony for Deutsche Grammophone, but after his summers at Marlboro, and the influence of Pablo Casals and Rudolf Serkin, he decided to pursue a career in chamber music, rather than kowtowing to an impresario like Sol Hurok.

In 1964, Shmuel's Curtis colleagues, violinists Arnold Steinhardt, John Dalley, and Michael Tree, founded the Guarneri

Quartet with cellist David Soyer at Marlboro. Five years later, in 1969, Shmuel and the French-Canadian violinist Pierre Menard founded the Vermeer Quartet at Marlboro. We never discussed the reason for their choice of the name, and left the critics to play with it in any way they pleased.

Pierre was a student of Ivan Galamian, and a marvelous player. He had a Gallic charm, was extremely intense, often hot-tempered, and, like Shmuel, was a perfectionist to the nth degree. Their musical union was nothing short of amazing. I found it baffling how Shmuel and Pierre, people so innately unlike in personality, were able to agree on so much in their playing. Note that I don't say that they "played as one," a commonly misused cliche; you wouldn't want that in a quartet. Their different styles complemented each other, like two sides of the same coin. Pierre had his own sound and style in solo playing (brilliant when required) and a distinctive use of vibrato in his quartet solos.

Their current cellist, Marc Johnson came from Lincoln, Nebraska, and studied at Indiana University with Janos Starker. He was clear as glass in his musical reasoning, and, like Pierre, was outwardly different from Shmuel. It was a second wonder the way they agreed on every musical point. Marc was one of the finest quartet cellists it has been my good fortune to sit next to. Hardly the cellist "grandfatherly" type, he was an excellent solo player who understood, as we all did, that there was no better place to make music than in a string quartet.

We met for a run-through, and it was a breeze to fit with these three superb chamber players. I sensed immediately that this would be quartet playing of the very highest level, and I saw no reason to turn them down. After we began rehearsing in earnest, the tightness of ensemble reminded me of the way the Composers Quartet met Milton Babbitt's technical demands. The uncanny ensemble this Quartet achieved was apparent in everything we played, from Berg to Beethoven, and beyond.

I would sometimes find tiny perplexing markings pencilled in the Vermeer's viola parts. I wondered if they used some secret code I needed to learn, until I realized they had been written by Nabuko Imai, in Japanese. My beautiful Guadagnini blended perfectly with the other members' equally fine instruments: Shmuel's Guarneri del Jesu (the maker of both Harold Kohon's and Leonard Sorkin's violins), Pierre's brilliant-sounding Nicholas Lupot violin (one of the greatest of the early 19th-century French makers), and Marc's David Tecchler cello, (Tecchler was a great Austrian maker from the early 18th century).

Since membership in the Quartet meant membership in the music department at Northern Illinois University in DeKalb, there were practical and financial matters to consider. Northern offered me tenure with the promise of a professorship by the second year, with a near match in my salary and work load. They offered Nomi an adjunct position on the piano faculty as well.

Before considering a move to Chicago, Nomi and I invited Shmuel to visit our home in Shorewood, and his gut reaction was, "You'd really sell a home like this to join us?" I really didn't want to commute (possible only by car) from Milwaukee to Chicago and even further to DeKalb. We had always thought of ourselves as New Yorkers, but we never had the opportunity to live right in Manhattan, so we felt that moving to a bustling, culture-loving metropolis like Chicago might be stimulating. Since inflation had raised mortgage rates to above 20%, selling our house took a long time. While we waited for it to sell, and before we found an apartment in Chicago, I made the boring and sometimes dangerous (in winter) 90-minute commute from Milwaukee to Chicago.

I had a rather large class of viola and chamber music students already in place at Northern, most of whom had been attracted to the rather bleak cornfields of DeKalb by the presence of the Vermeer. Quite a few went on to careers in music, like Richard Marshall, who became the violist of the Vermillion (perhaps influenced by Vermeer's name) Quartet, and later became the assistant principal of the Minneapolis Symphony, and Bruno Price, a young British cellist, who was a member of my chamber music class, became an important authority in the violin world. During a break at our first rehearsal, Marc, usually economical with words, asked me, "Did you guys in the Fine Arts used to say poems to each other when you rehearsed?" It was evident that prose was the chosen manner of communication in the Vermeer, and even that was used sparingly. It became clear why the Vermeer was so widely acclaimed. This was serious stuff, and our goal was nothing less than perfection. We would often play our parts for each other individually, which made it possible, for example, to show exactly where the least *smidge* of pullback would be appreciated. We often rehearsed in pairs (rather than all together) to work on intonation and clarity, and tried out particular passages in different ways, to see if we agreed about where the phrase was heading. We scrupulously analyzed and assessed everything we did, and it paid off.

Usually it was "lucky Pierre" who controlled the fine tuning knob of our intonational microscope. He would make a practice of playing an offending note, loudly and irritatingly, making the point that someone's pitch was suspiciously errant. Nobody was allowed to be even a hair off-pitch, before Pierre allowed us to move on. To enhance the mood of a major or minor key in works of the Classical Period we would intentionally raise or lower the interval of a third or a fifth, ever so slightly.

We adjusted our balance to a fare-thee-well. I sometimes felt that my Guadagnini was being overly shushed by Shmuel in some places, especially when I played the B natural on the G string (a particularly sweet spot on my instrument), but I mostly deferred to the collective opinion. We adjusted our bowing to achieve our unified sound, and didn't feel compelled to change our bows in the same places for the visual effect. It took years of living with our repertoire before we agreed collectively on what direction the music should take. We ran the whole gamut, using all the tools for interpretation in our toolbox: how sweetly, how harshly, how much faster, how much more slowly, how much louder here, and how much softer there. The response of the critics, and the requests for return engagement from our clients, proved that our infinite attention to detail paid off.

We normally rehearsed in Pierre's apartment, which was

located on a high floor of a Ludwig Mies van der Rohe skyscraper in Chicago. Van der Rohe's "less is more" concept of floor-to-ceiling walls of glass is somewhat frightening at first, but it does offer a stunning view of the city. Pierre was a most imaginative oil painter, and in the second bedroom of the apartment, which he used for his studio, there was usually something new and wildly original sitting on his easel. I regret not having acquired any of his canvasses, as Marc has.

Shmuel also lived nearby, so Nomi and I looked for an apartment to rent in the same Lake Shore Drive area. While we looked for something large enough for our needs, we rented a small apartment on the 51st floor of a high rise in the Loop area (and we also rented a small apartment in DeKalb for staying overnight on our teaching days). It was fascinating to see spiders free-floating outside the floor-to-ceiling windows of our temporary Loop apartment, but we really needed something large enough to contain Nomi's grand piano, and the antique furniture we had collected through the years.

Nomi came along on my first European tour with the Quartet while our Shorewood house was still on the market. After we returned we learned that a supposed "prospective buyer" had stolen some antique valuables out of a bedroom drawer. He was, in fact, a known thief. Several months later Nomi noticed someone standing outside and enjoying the beautiful exterior of our house, so she asked him in to have a look. He wound up buying it, which freed us to move into a large (3,000 sq. ft.) so-called "vintage" (1920s) apartment we found at 3330 Lake Shore Drive, across from Lake Michigan. An apartment with a lake view is certainly desirable, but the "Windy City" can offer some uniquely unpleasant surprises. Once, after returning from another European tour, we discovered that one of our bedroom windows had been blown out and then boarded up with plywood by the building's superintendent. There was still broken glass on the bedspread. When icy weather came to call, the city of Chicago set up ropes for people working in the Loop to hang on to, to prevent them from being blown away.

Chicago had an excellent bus system, and the bus stop right at our front door provided excellent access to the Art Institute, and the Magnificent Mile. The Outer Drive that follows the shore of Lake Michigan (complete with speed traps) made urban car travel a possibility (in contrast to New York's maddening bumper to bumper traffic), but I first learned about Chicago's traffic etiquette when a cop pulled me over for going 2 miles over the 20 mile-per-hour speed limit on one of its curved sections. Talking like a rube to the officer, I asked him quite innocently if there was anything *at all* I could do to remedy the situation. He responded by holding up his large motorcycle glove and told me to slip the $50 bill I just happened to be holding in my hand into its cuff. At the same time, he explained very carefully that I should "make off as if" (his exact words) I was giving him my driver's license to inspect, in case a fellow cop was watching.

Nomi calls me a "pack rat" for saving old datebooks (and the odd concert program I would slip into my viola case), but they do serve to tick my memory, which helps when writing a memoir. I found an elegantly-printed program showing that the Vermeer played Mozart's Adagio and Fugue, K. 546, Bartók's Quartet No. 2, and Beethoven's Quartet Op. 132 in a concert at the Palau de la Musica Catalana during the Festival Internacional de Música de Barcelona on October 20, 1980. Since my name is clearly printed on the program, along with the other members, it must have been during my first European tour with the Vermeer. Though I can't recall any other cities on the tour, I do recall standing one evening with my colleagues in a town square in Barcelona. I observed people removing their overcoats, making a pile of them on the ground, joining hands in a circle, and dancing slowly and solemnly to to the accompaniment of a group of nasal, odd-sounding woodwind instruments. I believe the sad music to which they danced was called the *fado*.

It was either before or after that tour that we played a benefit concert for the Boston Philharmonic Scholarship Fund on a Saturday night in New England Conservatory's Jordan Hall, one of the acoustically-finest halls in the country. The review by

David St. George, called us "Little known, but still great," and said, "The performance of chamber music on this level of imaginative creativity and musical understanding, of technical accomplishment, of communicativeness, of intensity and of humility is something that only a handful of the greatest instrumental groups have ever achieved." He didn't stop there. He wrote about "the perfect internal workings of the quartet, in which each player has a vital function and contributes something uniquely his own while never mistaking his role for that of a soloist." He remarked on the range of Shmuel's sound, bow control, and "purposeful, wonderfully subtle rubato," that can "spur players on to take risks, gambles, and ultimately greatness that they might not otherwise dare aspire to." He was most impressed by our analytical ability, and our sense of musical structure.

That program consisted of a Mozart Quartet, Janáček's Quartet No. 2 "Intimate Letters," and Beethoven's Op. 132. This was the very first review I received playing with the Vermeer Quartet. I thought the Fine Arts Quartet had been well received critically, but critics from every corner of the world seemed to swoon over the Vermeer. Aside from causing my head to swell, it assured me that my move had been a good one. The physical move from Milwaukee's Shorewood to Chicago's Lake Shore Drive, however, was a schlep of some magnitude. Our grand piano, our antique furniture, and other collectables we amassed during our 12 years in Milwaukee and our summers in Maine, had to be brought up to the sixth floor by means of the vintage apartment building's vintage freight elevator.

The normal concert season is akin to the academic calendar, running roughly from September to May or June. Like the Fine Arts Quartet, we played our home series of concerts at Northern Illinois University and repeated the program at Chicago's acoustically-excellent Goodman Theater the following night. Some of the highlights of our first 1981 European tour included concerts at the Festival de Musique Montreux-Vevey on January 17, Rotterdam on the 20th, and next day at Amsterdam's Kleine Zaal at the Concertgebouw. Nomi flew over from Chicago to visit the Rembrandt House Museum with me.

We returned to Chicago, and played Haydn's Op. 76, No. 1, Janáček's Second Quartet, and Mendelssohn's Op. 44, No. 1. at the Goodman on January 26. John Von Rhein's headline in the *Chicago Tribune* read, "New Violist with Vermeer Quartet Blends into Ensemble Like a Veteran."After writing about how much he admired and respected the group, he mentioned me, "So smoothly and intuitively did he (Zaslav) merge his own musical character with that of his colleagues . . . that you would have thought him a veteran." Heck, I thought I *was* a veteran, but why quibble? A more emotional reaction came from Marc's wife, Kathy Johnson. Standing backstage, she cried tears of happiness because the quartet was whole again. I felt good about that.

John La Tourette, the Provost of Northern Illinois University also felt good about that, and he wrote us a letter saying, "Von Rhein's warm welcome to Bernard Zaslav will, I am sure, be echoed by audiences throughout the country and I congratulate you all on your ability to achieve so rapidly such a total integration of your respective talents."

This letter shows just how supportive the University was of the Quartet. Unless the roads were impassable, Donald Funes, the Music Department Chairman, along with a mess of faculty, often came out to our Chicago concert to cheer us on. Donald's son, Matthew Funes, a good violist who was in my class, now inhabits the salt mines (movie studios) in Los Angeles. I was later told that when negotiating Northern Illinois University's offer against my previous salary at University of Wisconsin-Milwaukee, Provost Tourette told the number crunchers, "The Vermeer wants him, so just make it happen."

Shmuel's solo career and blend of virtuosity and musicianship signaled, from his first notes, that this group was of "star" quality. I have seen violinists walking about, muttering to one another about Shmuel's astounding technical feats, and I have witnessed them myself. There were times when Shmuel's music fell off the stand, or he missed a page turn, and he would continue playing without missing a note. Reviewers would comment on his technical prowess in almost every review. In some groups this might be some cause for envy, but we took it for the plus that it was, rather than a cause for dissension. What's not to like?

On February 22 we left Chicago's winter weather for sunny California to play a concert at Stanford's Lively Arts series (my future stomping grounds). Returning to cold reality, we played a concert on April 28th at Milwaukee's Pabst Theater (my old stomping grounds). Jay Joslyn, of the *Milwaukee Sentinel,* welcomed us by writing, "As varied as the program was, it contrived to showcase the familiar, big voice of Bernard Zaslav's viola." He might have been just a tad prejudiced, but many of my friends and ex-students came backstage to greet me and my new associates after my 12 years with the Fine Arts Quartet. John Von Rhein of the *Chicago Tribune* thought a concert we played in Grant Park was our best playing of the series, saying, "Velvety smoothness of ensemble, a controlled rhythmic abandon, and a shared commitment to the most minute detail of the musical design continue to define the Vermeer approach. Intellect and emotion meet in subtle equilibrium . . ."

On May 24 we played a concert for the Wiener International Festwochen 1981 in Vienna's Mozart-Saal, and a few days later we played an all-Schubert program in Friedrichshafen-Schnetzenhausen. Pinchas Zukerman, Shmuel's old friend, invited us to participate in his Carnegie Hall Festival Concert series on June 5th (they were having a Schubert festival that year). We played the *Quartettsatz,* D. 703, Pinky and pianist Mischa Dichter played the Duo for Violin and Piano, D. 574, and we ended the program with the Quartet No. 14, D. 810 "Death and the Maiden."

The review in the *New York Times* on June 7th (with a headline, "Two Dramatic Quartets for Strings by Schubert") read, "The Vermeer Quartet made much of the two scores' feverish intensity and electrically charged musical atmosphere. These were lean, tautly drawn, even driven performances that rarely attempted to produce conventionally pretty sounds, and for that reason the results were all the more true to the spirit of the music." The members of the Vermeer Quartet wisely held off recording until they felt ready to "engrave" their product for posterity. We decided to make these two Schubert Quartets, which are mainstays of the repertoire, the first pieces we would record.

Vermeer Quartet
Shmuel Ashkenasi, Bernard Zaslav, Marc Johnson, and Pierre Menard

The Vermeers summered happily on the rocky coast of Maine, playing a series of Bay Chamber Concerts at the old Rockport Opera house in Rockport, Maine (1981 was the 21st season of the series). We normally played four or five concerts on the series, depending on our schedule, and used our rehearsals and performances to prepare music for the following season. Pianist Andrew Wolf, who served as the artistic director of the series, usually played several concerts with the Quartet. The Wolf family has a long and time-honored history in Maine, and at the time they owned several historic houses that looked down on picturesque Rockport Harbor. Shmuel also owned a house facing the harbor, but the rest of the members of the Quartet had to find their own rented accommodations.

Nomi and I had a cedar-shingled shore cottage in Surry that we built in 1974, but it was a long drive north of Rockport. Instead of commuting for our many rehearsals and concerts in Rockport, we rented a local cottage that was owned by the Suzuki family in nearby Camden, and we rented out our Surry cottage to Raya Garbousova, our colleague from Northern Illinois University.

Raya, a superb cellist, was the dedicatee of Samuel Barber's Cello Concerto, and she premiered the work in 1946 with the Boston Symphony Orchestra under Serge Koussevitzky. I first heard her play a Town Hall recital when I was a student at Juilliard. Besides her romantic style and rich, vibrant tone, she was superbly endowed physically, and from my vantage point high up in the front-row balcony, I could observe her womanly charms to the fullest. It took the passage of a few years of friendship after I joined the Northern Illinois University faculty before I could tell Raya, without fear of offending her, about how I had viewed her décolletage from my high perch at Town Hall. Raya took the news in stride and giggled delightedly, saying in her rich Russian accent, "You know? Dmitri Shostakovich—*de same!*"

After renting the Suzuki cottage for two seasons, we sorely missed our own shore cottage, so I threw in the towel and decided to commute. When I returned to my Surry shore after a rehearsal. I sometimes found it necessary to vent my frustration (especially if that rehearsal seemed barely worth the effort) by digging for the delicious pisser clams that hid under the mud of our rocky beach.

Our Bay Chamber series ran from July 2 to August 27, and the list of distinguished guest artists included violinist Berl Senofsky, violist Abraham Skernick, cellists George Sopkin and Leslie Parnas, oboist John de Lancie, bassoonist Sol Schoenbach, French horn player David Jolley, and pianists Vladimir Sokoloff, Leonard Hokanson and Artur Balsam. In his review in the *Maine Times*, Elliot Schwartz wrote, "Actually, there have been some changes: the building now sports ceiling fans to help the summer air flow, and the Vermeer Quartet has a new viola player. Violist Bernard Zaslav is a well-known figure in chamber music and has integrated his playing into the total Vermeer ensemble perfectly. If his addition is any index of the way changes are made in Rockport, then the new fans were probably engineered by Rolls Royce. In fact, they worked very well, too."

After we played our first Bay concert of the 1981 summer season, Shmuel received a phone call from London. Felix Van Dyl, our London manager, told him that the young British conductor Simon Rattle was inviting us to play a pair of concerts at Queen Elizabeth Hall on his South Bank Summer Music series that August. Our Rockport schedule left us free until August 20th, so we thought it worth making the trip to London and back.

After hearing the news, I called my old violinist friend Emanuel Hurwitz, who had been made a big-shot CBE (Commander of the Order of the British Empire). He was given the honor because of his long career leading the Hurwitz and Aeolian String Quartets as well as the English Chamber Orchestra and the Melos Ensemble. We had become close back in my Fine Arts Quartet days, so he and his violist wife Kay asked Nomi and me to stay with them in their comfortable old house in Golder's Green. We had a few days in between concerts to enjoy much good talk and good food with Manny, Kay, and their cellist son Michael, not to mention our visits to London's art galleries, and Carnaby Street, where Nomi bought a Twiggy-inspired knockout of a dress.

We made a hit with the critics in London, a town that usually prefers its own above others, and doesn't hesitate to tell you what it does and doesn't like. Modesty prevents me from quoting what Alan Blyth thought of us in the *Daily Telegraph* on August 11th. But Paul Griffiths in the August 7th *Times* couldn't restrain himself: "Indeed the playing was so vibratingly [sic.] alive that only afterwards did I realize how much had been said: at the time there was opportunity only to sit on the edge of one's seat and be swayed by the fact and forceful mix of mood, colour and conflict.

Memory, however, retains images of the second [Bartók] quartet's demon scherzo as a dialogue of angular momentum and flowing, flowering gentleness, of the same work's finale as a play of emotion as graphic yet as ominous as the opera *Bluebeard's Castle*, of a sixth quartet filled with a hopelessness and barrenness more appalling than melancholy, of Bernard Zaslav's viola—here exulting madly in its banjo parodies, of Shmuel Ashkenasi's violin exchanging one disguise for another in the second movement, now crawling through a grim, grey spider's world, now whistling with a forced blitheness, as if through the teeth." Like the old E-type Jaguar (1961 to 1975) they don't make (or write) this kind of stuff anymore.

We played our last Rockport concert of the season on August 20th with pianist Leonard Hokanson, and then, as Abe Loft would say to us at midnight, after an exhausting day, we took the rest of the (night) summer off. Of course, we still had to prepare for the 1981–82 season.

Chicago's urban tempo was invigorating, and we made many new friends there. We also reconnected with a few old ones, like David Krupp, my "failed baritone" friend (turned attorney) who had hilariously mispronounced Ferde Grofé's name at Interlochen so many years before. Mark was working as a psychologist at the Veteran's Administration in Milwaukee, and Claudia married her mathematician boyfriend, and was living in State College, Pennsylvania.

Though we were less well-known in America, the Vermeer Quartet was especially well regarded in Europe. It was often said that we represented the best in American quartet playing, but some of the more sophisticated audiences and critics claimed that our playing was more European than American in character. Regardless of tradition or borders, we had our own voice.

The city of Manchester is only a train ride from London, so many faculty members from the Royal College of Music and the

Guildhall School in London also taught at the Royal Northern College of Music in Manchester. By the time I joined, the Vermeer Quartet had been giving master classes and performances there for many years.

After we finished our coaching, we played a concert of Haydn, Bartók, and Mendelssohn on November 2, 1981 for the Manchester Chamber Concert Society, and after a few more concerts in England, we went off to Römerbad-Musiktage Badenweiler to play two concerts at Klaus Lauer's historic Grandhotel Römerbad. This low-hilled spa town outside of Freiburg was the place where Herr Brahms was said to have taken his stately walks, hands behind his back, as he is often pictured. Perhaps he might have been deep in thought about his next symphony (or maybe a viola concerto, *efsher*?), but of course he might also have been fantasizing about Frau Clara Schumann, albeit in the *most* honorable manner.

The Grandhotel Römerbad was one of a chain of Die Kultur-Rezidenzen, known in English as the "Great Hotels of the World" (their modest description). Klaus Lauer, a highly perceptive music aficionado, presided over this unique in-house (more like "in-castle") vacation spot, which had been run for decades by his forbears, a long line of hoteliers. For perhaps $1,000 (which was a lot of money in the 1980s), a couple might spend a three-day idyllic weekend there, enjoying the fabulous food and even more fabulous accommodations, and they could attend Friday and Sunday evening chamber music concerts played by major chamber artists. Following the concert they could drive home leisurely in their BMWs, taking the Autobahn to Freiburg, Munich, or to their own private *Schloss* to lord it over the less well-heeled *Landsmänner*.

Klaus chose the music and the musicians he wanted, and saw to it that we were treated royally during our three days at the Römerbad. We were picked up and delivered to the hotel from the Freiburg airport by the hotel's fast limousine, a special-order Bimmer. Nomi, who always warns me to slow down when I drive over 60, sat contentedly (and unwittingly) as Klaus' driver sometimes hit well over 100 mph (or more than 44.70400 meters per second) in order to get us to our destination. In the mornings, a waiter would knock, roll in a cart bearing my breakfast, complete with starched napery and a big glass of ice-cold blood-orange juice (plus other delicious delicacies from their fabled kitchen) and arrange it on a table near my bed.

On Friday, November 13th, we played Stravinsky's Three Pieces for String Quartet and the Mozart Adagio and Fugue K. 546. At last I was able to meet (and hear) Nobuko Imai, the charming source of those mysterious pencilled Japanese markings in my inherited quartet parts. Nobuko was a top rank violist, and her performance that night of Stravinsky's tricky Elegie for Solo Viola was the best I had ever heard. Following the Stravinsky, she joined us to play the second viola part in the Mozart G minor Quintet, K. 516.

Mozart was one of the first composers to add a second viola part to the normal string quartet combination of two violins, a viola, and a cello. Adding a second viola part to the ensemble frees the quartet's violist to take part in a bit of dialogue with the first violin, while also expanding and enriching the group's total texture.

Beethoven (perhaps influenced by Mozart) has given us a single (but joyous) viola quintet, and Brahms (every violist's friend) wrote two highly-colorful works in this genre. Mozart's six magnificent viola quintets are generally regarded as the quintessence of his chamber music, and I was fortunate to have had the opportunity to record them with the Fine Arts Quartet, with Francis Tursi playing the second viola part. Teldec asked the Vermeer Quartet to record the six quintets with Nobuko as guest violist. What a luxury it would have been to record these masterworks for a second time (but it didn't come to pass).

On Saturday (and most of Sunday) we stuffed ourselves with gourmet food at Badenweiler, had great talks about music with Klaus, and took balmy walks in the countryside. For our Sunday concert we were joined by Heinz Deinzer, a wonderful clarinetist, who taught at the Freiburg Musik Conservatorium. The program included Stravinsky's Concertino for String Quartet, Mozart's Quartet in E Major, K. 428, Stravinsky's Three Pieces for Clarinet Solo, and the Mozart Clarinet Quintet in A Major, K. 581. I'm especially proud of the recording of the Mozart Quintet that we made later for the prestigious Orfeo label with Karl Leister, the principal clarinet of the Berlin Philharmonic, but Hans Deinzer was also absolutely wonderful in this work. The next day, knowing about my interest in autos, Heinz took me out for a spin in his vintage Citroen Maserati (what a car) to view the nearby ski slopes.

We began 1982 with performances in Kansas City, Missouri, and in San Francisco where we played a Haydn quartet and two Mozart viola quintets with Geraldine Walther, who was then principal of the San Francisco Symphony, for their Mostly Mozart Festival. I was mentioned in the review of our March 4th concert at the Wilshire Ebell theater in Los Angeles: "The addition of Zaslav allows the Vermeer—never a faint-toned group—to produce a strikingly homogeneous sonority, one of the largest and darkest in quartetdom."

We gave a concert in Chicago later that March, and then flew off to Frankfurt to play concerts in Emden (Germany), at the Concertgebouw, and in Geneva, where our performance on March 30th of Haydn, Verdi, and Bartók led critic J-J.R. (perhaps a young Jean-Jacques Roth) of the *Tribune de Genève* to pen, "How should I say it? For once the music was so totally fulfilled that words are only intrusive . . . Each note is fired with fever. More than a shattering dialogue, more than the largest vision and immense musical field, more than the particular sensual vibration and suppleness of a feline attack, the Vermeer Quartet, seems to have invented an aesthetic of passion."

After paragraph upon paragraph of superlatives (the reviewer claims that we reached Parnassus in the Haydn, explored both heaven and hell in the Berg, and visited La Scala in the Verdi), the review ends: "Even the most blasé people at Tuesday evening's concert had to feel the emotional grip. Perhaps the Vermeer Quartet repeats this exploit every night. For us it remains something exceptional."

We were invited to participate in the Aldeburgh Festival in Suffolk, England, that April. We played a concert in Snape Maltings Concert Hall, and taught at the Britten-Pears School for Advanced Musical Studies. From there we went off to London to play a BBC Lunchtime Concert at St. John's Smith Square. These noontime concerts were always well attended, and many of my musician friends joined us for lunch afterwards. The shop talk was international and stimulating, and the gossip was all about who did what bit of malice to whom, and how a particular musician was (or wasn't) sounding these days. Between April and our trip to Australia in May, I had another chance that year to play the Elgar cello concerto on viola, this time with Northern Illinois University's orchestra. Raya Garbousova made me feel worthy by saying that she approved of it on viola, which is quite a concession from such a cellist (and such an artist).

Our five-concert series in Australia was sponsored by Musica Viva, an organization founded in 1945 to promote chamber music (it's Australia's oldest performing arts organization). We needed to change planes in San Francisco in order to get from Chicago to Sydney, and when we landed in San Francisco, Pierre discovered that he had somehow forgotten his passport. We learned to put up with Pierre's artistic temperament and his quirks. He was a dual citizen of Canada and the United States, and was in the habit of not paying his United States income tax on time. Sometimes he didn't pay it at all. He was miles above such mundane trifles, and much more concerned about artistic beauty. When dining at a table with a particularly beautiful silver saltshaker, for example, he might decided to add the odd piece to his collection.

We were told by customs that Pierre would follow the next day after getting proper certification, so we boarded the Qantas flight minus one fiddler. Qantas Airline pilots enjoyed dipping their wings over Australia's Gold Coast City in Queensland before landing in Sydney. Since we couldn't rehearse without Pierre, the three of us enjoyed a free day in Sydney. I enjoyed the city's brisk pace (it reminded me of New York's Lower East Side), and visiting the Sydney Zoo, with its many different types of kangaroos. I also bought a lovely Australian black opal for Nomi at the hotel shop.

The next day we went, with some trepidation, to the airport. After all the passengers deplaned, we saw no sign of "lucky Pierre." We wondered if he even made it onto the plane in San Francisco. We asked a flight attendant to check the aircraft one more time, and she finally found Pierre sound asleep in one of the back seats of the plane. Our second violinist yawned his way down the steps of the aircraft, and we were back in business.

I was able to enjoy a performance of *Amadeus* at a Sydney bank's downstairs theater, and our concert in Sydney took place in their fabulous multi-winged Opera House. When we arrived for an acoustic dry run before the concert, there were kids bouncing a ball against the walls of this architectural wonder. They were treating the spectacular wings of this famous edifice the same way I treated the old Brooklyn stoops when I was a child. One would expect the sound of a string quartet to be lost in such a huge space, but when I did a sound check from the back of the hall, I discovered the acoustics were surprisingly good. The rest of our Australian tour consisted of concerts in Canberra, Melbourne, Brisbane, and all the way west to Perth.

After we returned to America, we played a concert at Tanglewood (July 15th, 1982). The reviewer from the *Berkshire Eagle* was impressed by our Haydn, Mendelssohn, and by Britten's Third Quartet (my favorite), but the humongous mosquito that was biting me during a long held note made a longer-lasting impression on me. After the last of our Bay Chamber Concerts, we flew to California to play a concert at Santa Barbara's Music Academy of the West Summer Festival, and then Nomi and I flew back to Surry, Maine for a well-earned vacation.

Since Shmuel was a celebrated musician, and a native Israeli, we were invited to play a series of five concerts in Israel. We began on September 6, in Tel Aviv, and were joined by pianist Joseph Kalichstein. Jake and Shmuel had known each other in their youth, and the horsing around in rehearsal was memorable. When Israeli audiences like something, they make no secret of it, and they liked the pairing of the Beethoven Quartet, Op. 130 (with the *Grosse Fuga*) and the Schumann Piano Quintet.

Our next European tour began in October with an annual date in Hannover to play for a concert series run by a medical doctor who was an amateur violinist (he always selected our program). In the midst of this constant rehearsing and performing, I had some pain in the index finger of my left hand that was starting to worry me. The doctor who ran the series sent me to Hannover's main hospital to be examined, but the hospital refused treatment unless I was willing to remain in town for at least three days. This wasn't possible with our schedule, so I thanked them and went on my way. I played on, in spite of the occasional spot of blood on my fingerboard, and when I returned to Chicago I received proper treatment.

The Vermeer recorded for Teldec, a German record company that hired expert *Tonmeisters* who knew all our scores thoroughly. They recorded us in an old (and otherwise unused) church that was hidden on a small alley, right in the center of West Berlin. Assistants moistened its centuries-old wooden floors every so often with mops (it had something to do with the acoustics). There were a few unreachable openings in the church's high ceiling, and every so often a fluttering pigeon or two forced a halt to the proceedings. The *Tonemeisers* placed cushions under Shmuel's energetic feet, so their sound wouldn't be picked up by the microphones.

Their attention to detail made a recording that reflected the Vermeer Quartet's true sound. Our first Teldec recording was of Schubert's *Quartettsatz* and his "Death and the Maiden" Quartet, and then we made recordings of the Dvořák Quartet No. 10, Op. 51 and Verdi's flashy E minor Quartet. We started our complete Beethoven cycle with Op. 130 (with the alternate last movement and the *Grosse Fuga*), Op. 127, and Op. 135 (though Op. 135 was recorded with another violist). Our first Beethoven recordings were released on LP (audiophiles still believe it to be the superior format). These, and all of the Vermeer Quartet's subsequent recordings, were issued later in the newer CD format.

The day before the start of five full days of Beethoven recording sessions, Nomi phoned to say that my mother had died. I knew that I couldn't disrupt our recording schedule and concert obligations (all over Europe) by flying to Miami to attend her funeral, so I kept my grief to myself, and the show went on as planned. We returned to Chicago after our final concert in Cologne, and had our last runout concert of the year in UCLA's fine Schoenberg Hall in Berkeley, California at the end of October. We returned to Chicago's winter, and our commute to and from DeKalb.

This energetic pace (and our good reviews) continued through all of 1983 and 1984, and we were doing well in America thanks to the work of Mariedi Anders Artists Management. Mariedi had wide experience in the field, and she always came up with worthwhile American dates that fit in well with our foreign schedule. When we were in the area, we would visit Mariedi at her lovely San Francisco home.

The highlights of our 1984 Chicago series included a concert with principals from the Chicago Symphony, flutist Donald Peck, clarinetist Larry Combs, and French horn player Dale Clevenger, and a concert of French music at the Rockport Opera House with Nomi, Pierre, flutist Thomas Wolf and harpist Alice Rideout. That program included a transcription of Jean Phillippe Rameau's *Pièces de Clavecin* for harp, flute, and viola, Debussy's Sonata for the same (then unique) combination, and Nomi and I played Darius Milhaud's Sonata No. 1. Among the other high points of the season were playing Louis Spohr's Concerto in A minor for String Quartet and Orchestra with the Grant Park Symphony under Christian Badea, and performing the Schumann Piano Quintet with the excellent Austrian pianist Walter Klien at the Kennedy Center for the Performing Arts. Mr. Klien, who also played it with us in Germany, brought something special to the work. Was his performance the *cleanest* of them all?

Notable events of 1984 included Ronald Reagan's landslide

re-election (and Walter Mondale never being heard from again), and the introduction of the first Macintosh computer from Apple. Though it might have seemed akin to the one foretold by George Orwell, 1984 was a bountiful year for me and my family. Mark, our son, was working as a psychologist at the San Francisco branch of the Veterans' Administration, and our daughter Claudia's husband James Drosen, had become an assistant professor at Penn State University. The Drosens were about to present us with Sarah, our first grandchild. Nomi taught a small class of talented piano students at Northern Illinois University, and the Quartet continued to win critical accolades. Some critics even lauded us over the Juilliard, the Guarneri, and the Alban Berg Quartets, but such comparisons are invidious and pointless: we played our best, which is all one (or four) can do.

Touring is the best method yet devised for seasoning a work, but it comes at a price. We were being offered more concert dates than we could comfortably handle, and in order to perform up to our standard, we had to set limits. I felt that I had reached my highest level, both technically and musically, but the Vermeer's very success was becoming problematic for me.

Differences are inevitable when four people work as intimately and spend as much time together as they do in a string quartet. Marc and I usually traveled together, while Shmuel and Pierre, who each had many European friends, would usually go their separate ways, and make their own travel arrangements. Once we reached the concert hall, the playing was the easy part of the game. I thrived on playing concerts, and learned much from the recording process, but I didn't know how much longer my body could withstand the rigors of travel and the abuse to my circadian time clock that came into play during our many European tours.* I was roughly 15 years older than my colleagues, and had been touring since the late 1960s.

All of this came to a head quite unexpectedly in late 1984. Shumel and I shlepped our fiddles and luggage through Chicago's O'Hare airport, after a flight from Frankfurt, and we fought the

---

* Research has shown that jet lag can cause up to a 50% loss of new neurons in the hippocampus, the part of the brain involved in memory (at least in hamsters).

crush to share a cab. There was a hell of a snowstorm (we were lucky to have landed), and both of us were beat and exhausted. The snow seemed several feet thick, and negotiating Chicago's Eisenhower Expressway through this mess was driving our cab driver nuts. His cursing told us that we would be lucky to get home at all.

Something in my gut caused me to blurt out, "Shmuel, I quit." I was as surprised as he was, but I said it, and realized that I meant it. We had achieved tremendous success during my five years with the Quartet, but success meant less to me than saving my physical body, my machine for living, which took precedence over everything else.

We discussed this at length at our next meeting. I promised to honor my contractual obligations until they found a substitute, and took some moral comfort knowing that I had given them sufficient time to audition other violists for my slot. They finally settled on Richard Young, a violinist friend of Marc Johnson, who was persuaded to switch to viola.

I discussed the possibility of a tenured teaching position with the music department of the University of Michigan in Ann Arbor, but with so many years of quartet experience in my quiver (and after 17 years of Midwestern weather), the thought of settling for studio teaching alone seemed stifling.

During the spring semester break, Nomi and I flew out to California to visit Mark. He was living in El Cerrito, working at the San Francisco Veterans' Administration, and loving the California lifestyle. We made the requisite tourist's drive south on beautiful U.S. 1 to San Diego, and then I called Stuart Canin,* my old friend from New York. Many years earlier, Stu, a marvelous violinist with a storied career, asked me to leave New York and join a quartet in Ames, Iowa. When he became the concertmaster

---

* In an unscripted 15-minute segment of Fred Allen's "Town Hall Tonight" radio show in 1936, 10 year old Stuart Canin played Schubert's "The Bee." Allen's comment, "A little fella in the fifth grade at school and already he plays better than Jack Benny" initiated the so-called Benny/Allen feud (they actually remained friends and mutual admirers). In 1945 when Stuart was in the Army, he was asked to bring his violin to Potsdam to play a private concert for Churchill, Truman, and Stalin.

of the San Francisco Symphony, he asked me if I was interested in a principal viola position in the orchestra. I was flattered, but quartets were more my game than symphony orchestras.

This time Stu told me that he was thinking of leaving the San Francisco Symphony, and moving to Los Angeles to work in the film industry. He suggested that I should do the same, and that we should form a string quartet together with cellist, Eleanor Slatkin, one of the founding members (with her husband Felix) of the Hollywood String Quartet.

We crashed at the Canin's Los Angeles apartment for a few days (it was in Brentwood), and we read through some quartets with Eleanor and one of Stu's violin students. Since they were all busy with studio work, playing quartets with this bunch wouldn't involve much in the way of touring, but the longer Nomi and I thought about living in Los Angeles, the less appealing it became. Tempting as it would have been to make a quartet with Stu and Eleanor, spending half my life driving on the Southern California freeways and playing commercial dreck wasn't the kind of future I had in mind. I had to tell them so, albeit regretfully. We thanked them, said our goodbyes, and flew back to San Francisco to stay with Mark for a few more days.

I heard that Andor Toth, my old colleague from my Cleveland Orchestra days, had also gone west. After he left Cleveland, he joined the Alma Trio, and founded the New Hungarian Quartet. He was currently a professor at Stanford University, where he conducted and taught orchestral studies. He missed his life in chamber music, so he formed the Stanford String Quartet with Don Erlich, the assistant principal violist of the San Francisco Symphony. Don decided to leave the Quartet after a year of trying to play in both the Stanford Quartet and San Francisco Symphony, so Andy asked me to join the Quartet. I had to give it some serious thought.

Nomi and I drove to Menlo Park to discuss this latest wrinkle. We stayed with Andy and his singer-wife Louise, enjoying their house and gardens, and I sat in with the Quartet (with second violinist Mayumi Ohira and the cellist Stephen Harrison). With

Andy at the helm, and my long years of quartet experience, this group felt like something worth pursuing further.

Stanford University gave birth to Silicon Valley and its innovations in technology. It always disdained being called "the Harvard of the West," and thought of itself, rather, as the burgeoning Pacific Rim entity for education. It was known to be well funded in other areas, but I did have questions about Stanford's dedication to the arts. I discussed the possibility of joining the Stanford faculty with the chairman of the Music Department, and found it odd that all they could offer me was a senior lectureship as a member of the quartet-in-residence. The meager salary wasn't anywhere near what I had enjoyed previously, but the idea of working with Andy, a highly experienced quartet player, enjoying California's climate and lifestyle, and creating what the University hoped would become a "world class" quartet seemed worth a gamble.

Although the Stanford Quartet (with its current membership) was slated to make its London debut in Wigmore Hall in April, extensive foreign touring wasn't likely to happen, if ever, so after the necessary formalities (and a private donation from a sponsor to double Stanford's small salary), I accepted their offer for the next academic year. In September 1985 I would be the new violist of the Stanford Quartet.

Nomi and I returned to Chicago, and I fulfilled the rest of my obligations with the Vermeer Quartet.

For the final concert of the 1985 Chamber Music Chicago series the Vermeer Quartet played Beethoven's last Quartet, his Op. 135. Shmuel asked his old Curtis pal (and leader of the Guarneri Quartet), violinist Arnold Steinhardt, to play the second viola part in two quintets, Beethoven's lighthearted Quintet, Op. 29, and Mozart's heart-wrenching G minor Quintet. Since I had resigned, our plans for recording all six Mozart quintets for Teldec (with Nabuko playing second viola) fell through. This concert was the last time that Shmuel and I traded the dialogue in the slow movement of the C major Quintet (one of the most sublime movements in all of chamber music), and those magical interchanges between viola and violin still ring in my ears as I write.

Robert C. Marsh wrote of our "eloquence of expression and depth of perception that carries music of this type to its greatest heights," in the *Chicago Sun-Times*. He went on to say, "One of the particular strengths of these performances was that they were given all the opportunity necessary to sing forth with full richness and every opportunity for the spacious development of their musical ideas. Too often they are played too quickly and much important detail is given only superficial statement."

I quote his review at length to point out something that was inherent in the Vermeer's philosophy, and I like to think that is has something to do with the spirit of Marlboro. In their exuberance, many young players may regard a composer's carefully-considered detail as mere underbrush, missing the forest for the trees, so to speak. While the Vermeers boasted loads of horsepower under the hood, Shmuel would switch into his wise-old-Israeli-owl persona and say, "Sometimes it pays to be a little boring." In other words, don't rush, young hot shot.

The Vermeer Quartet's guest artists at Badenweiler (March 6-9, 1985) included pianist Gilbert Kalish, Jan DeGaetani (singing Chausson's *Chanson perpétuelle* and the tail end of the Berg Lyric Suite), Hans Deinzer (playing the Brahms Clarinet Quintet), and Murray Perahia (a friend of Shmuel's who became a friend of mine) playing the Schumann Piano Quartet, Op. 47 (I prefer it over his Quintet). We received rave reviews from the concerts we played in Munich, Hannover, Braunschweig, and Frankfurt, including one that (as far as I can tell) spoke of "Mellowing of the Cat" and "Stylistic Transformation."

Murray Perahia was one of the directors of the Aldeburgh Festival, and he invited us to play there that summer. In *The Rest is Noise* Alex Ross describes Aldeburgh as "a windswept fishing town on the east coast of the British Isles," while E. M. Forster calls it "a bleak little place; not beautiful." I think (and Nomi agrees) that Aldeburgh's seashore doesn't hold a candle to the Maine coast. Herbie Handt, my old friend from Tilden High, the tenor-turned-conductor, who had made his home in Lucca, came up for the Festival. It had been decades since we last saw each other, and meeting at Aldeburgh gave us a chance to catch up and talk about that crazy trip to Sardegna we made together while my Bergonzi was being repaired.

For our first performance at the Aldeburgh Festival, on June 8th, we played the Dvořák Piano Quintet, Op. 81 with Murray. The world-famous pianist Mieczyslaw Horszowski (1892–1993) was scheduled to play a recital the next night, and Murray confided to us that his 93-year-old piano teacher was diffident about appearing. Murray remained with his mentor all through the day, encouraging him to go on. He finally agreed.

Mr. Horszowski emerged from the wings of the Snape Maltings concert hall haltingly that evening, and he walked to the piano at an extremely slow pace. He seated himself quietly on the piano bench, and seemed lost in thought. He opened the program with Handel's "Air and Variations on the Harmonius Blacksmith," continued with a few Scarlatti Sonatas, and walked off slowly to the applause. He returned to play his second group of pieces, walking a trifle faster this time. After some Bach Preludes and Fugues and a few Villa-Lobos pieces, he left the stage more energetically than before. There was a palpable snap to his step when he came out for his Chopin offerings. This Polish-born keyboard master traces his piano studies back to Chopin (his first teacher was his mother, who studied with Karol Mikuli, a student of Chopin). It was memorable to see and hear him play what he had played so well, and for so long. Murray mailed me a tape of the recital as a gift.

Benjamin Britten lived most of his life in the Aldeburgh area, and he and his life partner, the tenor Peter Pears, founded the Aldeburgh Festival in 1964. Our second Aldeburgh program included Britten's Quartet No. 3, my favorite of his three (by a slim margin). Perhaps one reason that violists love to play

Britten's music is that he was a violist who studied composition with Frank Bridge, who was also a violist.

The highlight of the festival was a personal invitation to the Vermeer Quartet from Peter Pears to visit the home that he and Britten shared for so many years, and to play a private performance of Britten's Third Quartet for him (and only for him). Britten was never able to hear the piece performed, because he died on December 4, 1976, just two weeks before the Amadeus Quartet gave the premiere. As we played, Pears sat on the sofa of their living room right in front of us, eyes tearing up as he listened. After the cello's final dying note, he gave us tea and showed us the original manuscript. The manuscript, written in Britten's incredibly neat hand, sat in a glass case in that very room. The whole episode remains a fitting salute to my deep love of all of Britten's music, and of the close affinity he had with Shostakovich during their later lives. In remembrance of that day, my back patio at home now boasts a delicate-but-thorny English hybrid rosebush named in Britten's honor.

After we returned from England, we played five concerts on the Bay Chamber Concerts 25th Anniversary series in Rockport, Maine. The first concert of the 1985 season included the Berg Lyric Suite (with soprano Bethany Beardslee), and between concerts in Rockport, the Vermeer played a concert at the Kneisel Hall Chamber Music Festival in Blue Hill. We played Mozart's Adagio and Fugue, K. 546, Berg's Lyric Suite (minus a singer this time), and Dvořák's rarely-played Quartet in D minor, Op. 34 at the Norfolk Chamber Music Festival at Yale on August 2nd, and the next day we played a concert on the South Mountain Series in Pittsfield, Mass.

On August 8th, 1985 I played my last concert as a member of the Vermeer Quartet. It also turned out to be my last concert with my dear comrade Pierre Menard. In 1993, when the Vermeer called me to be a guest artist to play the Mendelssohn Octet in Rockport, I found that Pierre had been replaced by the excellent German violinist Mathias Tacke. After the concert I visited Pierre for the last time at the home in Warren, Maine that he shared with

with his partner, John Ladley. Pierre died quietly at age 53, just a year later.

The Vermeers, with Mathias and Richard in the second violin and viola slots, continued their brilliant career until 2007. They went out with a bang by making a number of farewell appearances. Stretching out one's goodbyes reminds me of a story about the world-famous German tenor, Leo Slezak. He worked as a gardener before taking singing lessons, and with his repertory of 66 operatic roles he gained international fame. During a performance of Wagner's *Lohengrin*, a stage hand sent the swan prop off stage too early. Slezak watched his feathered transportation disappear into the wings, and ad-libbed to the audience, "Wann fährt der nächste Schwan?" (When does the next swan leave?)

"Mainely" Music

For Nomi and me, the singular magic of Maine remains strong in our hearts and memories, whether or not we were making music there. Since our early days of playing concerts in Hancock, Maine, with Claude Monteux and Matt Raimondi in the 1950s, Nomi and I have averaged about two months a year for the past fifty years summering "Down East." I figure that those summer months have totaled up to more than eight years of our lives. We have traveled to other seacoasts, like Turkey's Bosphorus, Carmel Beach, in California, and the stony shore of England's Aldeburgh. Their beauty wasn't lost on us, but Nomi and I would inevitably look at one another and say, "It's not Maine." For many years we rented a succession of very modest "camps," as the state-of-Mainers called their summer cottages, but we started to identify very deeply with Maine, and dreamed of building a modest place of our own there.

Before World War I, Bar Harbor rivaled Newport, Rhode Island, as *the* summer spot for the East Coast's wealthy class. The Neighborhood House, built in 1905 in Northeast Harbor, was the focal point for the town's social life. During the first decades of the 20th century it housed balls, theatrical productions, and concerts by pianists like Harold Bauer, Ossip Gabrilowitsch, Leopold Stokowski, and the violinist Fritz Kreisler. After this golden age, Mt. Desert Island remained culturally dormant, for the most part, until 1963, when the Mt. Desert Festival of Chamber Music began holding summer concerts. In 1974 assorted Rockefellers and other wealthy music lovers put a plan in place to restore the Neighborhood House, so that the Composers Quartet might have a venue for its chamber music concerts. By the 1980s the Neighborhood House was restored and expanded.

The Mt. Desert Festival continued to thrive through the decades. Matt Raimondi was named music director of the Neighborhood House series, and his wife Natalie kept things going as the heroic executive director. In 1991, 23 years after we last played together, the Composers Quartet invited me as guest violist on the Neighborhood House series to play three of the Mozart String Quintets (they didn't "stick mad," as kids in Brooklyn would say). Matt retired in 1996 after 33 years, but the summer series at Neighborhood House continues as before, with Natalie's vital energy and planning.

During the summer of 1972, Nomi and I stopped by George and Carol Sopkin's family cottage located in Round Pond, Maine (they had to alternate their vacation weeks at the cottage with Carol's siblings). Round Pond was a lovely village, but the Sopkins dreamed of having a place of their own. Later that summer I happened to hear that a large piece of shorefront property on Newbury Neck Road in Surry, Maine was up for sale (it was near the cottage Nomi and I were renting). Surry is ten miles from the town of Blue Hill, the home of the Kneisel Hall Summer Festival.

The Sopkins thought that it might be worth a look, so they drove up north to Surry with us, and loved the property at first sight. The realtor warned that there was an offer pending, but it hadn't yet gone to contract. Because of this technicality, Carol (being a real estate professional) was loathe to pursue the matter further, but it turned out that the sellers, the Smith family, had been friends of her family. I urged the Sopkins to make an offer if it really appealed to them, and the property became theirs.

The 15-acre parcel included a charming old antique-filled farm house on Newbury Neck Road, and roughly 350 feet of tidal shore across the road, which fronted Union River Bay, and gave access to the Atlantic Ocean. The Sopkins spent their summers in the farm house for a few years, while a local young "green" architect designed and built them a grand and spacious solar-heated, earth-bermed home in the woods, with a shore view of the Bay. George hung a magnificent chandelier (he bought it from the Vecchia Murano glass factory when the Fine Arts Quartet was in Venice) in the great room, and the Sopkins filled the place with Carol's inherited Chinese antiques. One of the bathrooms was completely papered with Fine Arts Quartet's programs and brochures, which made for interesting reading while sitting on the throne. After George retired, the Sopkins spent the rest of their days living happily in their uniquely beautiful Surry home.

The Sopkins were so delighted that I helped them find the property, that they sold off an adjoining strip of land to us for an absurdly low figure. Our new-found bit of earth had three acres of land and 125 feet of shorefront, which was everything we needed to build our own summer haven. Nomi had previously overcome a serious health threat, so this secluded bit of earth was to be our own *Heiliger Dankgesang* for nonbelievers. We took out a mortgage on our new property, and I quickly worked up a homemade approximation of a blueprint. Rodney Saunders, our 65-year-old Surry builder, and his 75-year-old helper, spent that winter building our dream cottage to my amateurish specifications.

I flew from Milwaukee to Maine that winter to check on their progress, and when I suggested a belated change of plan, Rodney replied, "No trouble a'tall," He cheerfully knocked out an already-framed window with a few strokes of his hammer, and made one large room out of two smaller rooms. Freda Gray, a soprano from Hancock that Nomi accompanied during our summer concerts, was married to the owner of a nearby lumberyard, so I ended up paying only 27 cents per linear foot for his best No. 2 grade knotty pine. Yes, we built the proverbial knotty pine cottage, complete with a cast iron "pahlah" stove to rest our feet on during the cold Maine evenings.

A quarter-mile long driveway connected the cottage to the Neck Road, which made it really isolated. Nomi could sunbathe in the nude on our deck, to be ogled only by the odd lobster. We drilled a well, installed electric and phone lines, and made sure we had proper drainage. Our pretty 30- by 24-foot cottage sat just eight feet from the deep tidal shore (it was still permitted in those years). It had one bedroom, a bathroom with a shower, a large combination great room and kitchen, a good sized sleeping loft upstairs, and a screened sleeping porch. Sitting on the 24-foot deck that faced the bay felt like being aboard a ship. Talk about your sunrises.

Cottage Interior with "pahlah" stove

The total cost of our cottage, including furniture and an upright piano, came to $18,000. We were only a few wooden steps from the rocky Maine beach, where I could dig tasty "pisser" clams, and Nomi could gather mussels. We could pick our fill of blueberries in our back field (for blueberry buckle), and down the road there was a fisherman (you need a license to lobster) who sold us the very lobsters and crabs that made their homes in front of our deck. Our small kitchen window looked directly out at Acadia National Park, where Cadillac Mountain is the highest point on the

North Atlantic seaboard. This was heaven on earth, and it was ours.

When the Vermeer Quartet performed at the Rockport Opera House, we rented a cottage near Rockport, but after I left the Vermeer to join the Stanford Quartet, Nomi and I were free to spend our whole summer at our Surry cottage, which was ten miles away from the Kneisel Hall Chamber Music Festival in Blue Hill.

Kneisel Hall is named for the celebrated Austrian violinist Franz Kneisel, who came to the United States in 1885, at the invitation of conductor Wilhelm Gericke, to become (at the age of 20) the concertmaster of the Boston Symphony Orchestra. From 1885 until 1917 he also led the Kneisel Quartet, the first professional string quartet in America. From 1905 until 1926, the year that he died, Kneisel was the chair of the String Department of the Institute of Musical Art in New York (which became the Juilliard School of Music).

Kneisel spent his summers in Maine, and in 1902 he brought some of his most gifted students to a school he was starting in the town of Blue Hill. Sascha Jacobsen, Samuel Gardner, Louis Kaufman, Marie Roemaet-Rosanoff, Joseph and Lillian Fuchs, William Kroll, Phyllis and Karl Kraeuter, and Carl Stern were among the musicians who have studied at Blue Hill.

In 1986 Roman Totenberg, the acting director of Kneisel Hall, invited me to join him, pianist Artur Balsam, and cellist Barbara Stein Mallow (Lillian Fuchs' daughter) as the guest violist for one of their concerts. The overworked faculty only had six string players (Abraham Skernick was their sole violist), so Roman asked me to assist Abe with his considerable teaching load. Other guest artists who came to Blue Hill that summer included some of my old friends like violinists Aaron Rosand, Jacob Krachmalnick, Werner Torkanowsky, and the Vermeer Quartet (performing with their new violist). Also appearing that summer was the pianist Seymour Lipkin, my friend from Interlochen, who soon became Kneisel Hall's Artistic Director.

Abe Skernick decided not to return for the following summer, so I took over the faculty viola position in 1987. That summer's lineup included our regular pianists, Seymour Lipkin and Artur Balsam, violinists Andor Toth (the first violinist of the Stanford Quartet that I joined two years earlier), Ronald Copes, Roman Totenberg (I played Martinu's "Three Madrigals for Violin and Viola" with him that summer), cellists Jerry Grossman and Barbara Mallow, and guest cellists Laurence Lesser, and Leslie Parnas.

The following summer the entire Stanford String Quartet was invited to Kneisel Hall as guest artists (at my suggestion). I performed the Shostakovich Viola Sonata Op. 147 (his last work) with pianist and conductor Tonu Kalam, whose father, Endel Kalam, had been a fellow member of the Cleveland Orchestra. In 1990 Nomi and I played a transcription for viola of Dvořák's Sonatina in G Major, Op. 100 (our first performance together at Kneisel Hall). The other guest artists included violinists Ruth Waterman, and Michelle Makarski, and cellist Yehuda Hanani. Win Pusey, the reviewer for our local newspaper, the *Ellsworth American*, singled me out in one concert by writing, "In the viola solo that opened the third movement (of the Fauré Piano Quartet in G minor), Bernard Zaslav poured out the warmest, most fluid tone that I have heard in a long time. What an artist!"

Violinists Toby Appel, Theodore Arm, and Eugene Drucker, were Kneisel Hall's guests in 1991, and violinist Andrew Dawes and violist Raphael Hillyer were guests in 1992. The Zaslav Duo performed an entire program in a special "Soloists of Kneisel Hall" series that year. We played Frank Bridge's "Two Pieces for Viola and Piano," the Nardini Sonata in F minor, the Bloch Suite (1919), and my adaptations of Mozart's Adagio in E Major, K. 261, and his Rondo in C Major, K. 373. 1993's guests included violinist Elmar Oliveira, violist Sandra Robbins, and cellist Ko Iwasaki.

The 1994 season featured works that were particularly adventuresome, especially for a performance of Witold Lutoslawski's 1964 String Quartet that I played with violinists Ron Copes, and Andy Dawes, and cellist Jerry Grossman. I first heard the Lutoslawski when it was performed by the Guarneri Quartet. It is an example of Lutoslawski's so called "controlled aleatorism," where the players may start together at various given cue points, and are then granted limited freedom with the notated musical "events" they are given to play. It isn't unusual for experienced musicians to get together at a summer festival to perform Beethoven's String Quartet Op.135, but taking on the Lutoslawski, with all of its looming pitfalls, and with so little rehearsal time, was quite a challenge. I think it received a most respectable performance.

As a historical note, on January 12, 1894, the Kneisel Quartet gave the premiere of Antonin Dvořák's String Quintet in E flat minor, Op. 97, in New York. In 1994, to celebrate the work's 100th anniversary, I performed it with violinists Elmar Oliveira and Ron Copes, violist Sandy Robbins, and cellist Barbara Mallow, and we sat beneath a historic photograph of Franz Kneisel that hung over the fireplace.

When Seymour Lipkin asked me to suggest another violinist for the Festival, I recalled that the Canadian pianist Anton Kuerti had spoken about Andrew Dawes, the first violinist of Canada's Orford Quartet. When Andew joined us that summer, we discovered that his G. B. Guadagnini violin and my G. B. Guadagnini viola were made just a year apart, so we pulled out a real finger-buster by Alessandro Rolla, his rollicking three-movement Duo for Violin and Viola Op. 9. Rolla uses an Italian street song for a middle movement that is fun to play, and is a real crowd pleaser. That summer's programs also offered piano trios by Charles Ives and Arthur Berger, Nomi and I performed Francesco Travani's First Viola and Piano Sonata, and Seymour Lipkin gave an eloquent performance of Bach's complete Goldberg Variations.

We taught private lessons and coached chamber groups nearly every day of the six-week season. The Festival attracted about 70 top-level students from schools like Juilliard, Mannes, New England Conservatory, and from colleges and conservatories in Europe and Asia. One year a group of Stanford students I brought to Kneisel Hall gave excellent performances of Schoenberg's *Verklärte Nacht* and Dvořák's String Quartet, Op. 106. Members of the faculty put their own programs together, and managed to fit rehearsals into full days of teaching and coaching. The audiences were loyal, rapt, and enthusiastic. They sat up close to the edge of the Kneisel Hall's cozy stage, and it felt as if we were nearly in the laps of our listeners.

My class had grown in size and quality after my many summers at Kneisel, and we really needed an additional violist to handle the load. When Seymour claimed that the budget wouldn't allow this, I had to tell him, regretfully, that 1994 would have to be my last summer at Kneisel (this was the same reason that my predecessor Abe Skernick left). I had enjoyed my eight years of teaching and playing with iconic artists like Roman Totenberg and Artur Balsam, but my old friend from Interlochen, Paskudnyak Pashaslavnick, was now driving the troika, and I couldn't handle the load by myself.*

When Nomi and I stayed in Maine through October, we would see the dreaded "leafpeepers" arrive in droves to see the foliage. To prepare for the winter we had to board up the large sliding windows of our cottage that faced Union River Bay because of the wicked nor'easters that came in from the Atlantic. Life wasn't all that easy during the mud months for the sturdy locals. When we opened the cottage up in the spring, I would ask our partially-handicapped trash collector how he had fared through the winter, and his invariable terse reply would be, "Jes' baahly."

Nomi and I spent 25 happy summers at our shore cottage in Surry, but the time came when we could no longer make the long trip from Stanford. Our kids loved Maine as much as we did, and were expert devourers of lobster. Eventually even they began spending their summers in different parts of the country, so we regretfully thought it best to sell our beloved cottage to a deserving couple of nice and appreciative Mainiacs, like ourselves. Our cottage's irreplaceable location right on the shore, Nomi's prized clam hod, and her upright Yamaha piano closed the deal, but our buyers soon turned our knotty pine cottage into more of a real house. It is not what we would have preferred, but while you can build yourself a castle, they're not making any more shorefront these days. That cottage remains deeply embedded in our hearts.

* Eventually Seymour got the message, and there have been two violists on the faculty every since.

FERMATA: "MAINELY" MUSIC

We continue to enjoy the visual record of our many years in Maine. Seven works by the narrative folk artist, Philip Barter hang on our walls. Philip started out as an ex-hippie of the Jack Kerouac school, and became one of Maine's most popular and prolific painters, selling almost eighty paintings a year. He worked as a lobster fisherman, picked mussels, dug worms, and hired himself out as a carpenter. He traded an old pickup truck for an acre of land in North Sullivan, where he built a little house and art gallery. After crossing the Singing Bridge over the Taunton River on Route 182, you follow a ramshackle road, and pass a small hand-painted sign on the right that simply says "Art."

Philip was influenced by the primitive style of the American painter and poet Marsden Hartley, and progressed to his own abstract style, often using multiple layers of plywood to simulate a sense of depth in his depictions of Maine's pink rocks, cartoon-like clouds, and its dark sea. Like his hero, Vincent Van Gogh, Philip signs only his first name to his canvases. He and his wife, Priscilla, have nine children between them, and their son Matthew, follows his father's calling. In a spread on Philip in the August, 1992 issue of *Down East* magazine, Philip, a "people person" who loves to explain his work, is quoted as saying,"Art is just a vehicle. The real art is people."

Philip's words resonate when we think of the other artists who made the art that hangs on our walls: the Picasso-esque double portrait that David Jackier, my high school pal, painted as a wedding gift, a passionate line drawing depicting a mad scene from Thomas Mann's *Death in Venice* by Wisconsin artist, Warrington Colescott, Tom Perkinson's feathery water colors that capture the lonely deserts of New Mexico, and Philip Barter's oils that speak of Maine, that unique corner of the world.

CHAPTER XV
The Stanford String Quartet:
Westward Ho!

Andor and Louise Toth put us up in their Spanish colonial home (with its lush gardens) in Menlo Park during my negotiations with Stanford. We weren't able to do much in the way of house hunting because of my remaining Vermeer Quartet commitments in Chicago. When Louise phoned us to tell us that she found a house for rent just down the street from their house, we rented it sight unseen.

The movers loaded the contents of our huge Chicago apartment, and we headed west in our dark blue 1978 Honda Prelude. The modest two-bedroom California bungalow Louise found for us included the obligatory (and leaky) outdoor hot tub, and a two-car garage, which we filled to the brim with our antique furniture from Maine. Stephen Harrison, the Stanford Quartet's strong cellist graciously shoved around our furniture, and our new lodging began to take shape. Local wisdom held that California's Bay Area didn't have "weather;" it had "climate," so we schlepped all our parkas and galoshes for no good reason.

The city of Menlo Park was originally the home of the Ohlone Indians, but by the time we arrived, its inhabitants were mostly monied Californians. The area's odoriferous greenery made for pleasant walks, but the overgrown creek bed nearby also offered convenient hiding places for burglars. We were not happy to learn that burglaries were a rather common occurrence in the area. The Toths made sure to use their burglar alarm, and when they were away, they played their radio loudly to discourage potential intruders.

We returned from a movie one evening, after our first month in the house, to find that our house (and several of our neighbors' houses) had been ransacked. The burglars came in through a side window, and headed straight for my office desk to look for cash and valuables. I walked in to find papers strewn about, and I was horrified to see my precious Guadagnini lying next to its open case. Thankfully, it was untouched (and thankfully it was still there). The burglars used our pillowcases to cart off clothing and fine shoes (they left the pillows behind), but perhaps they might not have known how to fence a viola. After living in New York and Chicago, where robberies were common, it is hard to believe that our first such experience would occur in semi-bucolic Menlo Park.

The Friends of the Stanford String Quartet was a non-profit volunteer organization that supported the Stanford Quartet's professional activities. One member, a playwright who was a dear friend, heard of our plight. She came to our rescue, and found us a large apartment, two floors below her own at 101 Alma Street, Palo Alto's only high-rise. We sold off many of our antiques to the local shops, and made our second move in as many months.

The chairman of Stanford's music department must have been mystified why, at nearly 60 years of age, I would leave one of the most prestigious chamber groups in the world, as well as a high-paying university professorship (with tenure), to become violist of a newly-formed string quartet at the academic status of a Senior Lecturer. If the Vermeer Quartet had been based in Europe, perhaps a member of the wandering minstrel class (such as myself) could have traveled from concert to concert exclusively by Iron Rooster. In fact, back in 1835, the Duke of Wellington lamented that the invention of the railroad "will only encourage the lower classes to move about needlessly."

There were, of course, reasons beyond simply avoiding jet-lag that prompted me to come to Stanford. Andor Toth and I had worked together under George Szell in Cleveland (he became the associate concertmaster after I left). The son of a Hungarian immigrant, a master shoemaker, who married a hotel maid, and wound up as a Bronx apartment house superintendent, Andy began life as a tough New York City kid. He claimed to have sprinted to violin classes as a child to escape neighborhood bullies. He attended the High School of Music and Art, where,

Andy said, "it was normal to walk around with a violin case."

Andy had quick reflexes ("Look, Ma, I'm dancing"), and seemed to do everything with an easy flick of the wrist. He was an intense, demanding, and enormously talented violinist, with an old-world sense of just how things should go, and no patience for ineptitude.

He met his wife, the soprano Louise Rose, at Juilliard (like Nomi and me), and in 1955 he began teaching at Oberlin College. He replaced Roman Totenberg as the violinist of the Alma Trio (with cellist Gabor Rejto and pianist Adolph "Usiu" Baller) in 1963, and in 1972 Andy and his son, the cellist Andor Toth, Jr., founded the New Hungarian String Quartet at Oberlin. Richard Young, who followed me as the violist of the Vermeer Quartet, was the second violinist of the New Hungarian Quartet. The Quartet enjoyed an international career, and they made especially fine recordings of Bartók and Schubert. The New Hungarian Quartet's career ended shortly after Andy joined the Stanford faculty in 1978.

Ars longa, vita brevis, may serve to motivate a member of a string quartet, but Joe Masteroff also had it right when wrote, "Money makes the world go round" for Joel Gray to sing in *Cabaret* (a show I played "longa" than I should have). Andy had a tenured position at Stanford, but the other members' salaries required additional outside funding from the generous Friends of the Stanford Quartet. My two previous quartet residencies had been appropriately funded, so I was secure enough financially to accept Stanford's extremely modest salary, but the resulting disparity in compensation was a sore point throughout the Quartet's existence (some of my former students were earning more than the salary Stanford provided).

My first hint of unrest came about in September, 1985 during my first Stanford Quartet rehearsal. Our second violinist, Mayumi Ohira, told us she was planning to leave at the end of the season in order to pursue a solo career. We were preparing an all-Beethoven program (Op. 18, No. 6, Op. 135, and Op. 59, No. 2) to perform at New York's Merkin Hall on October 15th. Playing these Beethoven staples was a combination of *chutspah* and *culliones* on Andy's part. It was a hell of a challenge for us to offer such an ambitious program for our first appearance before a New York audience, but we somehow came up smelling of roses. Tim Page's review of the concert appeared in the October 17th *New York Times*. He wrote of our "sturdy assertion," and described our playing as accurate, lively, always musical, and "imbued with what seems a single-minded sense of purpose."

The Stanford String Quartet 1985
Bernard Zaslav (viola), Mayumi Ohira (violin 2),
Stephen Harrison (cello), and Andor Toth (violin 1)

On November 24th, we were a last-minute substitution for my old gang, the Fine Arts Quartet, to play a concert in San Antonio, Texas. It turned out that the program they wanted was the very thing we had in stock: all-Beethoven. The review's headline read, "S.A. Chamber Music Society belts one out of ballpark." Larry Barnes relying on an overworked baseball analogy, wrote, "Like the home-run hitter, they turned a mood of disappointment into surprise and elation, jumping into an all-Beethoven program and leaving their audience deeply moved. The intensity that shimmered throughout the program was turned up to a rolling boil and the tight phrases cooked with a delicious mixing of the musical ingredients mentioned above." I'm not kidding; that's exactly what he wrote. It made me wonder what kind of a season the San Antonio Spurs were having.

For our next concert we played the Mozart Quartet, K. 589, the Shostakovich Quartet No. 7, and the Dvořák Piano Quintet Op. 81 (repeating the Scherzo as an encore) with our beloved faculty pianist, Adolph Baller at Stanford's Dinkelspiel Auditorium (named for a generous donor). Baller's facility, light touch, and his elevated musicianship set him apart from lesser pianists. Usiu, as everyone called him, was a Jewish pianist who was born in Poland. He performed with the Vienna Philharmonic at age 13. The Nazis did unspeakable things to his hands, but he survived and later came to live at Yehudi Menuhin's Alma estate in Los Gatos, California, and accompanied him in recitals around the world. Usiu was one of the fleetest and most sensitive pianists imaginable. Nomi and I became very close friends with him and his daughter, Nina, and we mourned his death in 1994.

We played the Haydn "Lark" quartet, Britten's lush Second Quartet, and Beethoven's Op. 59, No. 2 in San Francisco's large Herbst Theater on February 13th, 1986. A few days later Andy and I teamed up to play the Mozart Sinfonia Concertante with Stanford's excellent student Chamber Orchestra. We meshed easily, and enjoyed ourselves. Quite a few of our Stanford students played well enough to consider making careers in music, and a few have become professional musicians, but most of my own double majors wound up as geneticists, historians, or professionals in the computer world.

Nomi and I were practicing some viola and piano music on our 8th floor (a high-rise for that area) apartment on Alma Street, when she yelped excitedly, "Bernie, the piano is moving!"

I patently explained to Nomi that such a thing was impossible, no matter how hard you bang on a Steinway. Then I felt the next tremor myself, and wrote down that date, April 9, 1986. I realized that we were nearly atop the San Andreas fault line, but most Californians seem to take these little tremors in stride.

When Mayumi returned to Japan (where she married a violist), we hired Roy Malan, the concertmaster of the San Francisco Ballet Orchestra to replace her as the second violinist in the Quartet. Roy studied with Menuhin in London and with Efrem Zimbalist at Curtis, and in 2004 he wrote *Efrem Zimbalist, A Life*, a biography about his teacher (who was known as "Zimmy"). Eventually Roy married one of my former viola students from Northern Illinois University, who had come to California to try her luck as a freelancer.

Boris Berman, the powerful Russian pianist who was the acting Director of Music Spectrum I at Yale University, invited us to play a concert at Yale's Sprague Memorial Hall on November 16, 1986. We played Beethoven's Op. 133 *Grosse Fuga*, and then Boris and Elizabeth Sawyer played Beethoven's Op. 134 version of the same work for piano, four hands, which was an interesting juxtaposition. Violinist Sidney Harth and Boris joined us for the Mendelssohn Concerto in D minor for Violin, Piano, and Strings, and we finished up with the Schubert "Trout" Quintet. We repeated the program at New York's Merkin Hall on November 18th.

I persuaded the Quartet to learn Ben Johnston's microtonal Quartet No. 4, Variations on "Amazing Grace," a work the Fine Arts Quartet commissioned. It is a difficult piece to learn, but it never fails to engage an audience. We performed it on January 18th, 1987 at Stanford University's Dinkelspiel Hall, sandwiched between the Beethoven Quartet, Op. 18, No. 1, and the Brahms String Quintet, Op. 111. My former student Nancy Severance was our guest violist.

Nomi and I became friends with Arthur Barnes, the conductor of the Stanford Symphonic Band. Along with his many virtues as a pianist (he knew all the standards in their proper keys), composer, and conductor, he was a native Maniac. We often stopped to visit Arthur and Helene, his French Horn-playing wife, at their summer home in Boothbay Harbor on our way to Surry.

Art asked me to play Morton Gould's jazzy (and rarely played) Concertette for Viola and Band (written in 1943) on the same program as David Lang's "Aliens Kidnapped Me and Stole My Blood," a piece commissioned for the Stanford Symphonic Band by Stanford's Music Guild. Lang, one of the founders of New York's Bang on a Can Festival, graduated from Stanford in 1978. Art invited me the following year to play Berlioz's *Harold in Italy* with his Livermore-Amador Symphony across San Francisco Bay at Livermore. Livermore is the home of the National Security Laboratory, our nuclear deterrent, but thankfully the timpani player, who was having a ball in Berlioz's "Witches' Dance" movement, didn't register on their transcontinental radar.

After a concert on November 22, 1987, where we played the Mozart Adagio and Fugue, K. 546, Leoš Janáček Quartet No. 2 "Intimate Letters," and Beethoven's Op. 130, with the *Grosse Fuga*, Roy Malan delivered the bad news that he had to choose between staying with us or the Ballet Orchestra (which supplied his main source of income). The Ballet Orchestra won out, and this was our last concert with Roy. Once again we were faced with trying to find a proper second violinist for a position that didn't have much funding.

We were in luck: our call was answered by Zoya Leybin, a member of the San Francisco Symphony's first violin section.

The Stanford String Quartet in 1987

Zoya was a fine Russian fiddler who had a positive spirit, and a sense of determination that made her popular with her conductor and her colleagues. She said that she wanted to join our quartet, regardless of how much time and effort it would involve. She had the strength, the chops, and the musical insight of a real quartet player. She also worked very well with Andy, so we welcomed her into the fold.

On January 2, 1988 we played a concert for the Phoenix Chamber Music Society. Our first program with Zoya (with very little rehearsal time) included Webern's Five Pieces, Op. 5, Beethoven's Op. 130/133, and Dvořák's luscious Quartet No. 10, Op. 51. Nomi played the Brahms Piano Quartet in A, Op. 26 with us on April 11 (the rest of the program had the Shostakovich Quartet No. 1, and the Beethoven Quartet Op. 59, No. 3), and the next night we began a three-concert all-Beethoven series at San Francisco's Palace of the Legion of Honor, which got a wonderful review in the *Chronicle* from Joshua Kosman.

We performed on the oh-so-Californian Bach Dancing and Dynamite Society's Candlelight Concert Series in October. The people who ran the series took pride in "presenting exciting artists in the relaxed, rustic setting of the beautiful Douglas Beach House on Miramar Beach in Half Moon Bay." In fact, the testimonials on the printed program from Joel Krosnick of the Juilliard Quartet and John Dalley of the Guarneri Quartet indicated that they appreciated that laid-back lifestyle.

Nomi and I were getting into the California lifestyle, but apartment living was beginning to pall and Bay Area house prices were astronomical (and everyone wanted in). In order to snag "star" faculty members (house prices were far less intimidating in the area surrounding Harvard or Yale), Stanford was obliged to make affordable faculty housing available. Living in San Francisco would have meant daily freeway commutes to Stanford and back, so we opted for buying a spacious, well-designed, three-bedroom, three-bath condo on campus. It offers a bit of the outdoors with a rear patio garden nestled among California's redwood trees. It has a nearby pool and spa, and enough room for

Nomi's grand piano, as well as an office for me. We also have an interesting mix of Stanford faculty members for neighbors, like our provost, Condoleezza Rice, who is an amateur pianist. She occupied a condo near us, and we often met at concerts.

The Vermeer Quartet came to play a concert on Stanford's Lively Arts series in 1988, and the chairman of the law department (an amateur violist) invited some guests to his home on campus to hear the Vermeer play an intimate house concert. When Condi saw me hobnobbing in the kitchen with my former colleagues my stock rose quite a few points, in her estimation.

With some financial help from Stanford's Lively Arts, José Bowen wrote "Bathsheba and Her Suitors," a piece for flute and string quartet. The well-known jazz flutist Hubert Laws was interested in having our Quartet perform it with him and to take it on tour. We performed the work on a program with the Mozart Flute Quartet, K. 285, and the Debussy String Quartet. We premiered the Bowen piece at Stanford, and repeated the program on January 13th, 1989 at California State Polytechnic in Pomona, at UCSD in San Diego on January 14th, and later at UCSC in Santa Cruz on April 6th.

In 1988 Stanford commissioned William Bolcom, a Stanford alumnus, to write his Tenth String Quartet as part of the celebration of Stanford University's Centennial (involving a financial goal of one *billion* dollars). We gave its premiere (on a program that also had quartets by Schumann and Beethoven) at Stanford on January 25th, 1989, and repeated it at Boston's New England Conservatory on the 28th, at New York's Alice Tully Hall at Lincoln Center on the 30th, and at the Terrace Theater of the John F. Kennedy Center for the Performing Arts on February 4th.

This remarkable Quartet is written in a symmetrical arch form, with 17 small movements that are linked together. Bolcom tells us that the movements are "musically cemented together in much the same way as the arches of Stanford's inner colonnades," and indeed, their titles were printed in pyramidal form in the program. It is a strong and carefully-crafted work that is exciting to play. The work was favorably reviewed in the *Boston Globe* on January

31st, in the *New York Post* on February 4th ("Bolcom's Arch Triumphs") and in the *Washington Post* on February 7th.

It seems that I had been kidding myself in thinking that the Stanford Quartet wouldn't be doing any foreign travel. Andor had been in contact with Harry de Freese, a really warmhearted concert agent (a contradiction in terms?) from Amsterdam. Harry, who booked the Fine Arts Quartet's concerts in Holland, lined up four 1989 concerts in Europe for the Stanford Quartet to play. Two were in the Saarbrucken area of Germany; at the Bürgerhaus Dudweiler and at the Blieskastel Rathaussaal. One was a BBC concert in London at St. John's Smith Square, and the last was in Frankfurt at Amerika Haus. Except for the BBC concert, this was relatively small potatoes, compared to my previous quartet life, but the concerts went well, the reviews were highly complimentary, and Bolcom's new work attracted special attention.

It came as no surprise that, like Roy Malan, her predecessor in the second violin seat, Zoya was feeling the pinch of playing with us and holding on to her day (and night) job in the first violin section of the San Francisco Symphony. When she told us, sobbingly, that she would have to leave, I knew I would miss her.

I had some misgivings about our future. Our Quartet's brief history already included three second violinists who were unable to sustain themselves on Stanford's meager stipend, and Susan Freier, a Stanford alumna, who had been a member of the Chester Quartet, became our next second violinist. This midstream change in configuration made recording complicated. We were able to record the Bolcom Quartet with Zoya, and we recorded the rest of the music on the recording (Ben Johnston's Quartet No. 9, and Mark Neikrug's Quartet, "Star's the Mirror,") with Susan on April 24th, 1990 in Nicasio, California, at George Lucas' Skywalker Sound Studios.

THE STANFORD STRING QUARTET

*The Stanford String Quartet in 1988
Bernard Zaslav, Stephen Harrison,,
Susan Freier, and Andor Toth*

On October 17, 1989, just before the beginning of the third game of the World Series at Candlestick Park, a magnitude 7.1 earthquake hit the Bay Area. It was followed by a 5.2 aftershock a half hour later. It was the worst Bay Area earthquake since the San Francisco disaster in 1906. There was six billion dollars worth of damage throughout central California: several freeways were impassable, there were many fires, 62 people died, many were injured, and 12,000 people were left homeless. Several of Stanford's larger buildings required years of repairs and retrofitting, but because it happens to sit on a rocky foundation, Peter Coutts, the area where we live, is not subject to liquefaction. We were extremely lucky, and made it through with only a damaged lamp or two, but a few of our neighbors were hit slightly harder. This depended (of all things) on the direction their units happened to face. In case of possible aftershocks, we all camped outdoors that night, and were happy that we escaped unharmed.

My pesky index finger problem that acted up in Hannover while I was on tour with the Vermeer Quartet required further treatment. Dr. Robert Chase, Stanford's eminent hand surgeon, was skeptical about the outcome in removing a cyst under the nail plate, which was the cause of my problem. He left the choice up to his stalwart assistant, Dr. Vincent Hentz. With my blessing and no other, the valorous Dr. Hentz decided to go for it. His students surrounded us and took pictures of the process, and Dr. Hentz was successful in solving (in his words), "The Case of the Derelict Digit."

During our 1990 season we performed Haydn's Quartets Op. 54, No. 1, Op. 76, No. 5, Op. 74, No. 3, and Op. 64, No. 5, as part of a Stanford University Haydn symposium. Nomi joined us in the Dohnányi Piano Quintet (and got a nice mention in the review) for a concert at Southern Oregon State College in Ashland on April 7th (my 63rd birthday). Thanks to the efforts of Sheldon Soffer, our new New York manager, we repeated the program (which also included some Haydn and some Beethoven) for concerts at the University of the Pacific at Stockton, California, Pomona College in Claremont, California, and for the Vancouver Chamber Music Society.

All five of my previous quartets had to go through growing pains and weather internal storms before achieving any kind of meaningful residency, but the Stanford Quartet began in a university setting, and its salary inequality was built in from the start. Andy began to suffer some severe physical stress because of tensions in the Quartet caused by our constant changes of personnel (due to salary inequality). I was terribly saddened (but not surprised) when my friend of many years showed up one morning to say that 1990 would be his final season with the group he started.

While we were in the process of auditioning violinists to replace him, Andy stayed on for our six-concert series at the Sedona Chamber Music Festival in Arizona. In addition to concerts in Sedona, the magical Red Rock country known as "The Land of Enchantment," we also played in some smaller towns like Prescott, Winslow, Jerome (known as America's most vertical city), and windy Flagstaff. Some friends flew into Prescott just to hear Nomi play with us. Andy's forthcoming retirement from the Quartet was noted sadly in the review of his final Stanford concert with us on June 5th, 1990. We played the Mozart D minor Quartet, K. 421, the Bartók Quartet No. 6 (a fitting choice, in its anguish), and the Dohnányi Piano Quintet with Nomi.

Andy toured for several years as first violinist of the Takács Quartet after leaving Stanford, and then he and Louise retired to Friday Harbor (one of the San Juan Islands) in Washington State. Their cellist son, Andor Toth, Jr., died of cancer in 2002, and then Louise followed in 2005. Andy passed away in November of 2006. Our cellist Stephen Harrison described him well: "he had great personality and sweetness in his playing, and an energetic virtuosity that leaped off the stage."

Our continued search for a new first violinist proved to be extremely frustrating. We finally came up with an excellent candidate, but due to one of academe's maddening glitches, Stanford dropped the ball, and we lost the person who was our first choice for the position. I was at my wit's end. I called just about every American violinist I could think of, and then I tried Manny Hurwitz in London. Manny mentioned Phillip Levy, a remarkable young Welsh-Israeli violinist. He called Phillip a "one-off," and "some kind of a genius" (strong words indeed for Manny). A reviewer for the London Telegraph praised Phillip's Wigmore Hall recital, writing of his powerful playing, warmth of sound, consistently clear interpretive ideas, clean articulation, and his appealing tasteful and confident sense of style.

Phillip was a member of the Apple Hill Chamber Players, a group that spent its summers near Keene, New Hampshire, about 300 miles from Blue Hill, Maine. I called Steve to see if he and Susan could come to Blue Hill so we might all get together to audition Phillip for the few days that he could be at liberty from his duties at Apple Hill. Some local friends of the Kneisel Hall Chamber Music Festival put all three of them up at his ten-room "cottage," and after two days of intense rehearsing, we knew that Phillip was our man.

Phillip had commitments abroad, and wasn't immediately available, so we asked Ian Swenson, a faculty member of the San Francisco Conservatory, to step in and begin our season. Ian has great individuality in his playing, and is a delight to work with. He saved our necks by playing two local concerts with us on October 29th, 1990, and November 4th, as well as a third concert when the Fine Arts Quartet (with three new members) joined us for a program of Mozart Quintets and the Mendelssohn Octet at the Chamber Music in Napa Valley series. We celebrated old times with my old cellist friend Wolfie Laufer and his comrades, and imbibed a fair amount of Napa Valley's best vintages; but only after the concert.

The Stanford String Quartet in 1991
Bernard Zaslav, Stephen Harrison,
Susan Freier, and Phillip Levy

THE STANFORD STRING QUARTET

Phillip Levy was indeed one heck of a natural fiddler. I also found, from playing the Frank Bridge viola duo with him, that he played viola equally well. He was born in Cardiff, Wales, and studied in Israel and Europe. He led the London-based Locrian and Amphion String Quartets and had played some of Bartók's Violin Duos with Sir Yehudi Menuhin for a BBC television broadcast. Outwardly he appeared like an Edward G. Robinson kind of "little tough guy," but he was extremely warm and deep; a real mensch. We lost Andy, but we gained someone different in temperament and style, with equal, if not similar, musical talent. Andy was inclined to be secretive, and almost cunning in his approach to life, but Phillip was guileless and open. He had innate *ta'am* (taste) in his music making and in all his other interests.

Phillip was also slightly dyslexic, so he depended more on his ear than what was on the printed page. His instinct was to play a phrase before over-analyzing it. Nomi and I warmed to him immediately, like one of the family. When Phillip came to our condo, he looked at one of the Staffordshire platters from our collection that was hanging on the wall and exclaimed, "Hey, that's Tintern Abbey, near where I was born." Go figure! He continued to regale us with stories about his Army duty and his life in Israel. You had to love him; which we did, and still do.

A New York violin dealer called to tell me that my old friend Normie Carr (my pal from that Raymond Scott gig I played back in 1946), had passed away. Normie's wife put his violin on consignment, and the dealer wondered whether, for old time's sake, I might be interested in it, assuring me that it was a "Guadinarius." That's a musician's *nom de plume* for a "mutt," an instrument without proven parentage (and a step up from a "Stradinini"). This "maker" is not to be confused with the lesser-known "Notonius," a fiddle that (you guessed it) sucks. Normie had purchased the instrument from a questionable dealer many years before, when prices were much lower, and had used it through his career as a Los Angeles studio musician.

The instrument turned out to be as sweet as pecan pie, so I bought it. I was even inspired to put aside my viola and tickle it occasionally. Phillip had a very fair modern Italian violin, and when he played on my new toy, he fell for it. I was forced to part with the fiddle as a result, but it was in far better hands than mine, and Phillip sounded great playing on it in the Quartet.

Phillip was safely aboard as first violinist and Senior Lecturer, and we played our first concert with him on December 6th, 1990 at Stanford. The program included Mozart's D Major Quartet, K. 575, Joaquin Turina's "La Orácion del Torero," and Dvořák's "American" Quartet, Op. 96. We also played the West Coast Premiere of Ezra Laderman's "Talkin–Lovin'–Leavin" for alto recorder and strings, a piece commissioned by the American Recorder Society for their 50th anniversary. Judith Linsenberg was our guest for this performance.

We played the Schubert Quartet, Op. 125, No. 1, the Shostakovich Seventh Quartet (I seem to fancy all his odd-numbered quartets), and the Brahms Quartet Op.51, No.1 on January 25th, 1991 at Stanford, and we repeated the program on the 29th at the University of California, San Francisco. The rest of the season included performances of the Boccherini Quartet, Op. 33, No. 6, the Fauré Quartet (which we were planning to record), the Beethoven Quartet Op. 59, No. 3, the Mozart Quartet, K. 387, and Elgar's Quartet, Op. 83. Phillip had his first exposure to the "California Effect" through playing an outdoor concert series, called "Sunday in the Country" at the Wente Brothers winery in Livermore, where we had great wine and fabulous food.

In June, 1991, following our concert series in Sedona, an unsettling situation began to unfold at Stanford. Some severe budget reductions had been set for the School of Humanities and Science (the source of funding for the music department). Stanford's financial problems started to raise some hackles among members of the faculty, who were concerned about the performance aspect of music playing "second-fiddle" at research-oriented institutions. Stanford's newspaper published articles regarding the centrality of music in the "Stanford experience," and people argued that reducing or eliminating music from the performing arts would breed "general mediocrity." A post-doctoral fellow at the Department of Cell Biology wrote a letter with the headline "Stanford shouldn't settle for Harvard's lack of art," so we were not alone.

Stanford's music department employed far more academic musicians than performing musicians. Applied faculty members, like the four of us, were a slim minority. As the old saying goes, "the shortage will be distributed among the peasants." Many learned voices joined the general chorus of complaints about the idea of eliminating the Doctorate of Musical Arts degree, and people spoke about how important the Quartet was to the University's mission, its students, and to the community at large.

Thankfully, after all the commotion, things came out all right for us, and the funding problem was resolved. Our concerts continued to garner excellent reviews, and our Bolcom, Johnston, Neikrug album for Laurel Records was being widely praised by critics. We resumed our pilgrimages to Arizona in June for our concert series in Sedona, and our New York manager provided us with concert dates in Oklahoma City, at Idaho State University, and at Mills College in Oakland, California. We invited George Sopkin, my dearest friend from the Fine Arts Quartet (who made his home in Maine) to appear as a guest artist in Schubert's great two-Cello Quintet. "String Quartet moves to the sublime," was the review's headline. Mary Page Stegner, the widow of the revered Stanford faculty member, Wallace Stegner, asked us to play the same glorious Schubert work as a tribute to her husband. Stegner, who is not as well known in the eastern United States as he is in the west, is called the "Dean of Western Writers." He is famous for his novels and his nonfiction works about the American West, and won the 1972 Pulitzer Prize in Fiction for his novel *Angle of Repose*. We played the tribute concert at Stanford's Memorial Church on May 3, 1993, and Bonnie Hampton was our guest cellist.

We recorded an album of 20th-century music (Darius Milhaud's Seventh String Quartet, Op. 87, Frank Bridge's First Quartet in D, and Gabriel Fauré's Quartet, Op.121) for the Music & Arts label. Robin Stowell reviewed it in the April 1995 issue of *The Strad*.

His words about the Bridge Quartet, "The testing finale, agitated and intense but with some reflective solo comments from the viola, is managed in exemplary style" seemed to reflect the agitated intensity that had entered our daily Quartet life.

The Quartetto Italiano was undoubtedly one of the finest chamber groups ever to grace a concert stage. They were a brilliant-sounding group that had a long and valuable career, and they played the whole repertoire by memory.* The Quartetto Italiano was founded in 1945 by two violinists in their twenties, Paolo Borciani, and Elisa Pegreffi. They married each other in 1977 (after 32 years, perhaps they simply felt it was time), but the Quartet disbanded three years later. I know of several young groups with members who are married to each other, and they seem to survive quite happily in a quartet situation, at least in the short term. Unfortunately this was not the case for us.

Shortly after we auditioned Phillip, Susan and Stephen decided to divorce their respective spouses and marry each other (as a popular television comedian once blurted out, "Not that there's anything wrong with that"). Even though their marriage was, and continues to be, a successful one, it was not without consequences for the Quartet. With five personnel changes in eight years, the Quartet's chemistry had taken an unwelcome turn, and I knew it was time for me to leave the group.

I talked to the Quartet, and then I informed our dean about my decision to retire. Although ten years of academic service were normally required for a faculty member to be given full emeritus status, the provost, who recognized my many years in academia, made a special exception that allowed me to continue living on campus and have library privileges. The Quartet had accomplished quite a bit during my time. I am proud of our many performances and recordings, as well as the teaching I did at Stanford, and the musical prestige we brought to the University.

* I once heard the Smetana Quartet, a group that also played by memory, suffer an embarrassing moment of forgetfulness during a concert in Munich.

Phillip remained with the Quartet until 1998, and then he moved to Los Angeles to play chamber music and do film work. I miss the pleasure of playing with him, but we continue to keep in touch. Another violist joined and left, Stephen and Susan formed their own quartet (they called themselves the Ives Quartet), and the Stanford Quartet was replaced by the excellent St. Lawrence String Quartet from Canada.

During my 36 years as the violist of six extraordinary string quartets, I was able to work with excellent colleagues and play a vast amount of literature. I had the most interesting and varied existence imaginable. Nomi and I had always played the viola and piano repertoire between the cracks of my quartet life, but our Duo had taken a back seat for a long time. It was time for the Zaslav Duo to write its own chapter.

Oh, Fiddlesticks!

I rose to the bait when Hank Dutt, the violist of the Kronos Quartet (and a fellow bow nut), suggested that I include a fermata about viola bows. Matthew Michelic, my former student, came up with the title of this fermata.

The tool used for exciting vibrations out of stringed instruments began as a rudimentary hunter's bow. During the Middle Ages and into the Renaissance, it still looked like a hunter's bow, and it kept much of its archer's shape into the Baroque Period, but it took the Parisian-born watch maker turned bow maker (*archetier*), François Tourte (1747–1835?) to bend it backwards and make the first reverse-curved fiddlestick.*

---

* David Boyden and James McKean (who apprenticed at Nigo's shop) both wrote excellent books and articles concerning the transition from the early Baroque bow to the Tourte bow.

In order to achieve the proper curve (or camber) for the shaft of the bow, Tourte carefully heated a carved stick of Brazilian pernambuco wood (now an endangered species) over the flame of an alcohol burner. He also used dense ebony wood from Mauritius, ivory from the tusks of elephant (or often Siberian fossilized mammoth), mother of pearl, tortoise shell, metals like silver, nickel, brass, and gold (in varying specimens) for the frog, and between 150 and 200 strands of white hair from the tail of an Arabian horse. Tourte's work earned him the title the "Stradivari of the bow" from the acknowledged bow expert, Paul Childs.

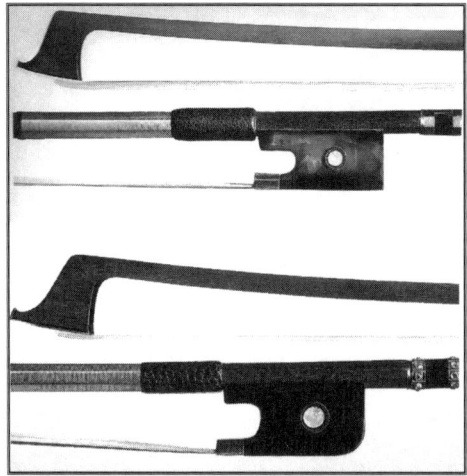

Heads and frogs of two viola bows

Plucked string instruments in Ancient Egypt, Greece, and Rome were mainly used to accompany singing or wind playing, because as melody instruments, these plucked instruments suffered the limitations of natural sound decay. Some people believe the principle of stringing a hunting bow with horsehair in order to draw sustained sound out of formerly-plucked instruments originated among Central Asia's nomadic horse-riding cultures. It then spread both westward through Islam and eastward, so that by the year 1000, the art of bowing concurrently reached China, Java, North Africa, the Near East and Balkans, and Europe. We do know that early bowed instruments were used in Islamic civilizations during the 10th century.

The best bow hair still comes from horses that live in cold climates (synthetic hair is touted today for its longevity, but it isn't generally used for fine instruments). Horse hair, when viewed under a microscope, has tiny barbs that allow for alternate partial adhesion (drag and release). If the hair has been sufficiently powdered with rosin, and is drawn across over a tightened string, the tiny barbs, alternately grabbing and releasing the string, cause it to remain in a state of constant vibration.

Because it was François Tourte who brought the bow to its highest state of evolution, France is considered the home of fine modern bowmaking. Many fine bowmakers came from the town of Mirecourt (France), but most of them moved to Paris, where the action was. The bow maker's art quickly spread to Germany (Markneukirchen), and England (London). English bowmaking families, like the Dodd and the Tubbs families, practiced their craft for generations. Now fine bows are made everywhere.

Like oboists seeking the perfect reed, violists are always on the prowl for the ultimate combination of weight, flexibility, and string "cling" in a bow. In order to activate its slightly thicker (and somewhat slower to respond) strings, our instrument is happiest with a bow that weighs between 65 and 73 grams, which is somewhat heavier than a typical violin bow. In order to pull every possible overtone out of the viola, a bow must hug the string as it is drawn. It must bounce easily for times when the music calls for our off-the-string spiccato strokes, and it has to play equally well at the tip as at the heel (or the frog, as it is also called). It also needs to have the right indefinable "feel" in the hand of the player, since size and musculature varies.

There has always been a far greater demand for violin and cello bows, and in the early days of modern bowmaking, there were fewer viola bows produced because of the smaller demand for them. Bows can also break quite easily* (usually at the thinner tip), so fine old viola bow specimens are rare

---

* I heard that Isaac Stern accidentally sat on one of his bows.

and expensive. I always used a cheap bow when working in a crowded Broadway pit.

Some bowmakers work alone, and some work as part of a shop. A. R. Bultitude, one of the bowmakers working for the historic W. E. Hill & Sons establishment in London, wrote a letter to a collector (on August 11, 1972) in which he explained that the bowmakers working at Hill were not permitted to brand their own names on the sticks. Bultitude went on to explain that the identity of the person in the shop who made a bow could be discovered by deciphering a secret code on the tip plate, where it could be concealed by the hair. Part of the romance of bow collecting lies in knowing these kinds of secrets about the makers, as well as information about the musicians who used their bows through the centuries.

Robert Mann, the former first violinist of the Juilliard Quartet, favored bows made by the French maker Eugene Sartory. In the 1940s you could buy a good Sartory, a tool of our trade, for about $150. Though I have owned two Sartory viola bows (one is currently being used by the violist of a major string quartet), I preferred playing bows by other makers, and I've been able to find some beauties during my travels.

My bow collecting began gradually. I first came across a useful bow to go with the Gaetano Chiocchi viola that Mischa found for me. It was branded Herman Richard Pfretzchner (1856–1892) of Markneukirchen, a town in Germany known for its tradition of musical instrument making. The Pfretzchner family of bowmakers was large, so I can't be certain that this bow was originally made by Herman Richard Pfretzchner, since it was quite inexpensive (which was what I could afford at the time).

Unlike most violin bows, viola bows can vary slightly in length. Those by Nicholas Maire (1800–1878) are often a few millimeters longer than usual, and bows by John Kew Dodd (1752–1839), one of the greatest of the English bowmakers (often called "the English Tourte") can be on the short side (often four to eight millimeters smaller), which is one reason why my petite-sized teacher, Lillian Fuchs, selected a Dodd.

In the 1950s I lucked into such a Dodd. It weighed 71 grams, had a beautifully-crafted eyeless frog and a rather bold head with an ebony tip liner (rather than the usual ivory). I was using the Dodd while I was sitting next to cellist Harvey Shapiro during a recording session with Stokowski for "In Dulci Jubilo, a Baroque Concert," that came out on Vanguard in 1967. Harvey and I looked at one another, and did a simultaneous double take; except for the size, Harvey's Dodd cello bow appeared to be a clone of my Dodd viola bow. Their bold heads were made in exactly the same pattern, and even looked like they were made from the same piece of wood. We immediately struck up a warm friendship, and made a point of sitting opposite each other thereafter.

Harvey had a tone "you could eat off of," as they used to say. He became the cellist of the distinguished Primrose Quartet in 1939, and was a member of the WQXR Quartet from 1947 to 1963. He joined the Juilliard faculty in 1970 (where he taught for 30 years, well into his nineties), and remains one of the world's most revered cellists. Harvey's taste in cigars and women rivaled his taste in bows. He married Rena Robbins, a member of the Metropolitan Opera's violin section, one of the best (and prettiest) violinists in town. George Szell once summoned Harvey to his New York hotel room, and after hearing him play, instantly offered him the position of principal cello of the Cleveland Orchestra, which he turned down for financial reasons: he needed money to support his family (the same reason I left). With his passing, we lost a truly heroic cellist and a master teacher, omnipresent cigar and all.

I discovered that smaller violas can be even more dependent on a bow's proper weight and flexibility than larger instruments when I began playing the Michaelango Bergonzi viola that Harold Kohon found for me. As part of the deal for buying the Bergonzi (that I didn't know was a Bergonzi at the time), I had to give, in partial trade, a bow made by Victor François Fetique (1872–1933). I hated to part with that Fetique; it was a prize winner in 1926, and was so stamped on the stick, but I wanted to own that wonderful viola. After that experience, I began to haunt every fiddle shop and bow maker I could find, both in America and abroad (where the pickings were better).

While I was subbing in a Broadway show in 1968, just weeks before I left New York for Milwaukee, I told my stand partner I was about to join a famous quartet. His response was to offer me an elegant bow made by William C. Retford (1875–1970) for only $250. It weighs 66 grams, has an octagon-shaped stick, a gold mounted tip, a tortoise-shell frog with a Fleur-de-lis shield insert, and a jewel-like gold and ivory button. After barely trying it, I bought it on the spot. Retford was one of London's finest bowmakers. In 1892, at the age of 17, he became an apprentice bow maker for the London firm of A. E. Hill & Sons, and worked there for 64 years.* I later learned that this Retford was once owned by Nicolas Moldevan, the violist of the old Flonzaley Quartet. My Retford bow is a dream to play. It's light and agile, and wants its head in spiccatto passages.

Before I left New York, Nigo found for me a wonderfully sensitive bow made by Louis Simon Pajeot (1770–1795) of Mirecourt. Pajeot's magnificently-crafted bows seem to have been strongly influenced by Tourte, and Joseph Roda, in his book, *Bows for Musical Instruments of the String Family*, considers them to be almost perfect reproductions. I enjoyed it for many years, and when it came time to part with it (the devil makes us do it, as we follow our elusive muse), the Pajeot went to a violist in the Milwaukee Symphony. This violist saved for many years to buy a truly precious bow like this one, and when it broke accidentally, his insurance company (true to form) gave him a hell of a time when he tried to collect on it.

A broken bow requires the attention of an experienced *archetier*, and can be quite frustrating to deal with. A graft (spline) can be inserted into a broken head, a frog can be relined or its tightening screw may be replaced, but repairs to the head or a replacement frog can compromise a bow's resale value. Prices for older bows that are intact and in excellent condition reflect their rarity and their value.

* In Bows and Bowmakers, a monograph he wrote at the age of 90, Retford muses about how the first fiddle bow might have been created.

I kept my eyes peeled for bows in every town with a fiddle shop while I was on tour with the Fine Arts Quartet. I was still playing my Bergonzi when I found Peter Paul Prier's shop in Salt Lake City, Utah. Peter told me in confidence that the main reason he relocated to Utah from Walter Hamma's shop in Stuttgart was for the skiing. He founded his Violin School of America there in 1972, and it was in his shop that I found my Dominique Peccatte (1810–1874) bow. It was boldly cut, played wonderfully and was in perfect condition.

I met some of Peter's students when I revisited his shop (they went on to become well-known lutiers), and it was there that I found the first of my three bows (lucky me) made by Guillaume Maline (1793–1850). Maline left Mirecourt to work at J.B. Vuillaume's shop in Paris. His bows can be breathtakingly beautiful in cut, and I find them sensitive to my every wish. His frogs, made in the rounded-edge Vuillaume style, bear Maline's own specially-elongated signature ferrule (the silver part of the frog that spreads the hair), which makes them instantly recognizable. Rare as they are, I managed to find two of them in America, and one at the shop of Etienne Vatelot in Paris. Mr. Vatelot, a brusque and imposing man, was one of the world's finest restorers of instruments. He was a widely sought expert on provenance, but the Maline I bought from his shop was disappointing, and I rarely played it. The first two had spoiled me.

While on another European tour, I walked into a dingy little violin shop on a side street of Den Haag, in the Netherlands, and I asked my usual question (expecting to be told that, of course, there were no worthwhile viola bows to be had). After some gentle coaxing (I offered to pay in American dollars), the shop owner came up with a bow made by Claude Thomassin (1870–1942), who had worked in Den Haag. He also brought out a bow stamped "Otto A. Hoyer Pariser," a bow maker I didn't know at the time. Hoyer worked in the Paris shop of Eugene Nicolas Sartory (1871–1940), and he modeled his bows after Sartory. After 1925 he did his business from Markneukirchen, one of the major instrument-making cities in Germany. I was already carrying two bows in my case, so fitting in two more took a bit of ingenuity.

When I opened the case of the Guadagnini viola that I purchased from Mrs. P. in 1974, I was thrilled to see that our deal had unexpectedly included a bow with a Vuillaume-style frog made by François Nicolas Voirin (1833–1885). It had most likely been selected by Émile Férir, the instrument's previous owner (before Mr. P.). It weighed 68.6 grams (the perfect weight), and seemed to be perfectly mated to this viola. Voirin's violin bows can often be rather slim and whippy, but this gorgeous viola bow (that was in perfect condition) was responsive to my every whim throughout its length, and could pull out every bit of the Guadagnini's sonic beauty. There was perfection, right in my hands, but being fickle (and greedy), I still lusted for more bows.

Nomi and I were often guests at Emanuel Hurwitz's home in Golders Green when the Fine Arts Quartet played in London. Each time I visited he would show me an absolutely pristine 72.2 gram James Tubbs bow that he was saving for his violist wife Kay. "But Manny," I begged, "Kay already showed me her own bows that fit with her larger viola. Couldn't you . . . ?" "No, I'm simply not ready to sell it," he said. To shut me up, he introduced me to a few of his other collector friends (read, nuts) in the neighborhood. From them, I picked up another Sartory, and two more bows that had come from the shop of W. E. Hill & Sons, an Edgar Bishop bow that weighed 65.4 grams, and a bow made by Albert Leeson. I learned from this crowd that many amateur British violinists seemed to enjoy trading off to play viola parts of an evening, so English makers wisely supplied them with small violas (my own preference). Manny's collector friends supplied me with a few smaller violas (for my students) made by Richard Duke, William Forster, Charles Boulanger, and George Craske. Though Craske is generally considered to be a rather minor maker, he is credited, by the firm of John and Arthur Beare, with making over 2,500 instruments.

It took five years of supplication for Manny to relent and finally sell me his magnificent Tubbs specimen. I tried every other Tubbs I could find while I was waiting for him to cave. Most were either too heavy or too soft, and a couple of the bows with their highly desirable "inscribed" frogs were really no better than average. The Tubbs family had several bowmakers, and their work varied in quality. Some bows are stamped W. Tubbs, and some are stamped E. Tubbs, and there is a great deal of confusion concerning their authenticity. My James Tubbs has the most elegant plain frog, a gold plate on the tip, and the gun-barrel view (for which one looks down the length of the bow to see if it is warped) and the winding near the frog confirm it to be one of his best. It was said that James Tubbs could turn out a bow in a day, but this was not one of those. He probably made it when he was working on his own (after he left Hill), when time was not a factor.

I happened into an unbelievably fresh bow (the whalebone wrapping near the frog looked looked like it had just been wound) that was made by P. Simon (1808–1882) when he worked in Vuillaume's shop. I found it at the shop of Emil Hjorth & Sons in Copenhagen while the Fine Arts Quartet was on tour in Scandinavia. I asked my usual question and expected the same old answer, but Hjorth's son told me that a collector in need of cash had just that morning left this virtually unused viola bow on consignment. It was a bit heavy for my taste, about 74 grams or so, but it pulled an incredible sound. I left a pile of U. S. dollars on the counter, and left the shop with what I thought was the most beautiful thing on wheels . . . er, with hair.

I stuffed the Simon into my crowded case and loved it to death, but it wouldn't work for me because it was reluctant to leave the string when I wanted it to. There are violists who are dying for the kind of sound that such a bow is able to produce, whether it wants to leave the string or not, so I reluctantly decided to offer it to the Chicago shop of Bein & Fushi.

As I stood waiting for the elevator in the lobby of 410 South Michigan Avenue (the Fine Arts Building), I struck up a conversation with an amateur violist I knew. I told him that I was bringing the Simon up to offer to Robert Bein, and he pulled me aside to a nearby bench and insisted on seeing the Simon before I went up. He took his viola out of its case, right there in the drafty corridor, and played the bow for about five minutes (the elevator users must have thought, "well, it takes all kinds"). My violist friend pulled out his checkbook, held the bow fast in one hand, and wrote out a check with the other. He would often come to see me backstage after our Fine Arts Quartet concerts at the Goodman Theater to tell me how this bow had changed his life. I still miss it, if only for its looks. Of course, when it came to looks, neither Ava Gardner nor Greta Garbo in her prime were in that league. Of course, back in high school there was my drama teacher Marjorie Dycke, but . . .

Once, when the Fine Arts Quartet played a concert in some German town (whose name I don't recall) a real old guy (maybe as old as I am now) came backstage at intermission, eyes sparkling and with a bow case in hand (that he handled as if it were pure gold). He opened it to reveal a really odd-looking early-Saxon bow with a wildly upturned nose (head), an elaborate ivory frog, and a shaft made of strongly speckled *Schlangenholz* (snakewood). He suggested that I try it right then and there, so I used it for the second half of the concert. He came backstage after the concert, and offered the bow to me for X German marks. I thought it over and decided against buying it, so we said our goodbyes.

He reappeared at our taxi window with his bow case in hand while we were preparing to return to the hotel. He had an intensely questioning look on his face, and I had a 1,000 mark bill in my pocket. I figured, "what the hell," and we exchanged both of these items through the window of the taxi, and drove off. My seat-mates thought I was nuts, but I simply couldn't say no.

When I showed the bow to Nigo, he told me he had seen such bows before; he had more respect for it than I would have imagined. And so does the excellent female violist in Texas who now owns it. There was also a nice bow by Joseph Arthur Vigneron (1851–1905) that I found during my European travels, and since living in California, I have purchased local bows made by Jack English of Santa Cruz and a prize-winning bow by Jian Ming Li of San Jose.

When the Fine Arts Quartet played in Saarbrucken I was told about Geigenbau (violin shop) Krause that was run by a young married couple. Herr Jurgen Krause made Baroque instruments and his wife, Angela Krause, was a sweet-faced bowmaker in her early twenties. Angela showed me some of her bows. They were beautifully made, weighed about 66 grams, and they were very playable, so I left the shop with two of them. I sold one to an excellent violist who wrote that he really appreciated it, and I kept the other in my studio. I once loaned that Krause to a student for an upcoming concert. He kept it for quite a while, and apologized for returning it with a repaired tip (he had accidentally broken it). No matter; it hadn't cost much, and it plays just as well, so I still keep it. When I returned later to the Geigenbau Krause, I learned that Angela had been quite ill as a result of pernambuco wood dust that had became lodged in her lungs. Thankfully she recovered.

Should you get the idea that I'm some kind of a bow-buying expert, please hold your applause. When I was living in New York, a dealer once showed me a gold-mounted bow with a flashy tortoise-shell frog that was stamped "Maire." Anyone else with the least bit of experience could see that, although it played well, it was an obvious fake. Nigo patiently explained this to me after I bought the bow. He told me that the bow was a nice Czech-made fraud, and that I should ask for my money back (of course I paid far too much for it in the first place, greenhorn that I was). The dealer had the *culliones* to say Nigo was wrong, so I was stuck with this glitzy lemon for far too many years. It finally has a happy home with someone who is clearly aware of its phoniness, but he liked the way it played, and he dug the gaudy frog.

I made another bow-related gaffe during my brief relationship with (now deceased) violist Louis Kievman. In the 1940s many of New York's most famous violists used to enter the teaching studio of Demetrius Constantin Dounis through the back door, lest the competition learn which of their rivals was doing the same. Dounis, an influential pedagogue of string technique was known to every fiddler in town for his unique approach to the violin, which was often guaranteed to leave you in physical pain (particularly if you are a violist). Kievman, as a violist, was curious about the Dounis method, and after studying with the great man, came out with his own viola method bearing the odd title, *Practicing the Violin, Mentally - Physically*.

Louis had a career as the violist of the Musical Art Quartet and the Stuyvesant Quartet, played in Toscanini's NBC Symphony, and retired to Pacific Palisades. When I came to California, he and his charming wife Elaine invited Nomi and me to his home for dinner.

Louis owned what is said to be the only uncut Gasparo da Salo viola in existence (most of Salo's violas, or *tenores*, were at least seventeen inches long). Louis' was highly decorated, and exactly fifteen and a half inches in length. I brought my similarly-sized Guadagnini that evening, and we had a ball, playing each others' violas and bows. Louis had an embarrassment of riches in the bow department. One of them was a rare viola bow by Tourte, and like most Tourtes I have played, they take a while to get used to. They seem to flex differently from other bows. Louis's viola Tourte was very light and thin, and I was surprised when he told me that he could part with it, and named a price of $3,000. He warned me that there was a problem with a bit of grain separation along the top of the stick, but I still took it with me to try.

I asked around, and heard conflicting stories about the actual worth of the bow, so I sent it to Dario D'Atilli in Florida (with Louis's okay) for an appraisal. Dario returned it, saying that the bow was a genuine Tourte, but the asking price was too high by about a third. I wasn't really smitten by its playing characteristics, and basically wanted to own it so I could boast that I had a real Tourte. I knew that I would never actually play it in public, so I asked Louis if he would reduce the price. He took it badly, and I felt I lost his friendship because of my ill-considered gaffe (he died in 1990, so I hope he will have forgiven me by now). This was quite a while ago, when prices weren't what they are now. In hindsight, I was really a damned fool not to have bought it, whether it was playable or not, because I just learned that a former student of mine recently paid an obscenely high price for a famous Tourte viola bow.

During one of the Vermeer's visits to the Royal Northern College of Music in Manchester, I happened to coach a student string trio that included Bruno Price, a young British cellist. Bruno followed the Vermeer back to De Kalb, Illinois, to study with our cellist, Mark Johnson. After he graduated, Bruno, who was always interested in instruments, spent about seven years working at Bein & Fushi's shop in Chicago, and another seven at Dietmar Machold's shop in New York. Bruno Price is now a widely-accepted authority in the violin world, and runs a shop, together with violinist Ziv Arazi, at 140 West 57th Street in New York (the former home of Jacques Francais).

Bruno chuckles when he reminds me that after the trio played their first movement for me at RNCM, the first comment I made to their violist Roger Benedict was, "Where did you ever find that green viola?" Indeed, the varnish of the odd-looking thing he was playing did have a distinctly greenish tinge in that studio lighting. Roger, who became the principal viola of the London Philharmonia, and is currently the principal violist of the Sydney Symphony, now plays a fine Carlo Antonio Testore viola made in Milan in 1753.

Since its inception, Stanford's "Lively Arts" series has been inviting a steady stream of visiting quartets to play concerts. Many violists from those visiting quartets (and even some violinists) make a regular point of stopping by my condo to try some of my bows on their own violas. Among these musicians were Roberto Diaz (who now owns the William Primrose Amati), Lawrence Dutton of the Emerson Quartet (Phillip Setzer, one of the violinists in the Emerson, tried one of my lighter viola bows on his beautiful Strad violin), Kazuhide "Kazu" Isomura (the superb long-time violist of the Tokyo Quartet), Geraldine Walther (the newest member of the Takács Quartet), Masumi Per Rostad (of the Pacifica Quartet), and violist Hank Dutt and violinist John

Sherba (of the Kronos Quartet). Others who have caught the virus include violists like my colleague Walter Trampler, Paul Neubauer (Walter's pupil), Ralph Fielding, and a few members of the San Francisco Symphony's viola section, like my former student, Nancy Severance, and the orchestra's co-principal, Yun-Jie "Jay" Liu (the river runs deep).

I doubt that any living pianist has listened to as many violists try as many bows as has my long-suffering wife, Nomi. I often try her patience by asking which of them she prefers for certain passages. Would she thereby qualify as an honorary bow nut?

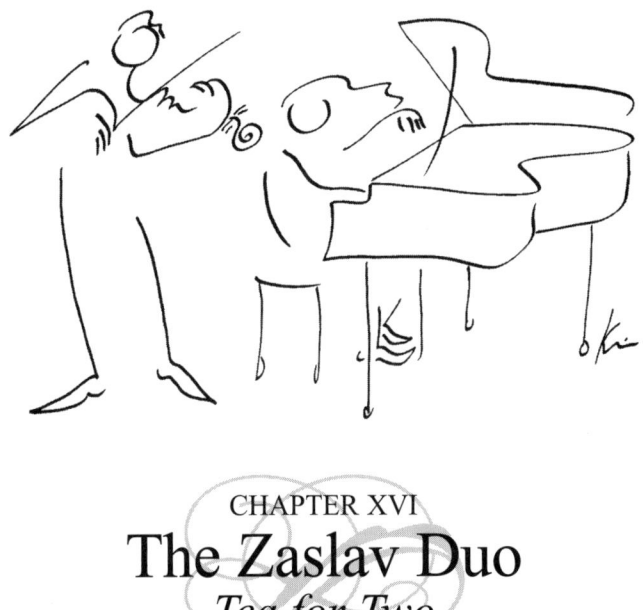

CHAPTER XVI
The Zaslav Duo
Tea for Two

Duos were a relative rarity in the 20th chamber music scene, especially viola and piano duos, but there were duos that had great success. A few duo-pianists have made their mark, like Ferrante & Teicher who performed and recorded their own extravagant arrangements of love songs and movie themes, and Luboshutz and Nemenoff, who performed and recorded original duo piano music from the classical repertoire.

It was common for two already-acknowledged soloists (usually, but not always, a string player and a pianist) to team up for a concert tour or a recording project. Some duos *en famille* had great success. Benno Rabinoff, for example, the last of Leopold Auer's violin students, and his wife Sylvia Smith (who studied with Paderewski, Simon Barere, and Rudolf Serkin), made a respectable international career as the Rabinoff Duo. Aaron Rosand and his wonderfully gifted wife, the pianist Eileen Flissler, gave many excellent recitals, and their recordings of the ten Beethoven sonatas (reissued on CD in 2007), remain unequalled.

During the 1950s Nomi and I tested the duo waters by giving a few New York recitals. In 1962, after appearing in various chamber music settings, we made our formal Carnegie Recital Hall debut as the Zaslav Duo, and continued to give recitals in New York. In 1969, one year after I joined the Fine Arts Quartet, Nomi and I gave a series of three duo recitals covering the various periods of the viola literature in the University of Wisconsin-Milwaukee's excellent recital hall. In 1974, when I acquired my G.B. Guadagnini viola (my new voice), I felt it was time for us to make our first official recording as a duo. The Fine Arts Quartet's recording equipment was already in place in the recital hall, and Orion Records, a small California record label, accepted our choice of repertoire. Orion coupled Darius Milhaud's First and Second Sonatas for Viola and Piano with my own transcription for viola of César Franck's A Major Violin Sonata on LP ORS-75186. To my knowledge, the Franck had never before been recorded on the viola.

Milhaud dedicated his less-often-played Second Sonata to the memory of Alphonse Onnou, the first violinist of the famed Pro Arte String Quartet of Belgium, who also enjoyed playing viola. It has three descriptively-titled movements: "Champêtre," a bouncy French pastorale, "Dramatique," which is more angular and stark, and "Rude," (rough) a movement similar in style and feeling to the Swiss composer Arthur Honegger, that gives a rather showy and intense ending to the work.

I had always wanted to transcribe music for other instruments to extend the viola repertoire. Lionel Tertis, William Primrose, Lillian Fuchs, and Paul Doktor all made successful transcriptions, but none of them had transcribed the Franck Sonata for viola. Perhaps they were of the same mind as Herbert Barrett who makes a point in *The Viola: Complete Guide for Teachers and*

Students, that transparency in the accompaniment is a deciding factor in the success of a transcription, and that a "sensitive pianist is something to be valued as highly as a collection of transcriptions from the Classical period." The Franck Sonata certainly does have a less-than-transparent piano part, but with Nomi at the keyboard, I had the courage to try my hand at it. I never played the Sonata on the violin, and Nomi and I both loved the work, and enjoyed the challenge. My sole liberty in transcribing it was to lower a few passages by an octave, and we were able to achieve proper balance without changing a single note of the piano part.

After the release of the recording in 1976, a congratulatory *Aérogramme* arrived from Madeleine Milhaud, Darius' wife (and cousin!). She wrote us from Paris to say, "Milhaud's intentions were well experienced and understood by you." She also added a postscript saying, "I would like to add that the record is excellent for both instruments." We were thrilled to receive a letter in May from Josef Gingold that read, "Dear Bernie and Naomi, Your recordings of the Franck and the Milhaud are superb!! I listened to the Franck twice and found it to be so beautiful, sensitive and technically perfect that I honestly can't think of more musical performance on records. Thank you for playing so wonderfully and my deepest appreciation. I love you!!" Imagine the joy we felt when we read this. We wondered why we had waited so long to make our first recording.

We also received a complimentary letter (what a surprise!) from William Primrose, the very king of the viola domain. He wrote about my "octavations," as he termed them. My friend Walter Trampler also sent me a letter, asking for a copy of my transcription of the viola part, and suggested I publish it, though I haven't so far.

There were also accolades from the press. The August 27th issue of the *Milwaukee Sentinel* called it "Album of the Year." In their Winter 1980 issue, *Devotee* named the LP "Debut Recording-Artist of the Year" and carried a florid review by Paul Elisha in their Winter 1980 issue that praised both the performance and the arrangement of the Franck, as well as the Dolby recording process (Orion's Super Stereo Sound recording).

The welcoming superlatives made two things clear to us: transcriptions for viola were no longer a no-no, and our Duo was beginning to be appreciated in some circles. Our obvious next choice was to record the two Brahms Sonatas, Op. 120. He wrote them in 1894 for clarinet and piano, and Joseph Joachim, the finest violinist of his time (and a composer who wrote excellent music for viola), suggested to Brahms that he should transcribe them for viola. These Sonatas have been usurped by violists, and are now staples of our literature. For this very reason, they are often played by violists who are too young to appreciate their innately reflective character (Brahms wrote them late in his life; just three years before he died). I feel that Brahms' marking of *Allegro appassionato* in the first movement of the F minor Sonata is best taken *cum grano salis,* and that his marking of *Allegro amabile,* which he uses for the opening movement of the E-flat Sonata, better defines the general mood of these late works. Nomi and I performed the E-flat Sonata for our 1962 debut. We are glad that we performed a lot of Brahms' other chamber music before taking the plunge and recording these masterworks.

Roy Christensen, who was a cello student of George Sopkin's at the University of Wisconsin-Milwaukee, worked in the recording booth when the Fine Arts Quartet made their recordings. Roy started his own record label called Gasparo, and released our recording of the Brahms Sonatas on that label. *Stereo Magazine* named it a "Recording of Special Merit" in their June 1981 issue, commenting on our "gorgeous tone, affectionate commitment, and enlivening give-and-take," and the *American String Teacher* called it, "the definitive recording of these two sonatas," and went on to describe how "the viola soars effortlessly in the long canzonas wonderfully backed by the piano. All the nooks and crannies of these works have been mastered and explored from all aspects of sound and rhythm." *Devotee Magazine* thought the album should be a collector's item, and in the July, 1981 issue of *The Strad,* Tully Potter wrote, "If I needed one word to sum up the performances of the Zaslav Duo here, it would be "loving." Mr. Potter went on to mention the apparent care that went into the preparation of the recording, "immaculate down to the last semiquaver," and commented on Nomi's "scrupulous placing of chords and pedaling" and my "supple phrasing." My beloved mentor Joe Gingold wrote us a second treasured letter (dated February 5, 1983) that read, "Your recording of the Brahms Sonatas is as beautiful, powerful and musical as one can ever hear it! Thank you for allowing me to share a great treat. As ever, your devoted Joe."

Considering Brahms' many heartfelt letters to Clara Schumann, I was surprised not to have heard from old Johannes himself. An email maybe, or a phone call—would it kill him?

After the release of our recordings, Baird Knechtel, a member of the Viola Research Society, invited the Zaslav Duo to give a recital at the 9th Annual International Viola Congress in Toronto. It was a significant event which Baird hosted very well. For ourconcert on June 14th, 1981 we played Elliott Carter's "Pastorale," the Brahms F minor Sonata, Milhaud's Second Sonata, and the First Sonata in E-flat major by Francesco Trevani, a 19th-century composer whose works I discovered on the shelves of the Musikhaus Doblinger in Vienna.

I knew many of the participants at this Viola Congress, including Steven Dann, Rivka Golani-Erdesz, Lillian Fuchs, Raphael Hillyer, Donald McGinnis, Myron Rosenblum, and my dear friend, Francis Tursi. On the morning of June 13th, the Russian violist, Feodor Drushynin performed Shostakovich's Op. 147 Sonata for Viola and Piano (his last work). Drushynin, the dedicatee of Shostakovich's Sonata, gave a performance that was directed more towards total faithfulness to the written notes, than to the emotional spirit of this monumental work.

Nancy Severance (who studied with me at Northern Illinois University), played the opening movement of Bach's Fourth Cello Suite for a master class that William Primrose gave later that afternoon, and was rewarded with a round of applause from the audience. Sitting right next to her, viola in hand, Mr. Primrose waited for the clapping to stop. He then turned to the audience, and asked, "Why are you applauding?" Everyone was flabbergasted by his remark, but Nancy kept her cool. Mr. Primrose proceeded, to the confusion of the audience, to tear her performance apart, unjustifiably accusing her of producing a "violin" sound. When he played his instrument to demonstrate a point, it was shockingly out of tune (Mr. Primrose had lost much of his hearing). I had never met the great man personally, and I had to struggle with my emotions about his public behavior when I was introduced to him after the class.

During the 1970s, Lucille Taylor, who played viola in a quartet with three of her siblings, drove every week from Benton Harbor, Michigan to the University of Wisconsin-Milwaukee to be coached by the Fine Arts Quartet. In 1989 the University of Redlands, California, hosted the 17th Annual Viola Congress, and Lucille, who was a member of the faculty, invited our Duo to play a recital. On June 22 we performed an arrangement of Pietro Nardini's Sonata in F minor, the (brilliant) Sonata for Viola and Piano by Hall Overton, a jazz pianist and an excellent composer on the Juilliard faculty (he was a rotten poker player), Charles Whittenberg's "Set for Two" (a premiere at the Congress), Ursula Mamlok's violin piece "From my Garden" that I transcribed for solo viola, Carl Reinecke's *Fantasiestücke*, Op. 43, and Richard H. Walthew's "Regret and Conversation Gallante," a charming British salon piece.

This Congress attracted many of my old friends and acquaintances including violists Paul Colletti, Alan de Veritch, Roberto Diaz, Czaba Erdelyi, Rosemary Glyde, Pamela Goldsmith, Martha Strongin Katz (to whom I loaned a C string), David Schwartz, and Karen Tuttle. Nigo, my lutier friend from New York was there, and we talked together while he eyed my Guadagnini viola, the one that he had assured me many years before, "is what it is." Nigo, who was one of the founding members of the Viola Society of America, died in 1997.

The remarkable Music & Arts catalog contains many CDs of refurbished recordings by famous artists of past generations, like

Sir Thomas Beecham, Wilhelm Furtwängler, and Bruno Walter. The Fine Arts Quartet's album of quartets by Milton Babbitt and Charles Wuorinen was in its catalog, so I asked Fred Maroth, Music & Arts' pioneering and farsighted owner, whether he might be willing to take on the Zaslav Duo. He took his first inexpensive gamble on us by re-releasing both of the two Brahms Sonatas and the Franck. After receiving critical attention, the CD release of album sold well, and Fred was interested in releasing more repertoire. After I retired from quartet life in the Fall of 1993, Nomi and I had the luxury of concentrating on new recording projects.

A recording engineer advised us to buy the newer type of SONY DTC-2300 tape recorder (or DAT, as it was called), and a pair of Neumann KM130 microphones and microphone stands. He also said that we would require the services of a recording engineer to monitor what was being played, keep a running log of the takes, and edit the finished product on a computer. Rather than hiring a recording engineer, I decided to learn to do the work myself, with the help of some friends.

James S. Koford (nicknamed "Shingle") and his wife Marcia purchased an unusual home high in the Monterey hills. They called it "Casa de Cielo," because of its 30-foot ceilings. A great circular area in their home that housed a nine-foot Mason & Hamlin grand piano proved to be an excellent recording space. Shingle is a Stanford alumnus who was then a technical executive working in a leading semiconductor company. In addition to his love for the organ, he is a piano devotee, and his "Casa de Cielo" houses five pianos, a few of which are mecanical reproducing pianos which he loves to take apart and put back together (properly). He most

Recording at Casa de Cielo

graciously spent many hours showing me how to use his Pro Tools editing program, a program that cost thousands at the time, and now comes free on a Mac.

I become close friends with Max Mathews, our next-door neighbor at Peter Coutts, after I retired from the Stanford faculty. He is an amateur fiddler and a sailor (he and his wife Marge once sailed from New Jersey to visit us in Maine), and he was the person responsible for creating the computer-generated swan song of the dying computer ("Bicycle Built for Two") used by Stanley Kubrick in *2001 A Space Odyssey*.

Max directed the Behavioral and Research Center at AT&T Bell Laboratories from 1955 to 1987, and from 1974 to 1980 he served as the Scientific Advisor to the Institute de Recherche et Coordination Acoustique/Musique (IRCAM), in Paris, France. In 1987 Max, joined the Stanford University Music Department as a Professor of Music (Research) in the Center for Computer Research in Music and Acoustics (CCRMA). The development of his computer-driven Radio Drum, was inspired by the work of the Russian scientist (and cellist), Léon Theremin, who invented the electronic instrument known as the Theremin in 1919. I was present at CCRMA when Mr. Theremin spoke there; his story about doing electronic spying for the Soviet Union is a real-life spy thriller. Max allowed me to use his lab at CCRMA to improve my computer skills and learn the newest computer-based recording and editing techniques.

While Nomi was busy at the piano, I served as a one-man crew for our recording sessions. I did the microphone set-up, ran the machine, kept the log, and played the viola part, while making decisions about how many takes we would need for my up coming editing process. As a kid, I remember playing a guitar while blowing into a harmonica I had fixed to my mouth, and beating a drum trap, all at the same time. That was for fun, but this was no laughing matter. Multi, multi, multitasking was my lot here.

Driving back and forth from Stanford to Monterey, plus setting up and then tearing down the machines and mikes, was extremely grueling. If we had an engineer paying attention to balance in a control room, it would have permitted me to concentrate solely on the task of playing the viola part. Doing it myself allowed me to have total control of the end product, but it came at a rather steep price.

I remembered hearing Leonard Rose play a wonderful performance of Ernest Bloch's *Schelomo* in Carnegie Hall with the New York Philharmonic many years before, so we chose Ernest Bloch's marvelous Suite for Viola and Piano for our first recording project at Casa de Cielo. Bloch played the viola (which immediately makes him a right thinker), and is considered to be the most important composer of Jewish music in the twentieth century. He was born in Geneva, Switzerland, on July 24, 1880, and within five months of his arrival in New York Harbor in 1916, he was hailed as a genius of the first rank. He wrote the Suite in 1919, and by 1921 his reputation as a composer, conductor and teacher was firmly established (he became an American citizen in 1924). Bloch regarded composition as an act of faith, and when asked about the source of his inspiration, he replied, "It is the Jewish soul that interests me, the complex agitated soul that I feel vibrating throughout the Bible . . . All this is in me and it is the better part of me."

The Fine Arts Quartet championed (and recorded) Bloch's quartets and his piano quintet early on, but by the late 1980s, his music had somehow slipped out of the repertoire. I got in touch with Dr. Robert Strassburg, an emeritus musicology professor at California State University in Los Angeles, and the writer of *Ernest Bloch: Voice in the Wilderness*. He generously offered to write the program notes for our upcoming recording. We discussed the choice of music for the CD, and in addition to music for viola, he suggested including some of Bloch's lesser known solo piano works, "In the Night, A Love Poem for Piano" (1922), and "Five Sketches in Sepia for Piano Solo" (1923).

Bloch wrote that his 1919 Suite has some perceived Jewish inspiration, but he did not consider it to be one of his "Jewish works." His inspiration was of places he had never visited in the

Far East, like Java, Sumatra, and Borneo. The movements of the Suite initially bore exotic titles (In the Jungle, Grotesques, Nocturne, and The Land of the Sun) but Bloch felt them to be incomplete and unsatisfactory. He "preferred to leave the imagination of the hearer completely unfettered, rather than to tie him to a definite program."

Bloch died in 1958 and left his Suite for Viola Solo unfinished. The four movements of the work are are linked together. He used Schoenberg's 12-tone method of composition for the opening three measures of the third movement, favoring intervals of fourths and fifths, but the work is otherwise tonal. Along with the two solo piano pieces, the recording also has the well-known *Suite Hébraïque* (1951), and the "Meditation and Processional," a piece Bloch wrote for Milton Preves, long-time first-chair violist of the Chicago Symphony (I knew him when we lived in Chicago).

The album was released in 1995, and it received a mixed response from the *American Record Guide* in 1997, but the reviewer in *Luister* Magazine, from the Netherlands, liked my performance of the unfinished Solo Suite. A reviewer in the French magazine *Diapason* wrote that the 1919 Suite was "music of majesty and subtle poetry, offering passages of great lyricism which offer the viola an opportunity to display it's beautiful sonorities." The *Diaposon* reviewer also thought it was "a very beautiful disk, not easily accessible, but fascinating." Well, "fascinating" wins over "lousy" every time.

In the *Journal of the American Viola Society*, David O. Brown remarked that my playing took him back to his early days of music listening, when there was a distinct style of playing that he loved so well (he referred to it as the Primrose, Vardi, Fuchs school of playing). Brown wrote, "Zaslav has the same sweetness of tone and phrasing and sensitivity of expression that meant so much to me then, and still does today. I was very familiar with his performances with the Kohon and Fine Arts Quartets but it's always nice to hear that musicianship translates to the solo repertoire as well. I also appreciated hearing Mrs. Zaslav play a couple of piano solos to fill out the disk. She is a consummate artist in her own right."

Tully Potter was also very happy with the album, calling the performances "magnificent." In a review in *The Strad* he mentions the intensity, breadth and power of the 1919 Suite, the "thoroughly idiomatic" *Suite Hébraïque,* and dilutes the compliments by writing, "Zaslav does about everything that can be done with the unfinished Solo Suite."

In deference to Sara Lee, nobody doesn't love Antonín Leopold Dvořák. Such was my thinking when I decided to transcribe 14 movements of his violin, cello, and vocal music for our next recording. It was a long shlep to write out all the clef changes and octave alterations, but when it comes to melody, nobody beats Antonín. If he were still around, I would give him a hard time for cheating his fellow violists out of a solo Dvořák work for the very instrument he played, but he did write wonderful lines for the viola in every one of his quartets (and I was fortunate to record them all). We are especially grateful for the 12th Quartet, Op. 96, (the "American"), where the viola gets the opening tune.

I found that his Romantic Pieces, Op. 75, the Sonatina, Op. 100, (works he wrote for violin); and the Rondo Op. 94, and "Klid" (Forest Murmurs) Op. 68, No. 5 (works he wrote for cello), translated easily to the viola. I also transcribed his Four Songs, Op. 2 for soprano (Dvořák wrote them for the lady he eventually married), and two from Op. 31. I also included my own adaptation of Kreisler's transcription of a popular Slavonic Dance, and the song everyone knows as, "Songs My Mother Taught Me," and called the CD "Dvořák's Viola."

The Dvořák CD sold out sooner than any of the others we did, so my guess about his popularity seemed to be on the money. Tully Potter admired the presentation of the disc, and wrote in *The Strad* that we played well throughout, and that "there is much enjoyable listening to be had from this disc," but other reviews were less positive. Margaret Barela's review in the September/October 1997 *American Record Guide* was rather critical. She said that my warm tone fit the selections, but that the music stayed in a narrow emotional comfort zone. She thought we played the music too safely, both technically and expressively, mentioning that only four of the 19 tracks had anything beyond a moderate tempo (she did have a point: there wasn't an *allegro molto* in sight). She thought the music was lovely, but thought the pacing made it difficult for her to keep her attention on the music, and closed by stating that the recording made a case for the viola to be "rightly considered a wallflower." She found it hard to believe that it was my intention (and she was right again; I hadn't planned on boring anyone).

Ms. Barela wasn't happy with our efforts, but one German critic was absolutely scandalized by my effrontery in daring to transcribe a single note of Dvořák. He called the album a "viola joke," but it still sold out faster than any of our other recordings.

I loathe viola jokes almost as much as I deplore television commercials, but since we're talking viola jokes, here's one that really makes me cringe: A violist comes home late one night to discover fire trucks, police cars, and a smoking crater where his house used to be. The chief of police tells him, "While you were out, the conductor of the symphony orchestra came to your house, killed every member of your family and burned your house down," to which the awed violist replies, "You're kidding! The conductor came to *my house*?"

Like some California chardonnays (in contrast to "Manischewitz Sweet Concord"), 1997 was a good year for Brahms' viola version of his two Clarinet Sonatas. Many violists were releasing new recordings of these works, so I thought it might worthwhile to reissue our 1990 Music & Arts CD, since it was no longer in print. I suggested to Fred Maroth that we should reissue our 1990 Brahms Sonatas once again, and combine them with a selection of other works of the period written for viola and piano by some of Brahms' students, friends, and colleagues. Fred liked the idea, so we made two-CD album (with a cover painting by Caspar David Friedrich) that we called "Brahms and Friends."

I enlisted Bernard Jacobson, my musicologist friend, to write the program notes. Thorough and elegant, they described each of the works and each of my chosen composers' relationships to Brahms. The first disc had the two Brahms Op. 120 Sonatas and Joseph Joachim's rarely-performed Variations for Viola and Piano, Op. 10, and the second disc held music (all originally for viola, and all rarely played) by Carl Reinecke (Three *Fantasiestücke*), Heinrich von Herzogenberg (Three Legends), Friedrich Kiel (Three Romances), Robert Fuchs (Six Fantasy Pieces), and Hans Sitt (Album Leaves). I had spread my net wide to find works by lesser-known composers to record, but I made a serious goof by failing to include a piece by the most obvious of all Brahms' friends: Robert Schumann. I wish we had included his *Märchenbilder*, Op. 113 (Fairy Tale Pictures), a work that we love and performed often.

The important Brahms scholar Styra Avins (her book *Johannes Brahms: Life and Letters* is published by Oxford University Press), was delighted with our musical choices, our performances, and Bernie Jacobson's notes, but, like Edith Eisler, she was baffled by the omission of the *Märchenbilder*. Nevertheless, this excerpt from Eisler's Amazon review is most complementary:

"Violist Bernard Zaslav and his pianist-wife Naomi are excellent, and they treat the music with total respect and love. The viola tone is beautiful, pure, warm, and expressive; ensemble and balance are first-rate. Their approach is lyrical, broad, expansive, noble, and inward, without external effects. The first Brahms Sonata is wistful, poetic, gracious; the second one smiles with autumnal benevolence. A worthy successor to the Zaslavs' Bloch disc on the same label, this is a splendid recording."

Donald Rosenberg, who wrote a review for the December 2001 issue of *Gramophone* Magazine, also liked the recording, and he makes a good case for recording music by Brahms' neglected friends; though he admits that "each score abounds in appealing romanticism and highly skilled craftsmanship," he writes that none of the pieces by his friends comes "close in quality to the Brahms sonatas." He also adds that, "the Zaslav Duo, further refutes the notion that the stringed instrument in the middle deserves to be the butt of jokes," and that, "Violist Bernard Zaslav and pianist Naomi Zaslav give everything exemplary consideration, probing the expressive depths even as they share musical thoughts with seamless vibrancy."

While such flattering reviews stroked our 70-year-old egos, we felt that our days of playing in public were coming to a close. We had enjoyed immersing ourselves in the music we loved, but the microphone must be the final arbiter.

There can be no better teacher than a microphone. Musicians often claim that the presence of an audience brings out their best performances, but I firmly believe that the recording process is still one of our most useful tools. It can be part of an unparalleled learning process, where a performer may experiment freely, without fear of failure, to shape a line in various ways. A recording can be a more personal statement than a performance, because the microphone permits the musicians to learn what pleases *them*, and allows them to rely less on the reaction of an audience.

Pianist Artur Rubinstein famously quipped that he could excuse many of his missed notes, as long as the piece he was playing was recognizable to the audience. Today's standards of excellence have become truly intimidating, and we have reached a point where a recording may not see daylight until it is note-perfect. Still, what moves the listener is a performance that best serves the music, rather than on that offers a mere display of a performer's technical prowess.

Making music with the one person you have lived and performed with for most of your life is different from working (and spending so much time with) three members of a string quartet. We had seen other "mixed marriages" (by which, I mean a marriage of two career musicians) splinter over ego issues.

Music has always been uppermost in both our lives. Nomi is naturally intuitive in her playing, and we shared an innate (and usually unspoken) approach to shaping a musical line (which is not to say that we agreed on every point). If a work presented technical challenges, we enjoyed displaying our individual virtuosity, when appropriate. Audience members often commented that we played together on stage as one, while our kids expected that a divorce lawyer might be called at any moment during our rehearsals. Mark, a professional psychologist, simply diagnosed me as an obsessive-compulsive, and he diagnosed Nomi as a hysteric; yet our performances seemed to be all sweetness and light to the general public.

Nomi played the Kofords' nine-foot Mason & Hamlin grand (Shingle and Marcia called that particularly piano "Sebastian") for the recordings we made in their home. She enjoyed its "feel," and eventually swapped her old Steinway model A grand for a new seven-foot Mason & Hamlin. Its rich mellowness lends itself naturally to Brahms.

In her free moments, Nomi would play her own beloved short Brahms pieces. I put away my viola for a while after we finished the Brahms and Friends album, and in fairness to the pianist who worked with me for so long, I donned my engineer's cap. The result was "The Intimate Brahms," an album of Nomi's 19 favorite later short pieces of Brahms. At Fred's suggestion, Nomi expressed her personal feelings about these pieces in the forward.

> This disk is the culmination of my long love affair with these late, most personal piano works of Brahms. *The Strad* wrote "Naomi Zaslav's scrupulous placing of chords and pedaling mark her out as a very fine Brahms pianist. If I needed one word to sum up the performances of the Zaslav Duo here it would be "loving." I hope that this same loving quality will be evident in my performances here, together with the pain and longing the composer felt in his later years. Brahms called his three Intermezzi Op.117 "three cradle-songs of my sorrows." In her journal Clara Schumann wrote about eleven of these new piano works that Brahms had sent her as being "full of poetry, passion, sentiment, emotion and with the most wonderful effects of tone. In these pieces I at last feel musical life stir again in my soul." The last time that Brahms ever saw his beloved Clara, she was at home, playing his Op. 118 piano pieces. What a wonderful gift from a composer, soul to soul!

John Bell Young wrote a review that captures the essence of Nomi's playing In the January/February 1999 issue of the *American Record Guide*. He calls her a solid, well-schooled musician with a beautiful tone and a creamy legato, and he notes her warmth and her honest and straightforward approach to Brahms. He likens her readings to those of Julius Katchen (such fine company), and even praises her choice of instrument.

My last swan had departed by 2004. Most of our Music & Arts CDs were out of print, and Fred Maroth didn't feel that pressing additional runs of our duo albums was worthwhile for such a small niche market. Nomi was in good physical and pianistic shape (of course, she bristles when I tease her about playing on a "percussion instrument"), but I wasn't about to inflict my 78-year-old fingers on a perfectly innocent microphone. My corporeal being was telling me, "Hey Bernie, it's time to hang it up. You've had a good run, so stop when you're ahead and let the younger ones take up the challenge." As comedian Joe E. Lewis said, "You only get to go around once, but if you play your cards right, that's enough." And the new generation is certainly doing a heck of a job. Many excellent violists, like Scott Slapin (and far too many others to name here) have taken up the baton of this particular relay race.

Nomi and I performed and recorded Milton Babbitt's 1950 "Composition for Viola and Piano" in the 1970s, around the same time that the Fine Arts Quartet recorded his Third Quartet (a piece that they commissioned). Our Duo's Babbitt recording hadn't been released, so I suggested to Fred Maroth that we release it, along with a few of our other previously-recorded works, on an album that would be a summation of the Zaslav Duo's recorded history. We put it together with the Franck, Milhaud, Dvořák, and Bloch, called it "A Viola Treasury," and Music & Arts released it in 2005.

I first met Milton Babbitt around 1965, when the Composers

Quartet played a work I particularly liked, his Second String Quartet (1959). At the time he was working in a sound-proofed room at Columbia University on 125th Street. It housed an enormous RCA Synthesizer that he used to create musical "events' from quick bunches of varying rhythms and pitches. He tested me to see if I could retain them and repeat them vocally after a single hearing (I guess I passed the test).

Milton and I renewed our acquaintance in Chicago, when he and his wife Sylvia attended the Fine Arts Quartet's premiere of his Third Quartet. Milton came to Stanford in the mid 1980s, and Judith Bettina, a member of Stanford's vocal faculty (and the daughter of my New York violist colleague, Jacob Glick) performed Milton's *Philomel* for soprano and synthesizer. Nomi and I performed his 1950 "Composition" at Stanford on the same program. We repaired to the requisite (for Jews) Chinese restaurant after the concert, and listened in awe to Milton's tongue try in vain to catch up to his wide-ranging mind, as he disgorged the latest baseball stats, or the original keys of pop standards. He also tossed off tidbits like, "My Second String Quartet is based on an all-interval series which is introduced interval by interval, as it were, with each new arrival initiating a development of the interval repertory acquired thus far, each development being argued in terms of derived sets." No matter how complex his speech was, his eyes, behind his dark horn-rimmed glasses, complemented the non-threatening curl of his lips.

He is termed a "maximalist" (compared to Morton Feldman, a "minimalist," who suspends time to the utmost lengths) because of his use of clusters of rhythm, texture, and harmony. I think of Milton's music when I look at a work of Jackson Pollack. Certainly they had very different approaches to their work: the painter dribbled and splashed paint in a seemingly haphazard fashion, while Milton insisted on controlling every note and every dynamic indication. Nevertheless, if they are given the time and the rehearsal they deserve, a pleasingly Pollack-like variegated texture seems to emerge from some of Babbitt's works. Milton once said in an interview, "I could never think of myself as a maverick, and I really don't mean in any sense, because I derived my work from such an immediate tradition as, well, as my transitivity to a long tradition. I mean, my music comes most directly from Schoenberg with a little bit of Webern maybe, and Schoenberg takes you right back to Brahms. I'm delighted to be taken right back to Brahms, because I can go there directly if not by way of Schoenberg."

Reviewers often evaluate the merits of serial music differently from the musicians who play it. Some reviewers considered our Babbitt "old school," and one claimed that, "However rigorously constructed, serial music can sound jarringly random, as if notes had been thrown into a blender and haphazardly spewed onto a score." A few carped about some of my notes in the higher register in the recording, but most of the reviewers were highly complimentary about our balance. Michelle Dulak Thomson, a writer for the *San Francisco Classical Voice,* thought of the Babbitt as "terribly innocent" even though she referred to it as "the sort of blips'n'bleeps piece that used to give other composers hives," while Robert Maxham of *Fanfare* thought that we made the piece "appealing without softening its melodic angularity or filing down its harmonic thorns."

The reissue was well-received in general. James Reel, in *Strings* called the disc "a superb recording of a suave partnership," and Tully Potter wrote in *The Strad,* "The violist Bernard Zaslav seems to have played in just about every string Quartet in the US at one time or another." He added that our version of the Franck Sonata has long been one of his "two favorite ways of hearing this work on the viola," (the other one was made by a French duo on another label). He thought that the Babbitt was "all too typical of academic Americana," and went on to write, "it is well played, though—better than it deserves."

Postlude

"Th-th-th-that's all folks!" PORKY PIG

My final public appearance as a violist took place on January 11th, 2004, when the Fine Arts Quartet invited me to perform as a guest artist for their concert on Stanford's Lively Arts Series at Dinkelspiel Auditorium. My cardiac problems, a hip replacement, and some vision loss made their presence felt, but what heavenly music I was privileged to play for my last outing as a performer!

The all-Mozart two-viola Quintet program the Fine Arts Quartet chose included the C minor, G minor, and C major Quintets, masterpieces of the chamber music literature. The Quartet's membership had changed since its founding 58 years earlier, but they retained the distinguished name, and continue to have a highly successful career. In 2004 their members were first violinist Ralph Evans, second violinist Efim Boico, violist Yuri Gandelsman, and the cellist was my good friend from 1979 (my last year with the Quartet), Wolfgang Laufer.

As I stood for the last time on the stage of Dinkelspiel Auditorium (an old German name that invariably produces a giggle), I remembered flying out of Milwaukee during a winter snowstorm to play a concert on that very stage with the Fine Arts Quartet so many years before. After performing these masterpieces all over the world, and recording them with Francis Tursi, I was playing the second viola parts for the first time in my life (while another violist carried the Torah), and I was playing them on the Stanford campus, which is my current home. Our two rehearsals were short, sweet, and to the point. There were no unplumbed depths to be uncovered here. We were all *landsleit* (fellow Jews) with a taste for the ironic, so we soon got on to the more serious business of joke-telling. I'm sure Mozart would have approved. The audience, filled with many of my friends, approved as well. They made it an especially memorable evening.

In 2005 Music and Arts released the 1975 Vox Box I made with Tursi and the Fine Arts Quartet, complete with informative notes by Abram Loft. These recordings have stood the test of time well. Reviewers praised them when they first came out, and praised them again when they were reissued. In November 2005 Michael Ullman wrote a review for Fanfare where he mentioned that, to his ears, we sounded at our best. He thought that the sound was compact and had the kind of distance that came with a live performance, and that altogether we had an "unaffected but flexible approach to Mozart." Ullman went on to say that our performances were "richly idiomatic" and that we "never rant" and we don't make the "composer patrician."

OUT OF THE CLOSET

Around the time that Nomi and I were recording our "Brahms and Friends" album, a call came from Lois Baum, the wife of David Krupp (my "failed baritone" friend). Lois, who worked for years at the Chicago Lyric Opera, was also working with Studs Terkel at WFMT in Chicago. While Norman Pellegrini, the station's long-serving program manager and smooth-voiced announcer, was searching for some of Studs Terkel's tapes in WFMT's forgotten "closet from hell," he came across some boxes of old Fine Arts Quartet tapes. These were master tapes made during live Fine Arts Quartet broadcasts from the studios of WFMT between 1967 (a year before I joined) and 1973. The boxes contained 24 unreleased (and forgotten) recordings of our on-air Chicago performances.

Maggi Payne, an accomplished audio engineer on the faculty of Mills College, refurbished enough of these tapes to assemble an eight-disc set (nine hours and fifteen minutes of music). I was the violist on 16 of the 24 works on those tapes, and my predecessor, Gerald Stanick played on the other eight. The album also included performances by French horn player Barry Tuckwell, and pianists John Browning and Naomi Zaslav. When the Music & Arts album was released in 2004, it included a 48-page booklet with commentary by Abram Loft, and many rare photographs. Its eight CDs include works by Beethoven, Haydn, Mozart, Brahms, Karel Husa, Seymour Shifrin, Béla Bartók, Paul Hindemith, and Jean Martinon.

A windfall from the past is always grist for the mills of record reviewers, and a small avalanche of nostalgia greeted this historical release. This grab bag of music from the Classical Period through the 20th century offers a mere snapshot of our routine. The presence of little-known music, and the rich assortment of guest artists, made for many long and insightful reviews.

In addition to a capsulized history of the Fine Arts Quartet, Robert P. Commanday of The *San Francisco Classical Voice* discussed the practicality of issuing boxed sets, praised the clarity of the recordings and the playing, and appreciated the spirit of the playing. He mentioned the value of the commissioned works among the treasures found in the closet, like Seymour Shifrin's Fourth Quartet, and Karel Husa's Third Quartet, and Jean Martinon's Second Quartet, and was convinced by the performance of Hindemith's Third Quartet that "Hindemith deserves revival."

Jean-Michel Molkhou from the French Magazine *Diapason* added praise for the group's naturalness, and praised our guest artists, particularly the pianist John Browning, and the French horn player Barry Tuckwell. Jerry Dubins of *Fanfare*, was both critical and nostalgic by turns. He preferred the Fine Arts Quartet's Mozart to its Beethoven, considered the tempos to be "on the cautious side," and found the intonation to be "really quite off." He said that the Fine Arts Quartet's "strongest forte is in Haydn." He went on to write, "They seem to capture that element of fun and jocularity in the music that eludes even some of the most note-perfect performances. Haydn's quartets are in some ways the perfect fusion of the medium and the message; and in them there is such inexpressible, life-affirming joy. It is here, more than anywhere else in this grand assembly of great works that the Fine Arts Quartet seems to be at home."

Elaine Fine, who wrote a review in the *American Record*

Guide, liked the Husa Quartet, and mentioned me in her review (this was before we knew one another): "I especially like the solo playing (particularly Bernard Zaslav's viola solos) and admire the focused emotional intensity of the ensemble."

Still more recorded goodies began to appear in 2006. Roy Christensen, the owner of Gasparo Records, sent me a belated copy of "Music of John Downey," a 1989 reissue of a 1976 Orion LP. John William Downey, my friend and colleague from the University of Wisconsin-Milwaukee, was a soft-spoken, naturally lovable, and talented jazz pianist and composer, born and raised on Chicago's south side, who went to Paris to study with Nadia Boulanger. His work was described by one scribe from The London Guardian, as "a combination of 'Hippie-Romantic' and early modernist." Gasparo's album contained John's Octet for Winds, "What If?," a work for chorus and orchestra set to a poem by e.e. cummings, "Adagio Lyrico" for duo-pianists, and "Agort" for woodwind quintet. The recording opened with "A Dolphin," a 12-minute vocal piece setting of an imaginative poem by John's Ukrainian linguist wife, Irusha Downey. I recorded it in 1976 at University of Wisconsin-Milwaukee with tenor Daniel Nelson. Israel Borouchoff played alto flute, Pavel Burda played vibraphone and percussion, and John conducted from the piano.

Underwater research during the 1970s found that the blue whale, (*Balaenoptera musculusis*), was the loudest animal on earth, capable of producing 188 dB, which is much louder than a jet (at an earsplitting 140 dB). Always looking for new and unusual sounds (John heard me use a practice mute in my studio and promptly incorporated it into a movement of his String Quartet), he asks in this piece for the viola to make "laughing glissandi" and produce shrieking effects, impersonating a dolphin (to the best of his imagination) by means of harmonics and scratchy slides played high up on the A string. John and Irusha visited us in Stanford before Irusha passed away in 2000, and John left us in 2004.

Another surprise arrived in the mail in 2006. Roy Christensen reissued the Fine Arts Quartet's 30th Anniversary Album album on his Gallante economy label. Using the master tapes, he added the Shostakovich Quartet No. 3 in F minor, Op. 73 (a favorite of mine, especially playing its fourth movement with George's Goffriller and my Guadagnini), and Prokofiev's Quartet No. 2, Op. 92. He also reissued John Downey's String Quartet No. 2, Ben Johnston's String Quartet No. 4 "Amazing Grace," and Ruth Crawford-Seeger's forward-thinking String Quartet of 1931. Without touching bow hair to string, 22 recorded works chronicling the world I inhabited, tracks I laid down over 30 years before, suddenly became available on CD.

I had been kvetching to my daughter about how difficult I found it to write a memoir, so she sent me a copy of *Inventing the Truth* for Father's Day. I noted that one of the authors was the distinguished cellular biologist, Dr. Lewis Thomas. In Dr. Thomas's best-known work, *Lives of a Cell*, he writes that he, himself, like all of us, started his life as a single egg. He warns the reader that an autobiography might prove to be no more than a linear account of one damn thing after another. He also advises not to select events that tilt only in one's favor. It sounds like perfectly sensible advice, but I'm not so sure that I have followed his advice to the letter. A musician's ego is fragile, at best.

During the 1970s Dr. Thomas made an unusual request of the Fine Arts Quartet. He asked us to record and film a portion of J.S. Bach's *Art of Fugue*. In 1962, six years before I joined the quartet, the Fine Arts Quartet, along with the New York Woodwind Quintet, recorded flutist Samuel Baron's unique transcription of this work. Bach's *Art of the Fugue* was probably written to be performed on a keyboard instrument. He did not indicate anything further in his 1745 manuscript. There have been several arrangements for various combinations of instruments, but Sam's use of the four strings and five winds in various combinations allows for a wide sonic palette of moods and colors. It seems that Dr. Thomas had been so enamored of this recording that he wanted to use a few of the twelve fugues and two canons for the film (including the one Bach left unfinished.

Perhaps Dr. Thomas was using the motion of the planets around the sun as a metaphor for Bach's musical cosmos. Music has its own internal logic; the order of the spheres might indeed invoke a harmony of sorts, so I'm guessing this is the message that Dr. Thomas wished to impart. We were flown to Baltimore to record a few of the movements in the George Peabody Library, a magnificent structure dating from 1878. The recording we made is out of print, but a meager edited portion made its way to YouTube.

Dr. Thomas's *Lives of a Cell* made a big impression on me when it came out in 1974. I always loved science as a kid, and hoped to make it my calling when I grew up. My summer at Interlochen Music Camp in 1944 really changed my direction. I graduated from Juilliard as a violinist, but the viola became my real passion. In that regard, I find it notable that quite a few of my viola students at Stanford University have had to make the decision between following, as a profession, the music they loved deeply, and other major interests. It's comforting to know that while most have followed other paths, they still play music for enjoyment. In fact, one evening I received a phone call from four of my former chamber music pupils who happened to be studying at Harvard at the same time. They called me one evening to say they were playing string quartets and said, "Let's call Bernie, and tell him what we're doing."

Well, isn't that what chamber music is all about? Wasn't this Papa Haydn's very purpose for writing quartets in the first place? As musical complexities reach the point where sight reading simply for enjoyment (*Hausmusik*) is sometimes not enough, we now have the odd construct of the professional string quartet that regularly deals with all sorts of musical complexities, and performs difficult works for the enjoyment of audiences all around the world. It's anyone's guess whether such a possibility could have entered Haydn's mind.

The Go-Between, L. P. Hartley's 1953 novel, starts with the statement, "The past is a foreign country: they do things differently there." I once heard the late historian Tony Judt quote this statement, and I understand that writing this memoir is really an attempt to tell the reader about my own special country. I started out as an overprotected kid from Brooklyn who loved music (as well as anything in print), and grew up in the aura of Arturo Toscanini, George Szell, and the Budapest Quartet. The great violinists of my era like Mischa Elman and Jascha Heifetz, are now mere reference points for today's students. Their heritage is mainly found in old books, CD reissues of rare recordings, or the odd YouTube clip, but when I started on the violin, they were the standard bearers. With today's overflow of varied input, we can easily dismiss lessons from the past. "That's so yesterday," is often used as a put down, rather than as an acknowledgment, "Oh, I see, so that's where it came from."

"*Ist es wahr*" (Is it true?) is a song from which Mendelssohn uses self-referential fragments as a unifying motive in one of my favorite quartets, his 1827 String Quartet, Op. 13 (I performed the piece in concert preceded, to good effect, by a Baritone singing the song). "Is it true?" is a perfectly legitimate question that a reader might properly ask me: How much of this "memoir" is true?

Time may have dimmed or clouded my recollections, but I can claim that what I have written here is what I saw and experienced; the way things looked and felt to me at the time. Ego, pride, and puffery may color what I have written; but in my mind's ear and eye, my memories are clear.

If I try to give the full flavor, the effect, delivery and rich croaking voice of Josef Gingold telling a story at Albuquerque's International House of Pancakes after playing a chamber music concert together, it wouldn't hold a candle to the way Mark Twain captures Jim's speech in *The Adventures of Huckleberry Finn*, but Gingold's cherubic smile, his half slitted eyes, and the way his lips curled, when he delivered a punch line about a student's performance or a conductor's errant manner, are etched in my memory.

The manner in which Menahem Pressler turned corners between phrases in a Schubert Trio, the unbearable beauty of that flute variation in Brahms' Fourth Symphony's final movement—such memories are forever locked up within me, and remain on call any time I push the buttons of my inner tape deck.

So, how are the kids? Isn't that what life on earth is all about? Doesn't the Red Queen's Hypothesis, Alice running faster and faster, finally dictate the evolutionary arms race between competing species?

Mark Zaslav

Our child-rearing days came a little early in our lives, but we certainly can't complain about the product. Our son, Mark, retired after 30 years as a psychologist with the Veterans Administration, and he is now in demand as a forensic witness (he also loves jamming on guitar with his similarly-minded lawyer friends). He and his wife, Jan, who is a nurse, live an hour away amongst the tall redwoods of Larkspur, in Marin County, and Madison, their 16-year-old daughter (tall and gorgeous), who writes intriguing short stories, is the apple of his eye. Our daughter, Claudia and her husband Jim (who loves to fish for walleye), live all the way hell-and-gone in the Upper Peninsula (Dah *You Pee*) in Marquette, Michigan. Jim is a business professor at Northern Michigan University, and Claudia plays first flute in the Marquette Symphony. She also writes their program notes (well done and catchy), teaches flute, and is a member of an excellent woodwind quintet. She is a Scrabble freak, gives poetry readings, and is in the process of publishing her first collection of poetry (I have included a sample as the Fermata called "Stage").

Their 26-year-old daughter Sarah is working towards a career in animal surgery, while their 23-year-old son Alex is a computer composer with a degree in electronic music from the University of Michigan in Ann Arbor (much luck to him).

So there's the lineup. We lucked out with our children, our grandchildren, and our marriage of 64 years (who says we're co-dependent?) Man is a social animal, and though we have left many friends in the East and the Midwest, our western migration ended on campus at Stanford, where we enjoy the University's diversity, its many cultural riches, its "climate," and the many friends we have made in California.

Claudia Drosen

Let me finish my tale with a word about the fantastic Guadagnini viola, born in Turin, Italy, in 1781, that had been my voice for so many years. One is never actually the "owner" of such a rarity. We are only brief custodians of these wonders of the instrument-maker's art, and I held this one in my hands every day from 1974 until 2007. My vision no longer allows me to read a page of music, and my aging fingers are ready to be put to pasture, but Giovanni's magical wooden box is holding up beautifully. In answer to a violist's prayer that "my" Guadagnini, rather than ending up on a collector's shelf, or being drowned out in the viola section of a symphony orchestra, might continue to sing on stage as a member of a string quartet, I'm happy to say that it now has a proper new home in Norway.

The prices of rare instruments have become too high for most musicians to afford, so Norway's Dextra Musica makes the rare stringed instruments in its collection available to deserving musicians. The ex-Villa, (and now) ex-Zaslav Guadagnini viola is now one of three violas in the Dextra Musical Collection. The 62-instrument collection, which also includes instruments by Guarneri del Gesu, Rugieri, and Stradivari (just to name a few), was featured at the 2010 Ole Bull Celebration in Bergen, Norway, and that Guadagnini viola I so treasured is handsomely.

Bernard Zaslav handing the Guadagnini Viola to Henninge Landaas, the violist of the Vertavo Quartet.

Oslo's Vertavo Quartet (four women who have worked together for 26 years) came to play a concert on Stanford's Lively Arts series in Dinkelspiel Hall on January 26, 2011, and I was there to *kvell*. They played works of Josef Haydn, Leoš Janáček, Gabriela Lena Frank, and Beethoven (his Op. 130, leaving out the *Grosse Fuga*), and the Guadagnini sounded forth, accompanied by a trio of three equally rare instruments, in the excellent hands of their violist, Henninge Landaas. Henninge visited with us the day before the concert, and I put the Guad beneath my chin for the last time. I adjusted the bridge to the proper secret spot (the way Nigo would have wanted it). After the concert, filled with joy, we said farewell to this wonderful group, happy that the Guad will continue to sing in string quartets for many generations to come.

Acknowledgments

My deepest thanks must go first to my long-suffering editor Elaine Fine for her unflagging patience, her clarity of thought, and her wide-ranging musical experience as composer, violist, violinist, flutist, teacher, writer and critic for the *American Record Guide*. I must also thank the composer Seymour Barab, my cellist colleague in the Composers Quartet, for his extremely valuable contributions and editorial help. I was surprised to learn that many more Yiddishisms had made it to the page than were normally in my mouth, so I thank him for those few he permitted me.

Robert and Becky Spitzer, the owners of Science and Behavior Books, are two of our closest friends. A musician's memoir would seem to be a far cry from the psychology books that they publish, but Bob offered to publish mine, and I am indebted to them for their willingness to include the two accompanying CDs of our music. I wish to thank Fred Maroth, president of Music & Arts Programs of America, and Roy Christensen, owner of Gasparo and Gallante, for their kind permission to include excerpts from works that had been released on their labels.

My heartfelt thanks go to James and Marcia Koford, who allowed us to use their Monterey home "Casa de Cielo" to record the Zaslav Duo's last five albums, and for Jim's generous technical help. Thanks also to Professor Max Mathews, my friend and former Stanford neighbor, who taught me how to edit my recordings using his studio at Stanford's CCRMA (Center for Computer Research in Music and Acoustics). I wish to thank Jonathan Norton, composer and audio engineer who studied at CCRMA, for his help in assembling the works for the two CDs.

I wish to acknowledge my teachers, Sasha Jacobson, Mischa Mischakoff, and Lillian Fuchs, and my beloved mentor Josef Gingold, along with the many wonderful colleagues mentioned in the memoir that I have been privileged to work with and learn from over the years.

Thanks to our poet/flutist daughter Claudia, who permitted me to insert her most intimate revelations about her father in "Stage." Finally, to Nomi, who allowed me to steal her away from Mme. Lhevinne's piano studio 64 years ago to become my wife, my duo-partner, and the mother of our children, I say thanks for your love and your musical talent.

Discography
134 Recorded Chamber Works (Listed chronologically)

The Kohon String Quartet Recordings with Bernard Zaslav

Berg, Alban. String Quartet, Opus 3. The Kohon String Quartet. LP record DL 730. Vox, 1962.
(Awarded the Grand Prix du Disque for Chamber Music, 1964, Charles Cros Societé, Paris.)

Hummel, Johann Nepomuk. Quintet for Clarinet and String Quartet, Carl Maria von Weber, Quintet for Clarinet and String Quartet. The Kohon String Quartet, David Glazer, Clarinet. LP record DL 960. Vox, 1963.

Dvořák, Antonin. String Quartet in A Major Op. 2, Quartet in a minor, Op. 16; Quartet in D minor, Op. 34; Quartet in E-flat Major, Op. 51; Quartet in C Major, Op. 61; Quartet in E Major, Op. 80; Quartet in F Major, Op. 96; Quartet in A flat Major, Op. 105; Quartet in G Major, Op. 106. The Kohon Quartet. LP records SVBX 549–553. Vox, c. 1963.

Brahms, Johannes. String Quartet, Op. 51, No 1; Quartet Op. 51, No 2; Quartet Op 67 No. 2; Robert Schumann. String Quartets Op. 41, Nos. 1–3. The Kohon String Quartet. LP record VBX 42/SVBX 542. Vox, 1964.

Ives, Charles. String Quartet No. 1 "A Revival Service," Quartet No. 2. The Kohon String Quartet. LP record DL 1120/STDL 501.120. Vox, 1965.

The Composers String Quartet Recordings with Bernard Zaslav

Johnston, Ben. String Quartet No. 2 and John Cage and Lajaren Hiller, HPSCHD. The Composers String Quartet. LP record H 71224. Nonesuch Records, 1967.

Weinberg, Henry. String Quartet No. 2 (with violist Bernard Zaslav), Kirchner, Leon, String Quartet No. 3 (with violist Jean Dupuoy). The Composers String Quartet. LP record MS 7284. Columbia Records, 1970.
(Henry Weinberg won a Naumberg Foundation award for this work in 1967.)

The Fine Arts String Quartet Recordings with Bernard Zaslav

Haydn, Joseph. String Quartets, Op. 50, Nos. 1 through 6, "Unfinished Quartet," Op. 103 (Volume 7). The Fine Arts String Quartet. LP record SVBX 595. Vox, 1968–1975.

Haydn, Joseph. String Quartets, Op. 76, Nos. 1 through 6 (Volume 8). The Fine Arts String Quartet. LP record SVBX 596. Vox, 1968–1975.

Haydn, Joseph. String Quartets, Op. 64, Nos. 1 through 6; Op. 2, Nos. 5 and 6; Divertimento, Op. "0" (Volume 9). The Fine Arts String Quartet. LP record SVBX 597. Vox, 1968–1975.

Haydn, Joseph. String Quartets, Op. 74, Nos. 1 through 6, Op. 3, Nos. 1 through 6 (Volume 10). The Fine Arts Quartet. LP record 598. Vox, 1968–1975.

Schubert, Franz. String Quartet No. 13, Op. 29, and Johannes Brahms, String Quartet No. 3, Op. 67: *The Romantic Quartets*. The Fine Arts String Quartet. LP record 3266. Everest, 1970.

Husa, Karel. String Quartet No. 2; String Quartet No. 3. (Commissioned for the Fine Arts String Quartet, and awarded the Pulitzer Prize for Chamber Music, 1969). The Fine Arts String Quartet. LP record 3290. Everest, 1971.

Wuorinen, Charles. First String Quartet, Milton Babbitt, String Quartet No. 3 (Both works commissioned by the Fine Arts Music Foundation of Chicago 1970–71). The Fine Arts Quartet. LP record S34515. Vox Box Turnabout, 1972.

Wuorinen, Charles. First String Quartet, Milton Babbitt, String Quartet No. 3. The Fine Arts Quartet. Reissue: Compact disc 707. Music & Arts, c. 2005.

Mozart, Wolfgang Amadeus. String Quintet K. 174 in B-flat Major; Quintet K. 406 in C Minor; String Quintet K. 515 in C Major; String Quintet K. 516 in G Minor; String Quintet K. 593 in D Major; String Quintet K. 614 in E flat Major. The Fine Arts String Quartet, Fraucis Tursi, viola. LP record SBVX 557. Vox, 1974.

Mozart, Wolfgang Amadeus. String Quintet K. 174 in B-flat Major; Quintet K. 406 in C Minor; String Quintet K. 515 in C Major; String Quintet K. 516 in G Minor; String Quintet K. 593 in D Major; String Quintet K. 614 in E flat Major. The Fine Arts String Quartet, Fraucis Tursi, viola. Reissue: Compact disc 1159–2. Music & Arts CD, 2005.

Shostakovich, Dmitri. String Quartet No. 3 in F, Op. 73, and Sergei Prokofieff, String Quartet No. 2, Op. 92: *Fine Arts Quartet 30th Anniversary Album.* The Fine Arts String Quartet (The Fine Arts Music Foundation of Chicago). LP record GS 203, Gasparo, 1978.

Shostakovich, Dmitri. String Quartet No. 3 in F, Op. 73, and Sergei Prokofieff, String Quartet No. 2, Op. 92: *Fine Arts Quartet 30th Anniversary Album.* The Fine Arts String Quartet (The Fine Arts Music Foundation of Chicago). Reissue: Compact disc GG 2024, Gasparo Gallante, 2006.

Adler, Samuel. String Quartet No. 6 "A Whitman Serenade." The Fine Arts String Quartet, Jan DeGaetani, soprano. LP record 608. CRI, 1979.

Beethoven, Ludwig van. String Quartets Op. 18, No. 1, Op. 59, Nos. 1 and 2, Wolfgang Amadeus Mozart, String Quartet K. 458, Horn Quintet K. 407, Joseph Haydn, String Quartets, Op. 1, No. "0;" Op. 2, Nos. 5 and 6; Op. 64, No. 6; Op. 76, No. 4 and 6; Op. 103, Op. 20, No. 5, Seymour Shifrin, String Quartet No. 4, Karel Husa, Quartet No. 3: *The Fine Arts Quartet at WFMT Radio: Radio broadcast performances.* The Fine Arts String Quartet, Barry Tuckwell, French horn. Compact disc 1154 (8 CD). Music & Arts, 2005.

Downey, John. String Quartet No. 2, Ben Johnston, String Quartet No. 4 "Amazing Grace," (commissioned by the Fine Arts Music Foundation of Chicago, Ruth Crawford-Seeger, String Quartet. The Fine Arts String Quartet. LP record GS 205. Gasparo, 1980.

Downey, John. String Quartet No. 2, Ben Johnston, String Quartet No. 4 "Amazing Grace," (commissioned by the Fine Arts Music Foundation of Chicago, Ruth Crawford-Seeger, String Quartet. The Fine Arts String Quartet. Reissue: Compact disc GG-1020. Gallante, 2006.

The Vermeer String Quartet Recordings with Bernard Zaslav

Schubert, Franz. String Quartet No. 14 "Death and the Maiden;" Quartetsatz. C minor The Vermeer String Quartet. LP record and Compact disc 6.24868 AZ. Teldec, 1983.

Dvořák, Antonin. String Quartet No. 10, Op 51, Giuseppi Verdi, String Quartet in E minor. The Vermeer String Quartet. Compact disc 8.43105. Teldec, 1983.

Brahms, Johannes. Clarinet Quintet in B minor, Op. 115, The Vermeer String Quartet, Karl Leister, Clarinet, LP record S 068–831. Orfeo, 1983.

Brahms, Johannes. Clarinet Quintet in B minor, Op. 115, The Vermeer String Quartet, Karl Leister, Clarinet. Compact disc C068–831A. Orfeo, 1983.

Beethoven, Ludwig van. String Quartet No. 13, Op. 130/133. "Grosse Fuge" The Vermeer String Quartet. LP record 6.42982 AZ , Compact disc ZK. Teldec, 1984.

Beethoven, Ludwig van. String Quartet No. 12, Op 127; No 16, Op. 135 (with violist Richard Young) The Vermeer String Quartet. Compact disc 8.43207 ZK. Teldec, 1986.

The Stanford String Quartet Recordings with Bernard Zaslav

Balcom, William. String Quartet No. 10; Ben Johnston, String Quartet No. 9; Marc Neikrug, String Quartet "Stars' the Mirror." The Stanford String Quartet. Compact disc LR–847. Laurel Records, 1992.

Milhaud, Darius. String Quartet No. 7, Op. 87; Frank Bridge, Quartet No. 1 in D minor; Gabriel Fauré Quartet in E minor, Op. 121: *Three Early 20th Century Quartets.* The Stanford String Quartet. Compact disc 823. Music & Arts, 1993.

The Zaslav Duo: Bernard Zaslav, viola and Naomi Zaslav, piano

Berry, Wallace. Canto Lirico for Viola and Piano. Bernard Zaslav, viola; Naomi Zaslav, piano. LP record SD 282. CRI, c. 1967.

Franck, Cesar, (arr. B. Zaslav). Sonata in A major; Darius Milhaud, Sonatas 1 and 2: *French Music for Viola and Piano.* Bernard Zaslav, viola; Naomi Zaslav, piano. LP recording ORS 75186. Orion Master Recordings, 1976.

Brahms, Johannes. Sonatas Op. 120, Nos. 1 and 2. Bernard Zaslav, viola, Naomi Zaslav, piano. LP Recording GS-215. Gasparo, 1980.

Brahms, Johannes. Sonatas Op. 120, Nos. 1 and 2 (reissue of above); Cesar Franck (arr. B. Zaslav), Violin Sonata in A major (reissue of Orion ORS 75186). Bernard Zaslav, viola; Naomi Zaslav, piano. Compact disc 626. Music & Arts, 1990.

Bloch, Ernst. Music for Viola and Piano: Suite for Viola and Piano (1919); Five Sketches in Sepia for Piano; Suite Hëbraîque for Viola & Piano; In the Night, A Love Poem for Piano; Suite for Viola Solo; Meditation and Processional for Viola and Piano. Bernard Zaslav, viola; Naomi Zaslav, piano. Compact disc 902, Music & Arts, 1995.

Dvořák, Antonin, (arr. B. Zaslav). Four Romantic Pieces, Op. 75 ; Rondo, Op. 94; Four Songs, Op. 2; Songs Op. 31, No. 4 and Op. 31, No. 5, Op. 55, No. 4; Sonatina in G, Op. 100; Klid, Op. 68, No. 5, Romance, Op. 11, Dvořák/Kreisler Slavonic Dance Op. 46, No. 2 Slavonic Dance: *Dvořák's Viola*. Bernard Zaslav, viola, Naomi Zaslav, piano. Compact disc 953. Music & Arts, 1996.

Franck, Cesar (arr. B. Zaslav), Sonata in A major (reissue of Music & Arts 626); Darius Milhaud, Sonata no. 2, Op. 244; "La Bruxelloise" from Quatre Visages (reissue of Orion ORS 75186); Antonin Dvořák (arr. B. Zaslav), Songs Op. 31, No. 4 and Op. 31, No. 5, Op. 55 (reissue of Music & Arts 953); Ernst Bloch, Meditation and Processional; Suite for Solo Viola (reissue of Music & Arts 902); Milton Babbitt, Composition for Viola and Piano: *A Viola Treasury*. Bernard Zaslav, viola, Naomi Zaslav, piano. Compact disc 1151. Music & Arts, 2005.

Brahms, Johannes, Sonatas Op. 120, Nos. 1 and 2 (reissue of above); Joseph Joachim, Variations for viola and piano, Op. 10; Carl Reinecke, Phantasiestucke for viola and piano, Op. 43; Heinrich von Herzogenberg, Legenden for viola and piano, Op. 62; Friedrich Kiel, Drei Romanzen for viola and piano, Op.69; Robert Fuchs, Sechs Phantasiestucke for viola and piano, Op. 117; Hans Sitt, Albumblatter for viola and piano, Op. 39: *Brahms & Friends*. Bernard Zaslav, viola; Naomi Zaslav, piano. Compact disc 1087–2. Music & Arts, 2006.

Selected Miscellaneous Recordings

Bach, Johann Sebastian. Jesu, Joy of Man's Desiring (from Cantata 147), Sinfonia (from the Christmas Oratorio), Sheep May Safely Graze (from Cantata 208); Antonio Vivaldi, Concerto Grosso in D minor, Op. 3, No. 10; Arcangelo Corelli, Concerto Grosso in G minor, Op. 6, No. 8: *In Dulci Jubilo A Baroque Concert*. LP record BGS-70696. Bach Guild, 1967.

Britten, Benjamin. Fantasy Quartet for Oboe, Violin, Viola, and Cello, Op. 2: *The Art of Harold Gomberg*. Harold Gomberg, oboe, Matthew Raimondi, violin, Bernard Zaslav, viola, Nathan Stuch, cello. LP record VCS 10064. Vanguard Cardinal, 1967.

Downey, John. What if?; A dolphin; Adagio lyrico; Octet for winds. Bernard Zaslav, viola, Daniel Nelson, tenor, Israel Bourakoff, alto flute, Pavel Burda, vibraphone & percussion, John Downey, piano (personnel on "A dolphin" only). LP record ORS 77267. Orion, 1977.

Downey, John. What if?; A dolphin; Adagio lyrico; Octet for winds. (Bernard Zaslav, viola, Daniel Nelson, tenor, Israel Bourakoff, alto flute, Pavel Burda, vibraphone & percussion, John Downey, piano, (personnel on "A dolphin" only). Reissue: Compact disc GSCD 276. Gasparo, 1989.

Naomi Zaslav, Piano

Brahms, Johannes. Ballade Op. 10, No. 1, Capriccios Op. 76, No. 1 and No. 8, Op. 116, No. 3 and No. 7, Romance, Op. 118, No. 5; Intermezzos, Op. 76, No. 3, 4, 6 and 7, Op. 116, No. 2 , 4 and 6, Op. 117, No. 1 and 2; Op. 118, No. 1 and 2 and Op. 119, No. 1 and 2: *The Intimate Brahms*. Naomi Zaslav, piano. Compact disc 1031. Music & Arts, 1998.

About the CDs

The works by Franck and Brahms were recorded at the University of Wisconsin-Milwaukee's recital hall. The recording of the Whittenberg comes from a recital at Stanford University's Dinkelspiel Hall, and we recorded the rest of the music at the home of Marcia and James Koford ("Casa de Cielo") where Nomi used their 9-foot Mason & Hamlin concert grand piano. I used my 1781 J.B. Guadagnini viola for all of these recordings.

Disc 1: The Zaslav Duo (Bernard and Naomi Zaslav)

Ernest Bloch (1880–1959)

Suite for Viola and Piano (1919)

    1 III Lento - Allegro - Moderato [4:20]
    2 VI Molto vivo [8:10]

Ernest Bloch, hailed as the foremost creator of Jewish music in the twentieth century, truly favored the viola. His Suite for Viola and Piano, which he also orchestrated, is one of his three greatest solo string compositions (the others are his 1916 cello rhapsody, *Shelomo,* and his Violin Concerto from 1938). Bloch first thought of the work as a suite of four symphonic poems. He tentatively titled the third movement "Nocturne" and titled the last movement "The Land of the Sun," but he was not satisfied with the names, and simply referred to them by their tempo markings. Bloch considered the last movement to be the most cheerful thing he ever wrote. All the works by Bloch on this disc were recorded on Music & Arts CD-902, *Ernest Bloch: Music for Viola and Piano*, released in 1995.

Cesar Franck (1822–1890)

Sonata in A Major for Violin and Piano (transcribed for viola by Bernard Zaslav)

    3 I Allegro appassionato [5:12]
    4 II Allegro [7:49]
    5 III Recitative- Fantasia (ben moderato) [6:24]
    6 IV Allegretto poco mosso [5:59]

Cesar Franck was 64 when he wrote his first and only Violin Sonata. It was a wedding gift for his compatriot, the great Belgian violinist Eugène Ysaÿe, and employs a highly-personal cyclic form, and a "cellular" technique of melodic development. His opening subject is a pure and haunting melody that takes a remarkable 27 measures to unfold.

The Franck was the first piece the Zaslav Duo recorded with my Guadagnini viola, and it was also the first recording ever made of the piece played on the viola. We recorded it in 1974 for Giveon Cornfield, the founder of Orion Master Recordings, and he coupled the Franck with both of Darius Milhaud's Viola and Piano Sonatas for *French Music for Viola and Piano*, LP ORS 75186. The album was released in 1976, and Fred Maroth, head of Music & Arts Recordings of America, re-released the Franck together with both of the Brahms Op.120 Sonatas in 1990 as CD-626, and released again in 2005 as Music & Arts CD-1151, *A Viola Treasury*.

Johannes Brahms (1833–1897)

Sonata for Viola and Piano Op. 120, No. 2

7 I Allegro amabile [8:29]

In 1894 the 71-year-old Brahms wrote his two Opus 120 Clarinet Sonatas (his last pieces of chamber music) for the clarinetist Richard Mühlfeld. When it was time for publication, Brahms made two editions of the Sonatas, one to be played on the clarinet, and one to be played on the viola. We recorded both Sonatas for Roy Christensen's Gasparo label, and the LP was released in 1980 as GS 215. Music & Arts re-released it on CD in 1990 (Music & Arts CD-626), and again in 2006 as Music & Arts CD-1087 (2), a two-disc album called *Brahms and Friends*.

Darius Milhaud (1802–1973)

Sonata No. 2 for Viola and Piano, Op. 244

8 I Champétre [3:58]
9 III Rude [2:41]

The second Milhaud Sonata is my favorite of the two because it is so much fun to play, spiky and gay by turns. "Champétre" translates as "pastorale," and has a rolling sort of French rural character, Dramatique (omitted here due to limitations of space) is more stark and angular, while Rude (rough) ends the piece in a rather showy and intense manner.

10 La Bruxelloise from "Quatre Visages" [2:44]

Milhaud dedicated his "Quatre Visages" to Germain Prevost, the violist of Belgium's Pro Arte Quartet, and each "visage" refers to a part of the world where members of the Quartet had lived. The crooning melody of "La Bruxelloise," and the way it curls through honky-tonk harmonies recalls Gershwin. Orion's LP ORS 75186 included both Sonatas and "La Bruxelloise," and Music & Arts re-released the Second Sonata and "La Bruxellose" in 2005 on Music & Arts CD-1151, *A Viola Treasury*.

ABOUT THE CDS

Charles Whittenberg (1927–1984)

11 Set for Two (1962) (Written for the Zaslav Duo) [5:10]

The viola part in Whittenberg's atonal piece uses extreme registers, and contains scoopy slides, fast tremolos, and the occasional restful bar, while the pianist chases her partner throughout this serial conversation. The concert was inadequately recorded when we performed the Whittenberg at Stanford, but we hope that you still enjoy this catch-me-if-you-can piece by our too-soon deceased composer friend.

The following works are some of my viola and piano transcriptions of music by Dvořák (released in 1996 on *Dvořák's Viola*, Music & Arts CD 953).

Antonín Dvořák (1841–1904)

Four Songs, Op. 2 (originally for soprano and piano)

12 II Andante con moto, "Twas wondrous sweet" [1:34]
13 III Andante, "naught to my heart can bring relief" [2:47]

I came across Dvořák's Four Songs for Soprano and Piano, Op. 2, in the Stanford music library, and transcribed the vocal parts of the songs for viola. These were love songs that he wrote in 1865 for his future wife, Anna Cermáková, and then revised in 1883.

Four Romantic Pieces, Op. 75 (originally for violin and piano)

14 III Allegro appassionato [2:22]

This is the third of four short pieces for violin and piano that Dvořák originally considered calling *Cavatina, Capriccio, Romance,* and *Elegy*.

Ernest Bloch (1880–1959)

15 Suite for Viola Solo (unfinished) [7:51]

In homage to Bach's magnificent unaccompanied works for violin and cello, Bloch begins the Andante with dramatic double and triple stop passages that release all of the viola's tonal resources. The gigue-like Moderato is followed by a dodecaphonic Andante that is full of pathos. In 1958 Bloch was living in Agate Beach, Oregon, and suffering from terminal cancer. He worked on the Suite during the last months of his life, and he died before he was able to finish it. Bloch only completed 25 measures of the fourth movement, marked Allegro deciso. Violists have cobbled together plausible endings, but I prefer playing only those notes that came from the composer's pen, and ending the Suite by playing Bloch's row of 15 accented quarter notes as they ascent ever upwards.

Disc 2: Bernard Zaslav with various String Quartets

With the Stanford Quartet

Gabriel Fauré (1845–1924)

String Quartet in E minor, Op. 121

    1 I Allegro moderato [6:16]

    Fauré's String Quartet was his only chamber piece without piano. At the age of 80, after a very distinguished career as organist, composer, critic, and teacher, he was ill, exhausted, and discouraged. This String Quartet was his last work, and he died without ever hearing it performed. The intricately polyphonic first movement has a dialogue between violin and viola. Philip Levy was the first violinist for this, the Stanford Quartet's last recording. It was made possible by a grant from the Friends of the Stanford String Quartet and also includes quartets by Frank Bridge, and Darius Milhaud. We made the recording at Pony Track Ranch in San Mateo County, California, and it was released in 1994 on Music & Arts CD-823.

With the Fine Arts Quartet

Dmitri Shostakovich (1906–1975)

String Quartet No. 3 in F major, Op. 73 (written in 1946)

    2 IV Adagio [5:15]

    1976 marked the 30th Anniversary of the founding of the Fine Arts Quartet. In this movement Shostakovich's dark ironic writing permits my colleague George Sopkin and myself to closely match the low string sounds of cello and viola. This recording commemorating the event on Roy Christensen's Gallante label (GG 1024) was made possible by a gift from Mr. and Mrs. Kenneth Montgomery on behalf of the Fine Arts Music Foundation.

Wolfgang Amadeus Mozart (1756–1791)

Quintet in C, K. 515 (with Francis Tursi, second viola)

    3 III Andante [9:48]

    Mozart's six Quintets for two violins, two violas, and cello rank as the highest examples of chamber music, and this Quintet, from 1787, embodies a combination of somber fatalism and sweetness. Abram Loft, my colleague in the Fine Arts Quartet writes of this movement, "The lyricism of the Andante is of so exalted an order that the two cadenza-like passages for the first violin and the first viola are free of any sense of virtuosity." Music & Arts digitally restored the original master tapes for our 1975 Vox LP recordings of the six Quintets, and released them in 2005 as CD-1159 (2).

Ruth Crawford Seeger (1901–1953) String Quartet (1931)

    4 I Rubato assai [3:09]
    5 II Leggiero, tempo giusto [1:55]
    6 III Andante [3:33]
    7 IV Allegro possible [1:51]

Ruth Crawford's single String Quartet is considered one of the finest modern works for quartet. I recorded the piece twice as a member of the Composers Quartet, but neither of those were released (they recorded the piece once again after I left). Our Fine Arts recording of her remarkable work was released in 1980 on LP for Gasparo, and re-released as a CD in 2006 on the Gallante label, GG-1020.

With members of the Vermeer Quartet

Antonin Dvořák (1841–1904)

Terzetto in C Major for Two Violins and Viola, Op. 74

    8 III Furiant [4:27]
    9 IV Tema con Variazioni [5:33]

Dvořák, who was himself a violist, wrote this lovely Terzetto in 1887 to play with two of his neighbors, Jan Pelikán, a violinist in the National Theater of Prague Orchestra, and his student Josef Kruis, who studied chemistry at the University. These two movements were recorded during a concert that Shmuel Ashkenasi, Pierre Menard, and I played on July, 24 1984, at the Bay Chamber Festival in Rockport, Maine. I regret that I was not able to obtain permission to reissue any of my Teldec or Orfeo recordings with the Vermeer Quartet for this disc.

With the Fine Arts Quartet

Wolfgang Amadeus Mozart (1756–1791)

Quintet in G minor, K. 516 (with Francis Tursi, second viola)

    10 I Allegro [8:20]

Mozart chose the dark key of G minor for his most grief-laden works. Various pairs of instruments interact with the first violin over a constant eighth-note pulse throughout this highly dramatic movement. This is also included on Music & Arts CD-1159 (2).

Ben Johnston (1926–2003)

11 String Quartet No. 4, "Amazing Grace" [11:14]

I first got to know Ben Johnston in 1957 while recording his Second Quartet with the Composers Quartet (Nonesuch Record's H 71224 in 1967). I found Ben's use of microtones and "just" intonation so intriguing that I asked the Fine Arts Foundation to commission him to write a quartet for us. The microtonal indications on the printed page look formidable, but Ben's amazingly varied set of variations always delights audiences. In one of his variations on the well-known hymn tune Johnston calls for bluesy bent notes and in another variation microtonal "mosquitoes" attack the tune fragments. At one point it sounds like the members of some barbershop quartet have gone mad trying to outdo one another, but it all ends resignedly in the major mode, *a la* Charles Ives. The Fine Arts Quartet gave Johnston's Fourth Quartet its Chicago premiere in 1974, and Gasparo released our LP recording in 1980 as GS 205. Gallante released it on CD in 2006 as CG 1020. Johnston's Fourth Quartet has also been recorded by several Quartets, including the Kronos Quartet.

Joseph Haydn (1732–1809)

String Quartet Op. 76, No. 4

12 I Allegro con spirito [6:13]

This is the opening movement of a Quartet called "The Sunrise" because of the way the first violin rises above the sustained chord held by the three lower voices. This is one of the 24 "lost" live performances from "The Fine Arts Quartet on WFMT Radio" on Music & Arts CD-1154 (8).

With the Stanford Quartet

Darius Milhaud (1894–1972)

String Quartet No. 7, Op. 87 (1925)

13 I Modérément animé [3:13]
14 IV Vif et gai [2:43]

In Milhaud's Seventh Quartet he combines rollicking brashness with a touch of Stravinsky-like jazziness. He wrote this lyrical and lighthearted work in Italy during his honeymoon voyage through Europe and the Middle East (while recuperating from a bout of illness). The viola interjects *assez rude* comments in the polytonal first movement, while the others go about their business. The contrapuntal finale bats the main theme around fugally (and gaily) from voice to voice, and lets it die away gradually towards the end, until Milhaud stomps on a final B-flat chord to say goodbye. This is also on Music & Arts CD-823.

Index

Note: Page numbers in *italics* indicate an illustration or photograph.

A. E. Hill & Sons, 372
Aaron, Henry, 219
Adam, Claus, 224, 242
Adderley, Cannonball, 189
Adler, David, 243
Adler, Samuel
   String Quartet No. 8, 298
Aeolian String Quartet, 319
Aitay, Victor, 255
Ajemian, Anahid,
   225–37, 239, 244, 246
Alban Berg String Quartet, 179
Alda, Alan, 142
Alda, Arlene, 142
Aldeburgh Festival, 324, 332–34
Alice Tully Hall, Lincoln Center,
   262–63
All Music Guide, 191
Allen, Fred, 48, 329n
Allers, Franz, 140–41
Alma Trio, 330, 349
Alsop, Lamar,
   174, *209,* 209–15, 247
Alsop, Marin, 211
Alsop, Ruth, *209,* 210–15, 247
Amadeus String Quartet,
   179, 248, 334
Amati, violins by, 225
Amati String Quartet, 179
American Ballet Theatre,
   260–61, 262
American Opera Society, 134
American Record Guide, 390,
   391–92, 396, 401–2
American String Quartet, 179
Amram, David
   music for *Splendor in the Grass,*
   239
Am-Rus (publisher), 52
Anderson, Ronald, 220

Angelou, Maya, 116
Ansermet, Ernest, 102
Antonini, Alfredo, 299–300
Appel, Toby, 342
Apple Hill Chamber Players, 359
Apple Tree, The (Broadway show),
   142
Arazi, Ziv, 379
Arcieri, Carlos, 159
Arditti String Quartet, 178
Arico, Fortunato, 208, 220
Arm, Theodore, 342
Arner, Leonard, 169, 174, 184
Aronoff, Shirley, 243
Artaria publishing firm, 280
Artist's Series Concerts, 206
Asher, Bob, 242
Ashkenasi, Shmuel,
   304, *307,*308–35, *317*
   solo career, 308, 315–16
Astor Hotel (New York), 10
Atkins, John, 208
Aubort, Marc J., 233
Auer, Leopold, 65, 67, 117, 381–82
Aumont, Jean Pierre, 141
Australia, 324–25
Autori, Franco, 81, 84
Avakian, George, 226n
Avins, Styra, 393
Avshalomov, Jacob, 169

Babai, Béla, 97
Babbitt, Milton, 199, 219, 220, *228*
   Composition for Viola and Piano,
   396, 397
   String Quartet No. 2,
   228, 230, 262, 397
   String Quartet No. 3,
   262–63, 275, 387, 396, 397
   string quartets, 250, 251, 254, 271

Babbitt, Sylvia, 397
Bach, Johann Sebastian
    Art of Fugue, 403–4
    Cello Suite No. 4, 385–86
    Cello Suites, 124–25, 158, 171
    Goldberg Variations, 343
    orchestral suites, 220
    trio sonatas, 208
    viola da gamba sonatas, 206, 257
Bach, P.D.Q., 172–73, 241
Bach, Wilhelm Friedemann
    Viola Sonata in C minor,
        207–8, 208, 257
Bach Dancing and Dynamite
    Society, 354
Bach Guild recordings, 174
Badea, Christian, 327
Badenweiler Festival, 332
Baez, Joan, 189
Bagot, Robert, 273–74
Bahlsen, Mrs., 272
Balestrieri, Tommaso,
    violins by, 252
Baller, Adolph "Usiu," 349, 351
Baller, Nina, 351
Ballet Orchestra, 353
Balsam, Artur, 319, 341, 342
Bang on a Can Festival, 353
Bar Harbor, Maine, 337–38
Barab, Seymour, 174, 225–37, 244
Barber, Samuel, 247
    Cello Concerto, 318
Barbirolli, John, 117
Bard, Ben, 184
Barela, Margaret, 391–92
Barenboim, Daniel, 106, 267
Barere, Simon, 381
Barnes, Arthur, 352–53
Barnes, Helene, 353
Barnes, Larry, 350–51
Baron, Samuel, 259, 403–4
Baroque music, 220–21
Barrett, Herbert
    The Viola, 382–83

Barrows, John, 164–65
Barshai, Rudolph, 22
Barter, Matthew, 345
Barter, Philip, 345
Bartók, Béla, 52, 218
    Contrasts, 208
    String Quartet No. 1, 237
    String Quartet No. 2, 320
    String Quartet No. 6,
        268, 269–70, 359
    string quartets, 103n,
        223, 251–52, 264–65, 274, 401
    Viola Concerto, 123
    Violin Duos, 361
Bartók, Peter, 123n
Barzin, Leon, 22, 181
baseball, 40–41
Bauer, Harold, 337
Baum, Lois, 400
Baumgartner, Roland, 292
Bay Chamber Concerts (Rockport,
    Maine), 317–20, 325, 334
BBC Lunchtime Concert (London),
    324
BBC Radio, 273
Beardslee, Bethany, 334
Beare, Arthur, 374
Beare, John, 292
Beaton, Cecil, 115
Beaumont, Guillaume, 273
Beaux Arts Quartet, 214–15
Beaux Arts Trio, 130
Becker, Carl G., 297–98
Becker, Carl G., Jr., 292, 293, 298
Becker, Jetta, 42
Becker House
    (Mountaindale hotel), 42
Beecham, Thomas, 387
Beethoven, Ludwig van
    Duo for viola and cello, 129, 207
    Grosse Fuga, 279–82, 326, 352,
        353, 354
    "Kreutzer" Sonata, 224
    Notturno, Op. 42, 207, 257

Piano Concerto No. 4, 102
Piano Quartet, 119
Serenade for Flute, Violin, and
 Viola, Op. 25, 119
String Quartet Op. 18, No. 1,
 256, 352
String Quartet Op. 18, No. 6,
 349–50
String Quartet Op. 59, No. 2,
 349–50, 351
String Quartet Op. 59, No. 3,
 168, 354, 362
String Quartet Op. 127, 237
String Quartet Op. 130,
 326, 353, 354, 408
String Quartet Op. 132, 314
String Quartet Op. 135,
 331, 343, 349–50
string quartets, 180, 247, 401
string quartets, late,
 178, 223, 262–63, 326–27
string quartets, Op. 18, 96, 261
string quartets, Op. 59, 178
String Quintet, Op. 29, 331
String Trio, 128
Symphony No. 5, 83, 105
Symphony No. 6, 105
Symphony No. 8, 105
Viola Quintet, 322
Violin Concerto, 105
as violist, 22
Beethoven String Quartet, 179
Bein & Fushi, 375, 379
Bein, Robert, 292, 375–76
Bell, Joshua, 95
Benedict, Roger, 379
Benny, Jack, 48
Berg, Alban
 Lulu, 102-103
 Lyric Suite, 274, 332, 334
 String Quartet, Op. 3, 192, 245
 string quartets, 223
 Violin Concerto, 267
Berganza, Teresa, 134

Berger, Arthur
 Piano Trio, 343
Bergonzi, Carlo, violins by, 225
Bergonzi, Michelangelo, violas by,
 128, 287, 293, 371–72, 373
Berkowitz, Ralph, 245–46, 259
Berkshire Eagle, 325
Berkshire String Quartet, 199, 254
Berlioz, Hector, 105
 Harold in Italy, 26, 353
Berman, Boris, 352
Bernsohn, Loren, 224
Bernstein, Leonard, 97
Berry, Wallace
 Canto Lirico, 205, 258, 266
Bettina, Judith, 397
Bialkin, Maurice, 170–71
Bickel, Theodore, 189
big bands, 7–14
Bishop, Edgar, 374
Black, Arnold, 62, 68, 69, 85, 141
Blassingame, Count Lurton, 72
Blitzstein, Marc
 Juno, 133–34
Bloch, Ernest
 "Five Sketches in Sepia for Piano
  Solo," 389–91
 "In the Night, A Love Poem for
  Piano," 389–91
 "Meditation and Processional,"
  390–91
 Piano Quintet, 258, 389
 Schelomo, 389
 string quartets, 251, 389
 Suite for Viola and Piano,
  263, 342, 389–91
 Suite Hébraïque, 390–91
 as violist, 22
Bloom, Arthur, 206
blue whales, sounds of, 402–3
Blyth, Alan, 319
Boccherini, Luigi
 String Quartet, Op. 33, No. 6, 362
Boehm, Joseph, 178

Bogin, Abba, 235
Bogin, Arthur, 174
Boico, Efim, 399
Bolcom, William
  String Quartet No. 10, 355–56, 363
Bolger, Ray, 62
Bolotine, Leonid, 132
Bolshoi Theatre Quartet, 179
Booth, Shirley, 133
Borciani, Paolo, 364
Boulanger, Charles, 374
Boulanger, Nadia, 402
Boulez, Pierre, 242
Bourouchoff, Israel, 402
Bova, Joe, 134
Bowen, José
  "Bathsheba and Her Suitors," 355
Boykan, Martin, 220, 236
  String Quartet No. 1, 234
Brahms, Johannes, 321
  Clarinet Quintet, Op. 115, 332
  clarinet sonatas (transcribed for viola), 392–94
  Clarinet/Viola Sonata, Op. 120, No. 1, 384, 393
  Clarinet/Viola Sonata, Op. 120, No. 2, 204, 257–58, 384, 393
  Piano Concerto No. 1, 106
  Piano Quartet in A, Op. 26, 354
  Piano Quintet in F minor, Op. 34, 245
  Serenade in A Major, Op. 16, 169
  String Quartet No. 3, Op. 67, 245
  String Quartet No, 3, Op. 67, 247
  String Quartet Op. 51, No. 1, 362
  string quartets, 188, 401
  String Quintet in G Major, Op.111, 260–61, 352
  symphonies, 106
  Symphony No. 3, 105
  Symphony No. 4, 105
  Variations on a Theme of Haydn, 106
  viola quintets, 322

Violin Sonata No. 2, Op. 100, 77
Brandeis University, 271
Brant, Henry
  Music for an Imaginary Ballet or Lightweight for Three, 132–33
Brehm, Alvin, 127–28, 174, 219
  Duo for Viola and Piano, 207
Breismeister, Ernestine, 231
Bridge, Frank, 334
  String Quartet No. 1, 363–64
  Two Pieces for Viola and Piano, 342
  Viola Duo, 361
Bright, Ernest, 113, 132
Britten, Benjamin, 247
  "Fantasie Quartet," 128
  String Quartet No. 2, 351
  String Quartet No. 3, 325, 333–34
  string quartets, 251, 274
  as violist, 22
Britten-Pears School for Advanced Musical Studies, 324
Broadhurst Theatre, 142–43
Broadway shows, 82, 115–17, 133–44, 165, 239, 242, 370
Brooke, Leonard, 300
Brooklyn College, 214, 239, 242
Brooklyn Dodgers, 40–41, 113
Brosa String Quartet, 178
Brown, Al, 117, 174
Brown, David O., 390–91
Brown, Hugh, 7–9, 82
Browning, John, 254, 274, 400, 401
Bruckner, Anton, 103
  Symphony No. 7, 105
Budapest Quartet, 93, 130, 166, 179, 186, 210, 260–61, 272, 279, 405
Bultitude, A. R., 370
Burda, Pavel, 402
Burnett, Carol, 134–35
Busch, Adolf, 130
Busch, Hermann, 130
Butler, Artie, 219
Buttons, Red, 43

INDEX

Caballé, Montserrat, 208, 295
Cabaret (Broadway show), 142–43
Cabrillo Festival of Contemporary Music, 211n
Cage, John
　HPSCHD, 233
Callas, Maria, 134
Calloway, Cab, 116
Canary Islands, 294–97
Candlelight Concert Series, 354
Canin, Stuart, 329–30
Capet String Quartet, 178
Capote, Truman
　The Grass Harp, 115–16
　The Muses Are Heard, 117
Carcassi brothers, 287–88
Carlstedt, Jan, 274
Carman, Eli, 167
Carnegie Hall (New York), 73, 102, 157, 162–63, 168–69, 196
Carnegie Hall Festival Concert series, 316
Carnegie Recital Hall (New York), 132, 169–70, 188, 192, 204–5, 218, 225, 229–30, 258, 269–70, 274, 382
Carnegie String Quartet, 209, 210–15, 239, 242
Carnegie Tavern, 145–56
Carpe Diem String Quartet, 179
Carr, Normie, 8, 12–13, 361
Carroll's Studios, 134
Carter, Elliott, 199, 219, 220
　"Pastorale," 385
　"Recitative and Improvisation for Four Kettledrums," 225
　String Quartet No. 1, 232
　String Quartet No. 2, 232
　String Quartet No. 4, 232, 237n
cartoon music, 17–18
"Casa de Cielo," *387,* 387–90
Casadesus, Robert, 98
Casals, Pablo, 130, 158, 166, 182, 220, 223, 308

Casals Festival, 166
Catskill Mountains vacation resorts, 42–43, 52, 118
Celibidache, Sergiu, 106
Center for Computer Research in Music and Acoustics (CCRMA), 388
Chadwick, George, 200
chamber music, as profession, 196–200, 250, 404–5
Chase, Robert, 358
Chausson, Ernest
　Chanson perpétuelle, 332
　Concerto for Violin, Piano, and String Quartet, 245
Chautauqua Symphony, 81, 84–88, 103–4
Cheltenham Festival, 266
Cherry, Philip, 118, 128, 224
Chicago, Illinois, 312–13, 320
Chicago Tribune, 315, 316
Childs, Paul, 368
Chilingirian String Quartet, 178
Chiocci, Gaetano, violas by, 78, 193, 370
Chissel, Joan, 266
Chopin, Fryderyk
　piano concertos, 105
Chou Wen-Chung, 219
Christensen, Roy, 293, 384, 402, 403
Civkin, Celia, 89
Civkin, Naomi. *See* Zaslav, Naomi
Claremont String Quartet, 179
Clarion Concerts, 131, 239, 242
Cleveland Orchestra, 21, 82–83, 89–107
Clevenger, Dale, 254, 327
Cliburn, Van, 131
Cohen, Gilbert, 132
Cohen, Isidore, 192
Cohen, Myron, 43
Colbert-Laberge Management, 256, 275
Coleman, Avron, 53

Coleman, Shepard, 53
Colescott, Warrington, 345
Coletta, Harold, 184
Colgrass, Michael
    Variations for Four Drums and
        Viola, 202, 203, 204, 207, 257
Colletti, Paul, 386
Collins, Dorothy, 8, 18
Coltrane, John, 189
Columbia Records, 165, 229
Columbia University, 186
Combs, Larry, 254, 327
Commanday, Robert P., 257, 401
Composer's Forum Concert, 205
Composers' Showcase, 132
Composers String Quartet,
    17, 223–39, 242, 243, 246, 262,
    294, 338, 396–97
Concert Disc, 251
Concertapes, Inc., 251
Coney Island, Brooklyn, 41, 71
Contemporary Festival, University of
    Wisconsin-Milwaukee, 259
contemporary music concerts,
    132, 186, 199–200, 205–6,
    218–20, 223–39
Coolidge, Elizabeth Sprague,
    179, 199, 248
Coolidge Quartet, 179
Cooper, Martin, 265–66, 267
Cooper Union (New York), 189–90
Copes, Ronald, 342, 343
Copland, Aaron
    "An Outdoor Overture," 58
Cores, Alex, 219
Crane Estate concert series, 246
Craske, George, 374
Crawford Seeger, Ruth
    String Quartet, 227–28, 250, 251,
        263, 403
CRI Recordings, 187, 266
Cross, Milton, 48
Curtis String Quartet, 179
Cuypers, violins by, 225

Daily Telegraph, 265–66, 267, 319
D'Alfino, Felice, 47
Dallapiccola, Luigi, 206, 229
Dalley, John, 308–9, 354
d'Ambrose, Jacques, 211
Damrosch, Walter, 38
Dane, Jean, 237n
Dangerfield, Rodney, 20
Dann, Steven, 385
Darack, Arthur, 254
D'Atilli, Dario, 293, 378
DaVinci Quartet, 301
Davis, Bette, 74
Davis, Emery, 118
Davis, Meyer, 118
Davis, Miles, 189
Davis, Sammy, Jr., 143
Davis, Virginia, 118
Dawes, Andrew, 342, 343
de Freese, Harry, 356
de Hartmann, Thomas, 205
de Lancie, John, 318
de Mille, Agnes, 133
de Veritch, Alan, 386
Debussy, Claude
    La Mer, 70
    Nuages, 99–100
    Sonata for Flute, Viola, and Harp,
        327
    String Quartet, 129, 249, 268, 355
Decca Records, 251
*Deconstructing Dad: The Music,
    machines, and Mysteries of
    Raymond Scott* (film), 18
DeCormier, Robert, 139–40
DeGaetani, Jan, 274, 298–99, 332
Dehmell, Richard, 231
Deinzer, Hans, 322-23, 332
DeMotte, Warren, 206–7
Dengel, Eugenie, 200
Dethier, Edouard, 73
Deval, Jacques, 141
Devotee, 383–84
Dextra Musica, 407-8
Diamand, Peter, 269

Diamond, David, 220
Diapason magazine, 390, 401
Diaz, Roberto, 379, 386
DiBiase, Edoardo, 8, 69
Dichter, Mischa, 316
Dick, Marcel, 94
Dietrich, Fritz, 25, 271, 283
Dinicu, Grigoras
   "Hora Staccato," 68
Dinkelspiel Auditorium (Stanford University), 351, 352, 399
Dodd, John Kew, 125, 370–71
Dodd family of bow makers, 369
Dohnányi, Ernst von, 119
   Piano Quintet, 358, 359
Doktor, Paul, 382
Donnell Library (New York), 205, 218
Dorati, Antal, 123n
Doring, Ernest, 289
Douglas, Melvyn, 133
Dounis, Demetrius Constantin, 377–78
Downey, Irusha, 402–3
Downey, John William, works of, 402–3
Downs, Hugh, 252
Drosen, Alex (grandson), 407
Drosen, Claudia Zaslav (daughter)
   birth and childhood of, 112–13, 120
   current life, 406–7
   encouragement of this memoir, 403
   flute studies of, 113, 193
   marriage of, 260, 287, 320
   in Pennsylvania, 320
   "Stage" (poem), 305–6
   at University of Wisconsin-Milwaukee, 260
   in Wisconsin, 241, 247
Drosen, James (son-in-law), 287, 328, 406–7
Drosen, Sarah (granddaughter), 328, 407
Drucker, Eugene, 342

Drushynin, Feodor, 385
Druzinsky, Eddie, 254–55
Dubins, Jerry, 401
Dubrow's Cafeteria (Brooklyn), 90
Duke, Richard, 374
Dunn, Thomas, 208, 242
Dupuoy, Jean, 237n
Dutch Mill Restaurant (Manhattan), 77–78
Dutoit, Charles, 22
Dutt, Hank, 16, 367, 379
Dutton, Lawrence, 379
Duvivier, George, 219
Dvořák, Antonín
   "American" Quartet, 268, 362, 391
   Piano Quartet Op. 23, 302
   Piano Quartet Op. 34, 334
   Piano Quintet Op. 81, 333, 351
   Sonatina in G Major, Op. 100, 342
   String Quartet No. 10, Op. 51, 326, 354
   string quartets, 187–88
   String Quintet, Op. 97, 343
   transcriptions for viola, 391–92, 396
   as violist, 22
Dycke, Marjorie (teacher), 54–55

Earle, Broadus, 224
earthquakes, 351–52, 357
East of Eden (film), 54
Eastman School of Music, 55, 58, 59–60, 301
Ebbett's Field (Brooklyn), 40–41
Eberl, Carl, 214
Eddy, Timothy, 232n
Edinburgh Festival, 266–69
Eger, Joseph, 224
egg creams, 135
Ehlers-Danlos Syndrome, 65, 171–72
Eisenberg, Maurice, 158n
Eisler, Edith, 393
Electronium, 17, 19
Elgar, Edward
   Cello Concerto, 22, 303, 324

"Introduction and Allegro," 303
Piano Quintet, 274
String Quartet, Op. 83, 362
Elisha, Paul, 383–84
Elman, Mischa, 37, 195–96, 405
Emerson Quartet, 275
Emil Hjorth & Sons, 375
Enescu, Georges, 181, 196
  as conductor, 103
  violin and piano music, 202, 204
Engel, Lehman, 136
English, Jack, 377
English Chamber Orchestar, 319
Erdelyi, Czaba, 386
Ericson, Raymond, 230, 294
Erlich, Don, 330
Escot, Pozzi
  "Movimentos for Violin and Piano," 225
Esterhazy Orchestra, 239
ETHEL, 179
Etlinger, Richard, 55–56
Evans, Gil, 189
Evans, Ralph, 399
Everest Records, 251
ExLax, jingle for, 171
Expo 67 (Montreal), 234

Fairbanks, Alaska, 271
Fanfare, 401
Fantasia (film), 173
Farnsworth, Philo, 248n
Fauré, Gabriel
  Piano Quartet, 342
  String Quartet, 362, 363–64
Feher, Ilona, 308
Feldman, Morton, 219, 228
  The Viola in My Life, 26
Férir, Émile, 291–92, 374
fermata, 15
Ferrante & Teicher, 381
Ferrante Brothers (builders), 44
Ferrer, José, 133
Ferrin, Richard, 56
Festival de Música de Cámara, San Miguel de Allende, Mexico, 300–301, 303
Festival de Musique Montreux Vevey, 314–15
Festival Orchestra, 239
Fetique, Victor François, 371
Feuermann, Emanuel, 249
Fiddler on the Roof (Broadway show), 141
Fiedler, Arthur, 22
Fielding, Ralph, 380
Fine, Elaine, 18, 401–2
Fine, Irving
  String Quartet, 271
Fine, Vivian
  Capriccio for Oboe and String Trio, 132
Fine Arts Foundation, 244, 262, 300
Fine Arts Quartet, *241*, 241–77
  25th Anniversary season, 264–65
  balance in, 268
  Bartók quartet cycle performed by, 103n
  Canary Islands concert, 294–97
  chemistry and rapport of, 249–50, 255
  in Chicago, 248–49, 251
  commissions for, 254, 352
  concert schedule of, 25
  domestic tours, 256, 271
  East Coast concerts, 258–59
  European tours, 253, 261–62, 264–66, 270–74, 276–77, 283–86, 294, 298, 302, 374, 375–77
  formation of, 198, 248
  Goodman Theater concerts, 253–54, 256
  guest artists, 254
  Jerusalem concerts, 294–95
  joint concert with Stanford String Quartet, 360
  as Laureates of Lincoln Academy of Illinois, 294
  local season, 253–54, 256–57

INDEX 431

management, 256, 271, 275
membership, 248, 300–304, 399
performances of Bartók quartet
  cycle, 251–52
radio performance tapes, 400–401
recordings by, 251, 272, 274–75,
  275, 283, 293, 322, 384, 387,
  389, 399–400, 403
rehearsal and teaching schedule,
  252–53
repertoire, 247, 251
reputation of, 234–35
Summer Evenings of Music series,
  246–47
television appearances,
  252, 256, 258
University of Wisconsin-
  Milwaukee residency,
  249, 252–53
Zaslav as guest artist, 399
Zaslav's audition for, 236–37
Zaslav's first appearance in
  Chicago with, 255–56
Zaslav's first official performance
  with, 245–46
Fisher, Steven D.
  Quartet No. 1, 227
Fleisher, Leon, 255
Flissler, Eileen, 382
Flonzaley Quartet, 372
FLUX, 179
Foldes, Andor, 218
Foley, Madeleine, 130
Folies Bergère, 13
Forster, E. M., 333
Forster, William, 374
Forsyth, Cecil
  Viola Concerto, 292
Foss, Lukas, 53, 218
Français, Émile, 287–88
Français, Jacques, 163, 194, 287–89,
  291, 292
Françaix, Jean, 119
Francescatti, Zino, 105, 167
Franck, César

String Quartet, 302
Violin Sonata, 382, 383, 396
Frank, Gabriela Lena, 408
Franklin, Benjamin, 200
Fredericks, Dr. Carlton, 71
Freier, Susan, 356–65, 357, 360
Fried, Miriam, 95
Friends of Music at Princeton
  University, 227
Friends of the Stanford String
  Quartet, 348, 349
Fritz Kreisler Memorial Concert,
  167–68
Frommer, Arthur
  Europe on Five Dollars a Day,
  159–60
Fuchs, Harry, 124
Fuchs, Joseph,
  73, 124, 126–27, 129, 206, 341
Fuchs, Lillian,
  22, 123–27, 124, 129, 179, 194,
  206, 236, 341, 370, 382, 385
Fuchs, Robert
  Six Fantasy Pieces, 393
Funes, Donald, 315
Funes, Matthew, 315
Funny Thing Happened on the Way to
  the Forum, A (Broadway show),
  141
Furtwängler, Wilhelm, 387

Gabrilowitsch, Ossip, 337
Gagliano, Josephus, violins by, 9, 107
Galamian, Ivan, 309
Galimir, Felix, 130, 218, 231–32
Galimir String Quartet,
  130, 178, 232n
Galitzin, Prince Nikolas, 262–63
Gallichio, Joseph, 185
Gallo, Johnny, 62
Gambling, John, 185
Gandelsman, Yuri, 399
Garbousova, Raya, 318, 324
Gardner, Samuel, 341
Garfield, John, 143

Gasparo da Salo, violas by,
    124, 125, 129–30, 194, 307, 378
Gasparo Records, 251, 384, 402
Geigenbau Krause, 377
Gelbloom, Gerald, 68–69
Gershwin, George, 59n
    Porgy and Bess, 116–17
Getz, Stan, 189
Giannini, Vittorio, 73
Giat, Sampson, 174
Gideon, Miriam, 220
    "Sonnets from Shakespeare," 225
Gilford, Jack, 134, 143
Gingold, Josef,
    94–97, *95,* 102, 105, 179, 245,
    245, 259, 385, 405–6
Giulini, Carlo Maria, 22
Gladwell, Malcolm, 128
Glazer, David, 188, 218
Glazer, Frank, 301
Glazer, Mia, 218
Glazunov, Alexander, 162
Gleason, Jackie, 135–37
Glick, Jacob, 204, 397
Glickman, Loren, 166–67, 174, 219
Gluck, Christoph Willibald
    Orpheus and Eurydice flute solo,
    62, 64
Glyde, Rosemary, 386
Goberman, John, 142
Goberman, Max, 165–66
Goffriller, Matteo, cellos by,
    158, 182–83, 252, 289, 293, 403
Goffriller, Matteo, violins by, 252
Golani-Erdesz, Rivka, 385
Goldberg, Alla, 53
Golden Boy (Broadway show), 143
Goldsmith, Pamela, 386
Golonka, Arlene, 136
Goltzer, Albert, 169
Goltzer, Doris, 169
Goode, Richard, 254, 274
Goodman Theater (Chicago),
    253–54, 256, 314–15
Goossens, Leon, 169

Gordani, Nina, 203
Gordon, Kenneth, 199
Gordon, Nathan, 85
Gorner, Peter, 254
Gorodnitsky, Sascha, 74
Gould, Morton
    Concertette for Viola and Band,
    353
Grainger, Percy, 55, 56–57
Gramophone magazine, 393–94
Grandhotel Römerbad (Freiburg),
    321–23
Granik, Arthur, 168, 169
Grant Park (Chicago), 316
Grant Park Symphony, 327
Gray, Freda, 339
Gray, Joel, 143, 349
Greenfield, Edward, 265, 271
Greenwich Village, 54
Greitzer, Sol, 242–43
Grieg, Edvard
    Piano Concerto, 105
Griffes, Charles, 200
Griffiths, Paul, 319–20
Griller String Quartet, 178
Grishman, Alan, 174
Grofé, Ferde, 22
    "Grand Canyon Suite," 57–58
Grokest, Dr., 171
Grossinger's Hotel (Catskills), 118
Grossman, Jerry, 133, 342, 343
Guadagnini, Johannes Baptiste, violas
    by, *4,* 25, 182n, 289–93, 296–97,
    310, 343, 378, 382, 403, 407–8,
    408
Guadagnini, Johannes Baptiste,
    violins by, 252, 343, 374, 386
Guardian newspaper, 265, 271
Guarneri del Jesu, violins by, 182,
    252, 299, 310
Guarneri String Quartet, 130, 170,
    171, 179, 199, 223, 308–9, 343
Gurdjieff Society, 205–6
Gusikoff, Isidore, 219

INDEX

Haber, Lou, 242
Hackett, Buddy, 141–42
Haenel, Frederick, violas by, 193
Hamma, Walter, 292, 373
Hanani, Yehuda, 342
Hancock, Herbie, 189
Hancock, Maine, 118–19, 224, 337
Handt, Herbert, 51, 54, 160–62, 333
Hanson, Howard, 55, 105
   Symphony No. 2, "Romantic," 58
Happiest Girl in the World, The
   (Broadway show), 139–40
Harper's magazine, 191
Harris, Barbara, 142
Harris, Roy
   "Soliloquy and Dance," 206
   Violin Concerto, 95, 105
Harrison, Guy Fraser, 55, 57, 58
Harrison, Stephen,
   330, 347, *350, 357,* 359–65, *360*
Harth, Sidney, 352
Hartley, L. P.
   The Go-Between, 405
Hartley, Marsden, 345
Haworth, Jill, 143
Haydn, Franz Joseph
   Seven Last Words, 166
   String Quartet No. 68, 256
   String Quartet Op. 33, No. 3, 267
   String Quartet Op. 64, No. 5,
   "Lark," 351
   String Quartet Op. 76, No. 1, 315
   String Quartet Op. 76, No. 4,
   "Sunrise," 245
   string quartets,
      103n, 166, 180, 238, 258, 358,
      401
   string quartets, Op. 76, 239
   symphonies of, 105
Heath, Percy, 254
Heifetz, Jascha,
   37, 59n, 65, 68, 69, 101, 117, 195,
   196, 405

Heiles, Anne Mischakoff, 59n
   Mischak Mischakoff: Journeys of a
   Concertmaster, 66
Henahan, Donal, 92-93
Henreid, Paul, 74
Hentz, Vincent, 358
Herbst Theater (San Francisco), 351
Herlie, Eileen, 136
Herzogenberg, Heinrich von
   Three Legends, 393
High Fidelity magazine, 188
Hiller, Lejaren
   HPSCHD, 233
Hillyer, Raphael, 242, 342, 385
Hindemith, Paul, 218
   Duo for Viola and Cello, 258
   Die junge Magd, 298
   Mathis der Maler, 53, 105
   orchestral music, 52
   Solo Viola Sonata, Op. 25, No. 1,
      206, 208
   String Quartet No. 3, 268, 401
   string quartets, 251
   Symphonic Metamorphoses, 102
   Des Todes Tod, Op. 23a, 274, 298
   as violist, 22
Hokanson, Leonard, 319, 320
Hollander, Lorin, 254
Holliger, Heinz, 169–70
Holliger, Ursula Haeneggi, 169–70
Holloway, Sterling, 115
Hollywood String Quartet, 179
Holz, Karl, 280
Honegger, Arthur, 382
Horszowski, Mieczyslaw, 130, 186, 333
Horvath, Josef Maria, 234, 236
"How Much is that Doggie in the
   Window," 170
Howard, Peter, 53
Howard High School (Wilmette),
   253, 256
Howe, George, 224
Hoyer, Otto A., 373–74
Huber, Klaus, 169

Huggler, Jack, 132, 220
   Sonata for Viola and Piano, Op. 49a, 203
Hughes, Allen, 257
Humeston, Jay, 231
Hummel, Johann Nepomuk
   Clarinet Quintet, 188
   violin and piano music, 202, 203, 204
Hungarian String Quartet, 179
Hunkins, Dorothy, 215
Hunkins, Sterling, 132, 215, 220
Hurok, Sol, 38, 308
Hurwitz, Emanuel, 319, 359, 374
Hurwitz, Kay, 319, 374
Hurwitz String Quartet, 319
Husa, Karel
   String Quartet No. 3, 255-256, 260, 263, 267, 401
   string quartets, 251, 253, 259, 290, 412, 413

I Had a Ball (Broadway show), 141–42
Ice Capades, 12–13
Ilmer, Irving, 248
Imai, Nabuko, 308, 310, 322, 332
Imbrie, Andrew, 251
Institute of Musical Art (Juilliard School), 7, 49
   atmosphere of, 73
   founding of, 60–61
   graduating class, 1946, *79*
   uptown location of, 61, 73
   Zaslav's years at, 60–79, 81
Interlochen Music Camp, 55–58, 59, 404
International House (New York), 73
International Society for Contemporary Music, 224–25
International Viola Congress (9thAnnual), 385
International Viola Congress (17th Annual), 386

Iowa String Quartet, 179
Isabella Stewart Gardner Museum (Boston), 231
Isherwood, Christopher
   Goodbye to Berlin, 142
Isomura, Kazuhide "Kazu," 379
Israel, Theodore, 116–17, 164, 174
Ives, Charles
   Piano Trio, 343
   String Quartet No. 1, 190, 193
   String Quartet No. 2, 190–91, 193
   "The Unanswered Question," 189–90
Ives Quartet, 365
Iwasaki, Ko, 342

JACK, 179
Jackier, David, *51,* 54, 55, 60, 90
   LUV LUV, 3, 55, 345
Jackson, Milt, 254
Jacobs, Paul, 225
Jacobsen, Sascha, 21, 59n, 61, 62–63, 179, 341
Jacobson, Bernard, 254, 393
Jacobus, Jan van, violas by, 184
Jahoda, Fritz, 224
Janáček, Leo?
   String Quartet No. 2 "Intimate Letters," 314, 315, 353
Jay and the Americans (rock group), 165
Jenkins, Newell, 131, 242
Jeunesses Musicales International, 234

Jian Ming Li, 377
jingles, 170–71
J-J.R. (critic), 323–24
Joachim, Joseph, 384
   Variations for Viola and Piano, Op. 10, 393
Joachim String Quartet, 178
Johnson, Harriett, 263
Johnson, Kathy, 315

Johnson, Marc, *307,* 309–35, *317*
Johnson, Mark, 379
Johnston, Ben, 220
  String Quartet No. 2, 233–34, 242
  String Quartet No. 4, 352, 403
  String Quartet No. 9, 356, 363
  string quartets, 250, 251, 254
Jolley, David, 318
Jordan Hall, New England
  Conservatory (Boston), 313–14
Josephs, Wilfred
  Viola Concerto, 264
Joslyn, Jay, 316
*Journal of the American Viola
  Society,* 390–91
Joyce, James, 141
Judt, Tony, 405
Juilliard School of Music. *See*
  Institute of Musical Art
Juilliard String Quartet,
  129, 130, 167–68, 179, 191,
  242, 248
June Music Festival, Albuquerque,
  245–46, 259, 263, 266
Juno (Broadway show), 133–34

Kalam, Endel, 342
Kalam, Tonu, 342
Kalichstein, Joseph, 325–26
Kalish, Gilbert, 332
Kalman, Lilla, 132, 215, 220
Kaplan, Melvin, 219, 274–75
Karlins, M. William, 205
Karr, Gary, 254
Kashkashian, Kim, 232n
Katchen, Julius, 396
Katims, Milton, 22, 78, 260–61, 268
Katz, Martha Strongin, 386
Kaufman, Louis, 341
Kaufman, Sidney, 174
Kay, Connie, 254
Kay, Richard,
  118, 131, *177,* 181, 182–91, 199
Kaye, Danny, 43

Kennedy, Edgar, 229
Kennedy Center, Washington, D.C.,
  271
Kerr, Walter, 116
Kiel, Friedrich
  Three Romances, 393
Kievman, Elaine, 378
Kievman, Louis, 377–79
Kipnis, Igor, 174, 220
Kirkpatrick, John, 189
Kittel, Nicholas, 182
Klemperer, Otto, 187
Klien, Walter, 327
Knauer, Baruch (Ben; uncle),
  32–33, 41–42
Knauer, Esther (maternal
  grandmother), 32–33, 39
Knauer, Selig (Samuel; maternal
  grandfather), 32–33, 42, 45
Knechtel, Baird, 385
Kneisel, Franz, 341, 343
Kneisel Hall Music Festival
  (Blue Hill, Maine),
  56n, 99n, 130n, 334, 338,
  341–44, 359–60
Kneisel String Quartet, 178, 343
Koford, James S., 387–90, 395
Kohon, Harold,
  177, 180–200, *192,* 226, 310, 371
Kohon, Isadora, 182
Kohon, Pauline, 182
Kohon String Quartet,
  118, 131, *177,* 180–200, *192,*
  210, 223
  chemistry of, 180–81
  first official ocncert, 186
  premiere of Ives's String Quartet
    No. 1, 190
  recordings by,
    187, 188–89, 190–91, 192
  rehearsa schedule, 181–82
Kolisch, Rudolph, 223
Kolisch String Quartet, 178, 223
Kolodin, Irving, 191, 192

Koltun, Loretta (aunt), 32–33, 39,
Kopf, Richard, 137
Korngold, Eric Wolfgang, 218
Kosman, Joshua, 354
Koussevitzky, Serge, 318
Krachmalnick, Jacob,
    95–96, 99, 105, 107, 174, 341
Kraueter, Karl, 341
Kraueter, Phyllis, 341
Krause, Angela, 377
Krause, Jurgen, 377
Kreisler, Fritz,
    67, 101, 167, 218, 337, 391
Krenek, Ernst, 218
Kroll, William, 137, 341
Kroll String Quartet, 137, 178, 186
Kronos Quartet, 16–18, 179, 301
Krosnick, Joel, 129, 205, 242, 354
Krupp, David, 57–58, 320, 400
Kuerti, Anton, 343
Kunicki, Raymond,
    177, 182–200, *192*
Kuskin, Charles, 174

La Maison Française (New York),
    202–3, 218
La Salle String Quartet, 179
La Tourette, John, 315
Laderman, Ezra, 220
    "Talkin'—Lovin'—Leavin'", 362
Ladley, John, 335
LaGuardia, Fiorello H., 46, 52
Lalo, Édouard
    Symphonie Espagnole, 95
Landaas, Henninge, 408, *408*
Lang, David
    "Aliens Kidnapped Me and Stole
        My Blood," 353
Lanner, Joseph, 34
Lansky, Paul, 220, 232
Lanson, Snooky, 8
Laredo, Jaime, 95
LaSalle Quartet, 223, 266
Lauer, Klaus, 321–23

Laufer, Wolfgang,
    301–2, *302,* 360, 399
Laurel Records, 363
Lavin, Avram, 96
Lawrence, Elliott, 143
Laws, Hubert, 355
Layton, Billy Jim, 220, 232
Leddy, Michael, 18
Lees, Benjamin, 274
Leeson, Albert, 374
Lehar, Franz, 34
Lehnhoff, Shephard, 248
Leigh, Vivian, 141
Leister, Karl, 323
Lenya, Lotte, 143
Lerdahl, Fred, 220
Lesser, Laurence, 342
Levarie, Sigmund, 214
Levens Hall (Cumbria), 273
Levin, Walter, 223
Levine, Julius, 127–28, 272
Levinson, Sam, 52–53
Levitan, Sam, 219
Levy, Gerardo, 174, 208
Levy, Phillip, 359–65, *360*
Lewis, Jerry, 43
Lewis, John, 254
Lewis, Robert, 115
Lewis, Uncle Dave, 191
Leybin, Zoya, 353–56
Lhevinne, Rosina, 73–74, 77, 90, 243
Libove, Charles, 174, 214
Lichnowsky, Prince Karl, 178
Lifschey, Marc, 85–86
Lifschey, Samuel, 85
Linsenberg, Judith, 362
Lipkin, Seymour, 56, 341–42, 343
Little Rumanian (Manhattan
    restaurant/night club), 46
Liu, Yun-Jie "Jay," 380
Lively Arts series (Stanford),
    316, 355, 379–80, 399
Local 802, Musicians' Union, 87–88
Loebel, Kurt, 95

INDEX

Loeffler, Charles, 200
Loft, Abram,
   241, 248–77, *255, 275,* 283–301,
   285, 320
   early career, 250
   How to Succeed in an Ensemble,
     250
   program notes, 400, 401
   resignation from Fine Arts Quartet,
     300, 301
   violin of, 252
London, George, 134
Longines Symphonette, 117–18
Lookofsky, Harry, 170
Los Angeles String Quartet, 179
Luboshutz and Nemenoff, 381
Lucarelli, Bert, 174
Lucca, Italy, 161–62
Luening, Otto
   Fantasia for String Quartet and
     Orchestra, 186
Luister magazine, 390
Lundy's Restaurant, Brooklyn,
   137–38
Lupot, Nicholas, violins by, 310
Lurie, Mitchell, 271
Lutoslawski, Witold, 250, 274
   String Quartet, 251, 342–43
Lynch, Ynez, 275

MacGowran, Jock, 133
Machold, Dietmar, 379
Maddy, Joseph E., 55
Maggini, Paolo, violas by,
   129–30, 264
Mahler, Fritz, 63, 77, 84, 218
Mahler, Gustav, 103
   Symphony No. 9, 105
Mailer, Norman
   The Castle in the Forest, 16
Maine Times, 319
Maire, Nicholas, 125, 164, 370
Maisky, Mischa, 182
Makarski, Michelle, 342

Malan, Roy, 352–53, 353, 356
Maline, Guillaume, 373
Maline, Nicholas, 277
Mallow, Barbara Stein,
   129, 130, 341, 342, 343
Mallow, Don, 130
Mallow, Jeanne, 130
Mamlok, Ursula, 205, 220
   "From My Garden," 386
   String Quartet, 225
Manchester Chamber Concert
   Society, 321
Mann, Robert, 301, 370
Marais, Marin, 202
Mariedi Anders Artists Management,
   327
Marlboro Music Festival,
   130–31, 308, 332
Marliave, Joseph de
   Beethoven's Quartets, 279
Maroth, Fred, 387, 392, 396
Marsh, Robert C., 254, 256, 332
Marshall, Richard, 310
Martin, Alan, *209,* 210–15, *214*
Martin Beck Theatre, 141–42
Martinon, Jean
   String Quartet No. 2, 401
   string quartets, 251
Martinu, Bohuslav
   "Three Madrigals," 206, 342
Masteroff, Joe, 349
Mathews, Max, 388
Maxham, Robert, 398
McCoy, Seth, 208
McCracken, Charles, 174
McGinnis, Donald, 385
McMillan Theater (Columbia
   University), 186, 218
Meier, Gustave, 225
Melos Ensemble, 319
Menard, Pierre, *307,* 309–35, *317*
Mendelssohn, Felix
   Concerto in D minor for Violin,
     Piano, and Strings, 352

Octet, 170, 360
Sonata in C minor, 257
String Quartet Op. 13, 269, 405
String Quartet Op. 44, No. 1, 315
string quartets, 274
String Symphony, 127
Mendelssohn-Bartholdy,
 George H. de, 187–88
Mennin, Peter, 103
 string quartet, 220
Menuhin, Yehudi,
 196, 267, 351, 352, 361
Merkel, Una, 136
Merkin Hall (New York), 349–50
Merrill, Bob, 136
Messiaen, Olivier, 103
Mester, Jorge, 22, 172–73
Metropolitan Museum of Art,
 concerts at, 126–28, 275
Metropolitan Opera Orchestra, 191
Miami Beach, childhood vacations in,
 43–44
Michelic, Matthew, 301
Mies van der Rohe, Ludwig, 312
Milhaud, Darius
 String Quartet No. 7, 363–64
 suite, 224
 Viola Sonata No. 1,
  327, 382, 383, 396
 Viola Sonata No. 2,
  382, 383, 385, 396
 Violin Sonata, 203
Milhaud, Madeleine, 383
Milk and Honey (Broadway show),
 165
Miller, Frank, 298
Miller, Glenn, band of, 53
Milstein, Nathan,
 38, 65, 66–67, 139, 167, 196, 246
 The Art of the Violin, 38
Milwaukee, Wisconsin, 259–60
Milwaukee Sentinel, 316
Milwaukee Symphony, 259
Mintz, Shlomo, 308

Mischakoff, Mischa,
 8, 21, 59n, 63–70, *64, 66,* 117,
 193, 250, 252, 370
 appearance of, 63–64
 biography of, 66
 with Chautauqua Symphony,
  81, 84–88
 frugality of, 67
 group classes, 67–69
 in NBC Symphony Orchestra,
  49, 63–64, 66–67, 69
 as Philadelphia Orchestra
  concertmaster, 70
 viola lessons with, 78, 81
Mischakoff String Quartet, 85
Mobley, Hank, 189
Modern Jazz Quartet, 254
Mohawk Trail concert series
 (Shelburne Falls, Mass.), 62
Moldevan, Nicolas, 372
Molkhou, Jean-Michel, 401
Möller, Max, 292
Monosoff, Sonya, 220
Montagnana, Domenico, cellos by,
 183
Monteux, Claude,
 115, 118, 119, 132, 224, 337
Monteux, Pierre, 22
Moog, Robert, 19, 134
Moore, Carman, 207
Moorman, Charlotte, 204
Morgenstern, Marvin, 142
Morgenstern, Vera, 142
Morini, Erika, 105, 167, 168, 196
Morse, Robert, 136
Mostel, Zero, 62, 141
movies, 1930s, 42
Mozart, Wolfgang Amadeus
 Adagio and Fugue, K.
  546, 322, 334, 353
 Adagio in E Major, K. 261, 342
 Clarinet Quintet in A Major, K.
  581, 323
 Divertimento, 224

Duo for violin and viola, 128
Flute Quartet, K. 285, 355
Oboe Quartet, 128, 169
Overture to *The Marriage of Figaro,* 83
piano concertos, 98–99
Piano Quartet in E flat, 245
piano quartets, 93
Rondo for violin in C Major, K. 373, 126, 342
Sinfonia Concertante for violin and viola, K. 364, 124, 126–27, 169, 303, 351
String Quartet in B-flat Major, K. 589, 351
String Quartet in D Major, K. 575, 269, 362
String Quartet in D minor, K. 421, 359
String Quartet in E Major, K. 428, 323
String Quartet in G Major, K. 387, 362
string quartets, 180, 247, 314, 401
string quintets, 264, 268, 338, 360
Symphony No. 40, 105
Trio in E-flat Major, K. 498, *Kegelstatt,* 113, 132–33
Viola Quintet in G minor, K. 516, 245–46, 322, 331
viola quintets, 399
Violin and Piano Sonata, K. 302, 74
Violin Concerto No. 4, K. 218, 105
Violin Concerto No. 5, K. 219, 77
as violist, 22
Mozart-Saal (Vienna), 316
Mt. Desert Chamber Players, 128–29
Mt. Desert Festival of Chamber Music, 235, 337–38
Mumm, Craig, 298
Munch, Cahrles, 102
Museum of Modern Art (New York), 190

Music & Arts label, 275, 364, 386–87, 392–94, 396, 399–401
Music Academy of the West Summer Festival (Santa Barbara), 325
Music Spectrum I (Yale University), 352
Musica Aeterna orchestra, 126–28
Musica Viva, 324
Musical Arts Quartet, 179
Musikhaus Doblinger, 385

Nadien, David, 163–64
Naegele, Philipp, 131
Nahat, Dennis, 260–61
Nardini, Pietro
Viola Sonata in F minor, 342, 386
National Gallery (Washington, D.C.), 188
Natwick, Mildred, 115
NBC Symphony Orchestra, 48–49, 63–64, 66–67, 81, 92, 94, 96, 246
Neighborhood House (Northeast Harbor), 337–38
Neikrug, Mark
"Star's the Mirror," 356, 363
Nelson, Daniel, 402
Nelsova, Zara, 286
Neubauer, Paul, 380
Nevele Hotel (Catskills), 91
Neveu, Ginette, 105
Neveu, Jean-Paul, 105
New Century Chamber Players, 132
New England Piano Quartet, 301
New Hellenic String Quartet, 179
New Hungarian String Quartet, 330, 349
New School for Social Research (New York), 206, 207, 218
New York, concert scene in, 217–21
New York City Ballet Orchestra, 209–10
New York City Center Ballet, 131

440 INDEX

New York Philharmonic, 98, 219, 242–43
New York Pick-up Ensemble, 172–73
New York Post, 263
New York Times, 188, 230, 257, 294, 316–17, 350
New York Woodwind Quintet, 254, 259, 403
New York World's Fair (1939), 46–47
New Yorker magazine, 275
Nickrenz, Joanna, 233
Nickrenz, Scott, 307–8
Nigogosian, Vahakn, 158–59, 162, 276–77, 287, 291, 372, 376, 377, 386
92nd Street YMHA (New York), 187–88, 218, 251
Nonesuch Records, 187, 233, 242
Norfolk Chamber Music Festival, 334
Norfolk Music School, 123–25, 128–29
Northern Illinois University, 308, 310–11, 314–15, 324, 327
Northwestern University, 249
Novaes, Guiomar, 105
Now, Voyager (film), 74
Nyfenger, Thomas, 113

Ober, William B., 190
O'Casey, Sean
  Juno and the Paycock, 133
Odessa (now Ukraine), 34–35, 38
Odets, Clifford
  Golden Boy, 143
Odoardi, Giuseppe, violas by, 194–96, 287
Offenbach, Jacques, 139
Ohira, Mayumi, 330, 349, *350,* 352
Ohmes, Allen, 199
Oistrakh, David, 38, 168–69
Oistrakh, Igor, 169
Ole Bull Celebration (2010), 408
Oliveira, Elmar, 342, 343

Once Upon a Mattress (Broadway show), 134–35, 141
O'Neill, Eugene
  Ah, Wilderness!, 135–37
Onnou, Alphonse, 382
Opperman, Cal, 144
Orchestra Hall (Chicago), 297–98
orchestras, status and wages in, 86–88
Orfeo label, 323
Orion Quartet, 232n
Orion Records, 382
Ormandy, Eugene, 208–9
Ostrovsky, Boris, 207
Ostwald, Lise, 114
Ostwald, Peter
  Glenn Gould: The Ecstasy and Tragedy of Genius, 114–15
  Schumann: The Inner Voices of a Musical Genius, 114–15
  Vaslav Nijinsky: A Leap into Madness, 115
Ouchard, Emile, 164
Ouspensky, P.D., 206
Ovcharov, Saul, 174
Overton, Hall
  Sonata for Viola and Piano, 386
Oxenberg, Allen Sven, 134
Ozawa, Seiji, 97

Pabst family, 247
Pabst Theater (Milwaukee), 316
Pacifica Quartet, 188n
Paderewski, Ignacy Jan, 101, 381
Page, Tim, 350
Pajeot, Louis Simon, 372
Paramount Theater (New York), 8, 10–14, 17
Paris, Jay, 204
Parmenter, Ross, 132–33
Parnas, Leslie, 318, 342
Parris, Robert
  Sonata for Viola and Piano, 203, 204

Patelson Music House (New York), 13
Paul, Les, 17
Payne, Maggi, 400
Pearl, Jack, 184
Pears, Peter, 333–34
Peccatte, Dominique, 373
Peck, Donald, 254, 327
Pegreffi, Elisa, 364
Pellegrini, Norman, 400
Pennario, Leonard, 271
Pennington, John, 225
Per Rostad, Masumi, 188n, 379
Perahia, Murray, 332–33
Perkinson, Tom, 264, 345
Perole Quartet, 179
Persinger, Louis, 73
Pfretzchner, Herman Richard, 370
Philadelphia Composers Forum, 231
Philadelphia Orchestra, 69
Philadelphia String Quartet, 179
Philharmonic Hall, Lincoln Center (New York), 172–73, 208, 242
Philladelphia Orchestra, 208–9
Phillips, Harvey, 230
Phillips, Karen, 26
Phillips Collection (Washington, D.C.), 203
Phoenix Chamber Music Society, 354
Phoenix Theater, 134–35
Piastro, Mishel, 117–18, 131, 181, 199
Piatigorsky, Gregor, 183, 246
Picasso, Pablo, 238
Picon, Molly, 181
Pidgeon, Walter, 136
Pintavalle, John, 174
Piston, Walter, 247
Pittsburgh Symphony, 81, 193
Plow That Broke the Plains, The (film), 174–75
Polar Bear Club, 71
Polikoff, Max, 242
Politi, James, 175

Pollack, Jackson, 397
Popkin, Mark, 254n
Potter, Tully, 384–85, 391, 398
Poy, Nardo, 214
Pressler, Menahem, 105, 275, 301, 406
Preves, Milton, 390
Price, Bruno, 310, 379
Price, Leontyne, 116, 117
Prier, Peter Paul, 373
Primrose, William, 22, 96, 123, 179, 303, 379, 382, 383, 385–86
Primrose Quartet, 96, 178–79, 371
Princeton University, 271
Pro Arte Quartet, 248, 254, 382
Prokofiev, Serge
  String Quartet No. 2, 293, 403
Pusey, Win, 342
Pythian Temple (New York), 165

Quartetto Italiano, 179, 364

Rabin, Michael, 139
Rabinoff, Benno, 381–82
Rabinoff Duo, 382
Radio Registry, 131
radio shows, 48, 400–401
Raimondi, Matthew, 118, 119, 128–29, 169–70, 174 175, 199, 206, 224–37, 337, 338
Raimondi, Natalie, 338
Raisin in the Sun, A (film), 239
Rameau, Jean Phillippe
  Pièces de Clavecin, 327
Ramor Quartet, 192
Rampal, Jean-Pierre, 252, 254, 258
Rattle, Simon, 319
Ravel, Maurice, 105
  "Introduction and Allegro, 255
  String Quartet, 267, 268
Raymond Scott Quintette, 17
RCA Victor, 48, 223
Reeves, George, 231

Reinecke, Carl
  Fantasiestücke, 386, 393
Reiner, Fritz, 131, 173, 193
Reinhardt, Django, 189
Reinhardt, Max, 74
Reinmacher, Eduard, 298
Rejto, Gabor, 349
Retford, William C., 372
Rhodes, Samuel, 231
Rice, Condoleezza, 355
Rideout, Alice, 327
Ringo, James, 62, 69
Ritchie, Stanley, 220–21
Robbins, Rena, 371
Robbins, Sandra, 342, 343
Robinson, Jackie, 40–41
Robison, Paula,
  113, 174, 193, 213, 254, 307–8
Rochberg, George, 229
Rochester Philharmonic, 157n
Rochester Symphony, 85–86
Rockport Opera House, 327, 341
Roda, Joseph
  Bows for Musical Instruments of the String Family, 372
Rodgers, Mary
  Once Upon a Mattress,
  134–35, 141
Roemaet-Rosanoff, Marie, 341
Rolla, Alessandro
  Duo for Violin and Viola, Op. 9, 343
Rollins, Sonny, 189
Rosand, Aaron, 299, 341, 382
Rose, Billy, 116n
Rose, Charlie, 211n
Rose, Leonard, 389
Rose, Louise, 91, 347, 349, 359
Rose, Philip, 301
Rosé String Quartet, 178
Roseman, Ronald, 169
Rosen, Joel, 74–76, 90, 103
Rosen, Michael, 258
Rosenberg, Donald, 393–94

Rosenblum, Myron, 385
Rosenman, Leonard, 53
Rosenthal, Lawrence
  music for *A Raisin in the Sun,* 239
Rosoff, Eliot, 219
Ross, Alex
  The Rest Is Noise, 332–33
Rotenburg, June, 127–28
Roth, Henry, 263
Roth, Mary, 263
Roussel, Albert
  Trio for Flute, Viola, and Cello,
  Op. 40, 132
Rovics, Howard, 205
Royal Northern College of Music
  (Manchester), 321, 379
rubato, 101–2
Rubinstein, Artur, 101, 394
Rudiakov, Michael, 298, 300
Rudie, Lazare, 8–9
Rufino, Charles, 159
Rule, Janice, 139
Russell, Andy, 8, 12

Sacconi, Simone, 158
Saidenberg, Daniel, 238–39
Saint-Saëns, Camille
  "The Swan," 94
  Violin Concerto No. 3, 105
Saks, Toby, 231
Salevitz, Dr. Isaac, 28–29, 34–35
Salmond, Felix, 73
Salzman, Eric, 219, 232
Samuel J. Tilden High School
  (Brooklyn), 51–58
San Francisco Classical Voice,
  398, 401
Sandler, Murray, 235
Sardegna, 161
Sarnoff, David, 49, 248n
Sartory, Eugène Nicolas,
  370, 373, 374
Saslav, Isidor, 38, 157
Saslavsky, Alexander, 38

Satz, Ralph, 52
Saunders, Rodney, 339
Sawakis, George, 242
Sawyer, Elizabeth, 352
Sawyer, Tom, 300
Schermerhorn, Kenneth, 258
Schickele, Peter, 172–73, 189, 241
Schlieps, Armin, 162
Schlieps, George, 162–64
Schnabel, Artur, 98–99, 102
   cadenza for Mozart concerto, 99
   Rhapsody for Orchestra, 98n
Schneider, Alexander,
   166–67, 220, 223
Schneider, Mischa, 237
Schneider Quartet, 166
Schneider String Quartet, 178
Schoenbach, Sol, 318
Schoenberg, Arnold, 53, 218
   String Quartet No. 2, 192
   string quartets, 223
   Verklärte Nacht, Op. 4, 231
Schoenberg Hall (Berkeley), 327
Schor, Joseph, 224
Schubert, Franz
   Duo for Violin and Piano D.
      574, 316
   Fantasy, 267
   Quartet in G for Flute, Guitar,
      Viola, and Cello, 132
   Quartettsatz D. 703, 316, 326
   String Quartet in A minor, d.
      804, 247
   String Quartet in D minor "Death
      and the Maiden," D. 810, 316, 326
   String Quartet in E-flat Major, Op.
      125, No. 1, 362
   String Quartet in G Major, D.
      887, 279
   String Quartet in G Major, Op. 161,
      256
   string quartets, 180
   String Quintet, 363
   Symphony No. 9, 105
   "Trout" Quintet, 272, 352
Schuller, Gunther, *226*
   Composers Quartet and,
      17, 225, 226, 229–30, 234
   string quartets, 271
   works of, 199, 220
Schulze, Richard and Theodora,
   162, 188
Schuman, Henry,
   128, 169, 174, 206, 219, 224
Schuman, William, 105
Schumann, Robert, 247
   Manfred Overture, 105
   Marchenbilder, Op. 113, 257, 393
   Ostwald book about, 114–15
   Piano Quartet, Op. 47, 332
   Piano Quintet, 274, 326, 327
   String Quartet No. 3, 256
   string quartets, 188
   Symphony No. 1, 102, 105
   Symphony No. 2, 105
   Symphony No. 3, 105
   Symphony No. 4, 102, 105
Schuppanzigh, Ignaz, 177–78
Schuppanzigh Quartet,
   177–78, 223, 280
Schwartz, David, 386
Schwartz, Elliot, 318
Schwartzkopf, Elizabeth, 134
Schweitzer, Raymond, 191–92, *192*
Scott, Raymond
   band of,
      7–8, 10, 11–14, 17, 77, 361
   as composer and inventor, 17–18
Scott Clavivox, 17
Scribner, Consuelo, 16
Seaman, Norman, 203–4
Sedona Chamber Music Festival,
   358–59
Segal, Cyrus, 175
Seidel, Toscha, 59n
Senofsky, Berl, 318
Serkin, Peter, 166, 231
Serkin, Rudolf,
   56, 98, 106, 130, 166–67, 218,
   223, 308, 381

Sessions, Roger,
  53, 199, 219, 220, 229
  From My Diary, 231
  String Quartet No. 2, 231
  Violin Sonata, 231
Settin, Joseph, 195, 287
Setzer, Phillip, 379
Severance, Nancy,
  301, 352, 380, 385–86
Shane, Rita, 103
Shanet, Howard, 186
Shapero, Harold, 105
Shapey, Ralph, 220
  String Quartet No. 6, 232–33, 294
Shapinsky, Aaron, 193
Shapiro, Harvey,
  96, 174, 179, 192, 371
Shapiro, Laurence, 301, *302*
Shawe-Taylor, Desmond, 275
Sheepshead Bay, Brooklyn,
  41–42, 137–38
Shellans, Hartley M., 47–48
Shepherd, Bruce, 189
Sherba, John, 16–18, 301, 379–80
Sherwood, Robert E., 141
Shifrin, Seymour
  String Quartet No. 4,
    256–57, 263, 401
  string quartets, 251, 254, 271
Shoobe, Lou, 219, 238
Shostakovich, Dmitri, 52, 318
  Cello Sonata, 208
  Piano Quintet, 245
  String Quartet No. 1, 354
  String Quartet No. 3, 293, 403
  String Quartet No. 7, 351, 362
  string quartets, 251, 271, 274
  Viola Sonata Op. 147, 342, 385
Shostakovich String Quartet, 179
Shot, Joseph, 174
Shubert Theater, 135–37, 142
Shumsky, Oscar, 96, 179
Siegel, Barry, 32, 41
Siegel, Minnie (Aunt), 91
Silberstein, Ernst, 94

Silfies, George, 208
Silva, Luigi, 129
Silvers, Phil, 141
Silverstein, Joseph, 94, 290–91
Simon, Geoffrey, 303
Simon, P., 375–76
Singer, Isaac Bashevis, 90
Sitt, Hans
  Album Leaves, 393
Skernick, Abraham,
  107, 318, 341, 342
Slapin, Scott, 396
Slatkin, Eleanor, 330
Slatkin, Felix, 330
Slatkin, Leonard, 22
Slezak, Leo, 335
Smallens, Alexander, 116
Smetana, Bedřich, 105
  The Moldau, 102
  String Quartet No. 1, 268
Smetana String Quartet, 179, 364n
Smith, Sylvia, 381–82
Snider, Duke, 113
Soffer, Sheldon, 358
Sokoloff, Vladimir, 318
Soldo, Joe, 242
Sollberger, Harvey, 205
Solomon, Maynard, 114, 189
Solomon, Seymour, 114, 189
Sondheim, Stephen
  A Funny Thing Happened on the Way to the Forum, 141
Sopkin, Carol,
  238, 243–44, 247, 255, 259, 262, 338–39
Sopkin, George,
  241, 247, 248–77, *249, 275,* 283–301, 318
  arm problems of, 298, 300–301
  bowing style, 250
  cello of, 252
  early career, 248
  with Fine Arts Quartet, 234
  Goffriller cello of,
    182n, 289, 293, 403

as guest artist with Stanford String
    Quartet, 363
Maine home, 338–39
Milwaukee home, 236–37
retirement, 300–301
samovar of, 262–63
Santa Fe property, 259
students of, 16, 384
trip to Caressa and Français Paris
    violin dealers, 287–88
Sorkin, Leonard,
    241, 248–77, *255, 275,* 283–303,
    302
    bowing style, 250
    early career, 248
    skills decline, 303
    violin of, 252, 310
Sorkin, Naomi, 260–61
South Bank Summer Music series,
    319–20
South Mountain concert series
    (Pittsfield), 259, 334
Southern Oregon State College, 358
Soyer, David, 169–70, 179, 199, 309
Spice, Irving, 242
Splendor in the Grass (film), 239
Spohr, Ludwig, 168
    Concerto for String Quartet and
        Orchestra, 186, 247, 259, 327
St. George, David, 314
St. Lawrence String Quartet, 365
St. Petersburg school of violin
    playing, 65
Stanford String Quartet,
    170, 341, 347–65, *353, 357, 360*
    European tours, 356
    founding of, 330–31
    at Kneisel Hall festival, 342
    membership,
        349, 352, 353–54, 356, 358–59
    recordings by, 363–64
    salary disparity in,
        349, 356, 358–59
Stanford Symphonic Band, 352–53
Stanford University,
    271, 316, 330, 362–63
Stanick, Gerald, 248, 400
Stapleton, Jean, 133
Starker, Janos, 309
Stark's (Brooklyn clothing
    emporium), 33–34
Steber, Eleanor, 220
Stegner, Mary Page, 363
Stegner, Wallace, 363
Stein, Gertrude, 69
Stein, Joseph
    Juno, 133–34
Steiner, Max, 218
Steinhardt, Arnold, 308–9, 331
    Violin Dreams, 96–97
Stepansky, Joseph, 248
Stern, Carl, 341
Stern, Isaac, 38, 167, 239, 303, 369n
Sterne, Teresa, 233
Stewart, Robert
    Sonata for Viola and Piano, 206n
    Trio No. 5, 206
Still, Ray, 254
Stock, Frederick, 22, 198
Stokowski, Leopold,
    70, 137, 164, 173–75, 337, 371
Stonzak, Morris, 82, 115, 219
Stowell, Robin, 364
Strad, The, 384–85, 391, 398
Stradivari, violins by, 252
Stradivari String Quartet, 179, 199
Stradivarius Studios, 158–59
Strassburg, Robert, 389
Strauss, Johann, the younger, 34
    Die Fledermaus, 140–41
Strauss, Richard
    Don Juan, 84, 92
    Don Quixote, 105
    Salome, 94
    Till Eulenspiegel, 105
Stravinsky, Igor, 220
    Concertino for String Quartet,
        245, 323
    Dialogues and a Diary, 279
    Three Pieces for Clarinet Solo, 323

Three Pieces for String Quartet, 245, 322
string quartets.
   See also specific quartets
   balance in, 268, 311
   decorum and chemistry in, 180–81, 249–50
   naming of, 178–79
   playing in, 22–23, 24–25, 280–82, 310–12
   repertoire, 179–80
   struggle for survival, 180, 198–99
Strongin, Theodore, 258
Strouse, Charles
   Golden Boy, 143
Sudock, Shirley, 225
Suk String Quartet, 178
Sullivan, Ed, 252
summer music camps, 196–97
Suppan, Adolph, 239
Susskind, David, 164–65
Sutherland, Joan, 134
Suzuki family, 318
Swallow, John, 206
Swed, Mark, 17
Swenson, Ian, 360
Swiss Music Library, 169–70
Sydeman, William, 220
Sylvern, Hank, 164, 219
Sylvester, Robert, 192–93, 199, 213, 254, 307
Symphony of the Air, 49, 131, 168–69, 173–75
Symphony Space (New York), 218
Szell, George, 83, 109, 218, 246, 348, 371, 405
   biography and career, 92–93
   as Cleveland Orchestra Music Director, 82–83, 92–107
   dislike of Brahms, 106
   emotional coldness of, 100–101
   perfectionism of, 93–94, 97, 106–7
   as pianist, 93
   programming innovations, 98
   rigidity as conductor, 101–2

Szigeti, Joseph, 97, 101, 196
Tacke, Mathias, 334
Takács Quartet, 359
Take Me Along (Broadway show), 135–37
Tanenbaum, Elias
   Trio for Flute, Tenor Violin, and Trombone, 132
Tanglewood Festival, 325
Tarack, Gerald, 127, 174, 208, 214
Taubman, Howard, 188
Taylor, Lucille, 386
Tchaikovsky, Peter Ilyich
   Symphony No. 4, 105
   Violin Concerto, 105
Tecchler, David, cellos by, 310
Teldec, 322, 326–27, 332
Telemann Society, 188
Terkel, Studs, 252, 400
Tertis, Lionel, 22, 303, 382
Testore, Carlo Antonio, 379
Théâtre des Champs-Élysées (Paris), 272–73
Theatre Maisonneuve (Montreal), 235
Theremin, Léon, 388
They Shall Have Music (film), 68
Thomas, Clara Fargo, 224
Thomas, Lewis, 403–4
Thomas, Sue, 208
Thomassin, Claude, 373–74
Thompson, Sada, 133
Thomson, Michelle Dulak, 398
Thomson, Virgil, 69
   music for *The Grass Harp,* 115
   music for *The Plow That Broke the Plains,* 174–75
Three Choirs Festival, Gloucester, 266
Tich, Judith
   Ruth Crawford Seeger, 228n
Times (London), 319–20
Toch, Ernst, 218
Today Show, The (TV show), 252, 261

Torkanowsky, Werner, 162–63, 341
Toscanini, Arturo,
    48–49, 63, *64,* 66, *66,* 69, 81, 83,
    93, 246, 405
Totenberg, Roman, 341, 342, 349
Toth, Andor,
    91, 330–31, 342, 347–59, *350, 357*
Toth, Andor, Jr., 91, 349, 359
touring, general thoughts on, 25–26
Tourte, François,
    367–69, 372, 378–79
Tovarich (Broadway show), 141
Town Hall (New York),
    73, 218, 231, 233, 242
Tramontana, Pete, 8
Trampler, Walter,
    140, 174, 224, 268–69, *286,* 380,
    383
Travani, Francesco
    Viola Sonata No. 1, 343
Tree, Michael, *286,* 308–9
Trevani, Francesco
    Viola Sonata No. 1, 385
Tribune de Genève, 323–24
Tubbs, James, 374–75
Tubbs family of bow makers, 369
Tucker, Sophie, 46
Tuckwell, Barry, 400, 401
Tully, Alice, 126
Turina, Joaquin
    "La Orácion del Torero," 362
Tursi, Francis,
    254, 260, 264, 268, 322, 385, 399
Tuttle, Karen, 131, 386
twelve-tone or serial music,
    98, 205, 212, 228, 396–98
Twentieth Century Innovations,
    229–30

UCLA, 327
Uihlein family, 247
Ullman, Michael, 400
Ulysses in Nightown
    (Broadway play), 141
University of Michigan, 329

University of Puerto Rico, 252
University of Wisconsin-Milwaukee,
    249, 252–53, 256, 270, 382

Van Druten, John
    I Am a Camera, 143
Van Dyl, Felix, 319
van Gelder, Rudy, 188–89, 193
Vanguard Records,
    114, 174, 187, 189, 251, 371
Vardi, Emanuel, 202
Varèse, Edgard, 23
    Poéme électronique, 219
Varga, Laszlo, 271
Vatelot, Etienne, 277, 373
Vatelot, Marcel, 158
Vaughan Williams, Ralph
    "Four Hymns for Tenor, Viola, and
        Piano," 208
    "The Lark Ascending," 126
Végh, Sandor, 130
Végh String Quartet, 178
Veigl, Karl, 218
Verdi, Giuseppe
    String Quartet in E minor, 326
Vermeer String Quartet,
    304, *307,* 307–35, *317,* 347
    Australia tour, 324–25
    balance, 311
    at Blue Hill, 341
    Boston Philharmonic Scholarship
        Fund benefit concert, 313–14
    change in membership, 334–35
    concert season, 314–15, 327
    differences, 328–29
    domestic tours, 323
    ensemble tightness, 309
    European tours,
        312–13, 314–15, 316, 320–23,
        326, 328–29, 348, 379
    farewell concerts, 335
    founding of, 308–9
    Israel concerts, 325–26
    in London, 319–20
    Maine summer concerts, 317–20

recordings by, 317, 326–27
rehearsals, 310–12
Stanford performance, 355
Vermillion Quartet, 310
Vertavo Quartet, 408
Vigneron, Joseph Arthur, 376
Village Gate (New York), 207–8, 218
Village Voice, 207–8
Villager, The, 206–7
viola(s)
   age and tonal quality of, 128
   Amati, 225
   Bergonzi,
      128, 225, 287, 293, 371–72, 373
   Chiocci, 78, 193, 370
   Gasparo da Salo,
      124, 125, 129–30, 194, 307, 378
   Guadagnini,
      4, 25, 128, 182n, 289–93,
      296–97, 310, 343, 374, 378,
      382, 386, 403, 407–8, *408*
   lack of repertoire for, 21, 200
   lack of respect for and jokes about,
      20–21, 392
   Maggini, 129–30, 264
   Odoardi, 287
   in string quartet, 22–23
   Testore, 379
   transcriptions and arrangements
      for, 22
viola bows,
   125, 163–64, 277, 367–80, *368*
viola playing, bow pressure, 125–26
Viola Research Society, 385
viola strings, 235–36
violin bows, 182
violin playing
   St. Petersburg school of, 65
   staccato stroke, 68–69
violins
   Balestrieri, 252
   Gagliano, 9, 107
   Goffriller, 252
   Guadagnini, 343
   "Guardinarius," 361–62
   Guarneri del Jesu,
      182, 252, 299, 310
   Lupot, 310
   Red Diamond Stradivarius, 62–63
   Vuillaume, 100–101, 182
violists
   composers and conductors as, 22
   Tertis's memoirs, 22
   young, 21–22, 379–80
Vivaldi, Antonio, 165–66, 202
   sonatas, 77, 206
Vogelgesang, Freddie, 143
Voirin, François Nicolas, 374
Von Rhein, John, 315, 316
Vox Records,
   187–88, 190–91, 192, 238, 251,
   399–400
Vox Turnabout label, 274
Vuillaume, Jean-Baptiste, violins by,
   100–101, 182, 373

W. E. Hill & Sons, 370, 374
Wagner, Richard, 105
Waldeck, Lew
   poem "The Carnegie Tavern,"
      145–56
Waldman, Frederick,
   126–28, 242, 275
Waldteufel, Emile, 34
Wallenstein, Alfred, 168–69, 173
Walter, Bruno, 98, 387
Walther, Geraldine, 323, 379
Walthew, Richard H.
   "Regret and Conversation
      Gallante," 386
Walton, William
   string quartets, 274
Wann, Lois, 132
Warfield, William, 116, 117
Warnow, Mark, 18
Warnow, Stan
   documentary *Deconstructing Dad,*
      18
Washington-Lee University
   (Lexington, Virginia), 206n

INDEX 449

Waterman, Ruth, 342
Weber, Ben, 220
Weber, Carl Maria von
    Clarinet Quintet, 188
Webern, Anton
    Five Pieces for String Quartet,
      Op. 5, 212, 245, 354
    string quartets, 223
Webster Hall (New York), 220
Wedge, George, 78
Weill, Kurt, 143
Weinberg, Henry, 220
    String Quartet No. 2, 229, 231
Weiss, Howard. *See* Howard, Peter
Weisshaar, Hans, 63
Welsch, Chauncey, 53
Wente Brothers winery, 362
West, Philip, 298–99
White, Jane, 134
Whittenberg, Charles, 220
    "Set for Two," 205, 206, 258, 386
Wiener International Festwochen, 316
Wigglesworth, Frank
    Duo for Oboe and Viola, 206
Wigmore Hall (London),
    252, 264–65, 331
Willecke, Willem, 81
Willis, Thomas, 299
Wilshire Ebell Theater (Los Angeles),
    323
Winer, Linda, 254
Winter Garden Theater, 133
Wolf, Andrew, 317
Wolf, Thomas, 327
Wolf family, 317–19
WQXR Quartet, 371
Wright, Frank Lloyd, 238
Wuorinen, Charles, 220
    Piano Trio, 205
    String Quartet No. 1, 274–75, 387
    string quartets, 251, 254
Wurlitzer, Rembert,
    168, 183, 184, 193

Xenakis, Iannis, 230

Yajima, Hiroko, 232n
Ying Quartet, 301
Yoshizato, Eiko, 69–70, *79*
Young, John Bell, 396
Young, La Monte, 220
Young, Richard, 329, 349
Young Audiences, Inc.,
    210–13, *213,* 239, 242
Your Hit Parade (TV show), 18
Ysaÿe, Eugène, 94, 246
Ysaÿe String Quartet, 179

Zappa, Frank, 19
Zaratzian, Harry, 131, 209
Zaslav, Bernard
    Albuquerque property, 259, 292
    appearance of, 72–73
    Bar Mitzvah of, 46
    big band gigs, 7–14, 77, 78, 118,
      361
    birth of, 31
    birth of son, 104
    Broadway gigs,
      82, 115–17, 133–44, 165, 239,
      242, 370
    Brooklyn homes, 111
    with Carnegie String Quartet,
      210–15
    Catskills vacations, 42–43
    with Chautauqua Symphony,
      81, 84–88, 103–4
    Chicago homes, 312–13, 320
    childhood hobbies, 36–37
    childhood homes of, 28, 44–46
    childhood of, 27–49
    childhood *pince-nez* worn by, 36
    childhood radio and record player,
      48–49
    childhood violin lessons,
      37–38, 47–48
    Cleveland homes, 91–92, 105
    with Cleveland Orchestra, 89
    Cleveland Orchestra audition,
      82–83, 92

450   INDEX

with Composers String Quartet,
  223–39
conducting study, 63, 77
as Distinguished Professor of
  University of Wisconsin-
  Milwaukee, 294n
driving of, 71–72
family background, 32–35
film-score recording gigs, 53–54
final performance, 399
with Fine Arts Quartet,
  234–35, 241–77
Fine Arts Quartet audition, 236–37
finger problems of,
  64–66, 171–72, 326, 357–58
first Carnegie Hall concert, 102
first live chamber music heard by,
  44, 47
first orchestral job, 81–82, 84–88
first trip to Europe, 159–62
first viola gig, 8–14
first violin recital, 52
as freelance musician in New York,
  21, 131–44, 157–75, 218–21,
  224, 239, 242–43
gardening hobby, 45–46
honeymoon, 91
Honorary Doctorate from
  Northland College, 294n
injuries and illnesses of,
  28–29, 35, 36
at Interlochen Music Camp,
  55–58, 59
IRS expenses, 183–84
Istanbul vacation, 276–77
jingles gigs, 170–71
Juilliard violin recital, 77
Juilliard years, 60–79
with Kohon String Quartet,
  118, 131, 180–200, 223
Maine vacations and homes,
  247, 317–20, 325, 334, 337–45
Manhattan apartment of,
  72
marriage, 89–91, 90

meeting and courtship of future
  wife, 75–77
memoir writing, 404–6
Menlo Park home burglarized,
  347–48
middle name of, 31–32
Milwaukee home and life,
  247, 259–60
move to California, 347–48
move to Chicago, 314
move to Milwaukee,
  238–39, 241–45
nickname "Buddy," 33–34, 35–36
Packard Clipper owned by, 91
paintings owned by,
  3, 55, 264, 345
Palo Alto home, 354–55
performance anxiety, 269–70
pictures of,
  7, 27, 31, 51, 79, 90, 177, 192,
  201, 209, 213, 241, 245, 249,
  255, 263, 270, 275, 285, 286,
  297, 302, 307, 317, 350, 357,
  360, 367, 408
in plumbing business,
  109–14, 120–21
quits Vermeer String Quartet, 329
as recording engineer,
  387–89, 395–96
retirement of, 364–65, 394–98
with Stanford String Quartet,
  331, 347–65
student concert passes, 73–74
teaching duties at Northern Illinois
  University, 310–11, 404
tenure at University of Wisconsin-
  Milwaukee, 270
trip to Caressa and François Paris
  violin dealers, 287–88
undergraduate schools attended by,
  42, 46–47, 49, 51–58
with Vermeer String Quartet,
  307–35, 331–35
viola bows of, 371–80

viola lessons,
  78, 81, 123–25, 128–29
violas owned by,
  4, 25, 78, 128, 157–59, 162,
  182n, 184, 193–94, 225,
  287–93, 310, 343, 374, 386,
  403, 407–8, *408*
violins owned by, 8–9, 361–62
Zaslav, Billy (brother), 32, 120
Zaslav, Claudia. *See* Drosen, Claudia
  Zaslav (daughter)
Zaslav, Gary (cousin), 46
Zaslav, Louis (uncle), 44
Zaslav, Madison (granddaughter),
  406
Zaslav, Mark (son), *104, 112*
  army exemption, 171–72
  birth of, 104, 109
  at Brooklyn College, 241
  childhood of, 118, 120
  current life, 406
  as psychologist, 320, 328, 395
  rejection for military service,
    61–62
  at University of Wisconsin-
    Milwaukee, 260, 287
  at Zaslav Duo debut recital, 204
Zaslav, Mary (née Malie Knauer;
  mother), *31, 33, 90*
  appearance and taste of, 33–34
  death of, 327
  early years, 32–33
  honeymoon, 91
  illnesses of, 70–71
  Juilliard audition, 60–61
  marriage, 89–91
  non-attendance at debut recital,
    204
  overprotectiveness of,
    28, 36–37, 51–52, 59–60
  personality of, 111
  piano playing of, 34
Zaslav, Naomi (Nomi; née Civkin),
  75, 104, 112, 201, 263

  adjunct position at Northern
    Illinois University, 310, 328
  appearance of, 75
  birth of son, 104
  childhood in Winnipeg, 101
  first trip to Europe, 159–62
  Istanbul vacation, 276–77
  as Juilliard student, 75–77
  in Maine, 339–41
  married life in Brooklyn,
    109, 111, 112
  performances with Duo,
    201–9, 257–58, 342, 381–98
  as pianist,
    24, 76, 118, 132, 302, 327, 354,
    358, 395–96, 400
  piano position at Cleveland
    Conservatory, 107
  pregnancy, 103
  travels on Fine Arts Quartet tours,
    286, 300
  travels on Vermeer Quartet tours,
    322–23
Zaslav, Nate (cousin), 46
Zaslav, Samuel (father)
  early years, 38–39
  emotional distance of,
    40, 41, 111, 121
  kidnapping of, 40
  name shortened at Ellis Island, 39
  non-attendance at debut recital,
    204
  plumbing business of,
    39–40, 109–12, 120
  stubbornness and hostility to new
    ideas, 110

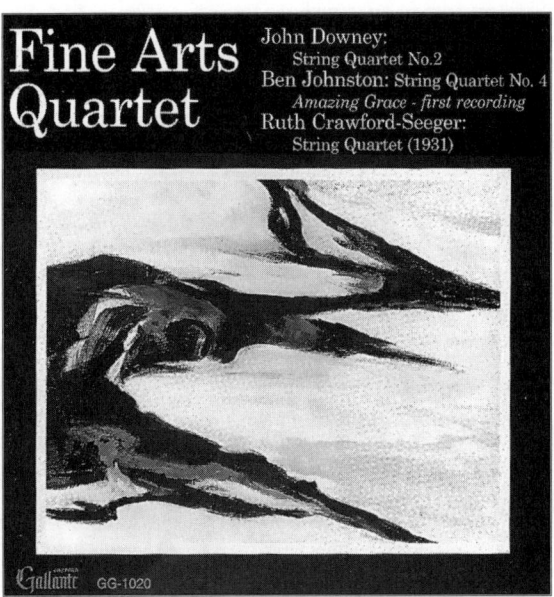

Fine Arts Quartet

John Downey:
　String Quartet No.2
Ben Johnston: String Quartet No. 4
　Amazing Grace - first recording
Ruth Crawford-Seeger:
　String Quartet (1931)

Gallante GG-1020